KINGDOM to
commune

PATRICIA APPELBAUM

KINGDOM to commune

PROTESTANT PACIFIST CULTURE *between*

WORLD WAR I *and* THE VIETNAM ERA

THE UNIVERSITY OF

NORTH CAROLINA PRESS

CHAPEL HILL

© 2009 The University of North Carolina Press
All rights reserved
Manufactured in the United States of America

Designed by Courtney Leigh Baker and set in Seria Sans and Whitman by Tseng Information Systems, Inc.

Olive leaves on title page © istockphoto.com/ Gregor Lajh

The paper in this book meets the guidelines for permanence and durability of the Committee on Production Guidelines for Book Longevity of the Council on Library Resources.

The University of North Carolina Press has been a member of the Green Press Initiative since 2003.

Library of Congress Cataloging-in-Publication Data
Appelbaum, Patricia.
Kingdom to commune : Protestant Pacifist culture between World War I and the Vietnam era / Patricia Appelbaum.
p. cm.
Includes bibliographical references and index.
ISBN 978-0-8078-3267-7 (cloth : alk. paper) —
ISBN 978-0-8078-5938-4 (pbk. : alk. paper)
1. Nonviolence—Religious aspects—Historic peace churches. 2. Pacifism—Religious aspects—Historic peace churches. 3. Peace—Religious aspects—Historic peace churches. 4. United States—Church history—20th century. 5. Nonviolence—United States—History—20th century. 6. Pacifism—United States—History—20th century. I. Title.
BT736.6.A67 2009
261.8'7309730904—dc22

2008037217

cloth 13 12 11 10 09 5 4 3 2 1
paper 13 12 11 10 09 5 4 3 2 1

THIS BOOK WAS DIGITALLY PRINTED.

Contents

Acknowledgments
ix

Introduction
1

1 "Character 'Bad'"
HAROLD GRAY
10

2 From YMCA to CPS
PACIFIST SOCIAL NETWORKS
25

3 The Protestant Heart
PACIFIST THEOLOGY
45

4 The Pacifist Vernacular
61

5 Performing Pacifism
WORSHIP, PLAYS, AND PAGEANTS
72

6 Swords and Plowshares
PACIFIST ICONOGRAPHY
89

7 "The Practice of the Presence"
PACIFIST SPIRITUALITY
110

8   Training for Peace
    RICHARD GREGG AND THE
    REALIGNMENT OF PACIFIST LIFE
    128

9   Milking Goats for Peace
    A NEW PARADIGM
    143

10 "Victories without Violence"
    PACIFIST STORIES
    163

11 "Bad Mother"
    MARJORIE SWANN
    184

    Epilogue
    203

    Appendix
    HYMN TEXTS
    217

    Notes
    221

    Bibliography
    281

    Index
    315

Illustrations

Armistice Day poster, ca. 1920 90

"Sermon on the Mount" cartoon, 1930s 93

"They Shall Beat Their Swords into Plowshares" poster, 1930s 95

Detail of "They Shall Beat Their Swords into Plowshares" poster 95

Blacksmith window, ca. 1929 96

Charles Lindbergh window, ca. 1929 99

Detail of Lindbergh window 99

Detail of Lindbergh window: signing of the Kellogg-Briand pact 99

Cover of Allan A. Hunter's *Courage in Both Hands*, 1951 100

Fritz Eichenberg, *St. Francis, Sermon to the Birds*, 1952 105

Fritz Eichenberg, *St. Benedict*, 1953 105

Edward Hicks, *The Peaceable Kingdom*, ca. 1833 106

Fritz Eichenberg, *The Peaceable Kingdom*, 1950 107

Marie Louise Rochon Hoover, *Christ of the Andes*, Christmas card, 1922 170

Acknowledgments

To acknowledge those who have supported and assisted this project is a happy exercise indeed.

First of all, I am indebted to the numerous libraries and archives whose collections have been available to me and to the staff members who know and maintain them. Thanks above all to the Swarthmore College Peace Collection; also the American Baptist Historical Society, Andover Harvard Library, Congregational Library, Franklin Trask Library of Andover Newton Theological School, Friends Historical Library, Krauth Memorial Library of the Lutheran Theological Seminary of Philadelphia, and the Schlesinger Library, Radcliffe Institute for Advanced Study. Special thanks to Jae Jennifer Rossman of the Yale University Arts Library; Tom Klute of Yale Media Services; Mary Louise VanDyke of the Hymn Society's Dictionary of American Hymnology Project; and Judith A. Gray of the American Folklife Center, Library of Congress. I am particularly grateful for access to the libraries of Amherst, Mount Holyoke, and Smith Colleges, and of the University of Massachusetts at Amherst.

This work would not be what it is without the people who shared their experience and perspectives in interviews and letters: Doris and Justin Hartman, Ted Klaseen, Tom and Anne Moore, Mary Page Raitt, Carol Swann, and Marjorie Swann. I am also grateful to the individuals and organizations who granted copyright permissions. A number of archivists, religious workers, and others helped me track down copyright holders; I thank them for their help and for much interesting conversation.

Of many teachers, colleagues, and readers, I wish especially to thank Margaret Lamberts Bendroth for her generous and perceptive readings and invaluable support. In the early stages of this work, Stephen Prothero offered not only intellectual direction but steady encouragement and good cheer. Much appreciation also goes to Dana L. Robert for early guidance and to Elizabeth Nordbeck for later insights. I remember the late William R. Hutchison with gratitude. The anonymous readers for the University of North Carolina Press provided careful readings and thoughtful comments that have greatly improved the final manuscript. I could not have asked for a better editor than Elaine Maisner, who manages to combine astute advice, tactful direction, and regular encouragement. Any errors that remain are, of course, mine alone.

Last, but far from least, my family has lived most closely with this project and with its sometimes harried author. First of all, my parents gave me the double gift of intellectual and moral education. Foot soldiers in the legions of good will, they have lived out their values with steadfast and often unseen devotion. My sister Lorraine Appelbaum has been an intelligent correspondent and steady supporter, and I am grateful for both. My daughter, Margaret Holladay, has endured with good grace innumerable dinner-table conversations and deadline pressures connected to this book. She brings light into my life every day.

My husband, William L. Holladay, is one of the rare people who have understood from the beginning why this subject mattered. He has been a constant intellectual and spiritual companion through the writing process. He also retyped the bibliography after a computer disaster, laid out the index, and assisted with innumerable details of documentation and manuscript preparation. In addition, he has washed dishes, done laundry, and provided, as occasion demanded, child care or teen transport. I hope the result will reward the efforts.

Abbreviations

AFSC	American Friends Service Committee
CNVA	Committee for Non-Violent Action
CO	conscientious objector
CORE	Congress of Racial Equality
CPS	Civilian Public Service
CSA	Council for Social Action (Congregational Christian Churches)
FOR	Fellowship of Reconciliation
ICBM	intercontinental ballistic missile
NCPW	National Council for Prevention of War
NECNVA	New England Committee for Nonviolent Action
SCM	Student Christian Movement
SVM	Student Volunteer Movement
TCF	Tuolumne Co-op Farm
WILPF	Women's International League for Peace and Freedom
WRL	War Resisters League
WSP	Women Strike for Peace
YMCA	Young Men's Christian Association
YWCA	Young Women's Christian Association

KINGDOM to
commune

Introduction

In 1946 the aging peace evangelist Kirby Page published a collection of nontraditional worship services in a volume hopefully called "The Light Is Still Shining in the Darkness." One of these services was dedicated to peace.[1] Some elements of the service would have been familiar to any mainline Protestant, such as readings from the Bible and an uplifting hymn. Other elements were less common—a period of silent meditation, for example. The Bible readings centered on the theme of following Jesus, and the nearest equivalent to a sermon was a long reading excerpted from an imaginative retelling of Jesus' life.[2] This reading incorporated paraphrased biblical texts on peace, love, forgiveness, and the Kingdom of God, including both the Old Testament "swords into plowshares" text and parts of the Sermon on the Mount.

The service also included two nonbiblical texts closely associated with peace and beloved of peace advocates. One was a "Negro spiritual," here presented as "I Ain't Gwine Study War No More."[3]

> Gwine lay down my sword and shield
> Down by the riverside,
> Down by the riverside,
> Down by the riverside,
> Gwine lay down my sword and shield
> Down by the riverside,
> I ain't gwine study war no more.

The other, which closed the service, was known as the Prayer of St. Francis:

> Lord, make me an instrument of thy peace.
> Where there is hatred, let me sow love;
> where there is injury, pardon;
> where there is discord, union;
> where there is doubt, faith;
> where there is despair, hope;
> where there is darkness, light;
> where there is sadness, joy . . .

Page's work is interesting not because it is original but because it is representative. The texts, ideas, and metaphors he assembled were well-known watchwords of midcentury pacifism, finding expression not only in reading and speech but in practice and symbolism. Because of this, they offer a revealing way into the subject matter of this book. I want to suggest, first, that pacifism is not a purely intellectual, moral, or ethical stance but exists in a matrix of culture and lifeways. Second, I propose that the culture of American pacifism as it exists in the early twenty-first century is historically contingent: it did not necessarily have to turn out the way it has.

Standard narratives of pacifist history, such as Staughton and Alice Lynd's *Nonviolence in America*, often assume that there is an unchanging category of "pacifism" or "nonviolence" that can be identified in diverse historical contexts.[4] But their approach overlooks the ways in which pacifism has evolved and has interacted with the various cultures in which it flourished or struggled. The Lynds and others apply a contemporary abstraction to acts and ideas that were much more complex, messy, and contingent in their own time. My intention here is to help the reader see pacifism through broader lenses, especially those of American religion, culture, and history.

Thus I argue first of all that religious pacifism was, and by implication is, a culture, not only an ethical or moral commitment. I trace continuity and change through cultural practices rather than through the usual approaches of intellectual and political history. I look at eight dimensions of the culture—social networks, theology, performance, iconography, individual spiritual practice, rituals of identity, narratives, and material culture. The book begins and ends with biographical chapters that reveal this continuity and change in the particularities of individual lives.

The book focuses on mainline Protestantism, which constituted the center of public religious pacifism in the United States during the large-scale peace movement after World War I. Most Protestant denominations during that period declared themselves opposed to war. Interdenominational groups like the Young Men's Christian Association (YMCA) fostered pacifism. Many of the more than one hundred peace organizations founded in the 1920s had significant mainline participation and leadership. This period of cultural immersion continued to shape both Christian and interreligious pacifism.

As World War II approached, however, pacifism moved from a central to a marginal position in mainline Protestantism and reshaped many dimensions of its culture. I argue that this change was a paradigm shift — a reorganization of cultural materials in response to built-up tensions and anomalies, a turn of the cultural kaleidoscope, not a radical innovation written on a blank slate.[5] The new paradigm, which took shape decisively between 1939 and 1942, had three principal characteristics: antimodernism, manifested in rural living, cooperative economics, and folkways; sectarianism, or self-separation from the mainstream, manifested in ritual and in stories of antiheroes; and a central emphasis on pacifism itself rather than on Christianity as the source of pacifism.

I suggest that Protestantism survived in pacifism in three ways. First, some groups of explicitly Protestant pacifists survived — for example, in denominational peace fellowships. Second, Protestantism survived as one of a number of options within the nonconfessional pacifism that predominated after 1960. Third, and most important, it survived in ideas and practices formed within Protestant pacifist culture, some of which later lost or severed their ties with the Protestant context.

In discussing pacifist culture, I also want to contribute toward a rethinking of mainline Protestantism. Over the last thirty years or so, the direction of growth in historical studies of American religion has been beyond the Protestant mainline. Much-needed works on evangelical and Pentecostal Christians, minority groups, new religions, and other forms of religious expression have displaced earlier assumptions about the normative nature of the mainline. Studies of the mainline have been correspondingly minimal. In recent years, however, a new scholarship has begun to emerge. Such writers as Leigh Eric Schmidt and David Morgan have incorporated ethnography, visual studies, material culture, and other methods into the study of history for a fresh look at the mainline. My work seeks to make a modest contribution to that conversation.

My narrative begins with an account of a World War I experience and concludes just before the Vietnam era. In this midcentury period, pacifist activity was most intense between the world wars, during the paradigm shift, during a brief revival after World War II, and in the late 1950s, as an antinuclear movement took hold. The materials in the book reflect this pattern, touching only lightly on the "nadir" of pacifism from 1950 to 1956.[6]

The book is both linear and circular. The first five chapters place more emphasis on the Protestant groundwork, the final four on the new paradigm. But, given the readily observable similarity in cultural themes between 1920 and 1960, every chapter traces movement through time. In many instances the chapters could be placed alongside one another, read as accounts of the same culture from different angles of vision. In other words, the reader may want to think of the book as a web rather than as a clothesline.

DESPITE THE PROBLEM of abstraction, a project such as this does need a working definition of pacifism. The broadest philosophical consensus defines pacifism as absolute opposition to war. But this leaves many questions open. Is "opposition" an internal moral commitment only, or does it require some form of action or practice? Is pacifism defined by refusal to participate as well as by moral opposition? Does opposition to war imply opposition to all violence? Are all forms of force violent? May a pacifist use physical force for personal self-defense? What about psychological force or coercion, in self-defense or otherwise? Does "violence" include social and economic as well as physical forces? Should opposition to war express itself in economic decisions about choice of work or consumer habits? What about paying taxes? Do all social causes conducive to peace properly belong under the rubric of pacifism?

Nor are pacifism's social boundaries always bright lines. It is true that some organizations, notably the Fellowship of Reconciliation (FOR), were theoretically limited to absolute pacifists. But many pacifists also participated in nonpacifist peace organizations, while others joined no organizations at all. Individuals slipped in and out of absolutist convictions or avoided committing themselves one way or the other. Absolutists disagreed among themselves, and argued endlessly, over definitions and implications of pacifism.

Most importantly, cultural materials were shared across boundaries. Books, prayers, songs, and posters were not rigidly divided between "peace advocacy" and "absolute pacifist" materials. Where definition is needed, then, I have relied on the consensus I mentioned above: pacifism is absolute opposition to all war. But lived pacifism has never been coterminous with any one organization, group, or ideological position.

Protestants are somewhat easier to identify. By "mainline" I mean seven culturally prominent denominations, most of them descended from or affected by nineteenth-century evangelicalism, that together constituted the center of American Protestantism in the first half of the twentieth century. These were the Congregationalists, Episcopalians, Methodists, United Lutherans, Disciples of Christ, Presbyterians, and Northern Baptists.[7] Methodists, Congregationalists, and Disciples had particularly strong pacifist factions between the world wars. Northern Baptists, Episcopalians, and Presbyterians also had a significant presence in peace activism.

In addition, I include Unitarians and liberal Friends (Quakers) in the study. Unitarians, of course, differed from the trinitarian mainline on an essential point of doctrine, the nature of the Christian God. But most, in the early twentieth century, professed Christian belief, participated in ecumenical activities, and were close to the mainline in piety, practice, and social location, while mainline Protestants by that time shared many of the liberal principles that Unitarians had pioneered. Among Protestant pacifists there is little meaningful difference between Unitarians and trinitarian Christians.

Quakers present a slightly different problem. Liberal Quakerism, located primarily in the Philadelphia-based Friends General Conference, had roots both in the mainstream evangelicalism of the nineteenth century and, with Unitarians, in early-nineteenth-century liberalism.[8] While chroniclers of Quaker history have often focused on Friends' exceptionalism, I would suggest instead that these Quakers occupied a sort of borderland with respect to the Protestant mainline. They had by the turn of the twentieth century moved some distance away from their original sectarianism, and over the course of the century they developed many social and theological connections with the mainline. On the other hand, their beliefs and practices remained distinctive enough that those who joined them as converts experienced Quakerism as different from other Protestant communions, and many midcentury mainliners regarded the Society of Friends as a model denomination different from their own. I propose that twentieth-century Quaker theology, mystical worship, and, after World War I, pacifism developed in a dialectical relationship with the Protestant mainstream. I have tried to trace that dialectic in this work.

In addition to denominational boundary crossings, Protestant peace materials crossed the boundaries between "religious" and "secular" contexts. Recent research has recognized the ways Protestantism has permeated American culture outside the boundaries of formal profession or membership.[9] In the pacifist case, Protestants participated in, and sometimes dominated, nominally secular peace organizations, while secular texts often included explicitly Protestant materials or were written to appeal to religious people. Here again, the discourses of Protestant pacifism resist complete identification with particular groups or individuals.

I have therefore found it useful throughout the study to think of Protestant pacifists as a folk group. A folk group is a group of "people who share some basis for everyday communal contacts, some factor in common that makes it possible, or rewarding or meaningful, to exchange vernacular materials in a culturally significant way." These materials comprise a wide range of modes of communication, including speech, written texts, gesture, ritual, music, and dress. Taken together, they constitute a "shared vernacular system of reference," a set of allusions and shared knowledge by which members of the group identify themselves and recognize each other and which differentiate the group from nonmembers. The materials typically exhibit a tension between tradition—a given way of doing things that supersedes individual taste, preference, and creativity—and dynamics, which encompass individual skill, variation, and "inventiveness" in using or performing traditional materials. The folk group further "[maintains] itself through its dynamics for a considerable time and . . . the expressive communications have thus become the educative matrix in which children of the group—or newcomers to it—are brought up."[10] In this view, Protestant pacifists constituted a subculture within and beyond the Protestant churches, defined by the use and exchange of these cultural materials rather than by formal profession or formal membership.

THEOLOGY, LIKE PACIFISM, calls for a brief discussion of definitions. Most Protestant pacifists were theological liberals. Although "liberal" has acquired a particular set of political and religious connotations in the early twenty-first century, historians use the term to refer to that form of Protestant Christianity that privileged reason and experience as sources of theological authority, affirmed the immanence of God and the general goodness of human nature, and emphasized ethics over doctrine. Liberal Protestantism was first identifiable as a movement in the early nineteenth century, reached its ascendancy between about 1875 and 1930, and survives into the present.

Liberals in their ascendancy were still very close to their evangelical heritage. Evangelicals constituted the mainstream of American Protestantism in the nineteenth century. They were Protestants who emphasized "the necessity of spiritual rebirth and a regenerate life of intense piety, moral purity, and public witness."[11] The rise of liberalism was largely a movement within the evangelical churches, and all parties took for granted the importance of the Bible and the centrality of Jesus Christ in human history. The polarization between evangelicals and liberals is a later phenomenon, although bitter controversy raged in the 1920s between liberals and fundamentalists.

Those opposed to fundamentalism were often called, or called themselves, "modernists." By this they generally meant that they welcomed modern knowledge about religion—biblical criticism, historical study, and study of other religions. Historians of ideas, however, have refined this definition, sometimes in divergent ways, and have not always agreed on the relationship of liberalism to modernism. William R. Hutchison's seminal work argued that modernism was an "impulse" in Protestantism that flourished during the period of liberal ascendancy. It was distinguished from general liberalism by its intentional embrace of modern culture and the conscious adaptation of religious ideas to it--the idea that God was immanent and revealed, not only in nature and persons, but in human society and its works.[12] More recently, Gary Dorrien has argued that all twentieth-century liberals were modernists, but he has argued for other distinctions among liberal theologians, which need not concern us here.[13]

In this book, I generally refer to pacifists as liberals, reserving the term "modernism" for its Hutchisonian meaning. The reader should bear Dorrien's insight in mind, however. Although modernism was muted after the 1930s, it did not disappear, and it was not necessarily the most significant criterion for distinguishing among liberal theologies. Moreover, many who referred to themselves as modernists used the term in its vernacular sense, meaning a wholehearted embrace of modern knowledge about religion— biblical criticism, historical study, and study of other religions.

KIRBY PAGE'S WORSHIP SERVICE points to some of the boundary lines on which liberal Protestants then stood: between formalism and flexibility, human effort and mystical experience, modernism and antimodernity.

And each of the texts carried multiple meanings, a network of associations and connections. The Francis prayer, for instance, reminds us that pacifists almost always mentioned Francis among examples of the committed religious life. They saw in him a model of many of the things they valued: *imitatio Christi*, nondoctrinal religiosity, resistance to institutions, direct and personal relationship with the divine, identity with ordinary people, community of goods, rural life, simplicity, and antimaterialism, as well as peace. Pacifist heroes from Gandhi to Glenn Clark were compared with him. Radical pacifists named a cooperative farm after him. Francis appeared in children's stories, conscientious objectors' statements, and spiritual autobiographies. An assessment of Civilian Public Service, a World War II program for conscientious objectors, declared, "If CPS were to have a patron saint, it would be St. Francis of Assisi."[14]

The song about "studying war no more" was usually accounted a "spiritual," a religious folk song with political overtones that emerged among African American slaves. The levels of meaning in white Americans' adoption of spirituals would make a study in themselves. Still, it is clear that when pacifists sang this song, they intended to signal not only opposition to war but respect for African Americans and solidarity with the oppressed. These ideals became inextricably intertwined with the ideal of peace.

Pacifists adopted both the prayer and the song from the wider culture. A stream of literature beginning in the late nineteenth century had presented St. Francis as an antiauthoritarian, mystical liberal, and the peace prayer circulated widely in Europe and the United States.[15] As for the song, a number of published versions had appeared during the 1920s, probably as part of the widespread reaction against war in that decade. The revivalist musician Homer Rodeheaver, the peace educator Florence Brewer Boeckel, and the poet and Americanist Carl Sandburg all included it in collections.[16]

Yet neither of these texts is what it is commonly believed to be. The peace prayer is not among the known writings of the historical Francis. It seems to have first appeared in French in 1913, in a Catholic devotional magazine. The earliest known English translation was in 1936. By that time, however, the saint's well-established following, the rising Protestant interest in personal devotion, and the threat of war ensured its popularity.[17]

And the song was probably not a slave song. There is no record of it before World War I, although traditional African American songs collected and published in the late nineteenth century sometimes used the refrain "down by the river," and at least one of those songs also referred to "war."

Elements of these songs may in turn have been borrowed from white camp-meeting traditions. All the early examples are associated with other melodies than the popular twentieth-century one. Neither James Weldon Johnson nor Howard Thurman included this song in his work on spirituals. Several sources credit Harry T. Burleigh, an African American singer, composer, and interpreter of black music, with publishing the song sometime between 1917 and 1922. Oral recollections, too, date it to that era. Sandburg, in 1927, cited reports that black Alabama families "sing it by the hour." And one of my own relatives claimed to have sung it in 1921 in, of all places, the Army Corps of Engineers.[18]

But this, of course, is the point. The people who published, sang, and recited these works were not interested in historical accuracy as much as they were interested in an experience and in a symbolic world. An appeal to history lent weight to that symbolic world but did not shape it, except perhaps secondarily. It is that world that this book seeks to capture — the elements of culture that affirmed pacifists' identity, urged them onward, and tied them to their deepest commitments and beliefs, to their past, to the future they hoped for, and to communities of the living and of the dead.

1 "Character 'Bad'"

HAROLD GRAY

The only way to overcome evil is by good—aggressive goodwill.—Harold Studley Gray, Character "Bad"

In 1934, in the midst of the pacifist travails of the 1930s, several books appeared that shaped pacifist memory and charted future directions. Vera Brittain's *Testament of Youth* was said to speak "for her sex, and for her generation" about the experience of the war.[1] Richard Gregg's *The Power of Non-Violence* offered a new paradigm for the relationship between pacifism and political action. But there is no better introduction to the mental world of midcentury American pacifists than Harold Studley Gray's *Character "Bad."*

Character "Bad" was an edited collection of letters written by a young man who turned to conscientious objection during the First World War and struggled with its implications. It circulated widely among pacifists and appeared on reading lists for Protestant youth groups through the end of World War II.[2] It introduces persistent themes of pacifist culture—liberal and modernist theological reflection, scrupulous ethics, consistent living, cooperative economics, rural life, prison, and fasting—as well as mutable or contested themes like conversion. Gray's social class, his religious affiliations, his associates, and his reading are also typical of pacifist culture. Even the title is indicative of pacifists' sense of exceptionalism, implying as it does a certain ironic pride in being "bad."[3] My primary concern here is not with the historical or biographical data the book presents but with what it reveals, as a text, about the culture of Protestant pacifism.

HAROLD GRAY'S LIFE

Harold Gray, the son of a Ford Motor Company attorney, was born in 1894 and grew up in Detroit.[4] He belonged to the Christian Church (Disciples of Christ), from which came a number of prominent pacifists, including Kirby Page, Charles Clayton Morrison, and Harold Fey. But much of his religious formation, especially in his teenage years and young adulthood, came from the interdenominational organizations in which he was active: the YMCA, Student Christian Associations, and Phillips Brooks House at Harvard. Because his secondary-school career was not particularly successful—owing, says his editor, to his extensive involvement in religious activities and a period of serious illness—Gray was already twenty when he entered Harvard College.[5]

The events recounted in this book occurred during the three years following Gray's sophomore year at Harvard. In the summer of 1916 he left college to volunteer as a YMCA secretary in England, working with German prisoners of war. While there he committed himself to pacifism. He returned to the United States in the fall of 1917 and registered for the draft, requesting exemption as a conscientious objector.[6] This request was denied, and he was inducted into the army in April 1918. As an absolutist, he refused to perform either combatant or noncombatant service. He exercised resistance in various ways, including a hunger strike. In October he was imprisoned in the guardhouse at Fort Riley, Kansas, after refusing to obey a military order. A court-martial later that month on charges of disobedience sentenced him to life in prison at Leavenworth, a sentence reduced to twenty-five years upon judicial review. Gray was imprisoned just after the Armistice and was transferred to Alcatraz in July 1919. In September 1919 the remainder of his sentence was commuted, and he received a dishonorable discharge with the written comment "Character 'Bad'".

Afterward Gray returned to a life of modest social service. Upon his release from Alcatraz, he completed his B.A. and M.A. in economics at

Harvard. He taught in China for several years, and in 1928 decided to "supplement [his] theoretical training with practical experience" by working in a bank.[7] The stock market crash and its consequences reinforced his interest in an alternative economic order, and in 1932 he set out to "realize the long-cherished dream" of founding a cooperative farm. In this he was fairly successful: his Saline Valley Farms were still operating as late as 1963.[8] Gray maintained membership in the Fellowship of Reconciliation, lectured occasionally about his wartime experiences, and took a public position against conscription during World War II, but was otherwise not particularly active in peace work.[9]

A few further notes are in order about the class and religious context in which Gray was situated. He was well-to-do, was well educated, and favored high culture: he attended the opera and theater, read poetry, and disparaged ragtime. His social status won attention from some military officers and judges; his captain at Camp Custer, for example, became "most friendly" when he realized that Gray "was a Harvard man and had been abroad." Gray's father had enough influence to get him an army desk job—which Gray of course refused—and made efforts to secure his release from prison.[10]

Gray's church was in a state of transition. Rooted in the Midwest and South, the Disciples of Christ were not generally considered part of the "mainline" until around 1900.[11] Their nineteenth-century forebears had not intended to found a denomination at all, but to restore the primitive state of the church, thereby eliminating denominational boundaries. Thus the Disciples had traditionally affirmed both the sole authority of the Bible and ecumenical openness. In the early twentieth century these emphases were increasingly in tension, with a liberal leadership embracing modern developments and a conservative faction moving toward fundamentalism.[12]

As for interdenominational activity, some commentators have claimed that the YMCA before and during the war was chiefly interested in personal religion, turning its attention to social issues only after 1918.[13] But this understanding draws too sharp a contrast. The personal religion of Gray's time was outgoing and activistic. It propagated an ethic of social service, a term that was understood to include missions and evangelism but was not limited to them. Gray's own activities with the YMCA in England are indicative: he mentioned evangelism but devoted the greatest share of his time to meeting the material and social needs of prisoners of war. Moreover, many in the YMCA were attuned to the Social Gospel ideas that had been widely embraced a decade before the war.[14]

On the other hand, Gray's story is itself a narrative of personal conversion and of its consequences. Conversion stories had long been a staple of pious speech and literature, originating in Puritan soul-searching and transposed into a different key for a broader American evangelicalism.[15] In this context they were probably familiar to Gray. But his narrative was not concerned with election or salvation, at least not directly. Instead, his conversion was to pacifism, and more broadly to social Christianity.

CONVERSION TO PACIFISM

Neither Gray nor his editor used the term "conversion." Yet Gray's account follows in every way the pattern of evangelical conversion narratives: a conviction of sin, a struggle culminating in surrender, and an ensuing sense of rebirth and assurance, subsequently tested for perseverance. Gray's conversion led him to a search for absolute consistency between belief and action based on freedom of conscience. Its outcomes were scrupulous ethics, suffering, and, by Gray's account, great happiness.

Like most conversions, Gray's had antecedents. He had been interested in the problem of peace as early as 1909. In July 1916, on board ship to England, he and his fellow YMCA secretaries—including the well-known evangelist Sherwood Eddy and his assistant, Kirby Page, both of whom were prominent pacifists in later years—engaged in prayer and "wonderful talks," which probably addressed social as well as spiritual issues.[16]

As the young secretaries encountered the effects of war in London, they turned their attention more directly to questions of war and peace. Informal discussions continued throughout the summer and fall. During the winter the secretaries agreed to hold a monthly seminar: they would read and discuss five hundred pages a month on "some topic connected with the present war."[17]

In this environment Gray came to an intellectual acceptance of pacifism. In October he wrote that "Kirby and I have been trying to thrash out the problem of whether a man is ever justified in using force to the extent of taking life." A few weeks later he declared, "I am a pacifist from the word go, if you mean by that one who is opposed to war under all conditions." In January Gray began reading and writing in preparation for his seminar presentation, a defense of the conscientious objector. "I am not the only man in the crowd that believes war is wrong," he remarked.[18]

But conversion involves a change of heart as well as a change of mind. The first signs of this change appeared in the spiritual turmoil that accompanied Gray's preparation of his paper. His prayer life, previously enthusiastic and meaningful, became dry: "Spiritually I am getting rusty. Instead of coming in contact with others and setting them on fire and thereby keeping myself aglow, I seem to be burning lower and lower." He felt a growing dissonance between his developing convictions and the society around him: "My presence is almost a stigma" at the hotel where he was lodged.[19]

Around the same time, Gray heard the Reverend W. E. Orchard preach "the greatest peace sermon I have ever heard" and sought him out for counsel. Like an evangelist seeking a convert, Orchard took an unusual interest in the young man; he immediately invited him to dinner, and afterward served as his pastor and adviser. Other mentors may also have played a role: Kirby Page later recalled that Sherwood Eddy arranged for Gray, Page, and others to discuss their concerns with pacifists Henry Hodgkin and Maude Royden.[20] Gray's edited text, however, refers only to Orchard.

The crisis began as Gray prepared to present his seminar paper. A few days before his presentation, a new idea struck him with such force as to realign all his previous thinking. In retrospect, it does not seem startlingly original. Gray thought that freedom of choice was the greatest sign of God's love for humanity. It followed that God, in Jesus, rejected all use of force in order not to deprive human beings of that freedom. Jesus therefore refused to establish a kingdom — even one of "love, peace, and righteousness" — by force, because even good ends could not justify evil means. For this refusal he was crucified. Crucifixion, then, is bound up with pacifism in Gray's view: "the world hated him [Jesus] and nailed him on a tree" because he would not lead his nation in "a just... war of liberation against... tyranny." In view of Christian observance, it is significant that Gray came to these conclusions on the night before Easter.[21]

The new idea triggered Gray's real conversion. "My idea is thoroly revolutionary and if I drive it to its logical conclusion ... it will result in some radical reforms in my own life.... The things which I have been feeling for the past six months but which I have been unable to express are now gradually settling down into convictions." His agonies grew intense as he tried to work out the consequences of his idea. The week after his presentation was "one of the greatest struggles I have ever known — a struggle which will determine my attitude not alone toward this war but toward the whole of life." In May he wrote, "I cannot describe my state of mind. There has been a terrible upheaval and it has brought me to God as I never knew him before." And in June, "My mind has undergone such an earthquake that even my dreams reflect my thoughts. . . . As yet I have not found a vocabulary to describe what has happened nor have I found anyone who can help me." And later, "I couldn't sleep more than a few hours each night."[22]

Gray's comment about "the whole of life" was important. He described his struggle tentatively as "the birth of a social self." Conscientious objection, a decision "between allegiance to Jesus or to the State," was one aspect of it. But allegiance to Jesus had wider implications. "I am beginning to apply Christianity to everything," he exclaimed, "with the result that either society or Christianity must sooner or later go smash as far as my own life is concerned."[23] Gray believed, then, that pacifist commitment did not stand alone but was necessarily linked to social, economic, and material life.

Ultimately Gray went to Dr. Orchard for reassurance, resigned his position with the YMCA, and went to stay with friends for a period of reflection. A few months later he began to act on his pacifist convictions. We will return to that story later on. For now, let us note that conversion produces a lasting change in worldview, called in traditional Protestant language "perseverance." Gray's perseverance was especially evident in two things: the fact that he never afterward wavered from his convictions, and his repeated expressions of great happiness, particularly during his imprisonment.

GRAY'S RELIGIOUS THOUGHT

There was an intellectual dimension to Gray's internal struggles. His thought had a great deal in common with modern Protestant liberalism, but it was not a systematic theology. There were no clearly stated principles, no defined terms, and no particular attention to developing a unified intellectual system. Nor did Gray refer to academic theologies or theologians. Rather, Gray's was a popular theology. It was derived from preaching and informal study in response to immediate problems of applied ethics, and it was visible in passing references, allusions, and assumptions as much as in expository statements.[24] Subsequent Protestant pacifism derived its theological thought from sources similar to Gray's, in similar ways, and with similar motifs and assumptions.

Gray's sources were both textual and social. I have mentioned the social sources: the nexus of activistic Protestantism, the university, the YMCA study group and informal discussions, and the guidance of older pacifists. Among textual sources the Bible, of course, was preeminent. Gray also made references to hymns, a favorite repository of Protestant piety. He read works by Harry Emerson Fosdick, Henry Drummond, and Phillips Brooks—all preachers and popular theologians, and all liberals, as were Orchard and Eddy, whom he heard viva voce. He mentioned Emerson's *Essays* and Tolstoy's *Resurrection* and *My Religion*, nineteenth-century forerunners of liberal Protestant pacifism. And he read Romain Rolland, a literary pacifist and critic of conventional religion.[25]

Gray's thought also suggests Social Gospel influences, which I discuss more fully in chapter 3. He shared much of the orientation of the Social Gospel theologians: he was concerned with the involvement of Christianity in the totality of life, including social and government systems, and he used the guiding motif of the Kingdom of God. It is scarcely conceivable that Gray had not encountered these ideas in his religious activism or university training. But even if he had not, his friend Kirby Page would have been a particularly strong influence: after studying various theories of the social order as an undergraduate, Page had embraced the Social Gospel theology of Walter Rauschenbusch and Washington Gladden, and he continued to advocate for it.[26]

It is important to note, however, that Gray nowhere identified himself with the Social Gospel or referred to its exponents or theories. This is a good example of how religious ideas are transmitted via a folk process among pacifists: they are "in the air," they are repeated, they are available, an individual may select and adopt them, but their derivation is not thought important, and individuals often experience their convictions as unique or distinctive.

Gray did make a few systematic expositions of his ideas: the seminar paper in 1917, the statement to his draft board, and his defense before the court-martial.[27] The last of these offers the clearest and most fully developed introduction to his theology of pacifism. Gray first rejected the myth of Germany as the sole aggressor in World War I. The real cause of the war, he said, lay in "the present, unchristian, materialistic social order in which we live." This social order is rooted in "sin in the human heart" and requires "regeneration"—defined as a softening of human hearts "in love towards one another"—to repair it. Thus, Gray retained the orthodox terms "sin" and "regeneration." But he understood sin to be both individual and social, and he interpreted regeneration in terms of the central liberal motif of love. He reinforced this interpretation when he said, "I believe that the establishment of a relationship of love with God and with our fellow men is the end or purpose of life."[28]

Gray then addressed the question of how this end was to be attained. One way, "the way of the sword," would be to "eliminate" evildoers, those who "work against" the relationship of love. Love itself, however, called for "the way of the Cross," which would entail "bearing with" the evildoer and accepting the consequent suffering in hopes of the evildoer's eventual repentance. This was how a loving God acted. Human beings might come to recognize God's suffering love "thru others who are living and preaching it." They would then change their ways, not from fear of punishment but "out of fear of wounding the heart of One who loves them and whose heart is cut by the sin they commit." And they "strive to act towards those who sin against them, as God has acted toward them."[29]

Gray was concerned, then, with the consistency of means and ends. Love, in his view, was both. As a means, it was not only morally correct but effective. Even though it might involve suffering, it would ultimately produce results.

It followed that he understood Christian life as *imitatio Christi*: Christians were to act like Christ, who acts like God.[30] Gray's editor borrowed Charles Sheldon's famous question, "What would Jesus do?"—from a bestselling work probably known to Gray as well.[31] It is also significant that Gray added "*living*" the way of the Cross to "preaching" it. Later in the statement he said, "I do not believe in war or in compulsory service under any circumstances, and I cannot live as if I did."[32]

Lived Christianity had been a continuous theme in Gray's thought. From Fort Riley he had written to his parents, "How I wish I could live the truth as I see it and please you both at the same time." But, he continued, "I simply cannot surrender my self-respect by living a lie." And in England he struggled with consistency of belief and action: "Do you realize that if there is no other way than war, Christianity is a failure, it is a lie?"[33]

Gray found in liberalism the warmth that observers usually associate with evangelicalism. He aligned himself clearly with modern critical study when he said of the other COs at Camp Custer, where he was first assigned: "Most of them take their Bible with painful literalness. There seems to be no one here who goes at the problem from a modern point of view."[34] But critical study was no sterile intellectual exercise. For him, as for most twentieth-century liberals, it was literalism that was sterile. His new idea, for example, "made [his] New Testament a living document instead of a 'scrap of paper.'" He continued, "The Gospels, particularly Jesus' teachings and the atonement, have become illuminated; God has been refound, in truth, a very living companion."[35]

Other religious themes important to Gray, though no more than implicit in the court-martial statement, are woven through his informal writings. These are the Kingdom of God, modernism, the historical Jesus, human nature and personality, sin and suffering, service, freedom, upward striving, and light.

Gray's references to the Kingdom of God echo the language of Protestant modernism as well as the Social Gospel. Early on, Gray wondered "how much [he was] willing to do to try and further Christ's Kingdom." And, "Even tho the present looks so black, it may mark the dawn of a new epoch for the Kingdom of God on earth if only even a few of us will dare to have faith." Later, arguing against conscription, he contrasted the Kingdom with the state: "God never conscripts men against their wills to serve Him and His Kingdom but always seeks to enlist them."[36]

Gray shared the modernist preoccupation with the historical Jesus and anxiety about his uniqueness. Jesus' "experience" had "assured him that he was indeed God's chosen; but he was no heavenly being coming on the clouds of heaven — he was a man." As such, his "life and teachings," not his divine nature, merited attention: "I am convinced we have fallen far short of grasping the teachings of Jesus." Jesus, as a human being, was tempted to use force to establish "a kingdom of peace and righteousness," but his "greatness" and "uniqueness" are apparent in his recognizing this as "a temptation of the devil."[37]

Gray also held a high view of human "personality," a favorite term of liberals that suggested uniqueness and individuality.[38] "How can a man help loving a God who respects his personality like that?" he asked. Similarly, he argued that war was wrong because it "violates men's personalities."[39]

It followed that he could be optimistic about human nature and capability. Human nature, he thought, contains "the spark of the divine." One of his early letters said, "The only way to overcome evil is by good — aggressive goodwill." Again, "There is only one way to drive out evil and that is with good." While his ideas about suffering tempered his optimism somewhat, he was nonetheless able to write from Leavenworth, "As fast as I have my eyes opened to the evil in men's hearts, God opens my eyes to the good which is there too, patiently waiting for the coming of love to make it blossom forth. I am often amazed even among the so-called religious c.o.'s how little faith they have in God and the power of love as the only way!"[40]

Gray also acknowledged sin and suffering. The root of the war, he said, was "selfishness [and] pride fostered by wealth . . . and the Gray family, H.S.G. in particular, carries a pretty good share of sin in this respect." Later he concluded, "For a Christian there is no such thing as 'a necessary evil' because the Cross reveals the fact that suffering . . . is to be preferred to participation in evil." Of soldiers he said, "If only these men had suffered as much in the interests of the kingdom of love as they have suffered and are suffering for war!"[41]

Historians of pacifism have sometimes overlooked the wide use of the term "service" at this time. Not only Gray but also his father—himself active in the YMCA and completely opposed to Gray's pacifism—took it for granted: "This war offers the greatest opportunity for real service which I suppose has ever existed." Gray used similar language for his hospital work at Leavenworth: "a wonderful opportunity for service." The term was familiar enough to serve as the basis of a comparison: "His [God's] Will for the present at least," Gray wrote to his father, "lies in martyrdom rather than service."[42]

Another important motif, which later pacifists explored in different ways, was freedom. While in military camp Gray bemoaned the inability of the soldiers to break out of conventional thinking about the war. "Christ is the only solution" to this problem, he said: in Christ, "we are no longer slaves but free." In prison, he referred to his personal sense of spiritual freedom: "I prefer spiritual freedom with physical bondage to physical freedom with even a wee bit of spiritual bondage." Charles Clayton Morrison, editor of the *Christian Century*, confirmed that sense when he inscribed a book: "To Harold S. Gray, in bonds but more free than the free."[43]

One final passage may serve as a summary, not only of Gray's theological ideas but also of the imagery of light and upward movement that liberal pacifists favored.

> The history of man is the record of his struggle for a larger life, his struggle from darkness into light, from falsehood to truth, in short his struggle for the perfection of life in God. In this struggle truth comes to him from within thru the heart to which God is able to speak when

man will listen. He sees a light and struggles to attain it; another sees his effort and he too comes to see the light and to struggle towards it; and slowly, very slowly sometimes, the world goes forward and up . . . because in the beginning one man or a few were true to the light they saw and by living it finally enabled all to see.

Gray adds, "Probably no man ever saw this so clearly as Jesus Christ, whose whole life and teaching were a protest" against favoring the "will of the majority" over the "still small voice of truth within."[44]

ACTION AND CONSEQUENCES

The narrative of Gray's conversion takes up less than half of the book. The remainder follows him through his efforts to act on his new convictions. His immediate plan of action shifted a number of times in the months after he committed himself to pacifism, but finally, in November 1917, he decided to return to the United States and face conscription. Once again, he reached this decision through reading and conversation, as he and his friend Evan Thomas studied the case histories of English COs.[45] In April 1918 he was called to Camp Custer in Battle Creek, Michigan.

Two aspects of Gray's subsequent actions are particularly important. One is the meaning of the body. Because control over the body, via conscription and internment, was the state's primary means of interference, the body was the ground of much of Gray's protest. Working, eating, wearing fatigues, gestures: these, more than speech or print, were the areas contested between "Jesus and the State."

The other is his decision-making process, which was characterized by minute examination of the implications of every action. The effects of the actions were less important: Gray was concerned with being true to "the light as he sees it," not with changing his immediate situation. In the long term, though, he did hope to persuade the authorities that conscription was wrong. There was a paradox, too, in Gray's careful decision-making, because he was engaged in a sort of endgame in which compromise was ultimately impossible. He knew what the result would be, sooner or later: "I shall be given some command and refusing to obey, I shall be court-martialed." And indeed that is what happened.[46]

One set of choices, as summarized by the book's editor, offers a good example of the kind of thinking Gray and others engaged in:

Should they obey any command given by an officer? Was obedience a condoning of the system they were determined to resist? If they were willing to maintain order and cleanliness about their cantonment, who should decide the boundaries of their grounds? What if the officers were to declare that the entire camp was within their province...? If they were to assist in the preparation of their own food, what was to prevent those in charge of the kitchen using their services for... the other barracks? And if this took place... what was their answer to the retort, that if they could cook for the soldiers they could do ambulance or farm service? If they were forced to cook their own meals, just what was their status in the army?[47]

At Camp Custer, Gray seemed to treat his situation as something of a lark. He was "very happy." He was with "a great bunch of men," had "heaps of fun" at recreation, and received "perfectly wonderful eats." True to his YMCA background, he also saw opportunities for "making converts," not just to pacifism but to Christianity.[48]

But he was serious about conscientiously scrutinizing his decisions. Upon learning that the other absolutists were taking care of themselves and their own barracks, Gray said carefully that he "could see no reason for refusing to share in this work, at least until I had given it a trial and had come to the conclusion that it was not the wisest policy." Called out for an emergency work detail two months later, he "began to feel uncomfortable about it" shortly after beginning, and, with a number of others, eventually refused to continue.[49]

Not long after this episode, a team of special examiners arrived at the camp to test the sincerity of COs and, where possible, reassign them. Most accepted alternative or noncombatant service. Gray, however, declared his "refusal to serve the government in any capacity whatsoever." Although he admitted that he had not fully thought through the reciprocal responsibilities of the individual, society, and government, he "felt that at present the highest service I could render my nation was in protesting" its course of action by "refusing to serve in any way and going to prison for it." He was sent briefly to Leavenworth and then, with about 120 other COs, to Fort Riley, Kansas.[50]

Here, both government pressure and Gray's scruples became more pronounced. He and others refused to work on building their own cantonment. "I am being held by the government and prevented from doing what

I feel to be God's will," he wrote, "and under such circumstances I do not feel that I can conscientiously coöperate with the government in keeping me here."⁵¹ Using this reasoning, he came to believe that he could not coöperate even to the extent of caring for himself, as he had done earlier. With two fellow objectors, Evan Thomas and Howard Moore, he began refusing to prepare his own food from the uncooked rations that were provided. "We decided that it was the government's business to keep us," he said, since the government insisted on their being there.⁵²

Not all the COs agreed on where to draw these lines, however. Nearly half did work on the cantonment. Most had no scruples about cooking until Gray and his friends raised the issue, and even then, not all were convinced. Gray's account of an early meeting of the COs verges on the comic: "Evan [Thomas] presided. It was over the matter of K.P. [kitchen police]: this service an ever increasing number of men was refusing to do on the grounds that they were serving a number of noncommissioned officers and a number of noncombatant C.O.'s. . . . All sorts of conditions were laid down by various men upon which their doing of K.P. depended. It was clear in a few moments that absolutely any agreement or any sort of coöperation among ourselves was impossible. Evan resigned and the meeting broke up."⁵³

The reason some of the absolutists refuse to serve noncombatants was that, in the absolutists' eyes, the noncombatants' complicity with the military system was more significant than their refusal to bear arms. Even within their own group, however, the absolutists drew lines so numerous and particular as to render them unable to act together. Brown rightly noted the COs' tendency toward "dangerous individualism." But he apparently overlooked its corollary: a kind of paralyzing perfectionism.⁵⁴

By this time Gray was no longer protesting against participation in war only. In articulating more fully his thinking about the individual and the state, he had come to the conclusion that individual liberty of conscience — by implication, obedience to God — took precedence over the state, the group, or "the will of the majority." The individual had a right and a duty to heed "the still small voice . . . within," to "follow the light as he sees it," to "perform the work we felt called upon by God to do." Any interference by the state with this right was illegitimate. "As for war," he wrote, "I feel there is room for an honest disagreement between men as to whether it is ever justifiable, but I cannot see how two men who profess to be dedicated to the truth should differ as to conscription."⁵⁵

This was the reasoning behind the hunger strike that Gray, Moore, Thomas, and Erling Lunde undertook in August 1918. "[We] are unalterably opposed to the principle of conscription.... We have ... determined to refuse to eat as long as we are kept from following the pursuits we feel called upon to follow in life," they wrote. But even this extreme action raised issues requiring further decisions. Gray, for example, worried that his action might be construed as upholding a right to suicide. Since he did not uphold such a right, he did not resist forced feeding. This freed him of the appearance of supporting suicide but left him open to the charge of cooperating with the government. Finally he abandoned the strike altogether. Lunde joined him; Thomas and Moore did not. Sixteen others also struck for a time, but for a different reason: "only for prepared food."[56]

An episode at Leavenworth similarly illustrates Gray's decision-making process and the importance of the body in his thought and action. Prisoners were expected to fold their arms when they encountered officers in the course of their work.[57] At first, Gray told himself that this was only a harmless gesture, intended "to assure an officer that a man did not carry concealed weapons." But, as with the work detail earlier, he grew uncomfortable. He came "more and more to feel that it [folding the arms] is an act of worship," not merely a functional gesture.[58] Such an act was, of course, incompatible with freedom of conscience, and Gray, with a number of others, stopped observing the practice. The prison authorities overlooked this small rebellion for a while, but later gathered about fifty of the protesters and gave them a direct command to fold their arms. They of course refused.

In connection with this incident, Gray echoed the language of his conversion. Though threatened with punishment, he said, "I have felt happier since things have come to a head.... I fear my conscience has been pricking me more than I realized." But the battle of conscience was not over yet. The prison authorities offered evidence that the gesture was purely a practical one, and Gray, feeling "upset" and "up in the air," decided to fold his arms after all. "I don't think I would enjoy solitary very much," he wrote, "unless my mind was easy on the cause of my being there."[59]

Was this admirable application of principle or destructive scrupulosity? Unwavering attention to the divine will, or unproductive hairsplitting? Dangerous individualism or flashes of insight? My purpose is not to make those judgments but to point out the emergence of a pattern—one that was also visible in the CO camps of World War II, in the postwar elaboration of nonviolent direct action, and, less directly, even in arguments over who was or was not a pacifist.

HAROLD GRAY'S STORY, as enacted during World War I and recounted in 1934, is an emblem of Protestant pacifist culture. Gray was an educated young man of the middle class, nurtured in a mainline church and in ecumenical youth organizations. His religious sensibility combined Protestant liberalism and modernism, all-embracing social concern, and the experiential intensity of conversion. In the tension between faithfulness and effectiveness, which was and is characteristic of Christian pacifism, Gray was inclined to favor faithfulness. This did not mean inaction, however, but scrupulous testing of every act for its fidelity to God's will and Jesus' example.

Gray's faithfulness was played out in bodily action, both on the large scale of resistance and imprisonment and on the small scale of gesture and self-care. In accepting the possibility of physical suffering Gray claimed to have found happiness and freedom. Some of his actions suggest in outline the rituals that pacifist culture later developed more fully, through which they expressed conscientious objection, moral purity, and group solidarity.

2 From YMCA to CPS

PACIFIST SOCIAL NETWORKS

For the extension of any cause, I have believed all my life and have tried to practice the threefold technique of the spoken word, the printed page, and the organization of men first in small, intimate, vital groups and later in national or international bodies.
—Sherwood Eddy,
A Pilgrimage of Ideas

Historians of pacifism have long known that Protestant participation in the peace movement between the world wars extended far beyond the "historic peace churches." Most mainline Protestant organizations took formal antiwar positions during the 1920s and 1930s. The Federal Council of Churches, the Presbyterian Church in the U.S.A., the Methodist Episcopal Church, and the Disciples of Christ acted as whole bodies. The Northern Baptist Convention and the General Council of the Congregational and Christian Churches strongly urged individual pacifist commitments, while the Protestant Episcopal bishops affirmed that "the cross is above the flag." Polls and public statements showed widespread cross-denominational pacifism. Smaller denominations and some southern churches also took pacifist stands. All affirmed that, as the Congregationalists put it, "the cleavage between the way of Jesus and the system of war is clear."[1]

This chapter looks at the social structures within which Protestant pacifism flourished—including but extending beyond the churches—and at the routes by which people became pacifists. One might envision pacifist culture as something like a spiderweb, with lines radiating outward from center to perimeter and crosspieces connecting the radii at various points. Thus Protestants exploring pacifism might begin at almost any point on the perimeter. They might follow one strand directly to the center or might travel along several of the crosspieces to other radii, but eventually they would reach the same center. And an impact at any point in the web would affect the whole thing.[2] We will see how those social structures and channels of transmission changed around 1940, one manifestation of the paradigm shift that was taking place.

THE PROTESTANT BASE

Most of the public figures in Christian pacifism were mainline Protestant clergymen. Harry Emerson Fosdick, a Baptist, preached pacifism from a nationally known pulpit; John Nevin Sayre, an Episcopalian, and John Haynes Holmes, a Unitarian and community-church pastor, led the FOR; Kirby Page of the Disciples of Christ was a popularizer and evangelist. A number of seminary professors and professors of religion were pacifists, including presidents Albert W. Palmer of Chicago Theological Seminary and Edwin McNeill Poteat of Colgate-Rochester Divinity School.[3] Ad hoc groups such as the Emergency Peace Campaign and the Ministers' No War Committee were spearheaded by Protestant clergy and were able to gather the signatures of clergy and church officials from all the mainline denominations; the latter committee claimed nearly 2,000 members in twenty denominations in 1941.[4] As late as 1942 an observer estimated that half of the "influential" clergy were pacifists.[5] Even among less prominent clergy, a substantial minority were pacifists: Kirby Page conducted a well-publicized survey in 1934 that found nearly 13,000 ministers, or about two-thirds of the respondents, opposed to any future war.[6] As in Protestantism generally, many pacifist clergy knew each other and worked together.[7]

Lay Protestants, too, were prominent in the interwar peace movement. The "secular" War Resisters League (WRL) was founded and managed by two Protestant laywomen, Tracy Mygatt, an Episcopalian, and Frances Witherspoon, a Presbyterian with Episcopalian sympathies. Frederick Lynch, a Congregationalist turned Quaker, founded the National Council for Prevention of War (NCPW). And mainliners, historic pacifists, and "secular" pacifists often worked together. For example, the *Pacifist Handbook* of

1939, a guide to conscientious objection, was a joint project not only of Quakers, Brethren, and Mennonites but also of Methodists, the FOR, and the Women's International League for Peace and Freedom (WILPF).

Moreover, "secular" organizations often used religious language, and when they did, it was usually mainline Protestant. For example, some of Florence Brewer Boeckel's instructional books on peace, written for the NCPW, included hymns, Sunday school lessons, and projects for church groups.[8] Similarly, a World Peaceways booklet on education included the texts of two "peace songs" recommended by John Haynes Holmes and mentioned a Congregationalist publication, *Educating for Peace*, in its bibliography.[9] Hegemonic mainline Protestantism, then, was widely taken for granted even in nominally secular contexts.

If there was a center to this Protestant pacifism, it was undoubtedly the Fellowship of Reconciliation. Founded in 1914 by the British Quaker Henry Hodgkin, the FOR began as an interdenominational Protestant organization for those opposed to all war. The U.S. branch was formed in 1915 and soon developed ties to Christian socialism and social-justice issues.[10] "When we come to the task of rebuilding a ruined civilization," said a 1918 essay, "what hope is there anywhere if not in the Christian Gospel?"[11]

In the inner circle of the FOR were Protestants whose names appeared repeatedly in pacifist writings and actions. The editors and managers of *The World Tomorrow* (1918–34), a periodical that served as the unofficial organ of the FOR, included Kirby Page, Devere Allen, Dorothy Detzer, Reinhold Niebuhr, George Coe, Halford Luccock, John Nevin Sayre, Henry Pitney Van Dusen, Sherwood Eddy, John Haynes Holmes, Paul Jones, and A. J. Muste. All were mainline Protestants, and almost all were clergy. The editorial board of its successor publication, *Fellowship* (1935–), was similarly composed, except for the conspicuous absence of Niebuhr. In 1940 it included Sayre, Muste, Allen, Detzer, Holmes, Jones, Luccock, and Page, as well as Episcopalians Walter Russell Bowie and Sarah Cleghorn; Baptists Bernard Clausen and Howard Thurman; Methodists Albert Edward Day, Georgia Harkness, and John Swomley; Congregationalist Allan Hunter; Quakers Douglas Steere and Richard Gregg (a former Congregationalist); and independent Protestant Muriel Lester.

On the other hand, the FOR was not entirely coterminous with Protestant pacifism. Although the large majority of its membership, and the tone of its religious language, was Christian and Protestant, the membership was officially opened to non-Christians in 1930. And it is likely that not all

Protestant pacifists joined the FOR: a steep increase in membership around the beginning of World War II suggests a large pool of sympathizers outside the official rolls, as this chapter shows later on.

THE MAKING OF PACIFISTS BETWEEN THE WARS

Colleges, Universities, and the Student Christian Movement

Social movements typically find new adherents among students, who tend to have some leisure, openness to new ideas, and questions about a life direction.[12] The peace movement of the 1920s and 1930s was no exception. Colleges and universities provided fertile ground for young adults' deliberations on war, peace, and pacifism. Resources and congenial fellow seekers were readily available for those who wished to explore the issues in depth.

During the 1930s, peace advocates regularly brought their cause before the public in peace-pledge demonstrations and annual student strikes. Mainline Protestant students joined in these actions. The strikes from 1935 onward were organized by a coalition of socialists, communists, and Protestants—the Inter-Seminary League and the National Council of Methodist Youth. At their height in 1937, 350,000 students participated.[13] On a smaller scale, male students on many campuses faced decisions about participation in ROTC and military drill. In one celebrated case, eight Ohio State University students were suspended for refusing to participate in drill in 1934. Three of them were Methodists, one a Congregationalist, one a Presbyterian, and only one a Quaker.[14]

But pacifist values were also transmitted in intense interpersonal settings. An important channel of transmission was the student Christian movement, a loose coalition of organizations such as the YMCA, the Young Women's Christian Association (YWCA), and the Student Volunteer Movement (SVM).[15] As one YWCA official later recalled: "Because the student Christian movement was part of the academic world where students and faculty members were constantly exposed to new learning, members were able to evaluate new ideas, rejecting some and incorporating others into their own value systems . . . convictions such as the acceptance of racial equality and the rejection of war spread quickly from one part of the movement to another."[16]

In the YMCA it was the student groups, more than the city or community branches, who concerned themselves with pacifism and other social issues. Around 1920 the student YMCA turned decisively in the direction of the Social Gospel, although, as we have seen, ideas of social Christianity had been percolating through the organization for some years before that.[17] Between the world wars the YMCA had a strong physical and institutional presence on more than 800 campuses.[18] College YMCAs were the loci of soul-searching discussions on "vital" religion and living an authentic Christian "way of life." One pacifist recalled "an average of forty-one discussion groups" organized each year through the YMCA on his campus, meeting in "dormitories, rooming houses and fraternities."[19]

The nature of a Christian response, and of one's own personal response, to war and militarism was one of the subjects of such discussions. During the 1920s and probably beyond, most of the student Christian movement secretaries were pacifists. The national organization promoted pacifism through the Association Press and the roster of speakers it offered, including Kirby Page, Howard Thurman, and, in the earlier years, Reinhold Niebuhr.[20]

The student YWCA similarly turned toward progressive social issues after World War I.[21] Women's Christian Associations were centers of intellectual stimulus and of social support for activism. Some students arrived at college already interested in questions of peace and social justice and sought out the YWCAs as a center. But the associations also invited and drew in students with no prior interest, often to life-changing effect. These women built networks of role modeling and practical action, even as they called on the resources of the male lecturers and writers who worked with the YMCA.[22]

Like the Christian Associations, the Student Volunteer Movement, which was originally concerned with foreign missions, shifted its identity and agenda after World War I toward the Social Gospel. Although its numbers were declining, the SVM continued to be a shaping force and a source of contacts for activistic Protestant students, some of whom embraced pacifism. For high school students, Christian Endeavor and denominational youth fellowships provided similar avenues for moving beyond the local church and coming to terms with social issues.[23]

Rank-and-file pacifists remembered these experiences. James Mullin, who came from a "rather conservative" Christian Church (Disciples of Christ) background, reported that his "horizons were expanded" during three summers of YMCA camp in the early 1930s by such leaders as Kirby Page and Sherwood Eddy.[24] Peace worker Mary Ellen Singsen first explored pacifism through the Smith College Peace Fellowship in 1936, and met her future husband, a Unitarian pacifist, at a student Christian movement conference the next year. Margarita Will, who married the prominent Methodist pacifist Herman Will, named YMCA-YWCA summer camps during the prewar and early war years as the most influential force in her pacifist development.[25]

Print and Publishing

Protestant pacifists came largely from the educated middle and upper classes and from a highly verbal religious culture (see chapters 3 and 4). Hence print media were an important locus of pacifist exchange and transmission. Printed works were channels of communication, means of circulating new ideas, and sources of "vernacular references." The print community then sustained already-convinced pacifists.[26]

Some pacifists first developed their convictions through reading. John Haynes Holmes, for example, said that he received his "education in pacifism" through "Jesus and his teaching," the examples of the Quakers and of St. Francis, and the writings of Romain Rolland and of Tolstoy.[27] These were typical choices for pacifists both before and after the paradigm shift.

Many of the pacifist books of the interwar period came from trade publishers such as Doubleday, Harper, George Doran, and Lippincott.[28] Religious presses also marketed pacifism: especially important were liberal denominational presses such as Pilgrim, Abingdon, and Beacon and the YMCA's Association Press. Friendship Press, the publishing arm of the Federal Council of Churches, issued works on peace education, and the more conservative publisher Fleming Revell published several of the mystical works that pacifists used, notably those by Brother Lawrence and by Frank Laubach.

Periodicals strengthened pacifist networks and communications. *The World Tomorrow*, edited by Kirby Page, was for many years the central ecumenical voice of Christian pacifism and socialism. It ceased publication in 1934 under pressure of financial losses and internal conflicts, but *Fellowship*, which the FOR launched the following year, continued in much the same role. At the same time, *The Christian Century* gave pacifism a sympathetic hearing and an influential platform. Its editorial policies, however, reflected wider opinion in the liberal churches and thus modulated the pacifist voice in the course of the 1930s.[29] Protestant pacifists also transmitted their ideas through denominational magazines, such as the Baptist *Missions* and the

Congregational *Social Action*, and through youth publications, notably the Methodist *Motive* and the student Christian movement's *Intercollegian*. Many pacifists read *The Nation*, edited by pacifist Oswald Garrison Villard, and numerous smaller or ephemeral publications circulated.[30]

The Lecture Circuit

"For the extension of any cause," said Sherwood Eddy, "I have believed all my life and have tried to practice the threefold technique of the spoken word, the printed page, and the organization of men first in small, intimate, vital groups and later in national or international bodies."[31] The twentieth-century lecture circuit—one form of the spoken word—has received relatively little attention from historians, but it was an important channel of communication and source of entertainment through at least the 1940s. Manuals for peace workers routinely recommended hiring a speaker as a means of publicity and recruitment.[32] Organizations such as the NCPW maintained speakers' bureaus; conferences publicized their keynote speakers and subsidiary lecturers; and authors and leaders undertook extensive speaking tours. The lecturer was often a writer and organizational functionary as well. For instance, Alvin Goddard served as executive secretary of the World Peace Commission of the Methodist Episcopal Church and delivered nearly five hundred speeches between 1928 and 1931, in venues including colleges, local churches, men's and women's clubs, Epworth League Institutes, and camp meetings.[33] Through the 1930s Kirby Page devoted approximately half of every year to speaking tours, the other half to reading and writing. In 1940, as pacifism came under increasing stress, he claimed to have traveled 17,000 miles and to have spoken in seventy-five towns, often giving as many as three talks each day at colleges, churches, and public meetings.[34] During three months of that same year, A. J. Muste, then an officer of the FOR, had ninety-eight speaking engagements. These included lectures, classes, and sermons for pacifist conferences, youth groups, labor and professional organizations, churches, and Quaker meetings, and the keynote speech for a student Christian conference.[35] Both the social institution of lecturing and the lecturer in person disseminated and supported pacifist convictions.

Conferences and Camps

Student movements, youth groups, churches, and peace organizations relied on another common institution: the regional or national conference.

"Stories abound," said one historian, "of the large summer conferences held at Silver Bay in New York, Blue Ridge Assembly in North Carolina, and Asilomar in California to discuss the major moral and religious issues of the day."[36] The Northern Baptist Convention annual for 1928 suggests the scope of the conference system at that time: the Women's Home Mission Society reported that it supplied funding for representatives to "six interdenominational and five YMCA student conferences" and to "33 of 40 Baptist summer assemblies."[37]

Pacifism flourished at such conferences. As an example, E. Raymond Wilson, later an officer of the American Friends Service Committee (AFSC) and of the Friends Committee on National Legislation, recalled as a turning point the SVM quadrennial conference in Indianapolis in 1923, which presented twenty-five speakers on issues of peace, economics, and race, and attracted some five thousand students. Wilson also recalled numerous "smaller rump sessions." At one of them, he said, Kirby Page made "an eloquent plea for total opposition to war based on the life and principles of Jesus. His talk . . . started me on a two-year struggle to reach the pacifist position."[38] Peace organizations themselves also relied on conferences. The FOR held an annual gathering. The AFSC was known for its "Institutes of International Relations," in some of which the Congregationalists' Council for Social Action (CSA) cooperated.[39] Activist Mary Ellen Singsen said she was "wrapped up and delivered to life-long peace work" after studying with Kirby Page at a 1937 institute.

The conferences also intersected with the American camping movement, which emerged around the turn of the century in connection with several other cultural trends. The recreation movement, Boy and Girl Scouting, nostalgia for the recently tamed frontier, and "muscular Christianity" all expanded on an earlier tradition of camp meetings for religious revival. Camps were thought to offer healthful engagement with the outdoors and an opportunity to exercise survival skills. More significantly, the separation they provided from the location and activity of everyday life was conducive to social bonding, decision-making, and self-dedication — functions that maintained and reinforced pacifist culture.[40]

The motif of camping occurred in several other areas of pacifism as well. It was probably one of the forerunners of pacifist interest in rural life and folk tradition. And during the 1930s, pacifists developed "work camps" as a form of social action. Participants lived in simple temporary accommodations while engaging in building or social-service projects. In this way camps, like conferences, fostered group solidarity and accommodated changes in pacifist cultural expression.

The Churches

To use a biblical metaphor, pacifists in the churches were like wheat growing with tares. On the one hand, mainline churches did much to disseminate general peacemaking and specifically pacifist ideas. There was strong "top-down" advocacy of pacifism through the clergy and denominational statements. Denominational agencies and publishing houses issued worship and educational materials devoted to peace. And, as we shall see, patterns of theological thinking often supported pacifist inclinations.

So it is not surprising to find pacifists attributing their convictions directly to church influence. Edward Burrows, a World War II resister, committed himself to pacifism while in college but traced the earliest origins of his commitment to his Episcopal and Presbyterian upbringing: "I had a traditional religious training, and I guess I take things very much literally; from very early, when they said you're supposed to love your enemies and so on, I took them at face value."[41] "I was a birthright CO," said one World War II objector, "since both parents were ministers and both were ardent pacifists."[42] Another said, "My background and training were in a Christian pacifist family.... From my earliest recollections war was a dreadful crime against humanity and was irreconcilable with the Christian ethic. Peace literature was always available in our home, and I grew up feeling that I could never participate in war."[43]

On the other hand, the churches had, at best, qualified success in making pacifists. A Council for Social Action poll in 1935 found that only 15 percent of Congregationalist laypeople considered themselves pacifists. The Methodist ethicist Walter Muelder observed that pacifism had never penetrated far into the "pews."[44] Margaret Calbeck, a Methodist activist, recalled that in 1939 "at the local church level, [one] might well be the only pacifist in his home congregation or family."[45] A conscientious objector said that until he received a draft call in 1940, "I really never prepared myself to deal with the matter of conscription into the armed forces, and church, school, home, and friends had never opened up to me the ideas of pacifism and non-violence. It now seems quite by accident that I was lead [sic] to examine the customarily unquestioned call to arms."[46] All this suggests that the mainline was no more monolithic in matters of pacifism and activism than it was in theology. Denominational promotion of peace issued in a range of responses from the noncommittal to the absolute. Pacifism itself accommodated both the converted and the nurtured.[47]

Nonetheless, religious pacifism between the world wars had deep roots in Protestant institutions. After World War I mainline leaders hoped to bring the whole church into the pacifist fold, and pacifists worked through existing Protestant structures—local churches, denominations, student associations, conferences—as well as through organizations dedicated specifically to peace. Although this top-down advocacy had uneven effects, many pacifists who came of age from the 1920s through the late 1940s cited Protestant institutions as instrumental in their moral formation as pacifists. In addition, the most prominent public advocates of peace were mainline Protestants, and mainline religious views were largely taken for granted in the public sphere.

Pacifism during and after World War II, on the other hand, has been characterized as "subversive" and "sectarian." From its base in mainline churches, large organizations, and favorable public opinion, pacifism became the position of a small and suspect minority located on the social margins. The change was not absolute: many Protestant pacifist organizations and channels of transmission survived through the 1940s and 1950s. But alternative structures and new emphases gained in importance. In sociological terms, pacifism shifted from a large-scale social movement to a set of abeyance structures, structures that preserve the lore and skills of a movement in small social units until conditions favor the movement's resurgence on a larger scale.[48]

THE CHANGING PARADIGM: "PACIFISTS FIRST
AND CHRISTIANS SECOND"

Thomas Moore (1924–2008) was a pacifist and social activist for most of his adult life. Moore came to pacifist commitment gradually and somewhat fortuitously. He grew up in Presbyterian and Congregational churches in Michigan and California without any particular awareness of pacifism, although he looked to one of his pastors as a general spiritual model. Moore's first "serious exposure" to pacifism came in 1942, when he was a student at the University of California at Berkeley. The conference of the student YMCA and YWCA, normally held at beachside Asilomar, was moved that year to the Pacific School of Religion, which is also in Berkeley. Moore attended and was especially impressed by two speakers—O. W. Mendenhall, president of the evangelical-Quaker Whittier College, and George Burcham, a Methodist minister who was later a co-founder of Tuolumne Co-op Farm. Very soon after the conference, Moore was drafted. His years in the Army Air Corps convinced him, he said, that "pacifists were right about war."[49]

His commitment manifested itself in several ways. When registration for the draft was reinstated in 1948, Moore insisted on registering as a conscientious objector instead of invoking the veteran's status to which he was entitled. At the same time, he joined the Society of Friends. In 1953 he resigned from a teaching post rather than take an oath of loyalty to the nation, as his employers required. He then spent a year at Tuolumne Co-op Farm, which was both a formative and a "healing" experience for him. Following marriage in 1954, he and his wife worked with a joint YMCA-YWCA in Pennsylvania, with the AFSC's International Student House in Washington, D.C., and with a campus YMCA-YWCA in Lawrence, Kansas.

Moore's story suggests the ways Protestant pacifism changed after 1940, and, at the same time, the often unremarked ways in which Protestantism remained alive in pacifism. Several factors contributed to the change in the movement's character. As the war approached, the broad base of the interwar peace movement weakened. Protestants and non-Protestants faced difficult moral questions. In the historical situation in which they found themselves, peace seemed to be antithetical to justice, and refusal to make war against Germany and Japan seemed likely to lead to further violence, not peace. Niebuhrian "Christian realism," which I discuss more fully in chapter 3, provided a theological justification for intervention. And, at the same time, the political and economic interests of nationwide organizations lay in the direction of compliance with government and public opinion. Thus as early as 1938, one pacifist remarked that the Student Christian Movement (SCM) was "a veritable battleground in many places."[50] Large organizations like the YMCA reduced their support of pacifism. Some peace-movement figures, such as Sherwood Eddy and WILPF leader Emily Greene Balch, found war to be the least of the available evils.[51] And the mainline denominations began to qualify or reverse their earlier antiwar positions. The Methodist reversal in 1941 came as a particular shock because of the size of the denomination, its commitment to liberal social activism, and, of course, the relatively large number of Methodist pacifists. Given the strong public support for the war effort, most of the interwar peace organizations collapsed in the early 1940s.[52]

Beleaguered pacifists banded together more tightly. Membership in the FOR grew by nearly 50 percent in the year following August 1940.[53] This fact suggests either that many pacifists existed who had previously avoided organizational affiliation or that many sympathizers had avoided definitive decisions or commitments until then. Within Protestant denominations, meanwhile, a number of new "peace fellowships" affiliated with the FOR sprang up—a staking out of separate territory that had not been necessary before.[54] None attracted large numbers; the largest, the Episcopal Pacifist Fellowship, counted only about 800 members at its height in 1944.[55]

Nevertheless, it appears that pacifist identity became an important point of distinction from other Protestants around the beginning of World War II. Pacifists entertained little hope of stopping the war, although there were brief "peace now" gestures in 1943. Instead, they turned their attention to postwar reconstruction, to the prevention of future wars, and to supporting conscientious objectors. More to the point, they developed a strong sense of exceptionalism and nonconformity, and the religious center of the movement shifted away from the mainline churches. New social networks included Civilian Public Service, peace "teams" or "cells," and a growing body of liberal Quakers. Pacifist cooperatives also took hold strongly during this period; chapter 9 looks at them in depth.

The CPS Experience

Protestant men of draft age faced a concrete decision: whether to register as conscientious objectors. Faced with the conditions of the war, many who had considered pacifism or had signed peace pledges abandoned their earlier ideals and entered the armed services. Some men, like Tom Moore, later became pacifists as a result of their military service.[56] Other young men reaffirmed—or discovered—an unwavering commitment to pacifism.

Most of this latter group entered Civilian Public Service, a government-sanctioned alternative service for religious objectors. Women also participated in CPS as staff members or wives. For all, it was an intense experience of enculturation. Though limited in duration, it was influential in shaping pacifist identity and the future course of pacifism. Participants in CPS were physically set apart, in prolonged contact with one another, with ample opportunity for education and discussion. Since they were not paid and were not eligible for military benefits, they shared a sense of principled sacrifice. Later, as the churches managing CPS camps became more enmeshed in compromises with the government, a growing minority of COs turned to radical protest or sympathized with it. Thus CPS first clarified the boundaries of the pacifist community and later contributed to the development of its radical wing.

Civilian Public Service was instituted in the Selective Training and Service Act of 1940 in response to lobbying from the "historic peace churches." This term, which refers to Friends, Mennonites, and Brethren, emerged only in the late 1930s, possibly in connection with the CPS negotiations.[57] Initially organized as work camps in forestry and soil conservation, CPS later added other projects, notably work in mental hospitals and service as "guinea pigs" for medical research. Most of the camps operated under the management and financing of the "peace churches," but since these bodies were acting on behalf of the government, the true extent of their autonomy eventually became the subject of bitter debate. At various times, Northern Baptists, the Methodist Commission on World Peace, the Association of Catholic Conscientious Objectors, and others also operated CPS camps.

Nearly 12,000 men participated in CPS over the course of its five-year lifespan. About half were Mennonites and Brethren, and 951 were Quakers. About an eighth of CPS men were other mainline Protestants, representing eight denominations. Of these, the greatest number were Methodists (673), who at times outnumbered Quakers in CPS, although they represented a very small proportion of all Methodists.[58] There were also about 200 each of Presbyterians, Congregationalists, and Northern Baptists, and some 300 from other bodies. Independent evangelicals, Jehovah's Witnesses, Catholics, Jews, and small sects were also represented.[59]

Support for mainline-Protestant objectors varied. The CSA, for instance, took responsibility for oversight of Congregationalist COs, but Northern Baptist support was almost entirely in the hands of one dedicated official of the home mission board.[60] Pacifist pastors maintained some contact with Protestant COs, as did public figures such as Kirby Page and A. J. Muste. All the denominations, however, fell short where financial support was concerned, despite repeated pleading from the COs' supporters for contributions.

Nevertheless, the camps were the locus of transmission of many postwar ideals. Pacifists who had been isolated and whose principles were sometimes inchoate learned to articulate them in the terms of the existing peace culture.[61] Educational programs in the camps fostered discussions of pacifist living, and several camps ran versions of a structured "school of community living" with instructors like Arthur Morgan and Morris Mitchell, whom I discuss further in chapter 9.[62] There was also opportunity for intensive study of nonviolent direct action. At one camp A. J. Muste instituted a "School of Nonviolence," with Gandhians Richard Gregg and Bayard Rustin, the Quaker mystic Douglas Steere, and others as teachers. Elsewhere, study groups and speakers discussed direct action. And the emerging trend toward protest and noncooperation in the camps after 1943 offered chances to practice it.

Peace Teams and Cell Groups

Pacifists who were not subject to the draft—women and older or exempt men—developed new modes of social organization around 1940. These emerged not from government action but from movements within pacifism. One such social structure was the pacifist cooperative, which was most often a farm but was sometimes an urban household.

The other was the "peace team." Beginning in the late 1930s, pacifists, especially but not exclusively in the FOR, tried to develop a network of small groups under this rubric. "Three or four [members] are enough," said Muriel Lester, "more than a dozen, probably too many. . . . Over the world are many vital experiments in such team work."[63] Advocates of peace teams thought that groups of three to twelve were the ideal size for intensive study, common prayer, and quick action on the local level. Richard Gregg, author of *The Power of Nonviolence*, compared peace teams to small military platoons for their cohesion and flexibility.[64]

The extent of participation in peace teams is difficult to judge. *Fellowship* reported regularly but unsystematically on local fellowships and in 1937 claimed that there were sixty such groups, but this number included local chapters of the FOR as well as peace teams. There appear to have been more peace teams in cities and on campuses than elsewhere.[65] As late as 1948 the body called Peacemakers set out to organize itself as a network of small groups, a fact that suggests the continuing appeal of the team model.

In the early 1940s the self-perception of such groups shifted markedly. In place of the word "team," with its overtones of action and athleticism, pacifists began to talk about "cells."[66] This term, probably borrowed from communism, implied secrecy, subversion, and a sense of threat. At the same time it harmonized with the imagery of organic growth favored by Richard Gregg and others. Douglas Steere called his first manual on small groups *The Peace Team* (ca. 1938) but titled its 1947 revision *Cells for Peace*.[67] In 1944 A. J. Muste referred evenhandedly to the "pacifist cell or team," perhaps reflecting language that was in the process of changing.

Muste thought the cell or team would be "the main line of development in the period ahead." The times, he wrote, called for a new way of life for the individual and for society, based in a spiritual revival nurtured in such intimate groups.[68] In 1948, Peacemakers agreed that members should belong to "disciplined cells" and should adopt "non-violence as a way of life," "right, spiritual values," and "simplicity in living."[69]

All of the groups I have discussed included mainline Protestants, and all engaged in religious activities of one kind or another, but none defined itself as Protestant except for the denominational fellowships. In CPS, cell groups, and cooperatives, group identity was based on pacifism. And one community, liberal Quakerism, forged a unique synthesis.

Pacifism and Quakerism

Liberal Quakerism became one of the important social spaces for the preservation and transmission of pacifist culture. This was in part because of its consistent official pacifism, but not entirely: the other "historic peace churches," Mennonites and Brethren, did not attract many converts or maintain as conspicuous a public presence as the Friends. Nor did the moderate-evangelical branch of Quakerism grow substantially during this period. The centrality of liberal Quakerism to pacifist culture resulted instead from a unique set of interlocking historical developments.

Quakerism was much admired in the mid-twentieth century by pacifist and other liberal Protestants, not solely for its pacifism, but also for its democratic ecclesiology, its mystical spirituality, and its reputation for social activism. This version of Quakerism—there were others—was located primarily, though far from exclusively, in the Northeast and in the meetings belonging to Friends General Conference. It interpreted the Quaker past through the lenses of nineteenth-century liberalism and of Protestant modernism.[70] These Quakers practiced silent worship and affirmed continuing revelation, an idea that left space for both inner spiritual experience and secular knowledge.

Since the early twentieth century, modernist Friends had engaged in conscious outreach and publicity to the political and ecclesial worlds, preeminently through the work of scholar and activist Rufus M. Jones.[71] A Haverford professor, cofounder of the American Friends Service Committee, and prolific writer and lecturer, Jones was also instrumental in founding the Wider Quaker Fellowship in 1936 as a locus for people interested in Quakerism but unable or unwilling to join formally.

Several other developments during the 1930s intensified these trends in liberal Quakerism. A small but steady trickle of pacifist converts from other Protestant churches contributed to theological cross-fertilization and brought new enthusiasm for social action. Quakers at this time were making both pacifism and group mysticism more central to their identity and public witness.[72] At the same time, small groups of "independent Friends" of similar mentality formed outside the existing denominational bodies. Toward the end of the decade, while other churches took account of neo-orthodoxy and "Christian realism," liberal Quakerism continued to be unabashedly idealistic.[73] In the face of the war, it remained officially pacifist.[74] After the war, its theological and ethical climate, and its spiritual practices, attracted substantial numbers of new members. The Nobel Peace Prize, awarded jointly to the AFSC and the (British) Friends Service Committee in 1948, confirmed Friends' prestige.

During the war and the postwar years, longtime peace activists and war veterans moved into Quakerism in substantial numbers. Membership in Friends General Conference grew by three to five percent a year between 1948 and 1955, with an astonishing ten percent jump between 1958 and 1959. By contrast, church membership as a whole in the United States increased by two and a half to four percent a year before 1955. Most of the Friends' increase was in New York and Philadelphia. New England Yearly Meeting saw little growth, but its character changed in the direction of liberalism.[75] Among new members, some were veterans repelled by war, some were Protestant pacifists discouraged by the lack of wartime support from their own churches, and some sought greater religious openness.

Quakerism, then, retained a theological liberalism that most other Protestants modulated after the war, and liberal and modernist Protestant pacifists found refuge there. In many instances it went even further: because of its emphasis on the human conscience, individual leading, and the human Jesus as ethical teacher, liberal Quakerism also made it possible for members to espouse a generalized theology that accommodated Christian confession but did not require it. As convert Tom Moore put it, "What I concluded from several years of [discussions in Meeting] was that some people were pacifists first and Christians second."[76] This is an apt summation of a post-1940 tendency of Protestant pacifism, one that we will encounter again.

Continuities

Some pacifist social structures made a smooth transition into the new paradigm. A number of Protestant pacifists continued to work within ecclesial structures. The denominational peace fellowships maintained the prewar movement's theology and culture in a direct way. The generally liberal college Christian Associations were instrumental in the brief postwar resurgence of pacifism. Individual Protestants continued to participate in every dimension of pacifist culture. Mainliners were still prominent in the FOR: of the *Fellowship* board members of 1940, ten were still contributors in 1958, along with Alfred Hassler, Margueritte Harmon Bro, Allan Knight Chalmers, and Henry Hitt Crane. And Harold Fey, the editor of the *Christian Century* from 1956 until 1964, was a Disciples of Christ pacifist like Kirby Page.

Print communication, too, was still central. Books and periodicals served as ways into pacifism, as private conversation partners, and as venues for discussion. A FOR publication for youth, *The Forerunner*, recommended nine books in its four-page inaugural issue in 1943. A CPS newsletter observed in 1944 that "almost everyone in C.P.S. got where he is because of something he habitually reads." Not only was reading matter "furtively glanced at during 'meditation,' worship services, and camp meetings," reading was "often regarded as an outward and visible sign of an inward and intellectual virtue."[77] Some years later Dan Seeger, a Korean War objector, said that he first encountered pacifism in the assigned texts for a college course. "And so I began reading more of Gandhi, Tolstoy, and Thoreau," he continued. "And in my isolated state in Queens, Long Island, not knowing there was any other CO in the world, I became a CO without knowing the word."[78] Seeger later became a Quaker.

Speakers and conferences also continued to be important modes of cultural transmission, but their subjects and sponsorship reflected the changing nature of pacifism. In 1943, for example, *Fellowship* evenhandedly listed summer conferences offered by denominational youth fellowships such as the Lisle (Methodist) and Pilgrim (Congregationalist) groups, by established peace organizations such as the AFSC and FOR, and by newer "way of life" groups like the Harlem Ashram and the School of Living, which

I discuss more fully in chapter 9.[79] The decentralized Peacemakers held regular conferences in the late 1940s and 1950s for mutual support, information, and discussion.[80] These cultural practices, then, persisted after the paradigm shift, even when their content had been modified.

RELIGIOUS PACIFISM BETWEEN the world wars was grounded in mainline Protestant institutions, and explicitly Protestant pacifism continued after the paradigm shift. Cultural practices such as reading and holding conferences also survived. But by the early 1940s, mainline institutions were no longer central to pacifist social organization and transmission. Instead, pacifists exchanged cultural materials through channels whose first concern was pacifism: organizations such as the FOR and Peacemakers; cooperatives, which functioned as a "way of life" for some and as models and way stations for others; loose networks of cells and personal contacts; and a "historic peace church" that succeeded in accommodating changed conditions.

The new paradigm also reflected a changing relationship to modernity. Modern organizational systems were characteristically large-scale and bureaucratic, and the nation-state was the characteristic way of organizing peoples. Interwar pacifism often reflected modern assumptions, for example when pacifists set up national organizations and when their activity and concern focused on agreements among nations. In the course of the paradigm shift, however, this model ceased to be desirable or normative for pacifists. Of course they did not altogether reject large organizations or international treaties, but their center of gravity shifted to the small, the local, the personal, and sometimes the transitory.

If the new paradigm was antimodern in organizational terms, and was in sociological terms a set of abeyance structures, what was it in terms of American religion? In many ways it resembled a sect. Protestantism, especially in America, has historically generated many small separatist movements, often in response to social or theological pressures.

A sect is an intensely committed religious group that emerges from a stable, settled religious body, usually one that has accommodated to the surrounding culture or is itself culturally dominant. The dissenting group is disinherited or disaffected in some way—it believes the larger body has departed from its founding principles, or it seeks to privilege a particular tenet of the faith, or it points to a neglected one. The sect is clearly related to the older group and may even claim to be its truest embodiment.[81]

Sects withdraw—to varying degrees—from the world and its institutions and values. Membership is often contingent on some form of new birth or explicit test of merit, and is in any case voluntary, except for children. High ethical standards and material austerity reinforce a sense of alternative values. In exchange for this marginalization, however, the sect offers an intense sense of fellowship and the promise of salvation. And many sects locate salvation at least partly in this world—in belonging to the community or in a changed or converted society. Sects often propose alternative systems of governance, economics, education, and recreation, and they develop cultures of their own. Thus far, then, sectarian theory seems to describe post–paradigm shift pacifism quite well.[82]

Yet Protestant pacifism differs from sects in very significant ways. These differences have primarily to do with boundaries. In contrast to the exclusivism typical of sects, Protestant pacifists permitted multiple belonging: one could be a member of a peace cell and also a Presbyterian, for example, or a cooperative farmer and also a mainline clergyman. Nor did pacifists embrace any one social or religious structure. A pacifist might be a Quaker, or a communard, or a CPS man, or all of these, or none. Pacifists also lacked explicit rules for discipline and expulsion, which, according to one theorist, is a defining feature of sects.[83] True, standards for pacifist practice functioned as a kind of discipline—but the standards either were implicit in the culture or were debated and contested; they were not universally acknowledged. And expulsion was unknown, except perhaps from scattered local groups.

Instead, I would suggest that the phenomenon that pacifism resembled most closely was fundamentalism. I refer to the early phase of fundamentalism's separation from mainline Protestantism, the 1920s through the 1940s, and I am thinking of social organization, not of theology or authority structure. Despite their differences in the latter areas, these two dissenting American Protestant movements were remarkably similar in the early stages of their formation.[84]

Fundamentalists in the late 1920s were beleaguered and defeated. From a position within the mainline, they had ultimately failed to convince it of the truth of their point of view. The mainstream was taking off in another direction. The result was separation—but it occurred gradually, unevenly, and incompletely. A fair number of fundamentalists continued to be members of their liberal mainline denominations, gathered in "conservative fellowships" or living in relative isolation as wheat among tares. On the other hand, fundamentalists at that time also consolidated a separate culture and institutional network, both of which had begun to evolve before the separation. Some of their tools were the same as pacifists': conferences, periodicals, and speakers.

But separation was never the ultimate purpose or agenda of fundamentalists. It was a strategy, a temporary means to an end—for them, restoring a Christian America. Similarly for pacifists: self-separation was partial, it consolidated an already evolving network, and it was a means, not a solution—for them, building a peaceful church and world. Pacifists had sectarian tendencies, but they were not like the Amish, who maintained peace and purity by keeping the world at a distance. Nor were they like the Unitarians, who built a new church out of a decisive point of disagreement with the old. They were a movement in abeyance, like fundamentalism, building strength for the next revival.

3 The Protestant Heart

PACIFIST THEOLOGY

God is love, and love is the only practical way of life.
—Shailer Mathews, The Faith of Modernism

"In the first three decades of the twentieth century, the agenda of America's elite divinity schools and Protestant denominations was set by liberals who advocated biblical criticism, reconciliation with science, ecumenical cooperation . . . and the social gospel," writes historian of theology Gary Dorrien.[1] By one estimate, in 1920 over a third of mainline pastors, and perhaps half of all mainline organizations and publications, promoted liberal views.[2] This was the environment that shaped mainline Protestant pacifist theology, with liberalism dominant but far from exclusive.

Most historians of pacifism have located the theological origins of twentieth-century pacifism in the nonresistance tradition. This assessment is not wrong, but it is incomplete: there were more immediate sources in the pacifist environment. This chapter surveys the most important of those sources—the liberal, evangelical, Social Gospel, and modernist movements—and looks at their most significant critique, neo-orthodoxy. The first section of the chapter focuses on the period before the paradigm shift, sketching the theological contexts of mainline Protestant pacifism. The second and third sections consider the way these various strands of thought found expression in two important cultural contexts—the works of popular writer and speaker Kirby Page, and the hymnody of peace.

Nonresistance

The idea of nonresistance was derived, at its most basic, from the Sermon on the Mount's directive against resisting evil (Mt 5:39, KJV). It was rooted in the early church—although its meaning in historical context is contested—and became a central tenet of one wing of the radical Reformation, surviving primarily among Mennonites, Brethren or Dunkers, and Quakers.[3] In the 1830s the New England freethinker William Lloyd Garrison advocated nonresistance for abolitionists; that is, they were to speak out against slavery but were not to resist the violence of civil authorities or unofficial mobs. Henry David Thoreau, Leo Tolstoy, and Mohandas Gandhi built on Garrison's thought, and their works were favorite texts of twentieth-century pacifists.

These works were important resources more than they were genetic forebears, however. Twentieth-century mainline Protestant pacifism arose from discovery and reinvention, not tradition, as we saw in Harold Gray's story and will see in others. Mainline pacifism originated primarily in reaction against war—particularly, but not exclusively, World War I—and in modern Bible study. It used late-nineteenth-century idioms such as evolution and social analysis, and its theology was postmillennial, unlike Garrison's premillennialism.[4] The earlier tradition of nonresistance thus served not as originator but as reinforcement and elaboration of ideas that emerged independently.

Mainline Theology

Twentieth-century liberal Protestantism was a complex and diverse movement with both intellectual and social dimensions, and space permits only an overview here. Liberal Protestantism at its height offered a religious response to the rapid changes and challenges of the nineteenth century—among them the emergence of modern science, the theory of evolution, historical criticism of the Bible, industrialization, urbanization, new technologies, and increasing contact with non-Christian religions. In part, the liberal movement was a search for a rational and reasonable faith in the face of these challenges. In another aspect, it was a reaction against Calvinism and its revivalistic descendants in favor of a God of unconditional love. "Although you may not believe in conversion, if you live in the spirit of love, you *are* converted," said the popular nineteenth-century preacher Henry Ward Beecher.[5]

There emerged a discourse of committed Christians coming to terms with the changing world. Broadly speaking, this discourse took a positive view of humanity and human nature. It favored a vision of God as immanent and close—accessible in the natural world and in humanity, and actively at work in the present world. It rejected external authority in favor of scientific and historical evidence on the one hand and personal experience, including spiritual experience, on the other. Within these broad outlines, liberal Protestant convictions could take the form of confident optimism, scientific rationalism, social activism, mystical inwardness, or even sentimentality—or some combination of all these elements.[6]

From liberal assumptions it followed that Jesus was not an atoning sacrifice or cosmic savior but a model and example, "the absolute ideal and principle of unselfish love," said modernist theologian D. C. Macintosh.[7] Ethical teachings, which did not depend on supernatural claims, took on added importance. Doctrine, church institutions, and customary practices were opened to question in the name of truth and modernity. "These formal exercises are not religion. At best, they are only one phase and manifestation of religion," said the Boston personalist theologian Borden Parker Bowne in 1910.[8] Since Christianity transcended the limits of doctrine and institutions, liberals thought, it was best understood as a way of life. The Chicago theologian Shailer Mathews wrote in 1925, "Now the teaching of Jesus given us in the critical study of the Gospels is exceedingly simple: God is love, and love is the only practical way of life."[9]

The idea of evolution proved useful despite its challenges. Many liberal Protestants came to see evolution as not only a biological process but a spiritual and moral one, through which humanity was growing toward its full potential—the Kingdom of God on earth. The theory of evolution also provided an explanation for the inconsistencies and troubling passages in the Bible. The well-known liberal and pacifist Harry Emerson Fosdick popularized this approach in *The Modern Use of the Bible* (1924), arguing that religious ideas had progressed from the "primitive" forms of the early Israelites to the pinnacle of their development in the Gospels. The highest point of this evolution was of course Jesus.[10]

Human evolution implied progress. Along with their general optimism about human nature, liberals well into the 1920s affirmed the idea of progress and assumed that the changing world around them was on an upward trajectory. Fosdick and others also spoke of "progressive revelation," meaning that divine revelation continued even though the biblical canon was closed. This concept, a favorite of liberal Protestants and Quakers, made room alongside biblical revelation for the advance of human knowledge and for religious insights beyond Christianity.

Progressive liberalism also built on its evangelical heritage. Theologically, this heritage emphasized the authority of scripture and the saving work of Christ. But salvation did not imply human passivity: mainstream evangelicalism insisted on the necessity of human decision and the competence of human will. Conversion narratives like Harold Gray's, recounting struggle and decision, were widely shared. And evangelicals were also energetic reformers, since converts were both obliged and freed to live a holy life. Liberals carried forward a favorable view of human will, ability, and action, which they directed toward spiritual convincement and social activism.

These larger patterns were important in pacifism, which was a cross-denominational movement. But some denominational particulars also supported pacifist convictions. Methodists, for example, had long emphasized the need for sanctification—growth toward perfection after conversion—and had therefore developed particularly strong traditions of activism and good works. Boston personalist theology was also influential among Methodists: this school of thought insisted on the absolute value of individual "personality," an argument often invoked against any form of killing. Baptists and Congregationalists remembered traditions of the gathered church, the church of "saints" distinguished from the world. Baptists were particularly suspicious of state interference in matters of conscience.

Across denominations, liberals' drive toward ethical action found particular expression in the movement known as social Christianity or the Social Gospel. First articulated in the 1870s, widely embraced between 1907 and 1916, and revived in the 1930s, the Social Gospel movement took its name from its conviction that the Gospel message applied not only to individuals but to social systems. This meant that society required salvation, that the social order was a legitimate concern of Christians, and that social problems arose not solely from individual moral failings but from institutions and societal structures. In particular, the human task was to build the Kingdom of God on earth. Social Gospelers assumed that the Kingdom had already begun working, though in slow and hidden ways. The calling of Christians was to bring it into the open, build it up, and cause it to increase. Metaphors of work and building abound in Social Gospel texts, as do images of evolution and organic growth.

Social Christianity was notably concerned with economic issues — poverty, labor, the working class, and urban conditions. Theorist Walter Rauschenbusch and others argued that capitalism was inimical to a Christian social order, because it fostered divisive competitiveness, corporate oligarchy, unequal distribution of wealth, and moral decay. They therefore advocated an alternative system — cooperation. This term encompassed everything from informal mutual assistance to international good will, but Social Gospelers were particularly interested in economic cooperation, for example in small-scale worker-owned enterprises like shops and farms. Many Social Gospelers embraced a moderate form of socialism that emphasized decentralized cooperative communities within a larger "cooperative commonwealth."

Thus the Social Gospel was simultaneously modernist — in its vision of the Kingdom of God emerging in human culture — and critical of modernity in its anticapitalism. This ambivalence was mirrored in pacifism. As I noted earlier, theological modernism, by one definition, embraced modern culture, found the divine revealed in it, and adapted religious ideas to it. But tensions around modernity, already present in the 1920s, played an important part in the paradigm shift in the late 1930s and early 1940s.

On the one hand, much of the popular peace literature of the 1920s and 1930s, both churchly and "secular," was modernist in its vision of peace as a function of progress. In this view, war was the final scourge to be eliminated from a generally enlightened society. Improved transportation and communication, better education, increased international understanding, international law, and the indelible lessons of World War I would, they thought, usher in a new era of harmony and cooperation. This line of reasoning found a potent symbolic representation in Charles Lindbergh, a subject we will return to later on.

On the other hand, pacifists' opposition to war was from the beginning a critique of modernity at a fundamental level, because modern war — its impersonality, its weapons technology, its involvement of civilians, its valorizing of the nation-state — was what generated the widespread pacifist reaction of the 1920s. In addition, the Social Gospelers and Christian socialists of the *World Tomorrow*, while undoubtedly hopeful, saw more to criticize in modern "progress," including the social ills of urbanization and the postwar humiliation of Germany. This faction took an early interest in Gandhi, as well as in urban communitarians like Muriel Lester and Christian radicals like Toyohiko Kagawa. Gradually a wider unease with modernity surfaced in the peace movement, manifesting itself particularly in folk arts and cooperative rural living. After World War II, resistance to the atomic bomb—the ultimate modern weapon—strengthened antimodern tendencies. Yet an element of optimistic progressivism survived through the 1950s, as we shall see.

A different, and more widely influential, critique of modern liberalism came from neo-orthodoxy. While this was a complex movement with no unitary point of view, in general terms it was both a theological response to the stresses of the twentieth century and a reaction against liberalism, modernism, and the Social Gospel. In the wake of World War I, European neo-orthodoxy rejected liberal notions of immanence and progress to affirm the otherness of God and the unique authority of the biblical revelation.

In 1932 Reinhold Niebuhr—a longtime pacifist, FOR board member, and friend of Kirby Page—published *Moral Man and Immoral Society*. Niebuhr soon came to be regarded as the chief spokesman for neo-orthodoxy in North America. In *Moral Man*, Niebuhr confronted pacifism and Social Gospel ideology head-on. He argued that, while individuals might live according to the rule of love, groups could not. Institutions and systems could operate only by the logic of power, and the best they could achieve was justice, not love. Liberal idealism was therefore useless in real politics, and the cooperative commonwealth, the community of love, was an impossibility. He further argued that Christians could legitimately use violence in the interest of justice. In later works Niebuhr continued to develop the themes of human sinfulness, irony, "tragic necessity," and "Christian realism." Christians, he thought, had a responsibility to act when justice was at stake, even when human action was inevitably imperfect and was conducted on the world's terms of sin and power.[11]

Moral Man sent shock waves through the world of liberal pacifism. It also exacerbated a conflict already brewing in the FOR over the use of violence in class struggle. This conflict has been well described elsewhere; suffice it to say that Niebuhr and others resigned from the board of directors, a minority faction left the FOR, and the remaining membership espoused nonviolence. Niebuhr's long-standing friendship with Page came to an end. As for the churches, they felt the effects of neo-orthodoxy more gradually, but by the late 1930s most liberal theologians at least conceded the legitimacy of its critiques, and some embraced it wholeheartedly. As international violence increased and war threatened, Protestant leaders found Christian realism and tragic necessity a more robust theology for the times than liberal pacifism.[12]

Yet the influence of neo-orthodoxy, too, was qualified. What emerged in the mainline churches was not so much a neo-orthodox hard line as a chastened liberalism.[13] Among pacifists, some theologians after 1940 rethought their arguments in order to address the neo-orthodox critique but remained firmly absolutist in their pacifism.[14] And common discourse among pacifists continued to focus on love, immanence, and action, with very little reference to these theological debates.

THE PROTESTANT HEART OF KIRBY PAGE

Harold Gray's friend Kirby Page (1890–1957) was both a model and a promoter of popular Protestant pacifism before World War II. John Nevin Sayre, longtime chair of the FOR, wrote, "Replies to a questionnaire [of FOR members], asking what books had influenced them most in the direction of Christian pacifism, put the Bible first and the writings of Kirby Page second."[15] The same survey placed Page first among influential pacifist lecturers; indeed he defined himself as a "social evangelist." In that capacity he was known to churches, interdenominational organizations, college audiences, CPS camps, and innumerable other audiences. He was also a writer, editor, and lecturer, a Disciples of Christ minister and a Christian socialist.

Page grew up in a struggling household in Texas. After several years' work for the local YMCA, he decided to prepare for the ministry and entered Drake University, where he encountered and ultimately embraced Social Gospel theology. He was graduated and ordained in 1915; he then served a church in Chicago while taking graduate courses at the University of Chicago. In 1916, YMCA evangelist Sherwood Eddy hired Page as his personal secretary. Page's international travels with Eddy during World War I brought him face to face with questions of war, peace, and pacifism, which he debated with Harold Gray and others. Ultimately he did commit himself to pacifism, and having done so, he never wavered from his conviction that "war is inherently and essentially a supreme violation of Jesus' way of life."[16] From 1927 onward, Page devoted his time entirely to lecturing and writing, with some financial support from Eddy. He edited *The World Tomorrow* from 1926 through 1934 and was an editorial contributor to *Fellowship* until his death in 1957.[17] His twenty-eight books made detailed criticisms of war, measuring its human and financial costs and recounting its horrors. The earlier books proposed mainly legal and political solutions to international conflicts, but as early as 1922 Page was interested in economic problems, and in the late 1920s and 1930s he shifted his focus toward economic alternatives to the capitalistic "war system." He also turned his attention toward prayer and spiritual growth: after 1929 a growing proportion of his books focused on such topics. In addition to studies of Jesus and a collection on "creative pioneers," he published seven manuals of spiritual practice and a collection of worship services.[18]

Throughout his public life, Page used evangelistic techniques and traditional Protestant theological categories to propagate social Christianity and, especially, pacifism. His arguments for the pacifist position were intended to convince and convert his audiences and conversation partners. Both in person and in print, he presented his ideas with the imaginative and dramatic rhetoric of the pulpit and the lecture circuit. His evocation of Jesus at Gethsemane, for example, gave emotional weight to pacifist theological arguments: "In the darkness of the night two alternatives appear before Jesus with the brilliance of the noon-day sun. Life or a way of life! He must choose. Live as his contemporaries live or die. . . . Out of the black silence comes light from the Eternal. A great quietness comes over Jesus. It is the will of God that a man should faithfully follow the way of love. The purpose of life is to build the divine community. The way to create the ideal society is to live today as if it is already a reality."[19]

As for Page's theology, it was typical of liberal Protestant pacifism. With respect to the Bible he argued that the "general character" of the human, historical Jesus was depicted in the synoptic gospels (Matthew, Mark, and Luke), even if details and quotes were inexact. He used the Bible above all as a model for imitation of Jesus' "way of life" and took this requirement very seriously: "Undivided allegiance to the task of establishing God's Home is what Jesus expects of his friends." Harry Emerson Fosdick agreed that Page was "engaged here in the high business of taking Jesus in earnest."[20]

Page held a similarly high view of human capability. "Jesus risks everything," he wrote, "upon the conviction that man, in spite of his present stupidity and cruelty, is God's Son and is capable of climbing to divine heights." He also thought the Christian life required arduous effort: "We can refuse to lower our ideals . . . never being satisfied with low aim and meager achievement, and ever being convicted of guilt, private and corporate, for failing to achieve more perfectly the ideal objective for ourselves and for society."[21]

Support for this arduous life, thought Page, would come from direct access to God. Page disparaged "ceremonial worship," drawing a parallel between the "paraphernalia of temple ritual" and the "existing system" of his own day. In contrast, Jesus "possesses an overwhelming conviction that God is near, accessible, and responsive. . . . Jesus lives continually in the conscious presence of the Father." For Jesus' followers to attain such a state, effort was required: "The heights of worship are reached only by a vigorous act of the will." As aids to worship Page advocated solitude, silence, and "beauty" as well as discipline.[22]

Despite his optimism, however, Page did not understate the prospect of suffering for those who imitated Jesus: living as Jesus does, as if the Kingdom has already come, is bound to offend those with an interest in "the existing social order," and persecution then becomes inevitable. Yet such living, says Page, is the only way to establish God's Kingdom, or "home," on earth. It is thus salvific for individuals and for society. Page was careful to distinguish this concept of salvation from that of fundamentalists, for whom belief in Christ's substitutionary atonement was essential. The true meaning of the cross was not atonement, he argued, but the "redeeming power of sacrificial love."[23]

Page's theology was closely bound up with practice. Adopting a way of life that seeks to imitate Jesus and enact his teachings is inherently active and embodied. Antiwar witness, social activism, persuasion, and evangelism were all integrated with thought. Less obviously, they were also integrated with modes of private spiritual practice that Page developed. These practices reveal another aspect of the Protestant heart of pacifism.

In many of his books, most notably the series on religious living published during the 1930s and early 1940s, Page provided methodical spiritual exercises designed to foster social activism and communion with God.[24] Usually he offered cycles of readings corresponding to the topics introduced in each book. In *Living Triumphantly* (1934), for example, some of the topics were heroic models, such as those who typically appeared in pacifist narratives; the "present economic order"; refusal to participate in war; and worship. Readings guided the users—individuals, families, or small groups—in "traveling these steps in cycles."[25]

Such exercises sometimes reached an extreme of personal discipline, as in Page's popular *Living Creatively* (1932).[26] In a bracing imperative voice, Page's table of contents identified eleven things the creative Christian should do. It was a formidable list. "Relieve human misery. Transform unjust social systems. Gain vision and serenity through silence. Seek beauty. Cultivate friendship and fellowship. Recover strength through penitence. Explore great biographies. Follow the noblest personality. Cooperate creatively with God. Run risks and accept penalties. Make wise use of time."[27]

Page then provided one hundred daily readings on these topics for use in meditation and discussion. He recognized that "there are not enough hours in the day . . . to enable us to devote adequate attention" to every creative activity every day. "It is obvious, therefore," he concluded, "that creative living depends in considerable measure upon the wisdom with which we divide up the twenty-four hours. Every wasted day constitutes an irretrievable loss, and every hour frittered away means unrelieved human misery."[28]

Having thus confronted the reader with his or her responsibilities, Page provided a series of charts on which one could keep track of how one was doing. For example, one could record "substantial, moderate, [or] negligible" accomplishments in various aspects of relieving human misery over the course of ten weeks. To chart one's "spiritual progress," one not only could record achievements in "penitence," "loyalty to Jesus' way," "recognition of cooperation with God," and "courage and sacrifice" but also could rate one's "quality of achievement" high, moderate, or low.[29] Whether or not anyone ever used these charts, the continued popularity of Page's work suggests that his methods were congenial to readers devoted to careful self-scrutiny and effort.

Around 1939, however, there was a noticeable shift in Page's writing. *Religious Resources for Personal Living and Social Action*, published in that year, echoed a number of neo-orthodox themes: sin and penitence, moral ambiguity, church and sacraments. In 1941 *Living Prayerfully* emphasized the spiritual basis of resistance to the challenges of the present world, with war on the horizon. Neither book signified a complete change in direction, but Page's confident tone became muted, and social action began to take a back seat to spiritual exercises. Undoubtedly Page's ideas were derivative, reflecting contemporary currents of neo-orthodoxy on the one hand and mysticism on the other. But they are indicative of pacifists' gradual turn away from humanistic optimism and reasoned persuasion in the face of growing worldwide conflict.

Yet Page's works on spirituality reinforced the values of pacifist culture: love, a way of life, service. They emphasized personal discipline and responsibility and expected personal spiritual practice to issue in direct communion with God. These themes were common to Page's evangelical roots and the Protestant mysticism that was developing at this same time. Nor was Page's work entirely "muscular"; Page advocated attention to natural beauty and fine art along with strenuous effort.[30] He and his successors in pacifist spiritual practice were also alike in insisting that right action was as important as right belief and that action should be consistent with belief. With this contention they simultaneously criticized fundamentalism, ecclesial institutions, and Christian complacency.

HYMNS: THE SON OF GOD GOES FORTH FOR PEACE

As recent scholarship has recognized, hymns can serve as signposts to Protestant mental worlds, as guides into those worlds and as representations of them.[31] Lacking a consistent tradition of visual imagery, Protestants have used music as a carrier of the biblical word and of the symbolic and emotional dimensions of religion. Hymnody has been a mode of popular expression and the center of many people's piety. The composition of religious verse and music has been available to, and used by, those excluded from official preaching and ministry, such as women and slaves. Hymns have also served as vessels of tradition and have conveyed instruction in theology and morals.

The antiwar sentiment of mainstream Protestantism between the wars is evident in hymns and hymn collections. Hymn texts illuminate the shape of pacifist expression, thought, and feeling. Twentieth-century peace hymns typically incorporate modernist or generally liberal theology, favorite pacifist biblical images, and the watchwords of pacifist religious life. Although there is little evidence for direct effects of peace hymns as instruction or exhortation, their presence in hymnals serves as a rough gauge of their popularity or of their perceived importance. A given hymn might be repeated and reused in additional sources, dropped from later hymnals, or referred to in individuals' testimonies.

Pacifist hymnody also participated in wider Protestant trends. Hymnals reflect both the interest in "service" and the shift from confident progressivism to a more reflective mysticism. In 1914 Louis F. Benson's important book *The English Hymn* had noted the ascendancy of the "hymnody of social service":

> It was, for instance, with an eye on the market that the publishing house which had chosen the high-sounding name of *In Excelsis* for its recent hymnal, called its new one *Hymns of Worship and Service* (New York: The Century Co., 1905). . . . The old hymn, "When I can read my Title clear," represents the old Evangelical Hymnody (no doubt at its extreme) in its individualism, its otherworldliness, its introspection. The new hymn, "Where cross the crowded ways of life," represents the new "Hymnody of Social Service" in its socialism, its this-worldliness, its concern for those who are not in church.[32]

Benson added, "We shall soon perhaps have *Hymns of Service and Worship* . . . then *Hymns of Service* . . . and then *Hymns of Social Service*."[33]

But by the early 1930s a change of course was occurring. *The Hymnal* of the Presbyterian Church in the U.S.A. (1933) introduced itself in this way: "This Hymnal has been compiled in response to a very general demand from the Church and in an endeavor to meet certain needs in devotional expression which are peculiar to our time. . . . [M]aterial has been added to give expression to certain new emphases in the religious thought of the present day, which concerns itself in such large measure, on the one hand, with social service, the brotherhood of man and world friendship, and, on the other, with the inner life, that mystical conception of the Christian life as 'hid with Christ in God.'"[34] These comments reflect the rising interest among mainstream Protestants in mystical piety alongside social activism, a theme that I take up again in a later chapter.

Most of the major denominations—including Quakers of the silent-worship tradition[35]—published new hymnals during the 1930s or early 1940s and again in the 1950s. The hymn collections, like responsive readings and other worship materials, were organized by topic.[36] Peace hymns generally constituted one section in a larger category such as "The Kingdom of God" or "The hope of a better world" or were grouped with related topics like "brotherhood" or "world friendship." At least two collections used the term "way of life" in section headings.[37] The volume with the greatest number of peace texts was published, oddly, in 1941. This hymnal was *Christian Worship*, a joint project of Northern Baptists and Disciples of Christ.[38] It is, of course, very likely that the hymnal had been in preparation for several years and expressed the temper of that slightly earlier time.

As for Quakers, no peace hymn in their collection is original to Friends, and all appear in at least one other Protestant hymnal. Of course this is not surprising for a body with no tradition of hymn-singing. But it is clear that the mainstream churches did generate a hymnodic tradition related to peace, and that Quakers saw no difficulty in using it.[39]

The official denominational hymnals are only half the story, however: much of the hymnody of peace and social action was disseminated through other vehicles. Mabel Mussey's *Social Hymns of Brotherhood and Aspiration*, first published in the liberal journal of social work *The Survey*, emphasized action, a spirit of uplift, and general moral principles, and avoided doctrine and "hymns of atonement, sin, and sacrifice."[40] Another nominally secular source was Florence Brewer Boeckel's "Books of Goodwill" series. Boeckel's purpose was peace education, and she had no formal religious affiliation herself, but she used Protestant religious material freely, including some hymns and songs. Similarly, the "secular" WILPF compiled at least one list of suggested peace hymns and worship books.[41]

"Youth hymnals" were another venue. Many were nondenominational, intended for the use of such organizations as Christian Endeavor and the YMCA.[42] These, too, were outward-looking, aspiring, and activistic — "leading [youth] out of self to the great world where love and service unite for the building of the Kingdom of God."[43] Significantly, the youth hymnals included folk songs and spirituals well before the official hymnals did so.[44]

Most of the popular peace hymns fall into three categories: those dating from the nineteenth century and earlier; those written in the twentieth century, generally after 1918; and twentieth-century revisions of older hymns that glorified war or used war imagery.[45] The nineteenth-century hymns retained an orthodox sensibility. Three widely used examples are Henry Baker's "O God of Love! O King of Peace" (1861), William H. Burleigh's "Lead us, O Father, in the Paths of Peace" (date unknown, before 1859), and Rudyard Kipling's "God of Our Fathers, Known of Old" (1897).[46] Baker's "O God of Love! O King of Peace" was written expressly "to be used in time of war" for the standard Anglican collection *Hymns Ancient and Modern*. The first and second stanzas connect the proliferation of war with human sin. The second and third reflect on divine power, and the fourth alludes to the communion of saints. "Lead us, O Father, in the Paths of Peace" by William H. Burleigh, a Unitarian abolitionist and temperance activist, does not refer directly to war. But it resembles "O God of Love" in its expression of dependence on divine power, mediated through "Christ, the true and living way," and it reflects on the contingency of the present life. Kipling's "God of Our Fathers, Known of Old" is a somber call to the British Empire for repentance and humility. The nineteenth-century peace hymns, then, are rooted in a dynamic of human sin, repentance, dependence on divine power, and the role of Christ as mediator.

By contrast, the twentieth-century hymns, though not uniform in their theology, shared a sense of this-worldly activism, human potential for good, heroism, and progress, and such watchwords as "good will" and "beating swords into plowshares." Three typical examples are Harry Emerson Fosdick's "The Prince of Peace His Banner Spreads" (n.d.), John Haynes Holmes's "God of the Nations, Near and Far" (1911), and John Oxenham's "Peace in Our Time, O Lord" (1938).[47] Fosdick's hymn alludes to traditional theology in asking for pardon and cleansing and in its second stanza's summary of the life of Christ. Yet humans are no longer sinners but "wayward folk." They are to "venture," to use "valor, skill, and power"; peacemakers are compared with warriors who "braved" and "dared." "Rancor, fear, and pride" will be replaced with "goodwill." Holmes's "God of the Nations, Near and Far" calls on the deity in the first and sixth stanzas, less for intimate guidance than for general blessing. The four middle verses ruminate on the state of the world. They refer to noncombatant "heroes" such as scientists and diplomats and to the international labor movement. Surprisingly, this hymn uses the image of Pentecost, uncommon among liberals. But it uses it to liberal ends — to describe the unity of the laboring class's "hundred tongues" and of peoples "from shore to shore."

"Peace in Our Time, O Lord" was, ironically, written in response to the Munich Conference of 1938. But this history, if known, did not prevent the hymn's survival among Episcopalians, Quakers, and, unofficially, Methodists.[48] Episcopalians perhaps appreciated the subtle trinitarianism in its references to power, "Living Christ," and "breath." Like Holmes and Fosdick, however, Oxenham offered a present-oriented and activistic sensibility: "peace in our time" is conceivable, and two of the four stanzas use the metaphor of "building."

The hymns that revised battle metaphors seem oddly heavy-handed (see appendix). Ernest Bourner Allen's "The Son of God Goes Forth for Peace" was an alternate version of "The Son of God Goes Forth to War."[49] Since the latter does not glorify literal war but uses it as a metaphor for the Christian life, Allen's purpose appears to have been to replace even language and imagery that seemed inimical to peace.[50] Allen's hymn incorporates many pacifist watchwords—love, brotherhood, service, and swords and plowshares. It also borrows from inspirational material: its phrase "to love, to lift" appears to allude to a popular youth hymn that declared, "I would look up, and laugh and love and lift."[51] In form, Allen's hymn is an extended meditation without a guiding metaphor or narrative. It is poetically awkward, for example, in the odd phrase "plowshares warm," rhymed with "harm."

Charles Coke Woods's "Peace Hymn of the World" is even more of a curiosity.[52] Of all the midcentury peace hymns, this one seems the most distant from present-day sensibilities. Set to the tune of "The Battle Hymn of the Republic," it replaces "His truth is marching on" with "Good will and peace to men." And instead of "Glory, glory, hallelujah!" it exclaims "Peace and friendliness forever!" It is possible that this phrase alluded to another revision of the "Battle Hymn," that of the Industrial Workers of the World, whose refrain was "Solidarity forever."[53] Still, the idea of "friendliness" is here set to a martial tune associated with rebellion, wrath, judgment, and liberation. Yet perhaps this radical reversal is itself part of the hymn's message.[54] Certainly the text is consistent with pacifist culture: there is the requisite mention of swords and plowshares, and the slip into treating them as a present possibility rather than a prophecy—"men *are beating* swords to plowshares." There are the themes of love and human kinship and the biblical reference to peace and good will (Lk 2:14).[55]

With all this in mind, it is not difficult to see the network of allusions in "O Hear Them Marching, Marching."[56] Like some of the other hymns, it subverts the imagery of battle, but unlike them, that imagery here constitutes the dominant metaphor: the "men of peace" march with "battle flags unfurled" under their "mighty captain." Their enemy, the "powers of darkness," is war itself rather than more general categories of sin or evil. The hymn reveals a progressivist sensibility in its language of struggling upward, building, and bringing in the "kingdom." It is activistic: even the meek participate in bringing in the "new regime." The hymn envisions eventual success: "they shall subdue the world." And the power by which this will be accomplished, the power the soldierly but gentle "legions" represent, is "good will."

AMERICAN PROTESTANTISM LAY at the heart of American pacifism in the twentieth century. Pacifism was fostered by individual Protestants in Protestant institutions through Protestant modes of practice and was intimately linked with Protestant thought. Harold Gray, Kirby Page, and their cohort had deeply Protestant concerns: freedom, the individual before God, Christian primitivism, the Bible, the twin poles of scripture and Spirit, energetic good works, evangelism, reform, sin, and regeneration. They sang hymns, heard sermons, wrestled with texts, read and wrote, discussed and prayed, and reached out to the unconverted.

Drawing on this heritage, which was evangelical in the broadest sense of that word, they also embraced modernism. They approved of critical study of the Bible, balancing this with affirmation of its essential truths as they saw them. Gray's conversion to social Christianity and Page's critique of the war system reflected systemic and sociological rather than private moral approaches to societal ills, even as their writings emphasized the centrality of individual conscience and responsibility in effecting social change. Both men, and their pacifist contemporaries, believed in evolution and progress, modern science and history, and worldly art and culture. With the wider liberal tradition, they affirmed a God whose primary attribute was love and a Christianity that was a whole way of life. They envisioned the Kingdom of God on earth.

This theology began to change in the late 1930s. Yet elements of it survived into the 1960s. The next chapter outlines this change and survival.

4   The Pacifist Vernacular

Believing in the creative power of love and good will to overcome hatred and prejudice, war and injustice, the Fellowship would make this way of life known in the world.
—Young People and a New World (FOR pamphlet)

In 1936 Kirby Page invited the British pacifist George Lansbury to conduct a speaking tour of the United States on behalf of the Emergency Peace Campaign. Among Lansbury's speeches was a radio broadcast in which he pleaded with "the nation" to "take the Gospel message at its face value": "Unless we are prepared to see the whole of our present civilization wrecked, we must turn to Jesus of Nazareth and without any reserve accept as true his statement that love and service are the law in life. . . . The Kingdom of Heaven is within us. Our duty is, by God's good grace, to bring that Kingdom out of ourselves and by our actions demonstrate that it is possible to live as Christ teaches us we should live."[1]

This was familiar language to pacifists. In fact, Lansbury's speech contained most of the "shared vernacular references" essential to pacifist culture. This chapter looks at the ways everyday pacifists appropriated and circulated biblical texts and theological assumptions to build their own unique cultural language, a language that was sustained through the paradigm shift. The chapter is not concerned with pacifists' reasoned argumentation as much as with the assumptions and allusions that they took for granted, used, and understood.

PACIFISTS AND THE BIBLE

Pacifists' use of the Bible was complex and even self-contradictory. Modern skeptical interpretation could become paradoxically literalistic in practice. Pacifists were thoroughgoing liberals in their willingness to look critically at scripture, and like other liberals, they commonly invoked its overall meaning rather than particular proof-texts. On the other hand, some of the deepest roots of Christian pacifism lay precisely in particular texts, and pacifist use of these texts could become its own kind of fundamentalism.

The Bible is a long and complex document, and any religious use of it requires some kind of interpretive strategy, if not always a conscious one. Christians take the New Testament witness as normative, of course, but even that is not simple. For example, New Testament teachings contain a tension between redemptive faith and obedient practice. And the text seldom distinguishes between teachings addressed to particular people or situations and those intended to be universal. Its relationship to the Hebrew scriptures (Old Testament) raises further questions, since those writings are also canonical for Christians. Should the Old Testament be regarded as authoritative in detail, as superseded, predictive, metaphorical? Christian approaches have varied enormously.

Nor is the biblical call to peacemaking unambiguous. There are clear pacifistic commands in the New Testament, but they appear in only two of the four Gospels, one of which also refers to conflict and battle. All the Gospels offer examples of nonresistance and reconciliation. Yet some epistles enjoin obedience to temporal authorities, the book of Revelation is a vision of cosmic warfare, and parts of the Old Testament describe Israelite conquests and defeats. Thus pacifist interpretation faced some critical dilemmas.

The "Life and Teachings" of Jesus

A national study group in 1923 asked, "In what measure are Christians as you know them really seeking to understand the life and teachings of Jesus?"[2] An admirer of Kirby Page said, "I never got away from his closely reasoned arguments that war was absolutely contrary to the life and teaching of Jesus."³ In 1940 David Dellinger, then a Union Seminary student and later a lifelong radical pacifist, said at his sentencing for draft resistance that war was "completely contrary to the best human intelligence and the teachings and life of Jesus."⁴

First of all, then, pacifists used the Bible as a guide to the imitation of Christ. They looked to Jesus' "life," "example," and "teachings" as the basis of religious life. They understood these to be portrayed more accurately in the synoptic Gospels (Matthew, Mark, and Luke) than in the more philosophical Gospel of John. They believed that Jesus both advocated and modeled absolute pacifism, and that Christians, as his human imitators and disciples, should—and could—do likewise.

This was true after the paradigm shift as well as before. Both Protestants and Catholics at the Fast for Peace in 1950 declared that they were guided by the "teaching and example of Jesus."⁵ A Congregationalist Bible study packet of the same era argued that the "personality of the historical Jesus," not meaningless "ritual" and "creed," offered the truest guidelines for right living. This course began with a reference to the whole sense of scripture: it said the Bible taken as a whole could provide "social principles applicable to our historical situation."⁶

Pacifists usually argued from the overall sense of Scripture. This approach, which was common to many liberals and reformers, allowed the application of general principles over apparently contradictory proof-texts—texts which in any case might be proven inauthentic by developments in historical criticism or science. It enabled liberals to distance themselves from fundamentalists, and it was compatible with the evolutionary approach. If Jesus was the high point of biblical history, then the records of his life offered the clearest distillation of that history's true meaning. Everything else in the Bible could then be evaluated according to its compatibility or incompatibility with Jesus' example.⁷ Fosdick wrote, "So long as a man knows the whole road [i.e., the whole Bible] and judges every step of it by the spirit of Christ, who is its climax, he can use it all. This is the finest consequence of the new approach to the Bible: it gives us the whole book back again."⁸

Emphasis on the whole sense of scripture, with "Jesus' life and teachings" as the standard for interpretation, gave pacifists a way to refute the biblical texts in which Jesus appeared to advocate violence. While these pacifist arguments differed in detail, their general thrust was consistent: even if Jesus drove the moneychangers from the temple, or said he had come to bring "not peace but a sword," or predicted "wars and rumors of wars," his life teaching as a whole pointed irrefutably toward peace, so these seemingly warlike statements were limited in their authority, or were in some way anomalous. This was the argument of John Haynes Holmes in *New Wars for Old*, for example, and of the syllabus of the National Study Conference on the Churches and World Peace in 1925.[9] It was also the overall approach of one of the most sophisticated works of pacifist biblical criticism, G. H. C. Macgregor's widely read *The New Testament Basis of Pacifism*.[10] This book, first published in 1936, had gone into four printings by 1941 and continued to be recommended for pacifists' reading lists after the war.[11] Macgregor made careful exegetical arguments against the usual interpretations of New Testament passages that appeared to sanction war or violence — such texts as Romans 13:1–7, Matthew 10:34, and Mark 13:7. In the same way, he argued that the overall trajectory of Jesus' life and teachings was pacifistic. Macgregor explicitly repudiated "a literalistic interpretation of either the Sixth Commandment or certain sayings of Jesus in the Sermon on the Mount."[12]

Despite his warning, however, pacifists often did take these texts quite literally. We can see this tendency, for example, in *Peace Study Outline: Problems of Applied Pacifism*, published in Philadelphia by a Quaker organization around 1941. On the one hand, this work follows the usual line of pacifist thought in saying, "As a whole the New Testament shows that the spirit of Christ is opposed to the spirit of war." Citing Macgregor, the authors argue that war cannot be justified on the basis of "the sayings of Jesus," since Jesus' whole life and actions clearly rejected violence. They also take "progressive revelation" for granted, asserting, for example, that "there is much in the Old Testament that is primitive and barbarous and therefore it cannot be used to justify war."

Yet the same document takes the Sermon on the Mount and other teachings at face value. "Jesus does not argue," it says flatly. "He states his own simple direct insights. 'Blessed are the peace makers,' 'Blessed are the meek,' 'Love your enemies,' 'Resist not him that is evil,' 'Whosoever smiteth thee on thy right cheek turn to him the other also,' 'Peace I leave with you; my peace I give unto you,' 'Whosoever would be first among you shall be your servant.' . . . [The] words of Jesus definitely indicate a way of life which cannot include war."[13]

All of this gives the effect of a kind of unthinking literalism, and that was always a possibility. But it also suggests, I think, that interpretation is not a wholly intellectual matter. The converted heart, the enlightened spirit, the practical witness—or the soul in search of these qualities—were also brought to bear on biblical interpretation, as they have been throughout Protestant history.

Favorite Texts

The favorite biblical texts of pacifists served not only as shorthand for the larger meanings of "Jesus' teaching and example" but as literal directions for behavior. They were, in addition, sources of visual and ritual symbolism, a subject I return to later.

The foundational text of pacifism was the sixth commandment: "Thou shalt not kill" (Ex 20:13, KJV).[14] The connection of this text to the peace message is of course obvious. But it may be instructive to contrast the pacifist understanding with other interpretive strategies. It is possible, for instance, to examine the Ten Commandments as a self-contained set of boundaries on behavior, or to consider their function in the Israelite community, or to take all the commandments at face value and undertake to follow them. The Moffatt Bible translation (1922–35) used the word "murder," not "kill," recognizing that Israelite law did not rule out war or execution.[15] Pacifists, however, typically accepted the King James translation and grouped the sixth commandment with texts from elsewhere in the Bible, applying the hermeneutic of peace that they understood to come from Jesus.[16]

But the sixth commandment was not the real heart of Protestant pacifism. That was the Sermon on the Mount, found in Matthew 5–7.[17] Some of its best-known texts speak directly to behavior in cases of conflict: "Love your enemies," "turn the other cheek," "resist not evil." These seemed to pacifists to be clear directives against participation in war. In contrast, other interpreters have seen them as applying only to interpersonal conflict, or only within the Christian community, or as overruled by such counsel as Romans 13:1–7. Pacifists also attended to the Sermon's treatment of material goods: "Do not pile up treasure on earth," "Consider the lilies of the field." They applied these texts to questions of economic relations and, later, to the issue of communal living.

Throughout the midcentury period and beyond, pacifists grounded their life and thought in the Sermon on the Mount. In 1925, for instance, the syllabus for an interchurch peace conference began with a section on "the spirit and teaching of Jesus," which opened with the consideration of the Sermon. In his 1941 draft-resistance statement Ammon Hennacy, then a nondenominational "Christian anarchist" and later a mainstay of the Catholic Worker movement, began with the premise that registration for the draft was contrary to "the principles of Jesus as given in His Sermon on the Mount: 'Love your enemies . . . turn the other cheek'"[18] The next year the communitarian Arthur Morgan, speaking at the Conference on Pacifist Farming Communities, cited the Sermon on the Mount as a symbol of the "values we hold highest."[19] The Quaker educator Amelia Swayne wrote in 1950, "We have had the example of the life of Jesus and the wonderful summary of his teachings, as presented in the so-called Sermon on the Mount, but we have not succeeded in making them a real part of our personal and national life."[20] Pacifists maintained the ideal of the Sermon on the Mount continually, believed that the ideal could be realized, and, in some cases at least, overlooked earlier failures to attain this goal.[21]

Another favorite text came from the prophets. Pacifists, like other social reformers, were aware that many of the ethical teachings attributed to Jesus drew directly on the Hebrew prophets who addressed the whole Israelite community with calls for righteousness and justice.[22] But one text in particular became a catchword. It appears in both Isaiah (2:4) and Micah (4:3): ". . . and they shall beat their swords into plowshares, and their spears into pruninghooks: nation shall not lift up sword against nation, neither shall they learn war any more."[23]

"Swords and plowshares" became a pervasive phrase. Numerous books and pamphlets used some variant of it as a title.[24] References to the text appeared in a message addressed to children in 1915; in the litany recited at the meetings of the Meadville, Pennsylvania, Fellowship of Peace in the 1930s; and as the epigraph to a Methodist youth institute in 1939.[25] Many peace hymns and liturgies used it, as we have seen. It was widely used in visual representation, as we will see in chapter 6. The image of "learning war" also had some reach. Curricula and study groups implicitly contrasted it with their goal of "teaching peace," and it was symbolically repudiated in the song beloved of pacifists, "I ain't gonna *study war* no more." As one commentator put it, "Young Europe has not wanted to 'study war' any more than has young America."[26]

These texts — "thou shalt not kill," "turn the other cheek," "they shall beat their swords into plowshares" — shaped the culture of pacifism at its most fundamental. We will encounter them, or their echoes, in pacifist spirituality, art, material culture, and practice.

PACIFIST RELIGIOUS PRINCIPLES

Together with biblical interpretation, pacifists developed an informal theology, a set of ideals and guidelines for the religious life. A distinctive pacifist discourse emerged out of words, phrases, and unstated assumptions that recurred frequently in pacifist speech and writing.

In listening to these voices we hear a few themes repeated again and again. These are the core ideas of vernacular pacifist theology. Pacifists maintained that true Christianity is a *way of life*, not a set of doctrines or an institution; that the *life and teachings* of Jesus are the model and guide for this way of life; that human beings are capable of emulating Jesus, and in so doing will build the *Kingdom of God* on earth; that *love* is the essence of divinity and the highest human value; that human *perfection* is possible and desirable. Love is manifested in *good will*, the right attitude toward interpersonal, interfaith, and international relations; and in *service*, the active work of love in the world. "Good will" is the only one of these themes that did not survive the paradigm shift with any strength, while *nonviolent direct action* supplemented *service* after the shift.

The idea of a "way of life" is a continuous strain in Protestant pacifist thought. Harold Gray's mentor, W. E. Orchard, wrote in 1918, "The Kingdom of God is at hand . . . [It is not] a system of theology . . . not a sentiment, a theory of life, a temper of mind, a type of character only, but a way of life."[27] Similarly, the 1923 study group mentioned earlier in this chapter argued that "Jesus typified and advocated a *way of life* which he asserted we all could live if we would."[28]

The "way of life" idea was also instrumental in the paradigm shift. In 1941 Methodists Jay Holmes Smith and John Swomley Jr. announced plans for a summer "training course in 'total pacifism'" at the Harlem Ashram: "We see this total pacifism in terms of (1) a way of life, in which we seek to live out the implications of truth and non-violence in all our relationships; (2) A goal for social reconstruction, a co-operative socio-economic order, approximating to the realization of the Kingdom of God on earth; (3) Non-violent action."[29] Smith and Swomley reiterated the themes of an actively practiced "way of life," peace, and right social order. However, they were selective about their retention of Christian language, and they added the new term "non-violent action."

The following year a group of conscientious objectors at the CPS camp in Coshocton, Ohio, wrote, printed, and used in worship an eleven-page pamphlet titled *A Way of Life*. They, too, reiterated the themes of a way of life, Jesus' example (and St. Francis's), creative action, and service. For them, the pacifist way of life was framed as Christian spiritual discipline.[30] But they reached beyond Protestantism to include a carefully formulated faith statement that accommodated non-Christian and rationalistic beliefs. It is worth noting that they understood themselves to be creating something original, personal, and fresh, not to be joining a movement or participating in a culture. Their statement, they said, was "a preliminary step in our quest for a way of life to which our lives may be completely dedicated."[31]

Nearly two decades later, the Vigil at Fort Detrick, a protest against biological weapons, issued a Christmas message for 1959: "At this season . . . we are particularly mindful of the manner of life revealed in Him, and to which he called all mankind. 'Love your enemies' and 'Return good for evil' are not unrealistic counsels. That way was always the way by which men could avoid mutual slaughter and share in abundant life."[32] A substantial number of mainline Protestants participated in the vigil, and the greeting made use of familiar Christian language, not only of love but of penitence. But it also incorporated more general references to "all mankind," "the moral law of the universe," and "the Spirit of God."

The phrase "way of life," then, initially meant fully embracing the Christian Gospel and subsequently evolved into something broader. After about 1940—as in the ashram and the CPS camp—it retained Christian associations but was no longer part of an argument about true Christianity. Instead, it was part of an argument about true pacifism. It connoted a whole-life commitment that pacifists understood to be more thoroughgoing than the public activism of the 1920s and 1930s, a commitment that was in turn a building block of a new social order.

Equally important to pacifists was the idea of love. Of course this ideal was already deeply embedded in the liberal Protestant mind, but it had a particular resonance for pacifists.[33] They believed that love was both the basis of the way of life Jesus taught and its outcome. Love was clearly the antithesis of violent conflict as a means of resolving differences, whether international or interpersonal.

Pacifists assumed that "Jesus' way of love" was an appropriate model for the social order as well as for individual persons.[34] Reinhold Niebuhr, in his pacifist period, alluded to "the task of organizing human society upon the basis of the principle of love" with "a God of love" at its root.[35] The FOR agreed that "love as revealed in Jesus is the basis of a true human society."³⁶ In about 1935 the Disciples Peace Fellowship said that its members were "determined to explore the possibilities of love for discovering truth, dispelling antagonisms and reconciling people, despite all differences, in a friendly society. They believe that love, such as that manifested preeminently in Jesus, must serve as a true guide for human conduct under all circumstances. They seek to demonstrate that love is an effective force for overcoming evil and transforming society into a creative fellowship."³⁷

After 1940, pacifists' claim to an ethic based in love, like the idea of a way of life, survived without Christian confession. For example, in 1959 a supporter wrote to an imprisoned pacifist, "I cannot feel that any evil effects can come from an action rooted in love."³⁸ A story for children, about a German soldier in World War II who was befriended by a Russian, made the point that the soldier ceased thereafter to "believe in Germany." Instead, the narrator of the story said, "He believed in love, dear heart, and there is nothing else."³⁹

Perfectionism showed in many pacifist cultural practices—the belief that the peaceful Kingdom of God could be established, the meticulous self-scrutiny of Harold Gray and his successors, the determination of pacifist mystics, whom I discuss in chapter 7, to be in constant communion with God, and the pacifist preoccupation with right living. Overt perfectionism was strongest in the 1920s; later, chastened by the events of the 1930s and aware of the neo-orthodox critique of pacifism, pacifists modulated their perfectionism somewhat. Yet it continued to exert a pull, even a temptation. In 1950, for example, A. J. Muste took on "one of the most serious charges against pacifism"—perfectionism—in a series of essays in *Fellowship*.⁴⁰ Even those who abjured perfectionism continued to see humanity as highly educable and improvable. And liberal Quakerism was largely unmoved by the neo-orthodox emphasis on sin and human contingency.

Before World War II, pacifists assumed that love should be manifested in both an attitude, good will, and a mode of action, service. It is difficult to overstate the ubiquity of the term "good will." In the broadest cross-section of the peace movement its use ranged from the Federal Council of Churches' Commission on International Justice and Goodwill to the celebration of Goodwill Day and the sentimental pageant "Good Will, the Magician."⁴¹ In absolute-pacifist usage it appeared in such contexts as the FOR's description of conscientious objectors as "pioneers of good will" and the story collection, edited by the Quaker Anna Griscom, called *Peace*

Crusaders: Adventures in Good Will.[42] The biblical referent was, of course, the text from the birth narrative in the Gospel of Luke: "Peace on earth, good will to men." By the postwar era, however, "good will" had largely fallen out of favor.[43]

As "mission," an older Protestant term, was likewise falling out of favor, the term "service" gradually replaced it in liberal discourse about Christian activity in the world. Originating in the Social Gospel, the idea of "service" found a particularly significant exponent in the American Friends Service Committee. This pacifist organization was founded in 1917, when three Quaker bodies separated by schism joined together for war relief, even though they could not agree on theology. Another source of the term was Harry Emerson Fosdick's *The Meaning of Service* (1920), the last volume in his trilogy on "the three meanings." It was reprinted ten times during the next thirty years. By that time "service" was well established. In 1942, for example, *Fellowship* listed work projects under the heading "This Summer for Service," and in 1949 a similar list was published by the Commission on Youth Service Projects.[44]

These words that were taken for granted, used in everyday discourse, are for present-day readers signposts to a mentality and a mental world. They suggest a vision in which, without aid of doctrine or clergy, the conscientious free Christian is led into a life of trust, peace, and care, a life in which perfection is possible. They suggest an intention of reforming and redirecting Christian communities so that the weight of the churches falls on the side of world peace. All this was a profound and powerful conception for many people. This conception, however, risked falling into naïveté and sentimentality, and it was vulnerable to Niebuhr's argument that it did not adequately address the dynamics of sin and of temporal power.

THE VERNACULAR THEOLOGY of Protestant pacifists arose from a primarily liberal matrix but developed its own particular set of cultural reference points and meanings. Around 1940, however, pacifism began to develop a theology and practice that could accommodate various faiths and unbelievers as well as Protestant Christians. This "umbrella theology" was, like Protestant pacifist theology, expressed in popular as well as learned terms — in a largely implicit set of shared assumptions about human life, moral action, and the holy. Many of these assumptions echoed Protestant liberalism — a loving, immanent, and accessible deity; the necessity of adopting a religious "way of life"; the central value of love in all relationships; the intention of building the good society and establishing peace.

The difference was that umbrella theology was organized around pacifism itself, not around Christian confession. Protestant modernism ultimately raised the question, "But why Christianity?," and post-1940 pacifism implicitly answered that it was not essential.[45] In one sense, this was a radical departure from tradition. From another angle, however, the change was not very great: in the end, almost the only difference between popular mainline theology and pacifist "umbrella theology" was that Jesus had become optional. As Alcoholics Anonymous replicates an evangelical conversion experience but substitutes sobriety and a "higher power" for Christ, so pacifists retained the shape of liberal Protestantism but began to organize their religious culture around pacifism rather than Jesus.

Such a conclusion is subject to divergent historical and ideological interpretations. Some will find in it confirmation that liberalism is a slippery slope toward unbelief. Others, on the contrary, will argue that American secular institutions maintain a subliminal religious bias carried over from their Christian and Protestant origins. Still others will maintain that pacifism is inherently universal and will therefore argue that Protestants were merely, and correctly, getting out of the way.

I prefer the metaphor of the Protestant heart. Liberal Protestantism contributed decisively to the shape of late-twentieth- and twenty-first-century pacifism and continued to participate in it after 1940. At the same time, by its openness, it enabled pacifism to slip its Christian moorings, or, depending on one's point of view, to open its umbrella over all faiths and none.

5 Performing Pacifism

WORSHIP, PLAYS, AND PAGEANTS

We could not remember Beethoven and sing war songs.
—Georgina Johnston, "Building for Peace"

Pacifist culture was highly verbal, but pacifism was not expressed in words alone. It was also performed. Harold Gray enacted his pacifism in legal and practical actions and in symbolic and ritual gestures. World War II objectors planted trees, volunteered for research projects, and experimented with communal living. But these examples tell us little about activists in peacetime; about those who were not subject to military service; about group or community performance; or about performance as a means of influencing public opinion or educating children. All of these were forces in pacifist history.

The range of pacifist performance is wide. Individuals and groups enacted their pacifism for intimate gatherings and for the larger public. Speeches, discussion, marches, picket lines, rallies, and public pledges emerged early and remained standard forms of pacifist action. Colorful public gestures, such as an international exchange of peace dolls in 1927, appeared alongside advertising, public relations, and film. Especially after World War II, nonviolent direct action, building on Gandhi's examples, touched the boundaries of sacred ritual on the one hand and street theater on the other.

In this chapter I focus on the interwar period and on three modes of group performance that were widely used and familiar cultural idioms and were engaged in conversation with Protestantism. These were worship services, plays, and pageants. Later chapters will look at the rituals of "training for peace," at cooperative living, and, briefly, at nonviolent direct action. In this initial exploration of performance, I consider the written texts of readings, liturgies, and scripts; the gestures, actions, and visual signals through which the texts were embodied and enacted; and the effects of word and embodiment on participants and audience.

David Glassberg's analysis of Progressive Era civic pageantry is instructive for the study of Protestant and pacifist performance. Civic pageants, says Glassberg, used both text and performative action to form collective identity, build solidarity within a community, inculcate common values, and educate the public. Pageant producers expected both performers and audiences to be affected. Borrowing from progressive-education and recreation theories, they assumed that performers would absorb ideals through creative, expressive participation in acting them out. At the same time, audiences were to absorb these same ideals through the power of spectacle and vicarious participation. Thus pageants functioned on one level as experiments in mass persuasion. Advocates for reform learned from them to use a combination of instruction, spectacle, and ritual to "inform public opinion, evoke public sentiment, and spur public action."[1]

At the same time, the ideology and practice of pageantry led to a "blend of progressivism and anti-modernism, customary civic religious ritual and the promise of artistic innovation."[2] Pageant producers typically embraced progressivist ideals and modern art forms, including dance and stagecraft. But on the other hand, they rejected commercialized or, in their view, coarse popular entertainment in favor of folk arts, which they understood to be the popular voices of less commercial, less fragmented eras. Glassberg's description of pageantry fits pacifist performance with remarkable accuracy, especially if one substitutes "churchly" for "civic religious" ritual.

Because performance encompasses word, ideology, allusion, and practice, the uses of pacifist performance extend in several directions. Performance was first of all a form of folklore: it quoted and creatively restated the vernacular reference points of Protestant pacifist culture.[3] Second, it constructed a symbolic world and explored diverse meanings of symbolic language, much of it Christian. In addition, it was a way of experimenting, tacitly, with religion in a broader sense than Christian confession: as ritual, group experience, and the absorption of ideas through bodily action and participation.

In speaking of ritual, we should recall that Protestants generally resisted or rejected the idea of ritual, largely because of Protestantism's historic opposition to Catholicism. For Protestants, action without explanation was as much suspect as pictures without words.[4] "Ritual" in Protestant parlance generally meant routinized, meaningless repetition, often imposed by some distant source of authority. Protestants did not think of ritual in the ways that scholars in the present time have learned to do: for instance, as an experiential means of attaining group cohesion, or as the enactment of a religious vision, or as an affirmation of continuity with the past.[5]

Yet many Protestant practices in fact drifted in the direction of ritual. For instance, mainliners readily accepted church drama; church groups performed plays in youth gatherings and at evening services. Most mainliners regarded drama not as religious practice per se but as an art form, a fresh medium for exploring religious ideas. And, since plays were as much verbal as performative, they were generally within the margins of acceptability. Pageantry went further toward exploring ritual action and visual symbolism, though pageants, too, often accompanied symbolism with explanation. Again, they generally took place outside the boundaries of what was called "worship," or were carefully circumscribed within it. Indeed, Protestant religious services themselves had ritual elements, such as the movement of liturgy toward an altar call or offering, or the emotional power of familiar hymns. And peace advocates sensed the power of civic rituals and the need to counteract them with an internationalist sensibility. But mainline Protestants seldom came to terms explicitly with the implications of dramatic ritual for the practice of worship.[6]

These traditions—civic and religious drama, pageantry, and public ritual—lay behind interwar peace performance. The peace rituals of this period fostered group identity and sought to affect public sentiment: they taught and acted out the Protestant culture of peace.

Worship

Worship services devoted to peace before about 1940 generally followed a free-church format, which also reflected the denominational location of a considerable number of pacifists. Many free-church hymnals also served as worship books, providing orders of service, prayers, responsive readings, and similar materials.[7] Since Calvinist, evangelical, and liberal traditions all rejected set lectionaries and minimized observance of the canonical year, the hymns and readings were usually organized around theological topics, social issues, and national holidays, in addition to Christian holy days. Responsive readings were composed of selections from the Bible. Often these were not complete pericopes but were edited and arranged to suit the topic at hand.

A typical example for the interwar era is *The Methodist Hymnal* (1935), a joint publication of three Methodist bodies. This volume provided a year-long cycle of responsive readings on themes ranging from "God's Unsearchable Greatness" to "Family Religion." In addition, it provided readings for holy days from Christmas to Pentecost, for days of thanksgiving and commemoration, and for social concerns such as missions, peace, and temperance.[8] Its responsive reading on peace combined two selections: Micah 4:1–5, which is one of the "swords into plowshares" passages, and Isaiah 65:17–19, 21–25, which includes an image of the "holy mountain" where wolves will eat with lambs. Another hymnal took selection and conflation even further—in the Northern Baptist-Disciples hymnal *Christian Worship* (1941), which I mentioned earlier for its numerous peace hymns, the reading on peace incorporated seven different texts. Among them were Micah 4:3–4 and parts of the Sermon on the Mount.[9]

The structure of most worship services was derived from the evangelical-revivalist pattern. In this model, Bible readings, hymns, and prayers set the mood for a climactic sermon near the end of the service, followed by an altar call. This last survived in the Methodist orders of worship as an "invitation to Christian discipleship." Other midcentury liturgies built up to the sermon but concluded with singing or prayer.[10] Theoretically, the evangelical pattern left room for considerable flexibility before the sermon.

Several characteristics of this mode of worship will be important as we consider later developments in pacifist religious life. First, the worship books use the Bible to highlight particular texts and subjects more than evolutionary progression or overall meaning. Second, the rites are heavily verbal, even verbose, with lengthy prayers and readings, hymns of four or more stanzas, and substantial sermons. Thirdly, the worship emphasizes human initiative. The shape of the liturgy is meant to stir up pious emotion and lead to commitment, and its flexibility permits adaptation to local circumstances. Much of its content presents human concerns to God, not the reverse. By way of comparison, other forms of Christian worship may be intended to call down divine presence, induce otherworldly experience, await divine initiative, or anticipate judgment.

Worship books intended for youth services or lay devotions were more likely than the official hymnals to depart from custom.[11] Their contents often included nonbiblical readings from both religious and secular sources, particularly literary classics. And a number of services used nonverbal materials such as paintings, decorations, and lighting effects.[12] *The New Hymnal for American Youth* (1930), for instance, includes in its services the usual responsive and unison readings but adds collections of "prayers and high resolves" and "devotional poetry and prose." These additions quote such authors as Tennyson, Whitman, and even Rabindranath Tagore, as well as popular favorites like Edwin Markham and Henry Van Dyke. Hymns and readings are arranged under broad theological headings (the persons of the Trinity, eternal life, and so on) and morally and socially oriented headings: "The Christian Way of Life," "Thy Kingdom Come." Within these groupings, the materials reflect on a constellation of issues reminiscent of Kirby Page's concerns: nature and the outdoors; beauty; "the temple of the body," health, and "clean living"; gendered moral virtues such as courage and loyalty on the one hand, motherhood and "home shrines" on the other; faith, truth, goodness; and imagery of light. These themes recur in pacifist sources, as we shall see.

Three Protestant Peace Services

While the denominational hymnals provide calendars and responsive readings, they leave it up to local pastors to add hymns, prayers, and other elements to make a complete service. But some other sources offer whole freestanding peace liturgies. Here we see not only text and liturgical shape but gesture, dramatic action, and visual imagery. In reaching for innovation, these sources melded Protestant patterns with the emergent culture of peace in diverse ways.

The *New Hymnal for American Youth* included a service for Armistice Day and Peace Sundays titled "The Human Race: A Ceremonial of Maps." The service stays fairly close to the verbally based free-church model. It begins with a meditation, given by a leader, on maps as symbols of what all nations have in common. A hymn follows. Then come a responsive reading composed of Isaiah 11:6 and a poem; a unison prayer; and another hymn, all on children and world friendship. Next comes a responsive reading composed of proverbs from many nations, concluding with the "swords and plowshares" text. But the "ceremonial" also includes visual and dramatic elements; a rubric says, "This service may be visualized by using a large flat map of the world and, during the progress of the service, placing lighted candles in sockets or clamps prepared to receive them at the countries indicated."[13]

The climax of this service—the functional equivalent of the sermon and altar call—is a trio of peace pledges. Between a general "Pledge of Good Will and Love toward All" and a specific "Pledge of this School or Congregation," participants are to repeat three articles of the Kellogg-Briand Peace Pact of 1928.[14] Afterward come a prayer, to be read silently, and a unison dismissal. The congregation, then, participates in a peace pledge, a gesture that emerged into wider public use in the 1930s.[15] Indeed, its use here suggests that it may already have been familiar to young Protestants before they began to participate in peace-pledge movements. And the Kellogg-Briand Pact, a signal event for peace activists, is here elevated into a sacred text.

In a different vein is the "Office of Commemoration for the Dead who Died in the Great War and of the War Resisters' Pledge of Brotherhood to All Mankind" (1932, revised 1935), by Tracy Mygatt and Frances Witherspoon. This was intended as a Jewish-Christian Armistice Day service, and it was well received, at least as a text: it was published in two periodicals, and the nominally secular War Resisters League printed copies for sale.[16] Mygatt, an active pacifist, was both a committed Episcopalian and a dramatist, and her background shows.

Like the free-church services, the Office is wordy. It includes five speeches, blending exposition and exhortation, on aspects of political action for peace: conscientious objection, the Kellogg-Briand Pact, and several others. Interspersed with the speeches are prayers, litanies, and pledges. Many of these use language reminiscent of the Book of Common Prayer as well as the King James version of the Bible. Theologically the Office aims at an interfaith position: the service invokes God the Father but also includes an oblique reference to Jesus, as "Him who lived to preach peace." A speech written for a participating rabbi calls on the Old Testament patriarchs and prophets, including one who "cried . . . 'Beat your swords into plowshares, and your spears into pruning-hooks!'" Mygatt has altered the quotation from a prophecy to an imperative.

The service moves outside words and exhortation, however, by including dramatic effects drawn from the vocabulary of pageantry. Among these effects are lone trumpets, torchbearers from four directions, movements of flags, ritual inquiries and responses, and more. Here, for example, is a dramatized litany of thanksgiving:

> [Assisting minister:]
> ... Yea, verily, upon the darkness of the green earth, war-torn and anguished though it is in this year of 1935, we see ever new signs of hope. And these, O people here assembled, and you, O Torchbearers of Liberty from War, I call you to salute in gratitude!
> For the English group of Oxford militants, who have publicly expressed their refusal of war service:
> *(Here the four Torchbearers shall say, as they raise their torches:)*
> By this, our torch of sacred brotherhood, we offer thanks!
> *(And the Assisting Minister shall continue:)*
> For the "Drill-Resisters," here at home in the universities of Maryland, California, Ohio State, Missouri, who, rather than accept compulsory military training, have sacrificed worldly advantage and academic degree:
> *(And here the four Torchbearers shall say, as they raise their torches:)*
> By this, our torch of sacred brotherhood, we offer thanks!

This service places the symbolic touchstones and political expressions of pacifist culture in a new framework: Anglican rhetoric and rubrics, an effort to reach beyond Christianity, and ritual gestures and symbols borrowed from the stage.

Finally, I want to look at the peace service from Kirby Page's *The Light Is Still Shining in the Darkness* (ca. 1946), which I mention in the introduction. Although Page published this collection of worship services well after the paradigm shift, the peace service can be read as a transitional piece. It made the materials of the earlier Protestant pacifist culture available to a new generation during the brief postwar enthusiasm for peace, and it is an unusually rich and dense example of the crosscurrents in pacifism in the 1940s.

The collection placed peace among other characteristic concerns: nature, beauty, Jesus, the cross, prayer, fellowship, and social action. In opposition to formalism, Page expressed a desire to create a "spirit of worship" and a "vital experience of communion with God."[17] Some of the services included a period of silence, presumably to accommodate the trend toward meditation and mystical prayer. Yet much space was still devoted to effort and activity.

The peace service begins with readings from the Bible—six texts in three different translations—by the leader, on sacrificial allegiance to Jesus.[18] A hymn, Earl Marlatt's "Are Ye Able" (1926) reinforces the theme: "Lord, we are able!" says the refrain. Then comes the sermon equivalent, incorporating allusions to favorite pacifist texts and ideas. "There was scarce light enough to see the face of Jesus, but his voice rose clearly out of the darkness: 'To what shall I compare the power of love?,'" it says.[19] In response, the group sings the African American song about refusing to "study war." Then come two hortatory readings—a poem by John Oxenham, author of the hymn "Peace in Our Time," and a prose piece from Ignatius Loyola. The first reading says: "Who answers Christ's insistent call / Must give himself, his life, his all / Without one backward look." The second adds: "To give and not count the cost; to fight and not to heed the wounds; to strive and not to seek for rest." Participants are then invited to "listen to the still small voice" during a period of silence, which concludes with the hymn, "Make Me a Captive." Finally, the group recites the prayer attributed to St. Francis, "Make me an instrument of thy peace."

The textual content of this service, then, introduces or reiterates a number of pacifist cultural touchpoints. It reflects favorite liberal sources and also reaches beyond them. And, despite the avowed search for communion with God, the service is full of human effort and will.

It also has an evangelical substructure. It begins with preparation for commitment, continues with emotional reflection on Jesus, and climaxes in exhortation. The period of silence, which at first glance seems very far from the explicit, highly structured call for response at a revivalistic service, is in fact an inversion of it: it is pretty clear what the listener is expected to hear while silently "listening." Prayer and song then reinforce the message and close the service. Thus this performance connects liberal theology and mystical spirituality with the evangelical roots of the mainline—and beyond that, with an evangelistic attitude that persisted in pacifism, albeit in muted forms.

Plays

In 1968 a reviewer in *Fellowship* mentioned three "really pacifist"—as opposed to merely to "antiwar"—plays that had been produced in the professional theater. The plays were Charles Rann Kennedy's *The Terrible Meek*, Tracy Mygatt's *Good Friday*, and *If This Be Treason* by John Haynes Holmes and Reginald Lawrence. All were produced before 1936, and all were written by Protestant pacifists, two of them well-known leaders.[20]

The reviewer did not, however, mention the hundreds of minor "peace plays" written for professional and, especially, amateur performance. Drama was an important and widely used mode of pacifist practice throughout the interwar period and into the early 1950s, after which it survived mainly as an educational medium for children and youth.[21] Lists of resources in manuals for peace action generally broke down into three categories: materials for worship, materials for discussion, and plays. Protestant organizations and "secular" peace societies—the FOR, the Federal Council of Churches, the Woman's Press of the YWCA, the NCPW, World Peaceways, and others—compiled and published "peace plays," as did general theatrical publishers such as Walter H. Baker and Samuel French.[22]

Pacifists were not unique in this; drama was a common cultural idiom of the period.[23] Though challenged by the movies, the professional stage attracted substantial audiences and was a closely observed benchmark of high culture. Theater was also a participatory art form: amateur and community troupes and guilds were common. Nontheatrical groups often ventured to perform plays related to their missions.

It is particularly important to note the widespread interest of Protestant churches in drama. Although most of them overlooked or resisted the dramatic possibilities inherent in liturgy itself, mainline Protestants used plays and pageants not only for education and recreation but in worship, especially in services outside Sunday morning. H. Augustine Smith, the compiler of hymnals, bore the title Professor of Church Worship, Music, Hymnody and Pageantry at the Boston University School of Theology. Newton Seminary offered training in "pageantry" as part of its religious-education program in the 1920s. Elizabeth Miller Lobingier's *Dramatization of Bible Stories* was reprinted every year between 1918 and 1934. And one author, discussing "the possibilities of using drama in Christian and peace education," noted, "In summer communities, camps, and hundreds of conferences from coast to coast, plays will be used as a form of recreation," for their "educational value," and "in fewer instances . . . as contributory to a moving experience of worship."[24]

The contents of the plays relied on a fairly consistent pattern of themes, motifs, and literary and dramatic devices. Many plays dramatized the horrors of war. Staged presentation made the depiction of war's effects more graphic, if no more emotional, than lectures or sermons. Not only soldiers but civilians were characters; for example, Frederick G. Pohl's *Gas* imagined gas bombs being dropped on New York City, and Beulah Marie Dix's *Where War Comes* had children portray starving, cold, and motherless war victims.[25]

Plays that emphasized the blessings of peace often relied more heavily on symbolism. Florence Brewer Boeckel's play for children, *The World's Christmas Tree*, drew on the ideology of "international friendship"—the cultivation of peace through studying and sampling other nations' folk practices—and alluded to the benefits of modern transportation and communication. In the play, an American child, left alone on Christmas Eve, magically summons children from many lands, who describe and share their games, toys, and Christmas customs. At the climax of the activity, Santa Claus appears and speaks metaphorically of the earth as a "Christmas pack," from which children should keep "giving things back and forth to one another." Hazel MacKaye's popular *Good Will, The Magician* is similar in tone and content. It concludes with a verse that includes the eschatological lines, "When children's friendships are worldwide, / New ages will be glorified."[26]

Other plays were more political. Holmes and Lawrence's *If This Be Treason* revolved around an imaginary, but conceivable, threat of war precipitated by a Japanese attack on the Philippines. The play's contention was that war could be averted by the will of the common people combined with the action of heroic single figures—in this case, a pacifist president of the United States and a popular Japanese leader modeled on the Christian activist Toyohiko Kagawa. In amateur theater, the Meadville Fellowship of Peace sponsored a dramatic production based on testimony before Congress in the Nye Committee hearings, which investigated profits from sales of armaments during World War I.[27] Plays like these relied more on dramatic realism than on symbol and allegory.

Holmes had a professional collaborator for his play. Other scripts were equally concerned with possible real-life situations but lacked equally skillful realization. Some amounted essentially to staged discussions. Many were didactic in tone. There are such lines as, "To prepare only *brings* war! War *need* not come!"[28] and "I guess that's what Dr. Harry Emerson Fosdick meant when he said in that fine Armistice Day sermon of his, that Christians ought to become 'politicians of Peace'!"[29]

A number of plays built their narratives around Christ figures with a fairly wide metaphorical reach. In Kennedy's *The Terrible Meek*, for example, the action revolves around an executed innocent, already dead. The dialogue on stage is between the military captain who ordered the execution, a soldier who is just "doing his duty," and the victim's mother. In the end the captain refuses to obey further orders to kill, becoming, in effect, a conscientious objector—and by implication, the next to be executed. In Mygatt's *Good Friday* the Christ figure is the conscientious objector. The play is based on the case of an objector from a small sect who died after mistreatment at Alcatraz and Fort Leavenworth.[30] Again, most of the action occurs among the bystanders: a cynical doctor who repeats the usual slurs against objectors and a jailer who is racked with guilt. The objector, meanwhile, stands with his arms outstretched as on a cross, and the jailer finally recognizes in him "the face of Christ." Mygatt implies that the jailer, like Kennedy's captain, will be converted and forsake his evil ways. In Jean Milne Gower's *That Unknown Guy*, on the other hand, the Christ figure is the "unknown soldier," and the motif is essentially a post-resurrection appearance. A young society woman, contemplating the tomb of the unknown, meets a figure who appears to be a discharged soldier. Eventually it becomes clear that he is the unknown soldier himself. When the woman recognizes this, she refers to the disciples' encounter with the risen Christ on the Emmaus road (Lk 24:13–35). "His Spirit still walks the earth," she says, and rejects her wealthy fiancé to pursue higher ideals, peace first among them.[31] In all three plays, Christ is identified with sacrifice and with the power to move others to change.

Many plays reworked or repeated familiar material. Some dramatized stories that were already in circulation among pacifists, especially "The Christ of the Andes" and William Penn's treaty with the Indians (see chapters 6 and 10). Plays also used known motifs: lessons on the international sources of household products, stories of "enemy" soldiers who become friends, and others.[32] At least four plays besides *That Unknown Guy* used the theme of the unknown soldier. Two of these were based on sermons: Fosdick's "My Account with the Unknown Soldier" and an Armistice Day sermon by John Haynes Holmes. The third dramatized Bruce Barton's essay "Unknown," and the fourth was another presentation of the unknown soldier as a Christ figure.[33]

The motif of swords and plowshares also appeared in various forms.

The pastor of a church in Framingham, Massachusetts, wrote "a dramatization entitled 'The Sword and the Plowshare'" for use at Armistice Day services.[34] Dorothy Clarke Wilson's play *The Friendly Kingdom* (1940), a childlike allegory, also uses this image. A boy king, newly crowned, "follows the commandment, 'Thou shalt love thy neighbor as thyself.'" His policy is to build schools, help a nearby nation afflicted with famine, gain friendship by treating others as friends, and so on. He has ceremonial swords replaced with green branches and military swords replaced with hammers, shovels, and, of course, plows.[35]

Performances were not limited to the stage, however. Some plays were set in a larger performative framework or crossed boundaries between players and audience, between stage and world, or between media. *The World's Christmas Tree*, for example, had a sacral framework. Boeckel directed producers of the play to prepare a sign reading "Suffer little children to come unto me" (Mk 10:14). This was to be placed above the stage, "but not actually forming part of the stage decoration." It was above and outside the fictional dramatic action. In such a setting, the play, like a sermon, explicated and reflected upon the scriptural text, which was presented as "real" and immutable. Also like a sermon, the dramatic action elicited a ritual response from the audience: the players collected a "goodwill offering" just before the end of the play, as an offering is collected near the end of a free-church worship service. Here dramatic action moved out into nonfictional reality. Louis Wilson's *The Testing Hour* weakened the boundaries in a different way. The script, published to acclamations from prominent pacifists such as Holmes and Ernest Fremont Tittle, specified that a church was to be used as the setting. The dramatic action began before the audience entered the "theater," with actors playing newsboys on the street outside. Other performers handed the audience real antiwar pledge cards.[36] Thus the audience, gathered in sacred space, was required to make a real response to a fictitious test. In addition, sermons and drama sometimes changed places: I have mentioned how Fosdick's and Holmes's sermons became plays, and how plays could take the place of sermons.

Plays, then, repeated pacifist political concerns, drew on pacifist practices and approaches to problems, used familiar symbols and stories, and integrated pacifism with Christian narrative. Performance venues ranged from the professional stage to the Sunday school. We will return later on to the meanings of performance as practice.

Pageants

Pageants were large-scale performances that relied on symbolic or allegorical figures, visual effects, and formalized speech. They reached their height as an Anglo-American fad between about 1890 and World War I and survived well after that heyday. At their root was the urge to reclaim an authentic national and community past, including popular art forms that were not crude or commercial. Advocates cited Greek drama and medieval mystery plays as antecedents. The Arts and Crafts movement fostered and legitimated these uses of history.[37]

In the United States, one of the functions of pageantry was to solidify local and national identity: "community pageants" were most often historical or patriotic in nature.[38] They were usually performed by large numbers of adults.[39] After the war, the pageant declined slowly as community performance and shifted gradually toward a children's format. Protestant churches began to see the possibilities of pageants for dramatizing Bible stories and moral teaching, especially outside Sunday morning worship. One source offered pageants as a solution to "the problem of the evening service."[40] Another noted hyperbolically that "the number of missionary plays and pageants which have been published is unlimited."[41] And one of the few venues where pageantry survives into the twenty-first century is, of course, the ubiquitous Sunday school Christmas pageant.

"Peace pageants" used familiar visual symbols of peace, a subject I discuss again in chapter 6. The figure of Peace, said one young performer in 1935, "should wear a long white robe and be very ladylike, like an angel."[42] This feminine figure might carry an olive branch or a dove.[43] The nations of the world often appeared as characters: typically, the player would dress in the folk costume of that nation and proclaim its contribution to international good will, to the food supply, or to technological developments.[44] Allegorical figures included Famine, Poverty, and Oppression, which were associated with war, and Engineering, Fine Arts, and Brotherhood, associated with peace.[45] Images of swords and plowshares appeared, and hymns often served as musical accompaniment.

Typical of the genre was a pageant whose script was published in 1915 but was still "highly recommended" in 1930:

> War comes upon the stage accompanied by two trumpeters and followed by Crime, Famine and Pestilence. As the trumpets blow, the

Farmer, Carpenter, Teacher, Scientist and others enter with members of their families. Each feels the obligation to go to war. War hands each one a sword and says, "Kill them!" As they draw their swords, Peace, Justice and Wisdom enter, followed by Social Service. As Peace overcomes War, all swords are put up except that of the officer, who is the last to submit. In answer to the question of how Peace may be kept with us always, twelve Judges appear representing an International Court. The pageant ends with groups from all nations, singing together a hymn of peace.[46]

A New Jersey high school concluded a year of "education in worldmindedness" with a short pageant in 1928. It opened with the figure of Charles Lindbergh—a well-known "hero of peace"—followed by "five primitive men." These represented "five races of mankind, blindly following Education and Good-Will hither and thither, trying to find their mother, World Unity." Lindbergh then transported them to the Hall of Justice, where they found Unity accompanied by Justice, Love, Truth, Science, and Peace. Thus the pageant suggested that through education, good will, and technological progress, humanity was to arrive at unity and enjoy its benefits.[47] The figure of Lindbergh here carries multiple meanings. Flight signifies not only advancing technology, as noted, but also internationalism, in the form of improved travel and communication among nations. Flight is assumed to be benign: the idea of air war has not yet coalesced. Lindbergh himself is the modern hero, the independent individual actor. And the technologically advanced individual leads "primitive men" to civilization, in this case the civilization envisioned by pacifists.

In 1939 the Metropolitan Federation of Daily Vacation Bible Schools presented a pageant at the Temple of Religion of the New York World's Fair.[48] Four years earlier this organization had run a citywide Vacation Bible School program on peace.[49] Among the program's projects were a number of pageants and plays emphasizing ways of building a peaceful world. The 1939 pageant, however, had a more desperate tone, clearly conscious of the threat of imminent warfare.

In speaking to this threat, the pageant drew on a number of favorite Protestant pacifist motifs. It used hymns that were generally thought suitable for peace services: "In Christ There Is No East or West," "Once to Every Man and Nation," and "Brother, Sing Your Country's Anthem," as well as the irenic "America the Beautiful." It also quoted or alluded to favorite biblical texts: "swords into plowshares," "blessed are the peacemakers," and "peace I leave with you" (Jn 14:27). The pageant enacts a dialogue between "those who accept" the call to war and "those who seek" another way. It begins by contrasting peaceful and warlike uses of the same skills. Weavers, for example, are called from making clothing to making army canvas; builders are told to construct barracks instead of schools. The pageant also raises the question of drafting women, as stenographers, secretaries, and even mothers are called to war work. Finally, members of various groups reject the call and join a chorus of "Peacemakers." Mothers lead the way, saying that their children "all knew the same games. They taught each other their native songs," a clear reference to "international friendship" activities. Musicians, artists, inventors, scientists, and some women workers follow, each with a line like, "We could not remember Beethoven and sing war songs" or "We could not remember Raphael and [create] war posters." The concluding hymn, "We Would Be Building," maintains a Social Gospel sensibility, alluding to the craftspeople seen earlier, to constructive activity, and to progress and creativity.[50] This pageant, then, uses allegory, sentiment, and familiar reference points as others do. But its oblique introduction of the question of resistance and refusal suggests the coming shift in pacifist thinking, as does its question about the right use of craft.

Performance and Results

What were the effects of all this? Despite pacifists' intention to spread their message through performance, there is little evidence that drama was successful as a means of evangelism. Pacifists' autobiographies rarely mention plays as a source of influence in their decisions. Nor did the professional theater bring in many new adherents; Holmes wrote that *If This Be Treason* "was acclaimed by those who agreed with its thesis and quite generally ignored by the theatergoing public."[51] Drama may have been somewhat more effective as instruction: "Certainly the meaning of the story becomes clearer as children act it over and over again," said a prominent pacifist educator.[52] Another study, however, indicated that "peace education," including plays and pageants, had at best ambiguous effects.[53]

I suggest instead that the performance of plays and pageants had its greatest effect within the pacifist community, as ritual, transmission, and bonding. In antiliturgical Protestant churches, the adoption of drama and especially of pageantry suggests a hunger for a richness of symbolism, a mode of bodily participation, and a visual dimension that were otherwise limited. This symbolically rich activity was tightly restricted in Sunday morning worship but was embraced in secondary services, small groups, church schools, and other settings.[54]

Drama also ritualized pacifist conviction. It was, in Catherine Bell's definition, a form of pacifist action differentiated from everyday activity and privileged, denoted as special and distinctive.[55] As in the pageants Glassberg studied, it was not only the public performances that were thus privileged, but the prior acts of preparation and participation. They were "medicine for mind, body, and soul," as one early instructor put it, "a community tonic that will effectively revive a [community] which may appear to be walking in its sleep."[56] An advocate of religious pageantry concurred: "No group of people can participate in a community-wide pageant or drama without engendering a broader sympathy and obtaining a more extended vision."[57] For pacifists, drama offered an occasion for group reiteration of their commitments, both verbally and physically.

Finally, the ritual preparation and performance of drama was a means of transmission of pacifist culture.[58] It educated and trained children and newcomers, putting the stories and arguments of pacifism in their own mouths. It was cathartic: it raised the questions directed against pacifism and disposed of them. It provided reinforcement for participants and for sympathetic audiences. It created a sense of solidarity through intensive work on a common project. It consolidated relationships and reaffirmed the group's religious mindset.[59] These ways of enacting pacifism were foundational for pacifist culture.

Looking Ahead

Pacifist performance changed drastically in the course of the paradigm shift. While staged dramas and carefully constructed liturgies never disappeared, they did give way to the public performance of war resistance in nonviolent direct action. Nonviolent direct action emerged most immediately from Gandhi's practice of rooting nonviolent political action in a matrix of symbol, ritual, and material objects. It also drew on American traditions of nonviolent protest developed in the suffrage, labor, and peace movements—marching, picketing, hunger striking, and similar gestures. The Congress of Racial Equality (CORE) from 1942 onward and the Committee for Non-Violent Action (CNVA) from 1958 reinterpreted and enculturated these forms of street drama for the American pacifism of their time.[60] Less visible, but equally important, have been the rituals of identity, internal to pacifist groups, which we will discuss in chapter 8. Some of the most creative and influential practitioners of nonviolent direct action, particularly after 1960, were Roman Catholics. We can at least speculate that Catholicism's frank embrace of ritual action, as compared to Protestant ambivalence, was a factor in their grasp of its possibilities.

6 Swords and Plowshares

PACIFIST ICONOGRAPHY

> *They shall beat their swords into plowshares, and their spears into pruninghooks: nation shall not lift up sword against nation, neither shall they learn war any more.*
> —Isaiah 2:4 (KJV)

In an Armistice Day poster from about 1920, headed "Let Us Have Peace," a mother and child sit enthroned in front of a semicircular border reminiscent of a halo, with a city skyline in the background. On one side of them stands a man holding a book; on the other, a man with a hoe. A dove hovers overhead. In the left foreground is a pile of the implements of progress, such as books and a telescope. The right foreground is dominated by a plow.[1]

An iconography of peace—a vocabulary of peace imagery—grew up with the interwar peace movement. In this poster we see many elements of that vocabulary: the dove; peace as a mother; the plow, perhaps "beaten" out of swords (Is 2:4); the allusion to familiar Christian iconography, here the Virgin Mary and the Christ child. We also see elements more characteristic of 1920 than of 1960: the city, which would have suggested to its viewers both the kingdom of God and the locus of human civilization; and the tools of scientific progress, symbols of peace for a modern era that had not yet encountered the atomic bomb.

Armistice Day poster, source unknown, ca. 1920. Image courtesy of Swarthmore College Peace Collection; photograph by the author.

Peace iconography was Christian insofar as it drew from the history of Christian art. It was Protestant insofar as it drew from existing Protestant cultural practices, such as the designing of church buildings, the display of artifacts from the mission field, or the use of familiar biblical references.[2] Much of this iconography, however, also appeared in "secular" contexts. It was shared by pacifists and nonabsolutist peace workers and maintained continuity after World War II, even while a more distinctively pacifist iconography emerged alongside it.

David Morgan, a historian of Protestant visual art, has argued that Protestant art has generally been tied closely to text. He notes that those ties began to loosen around the middle of the nineteenth century, as Protestants began not only to recognize but also to embrace the power of images alone. Protestant thinking did not undergo a complete reversal, however; Protestants remained ambivalent and often inarticulate about the power of images presented without verbal explanation.

Morgan has also described the late-nineteenth-century "sacralization of art," in which educated people began to attribute to art the powers of civilization, truth, and spiritual enlightenment. Art came to be seen as necessary food for the cultured soul and mind. The cultivation of taste and the transmission of an educated aesthetic sensibility became part of self-definition within the social class of which many mainline Protestants — including pacifists — were a part.³

So it is not surprising that the idea of beauty, the study of "high" art, and the use of visual symbolism were part of the lives and activities of many Protestant pacifists. Kirby Page strongly urged social activists to make "beauty" a part of their spiritual self-culture. Educated CPS men read Shakespeare or listened to classical music. Harold Gray went to the opera and eschewed jazz.

In another sense, however, Protestant pacifism was thoroughly aniconic. The pages of *The World Tomorrow*, for example, give no indication of a unifying visual language. There are sketches of important people, pictures of buildings, cartoons, and the like, but no overall pattern of visual references. The essays *The World Tomorrow* published on art were primarily concerned with fine or high art and its spiritual qualities, not with ways of developing art forms integral to social activism. Like Protestant culture generally, the culture of Protestant pacifism was strongly verbal.

And yet, once one begins to pay attention, one sees Protestant uses of imagery everywhere. Stained-glass windows and neo-Gothic statuary developed iconographic languages for progress and peace. Mainliners produced greeting cards and postcards devoted to peace. Bruce Barton, son of a Congregationalist clergyman and author of *The Man Nobody Knows*, initiated the use of advertising techniques in peace activism — and the result was World Peace Posters, later an influential organization called World Peaceways.

This Protestant iconography remained, as Morgan suggests, closely tied to words — the biblical Word, explanatory words, liturgical words, and stories. Indeed, in the pacifist case, the iconographic vocabulary shifted back and forth between word, dramatic enactment, and visual image. St. Francis, for instance, appeared not only in church statuary but also in story collections, plays, and the name of a cooperative farm. Yet this Protestant iconography carried forward earlier traditions in that it functioned as a reminder; its symbols and juxtapositions provided shorthand versions of narratives and moral lessons.⁴

There is not space here for a complete catalog of Protestant pacifist iconography. Questions of the cultural production and reception of pacifist images also await fuller treatment. This chapter has a more limited purpose — to outline the most widely used and widely recognized pacifist imagery, the fundamentals of the iconography. These fundamentals fall into four categories: the Bible visualized, especially the image of beating swords into plowshares; heroic and hagiographic images; gardens; and the Peaceable Kingdom. These images cross the boundaries of the paradigm shift in time and content.

The Bible Visualized

Some of the most enduring Protestant ways of representing peace referred to the Bible. The first of these — a dove carrying an olive branch — is probably the oldest symbol of peace in western art. The early Christian church used representations of Noah's dove as signs of peace and reconciliation between God and humanity after the flood. Doves were traditionally seen as loving, harmless, and gentle, and they were associated with those qualities in classical symbolism. The Gospel reference to being "innocent as doves" (Mt 10:16) reinforced this meaning. Even more commonly, Christian art used the dove to represent the Holy Spirit. This association was based on the story of Jesus' baptism, but it also occurred in other biblical texts.[5] The interest of many pacifists in mysticism, with its central theological emphasis on the Spirit, suggests a reinforcing connection between the two meanings of the dove.

The Sermon on the Mount was used regularly during the 1920s and 1930s in political cartoons and posters — "secular" venues that still assumed a general familiarity with the New Testament text. One cartoon, probably dating from the 1920s, showed a manuscript with the heading "Sermon on the Mount" overwritten by a rubber-stamped phrase, "Army Censored."[6] This image alludes not only to the suppression of love and forgiveness, but also to the restriction of free speech and the proliferation of untruth that, pacifists argued, inevitably accompanied war.[7]

A very widely used image from the early 1930s depicted the "mount" as a pile of cannons, missiles, battleships, and other implements of war. Perched precariously and distantly on top was a ragged man selling apples. This ambiguous Depression figure might be read as Christ, as a personification of the sermon itself, or as the poor who are called "blessed" — in this case with considerable irony. No matter what the figure's meaning, this cartoon makes an explicit connection between war and economics, thereby reinforcing a well-known liberal argument for peace.

The National Council for Prevention of War used the image in 1931 as part of a poster campaign in preparation for the 1932 Disarmament Con-

The Sermon on the Mount

"Sermon on the Mount" cartoon, from poster, Peace House, 1930s. Image courtesy of Swarthmore College Peace Collection; photograph by the author.

ference.[8] Florence Brewer Boeckel explicated its meaning in a booklet accompanying the program.[9] New York's Peace House reissued it as a poster with a quote from Harry Emerson Fosdick printed below the image.[10] And it appeared in 1935 in the widely used *"Halt!" Cry the Dead*, which gave the New York *World-Telegram* as the source of the cartoon.[11] Clearly it struck a chord—in part because economic and humanitarian arguments against war outlasted the free-speech ones that the first cartoon made.

But the most distinctive of the Word-based images was the prophetic vision of beating swords into plowshares: "They shall beat their swords into plowshares, and their spears into pruninghooks; nation shall not lift up sword against nation, neither shall they learn war any more" (Is 2:4 and Mi 4:3, KJV). Unlike the dove, this image has no long tradition in Western or Christian symbolism.[12] Yet it was ubiquitous in twentieth-century peace art. Like the Sermon on the Mount, it was basic to Protestant pacifism but overflowed those boundaries to appear in secular, nonabsolutist, and Catholic contexts.

Within the limits of iconographic consistency, the image was open to endless imaginative variation. A 1919 broadsheet, reprinted from the *New York Tribune* of Easter Sunday, 1919, urged people to join the League of Free Nations Association "for the building of the New Kingdom." The center of the broadsheet is filled with text. In the right border is a standing Christ figure from whom rays of light emanate across the printed text. Across the top of the sheet are war scenes; down the left border spill guns and swords as far as the point where the rays of light cross the page. Below that point are scythes, spading forks, and sickles, and across the bottom of the page a man plows a field with oxen.[13] An undated Methodist Peace Fellowship poster interpreted the text somewhat more freely, but by quoting it across the top, it made sure the audience would not miss the point. The image, in an industrial-art style, shows a male worker at a set of factory controls. Implements of war fly into a hopper above him, and his machinery transforms them into wheelbarrows, teakettles, and furniture. Below are scenes of peacetime productivity: factories, farms, laboratories, houses.[14]

Church iconography made free use of the image. A window in Trinity Methodist Church, Springfield, Massachusetts, which was built in 1929, shows a blacksmith hammering a sword on an anvil, with a finished plowshare beside it. The text says simply, "Peace." This window is one of a series representing "The Final Triumph of the Kingdom"—an implicit association of peace with liberal theology. Another Methodist church window elaborates on the metaphor, depicting "a sower, a reaper, [and] a child standing beside a cannon" alongside the "blacksmith beating swords into ploughshares."[15] Here, peace is associated with farming and children, each of which in turn carries a range of implications: farming and rural life, with their overtones of purity, independence, and anti-industrialism; original innocence and final harvest; childlike innocence, children as bearers of peace, and the need to protect children from war.

Ecclesial use of the image continued after the Second World War. When the Community Church of New York, whose longtime pastor was the well-known Unitarian pacifist John Haynes Holmes, constructed a new building in the late 1950s, it included a statue of the prophet Isaiah "snapping a sword to bits and holding up the broken pieces as he stands beside a

"They Shall Beat Their Swords into Plowshares" poster issued by the Methodist Peace Fellowship, 1930s. Note the farm scene at lower left and the scientist at lower right. Image courtesy of Swarthmore College Peace Collection, reproduced by permission of United Methodist Church General Board of Church and Society; photograph by the author.

Detail of "They Shall Beat Their Swords into Plowshares" poster, Methodist Peace Fellowship, 1930s. Image courtesy of Swarthmore College Peace Collection, reproduced by permission of United Methodist Church General Board of Church and Society; photograph by the author.

Blacksmith window, ca. 1929, Trinity Methodist Church, Springfield, Mass. Reproduced by permission of Board of Trustees, Trinity Methodist Church; photograph by the author.

ploughshare in the fields."[16] This piece accompanied existing statues of other pacifist icons: St. Francis and Gandhi.

Artifacts also made use of the iconography. Sometime after World War I, an unknown person made a spent artillery shell into a table lamp, with the "swords into plowshares" text inscribed on a metal band around the base.[17] An even more literal rendition of the text was a "peace plow" made of discarded Civil War swords. While it predated the period covered in this work—it was made for the Centennial Exposition in Philadelphia in 1876—photographs of the plow figured prominently in displays of "peace symbols" during the 1930s. Organized by WILPF member Zonia Baber, these exhibits and related booklets circulated to "schools, churches, conferences, [and] missionary societies."[18]

The passage was dramatized, too. For instance, a float in an Armistice Day parade in St. Louis in 1934 carried "six or eight boys hammering on anvils, blowing bellows, et cetera" with a sign displaying the biblical text.[19] The pacifist farms of the late 1930s and 1940s literalized the association of plowshares with peace and added connections with Francis, saint of the natural world, and Gandhi, the peasants' advocate.[20]

Why was this image so durable in mid-twentieth-century pacifism? For one thing, it was concrete and easy to visualize. Unlike "Thou shalt not kill" or "Blessed are the peacemakers," it called up a mental picture immediately. Beyond that, it had a wide metaphorical reach. Swords stood for weaponry and, by extension, war, battle, and public action. Plows evoked other values: peace, by contrast with the implements of war; productivity, because of their use in food production; and the primitivist ideal of rural life, farm work, and land. Because both swords and plowshares were products of human manufacture, they called to mind public discussions about the enmeshment of industry with war, and the contrary association of handcrafts with peace.[21]

Above all, beating swords into plowshares is an image not only of peace but of transformation. It is a small narrative about a process. To twentieth-century pacifists it suggested positive action, as opposed to the passive suffering implied in the Sermon on the Mount. And the narrative offered a positive outcome, a happy ending.[22]

Protestants, then, did not resist making biblical texts into visual images. They used the images for self-representation, persuasion, and religious formation. Since the images were not confined to institutional Protestant settings, it is clear that their users expected them to be recognizable to "secular" audiences. Verbal imagery from the Bible became visual and dramatic in a largely, but not uniformly, Protestant world.

Iconic Heroes

In the same progressive Methodist church where swords were iconographically beaten into plowshares, there is a stained-glass window of a modern saint. The term "saint" does not appear anywhere, but the image follows the iconographic conventions for portraying holy figures in stained glass: the picture of the person is surrounded by identifying symbols, sacred text, and signs that recall narratives.

The "saint" is Charles Lindbergh, an immensely popular public figure whom the burgeoning peace movement appropriated for its own purposes.[23] The window depicts Lindbergh standing, dressed in aviation clothing. The words "Good Will" appear on a banner behind his head. Circular insets in the two upper corners of the window show, respectively, a map of the world marked with latitude and longitude lines and a flying airplane, which casts a cruciform shadow on the ground. Allusions to Lindbergh's nickname, the "Lone Eagle," appear in the stylized image of an eagle at the top center and in a biblical text, "They shall mount up with wings as eagles" (Is 40:31). A rectangular inset beneath Lindbergh's feet depicts the signing of the Kellogg-Briand Pact in 1928. Lindbergh appears here amid a network of religious associations: the Bible, the cross, the saint as bearer of the cross, the multiple meanings of the eagle, the theological virtue of good will, anecdotes of his life and accomplishments, and a larger narrative of international peace.[24]

Lindbergh was an example of the "hero of peace," a type that emerged during the late 1920s and survived into the 1950s.[25] "Peace heroes" material, literary and visual, provided alternatives to the military model of heroism and sought to show that progressive and humanitarian activities ultimately contributed to world peace. So, in place of soldiers and conquerors, peace advocates offered scientists, inventors, explorers, artists, social reformers, and missionaries.[26] Many practiced "moral equivalents" of war, such as the "conquest" of nature or disease. Heroic individualism was the predominant ideology. Courage, perseverance, resourcefulness, inner strength: these were offered as the qualities of peaceful heroes. Even the less aggressive virtues of creativity and concern for others were presented as individualistic ideals. Works about women, though rarer, tended to follow this pattern as well.[27] Most of these books were issued by secular publishing houses for nondenominational audiences and took for granted a mainline-Protestant religious perspective. A number of the 1920s peace heroes appeared as late as 1953 in a Quaker collection for youth.[28]

But this liberal model, though never entirely rejected, was soon moderated by pacifists' growing concern with economic issues and with consistent modes of living. In the course of the 1930s, the culture began to generate new models of heroism. The earlier lore conceived of a peace hero as performing groundbreaking work that was not war and that might contribute indirectly to peace. The new hero worked intentionally for peace, both international and interpersonal, and conducted a way of life consistent with this commitment. In a sense, the new heroism retained the individualism of the older model: most stories presented the hero's action as single-handed, privately inspired, unprecedented, and countercultural. The difference was that individual action in the newer stories often issued in some form of community.

The new hagiography most often pointed to St. Francis, Mohandas Gandhi, Toyohiko Kagawa, and Muriel Lester. St. Francis and Gandhi have continued to be familiar figures into the twenty-first century. Kagawa was

Detail of Lindbergh window, ca. 1929, Trinity Methodist Church, Springfield, Mass. Note the airplane, the cruciform shadow, the eagle, and the globe. Reproduced by permission of Board of Trustees, Trinity Methodist Church; photograph by the author.

Charles Lindbergh window, ca. 1929, Trinity Methodist Church, Springfield, Mass. Lindbergh is here symbolically connected with good will, the Kellogg-Briand pact, and Christian iconography. The text to his left is "They shall mount up on wings as eagles" (Isaiah 40:31). Reproduced by permission of Board of Trustees, Trinity Methodist Church; photograph by the author.

Detail of Lindbergh window, ca. 1929, Trinity Methodist Church, Springfield, Mass. Signing of the Kellogg-Briand pact (note text, "Peace Pact 1928"). Reproduced by permission of Board of Trustees, Trinity Methodist Church; photograph by the author.

The cover of Allan A. Hunter's collection Courage in Both Hands (New York: Fellowship of Reconciliation, 1951) juxtaposed photographs of Toyohiko Kagawa, Albert Schweitzer, Muriel Lester, Mohandas Gandhi, and Frank Laubach, and a sketch of Albrecht Dürer's Praying Hands. Reproduced by permission of the publisher from a copy at Lutheran Theological Seminary of Philadelphia.

a Japanese convert to Christianity who lived and suffered with the poor and advocated pacifism, cooperative economics, and labor unions. Lester was an influential pacifist as traveling secretary of the International FOR from 1934 until 1956, and she had earlier built up an urban intentional community. Both were known for their spiritual insight as well as for their activism. We will encounter them again in chapters 7 and 10.

A 1951 image of this pacifist sainthood is representative. It is iconographically minimal—five black-and-white photographs of faces, in a single horizontal line. It appears in close association with text—on the cover of a book, in fact. The "saints" here are Albert Schweitzer, Kagawa, Lester, Gandhi, and Frank Laubach, a missionary and mystic (see chapter 7). The book, Allan Hunter's *Courage in Both Hands*, was a revised and expanded version of an earlier work, *Heroes of Good Will*.[29] Both titles recalled earlier ideals of "heroes of peace" even as the content and illustrations reflected shifts in the meaning of heroism.

Both the titles and the illustration associate courage, heroism, and good will with pacifism, social action, and mysticism. Through Schweitzer and

Laubach, these ideals are linked to an older Protestant narrative of missionary work, particularly of a humanitarian or scientific kind. But the real emphasis of the new heroes is identity with and service to the poor. The illustration suggests voluntary poverty through Lester, Gandhi, and Kagawa, and communitarianism through Lester and Gandhi. It is also an image of religious affiliation, rooted in Protestantism but extending across denominational and interreligious boundaries. The connecting spiritual strand is not formal affiliation but mysticism.

To take another example, Fellowship House, in Philadelphia, installed a series of murals sometime in the late 1940s depicting most of the new-heroism pantheon. Fellowship House was an interracial project initiated by Quakers and managed for many years by Baptist pacifists Marjorie Penney and Herbert Haslam. The stated purpose of the murals was to make the House's aims more accessible to children, since verbal explanations were often lost on the very young. The subjects included St. Francis, Gandhi, and Kagawa; Lillian Wald, a woman of the settlement movement; two bridging figures, Schweitzer and William Penn; and Jesus.[30] Most of the figures and social movements represented on Allan Hunter's book cover, then, were here linked with each other in an iconic depiction of fellowship, peace, and urban social service.

Peace and Gardens

A counterpart to human heroism and urban poverty in pacifist iconography was nature, particularly nature cultivated in the form of a garden. This image has, of course, profound and fundamental meaning in Western and Christian spirituality. The garden is the Edenic beginning; it represents the time when God, humanity, and nature were at peace with one another and humanity was innocent of evil. The expulsion from Eden, according to the biblical story, marked the beginning of an adversarial relationship between humanity and nature. More, it was the beginning of conflict between persons, since the story goes on to say that one son of Adam and Eve murdered the other.

The garden as a peace symbol appeared early in several commemorative "peace gardens." These attracted moderate attention: they were included in Zonia Baber's displays of "peace symbols" and elaborated upon in Elizabeth Lobingier's work for Christian children's education.[31] One noteworthy garden straddled the border of the United States and Canada, calling attention to the Rush-Bagot Treaty that left that border unarmed.[32] But these were gardens focused straightforwardly on international peace; any deeper resonances were left to the visitor.

A later and more complex example was the Peace Garden project of the 1950s in Lemont, Illinois, which sought metaphorically to cultivate peace by growing seeds from around the world. Its documents show a network of associations between gardens, innocence, Christian missions, and serious pacifist activism. Its tireless volunteer director, Mary Phillips, was a Methodist and a member of WILPF. She acquired seeds initially from Methodist missionaries and later from individual citizens, with the aim of building concrete connections between nations.[33] Peace Garden literature reinforced the suggestion of original innocence by identifying children with flowers as subjects of growth.[34]

Some might object that the Peace Garden represented nothing more than a timeworn juxtaposition of children, flowers, and happy ideals. But Mary Phillips was no mere sentimentalist. She promoted inner-city interracial projects, held observances of Hiroshima Day, and called attention to radical antinuclear actions. Peace Garden gatherings for work or celebration often recalled pacifist ritual by including discussions, folk dancing, and the singing of folk songs and spirituals—rituals I discuss more fully in chapter 8.[35] And the imagery of growth was common to religious liberals and radical pacifists.

A more far-reaching manifestation of the garden was the farm. Pacifist cooperatives, especially after the paradigm shift, recalled the Edenic garden of peace at the same time that they were places of exile, refuge, and resistance. Agrarian self-sufficiency offered moral freedom: freedom from enmeshment with the society that produced war. And it modeled a different kind of life, one that enacted peace in every dimension. (See chapter 10.)[36]

These gardens were not purely Edenic. As with Adam in exile, the "sweat of [one's] face" (Gn 3:19) was still necessary to survival; the farms required long hours of hard work. And the rural co-ops, like the Peace Gardens, generated protest and resistance as well as renewal and safety. But the association of peace with cultivating the land was powerful, and it emerged again in the work of a seminal pacifist artist after World War II.

The Peaceable Kingdom

The woodcut prints of Fritz Eichenberg offered fresh expressions of pacifism for the post-1940 era. Eichenberg (1901–90) was an assimilated German Jew who emigrated to the United States in 1933. Already an experienced graphic artist, he became well-known for his book illustrations, particularly of literary classics. He was also a distinguished teacher: he taught at the New School for Social Research, at the Pratt Institute, where he founded the Graphic Art Center, and at the University of Rhode Island.[37] Most significant for our present purposes, however, is his creation of a body of work at the intersection of art, peace, social action, and religion.

Following a period of personal crisis in the late 1930s, Eichenberg became a Quaker in 1940. He was drawn both to Quaker spiritual practice and to pacifism and social action.[38] In 1949 he attended a conference on religious publishing at Pendle Hill, a Quaker study center, where he was introduced to Dorothy Day, the founder of the Catholic Worker movement.[39] This was the beginning of a fruitful collaboration. Day invited Eichenberg to contribute to the movement's newspaper, the *Catholic Worker*, and he ultimately published over one hundred prints there. He also published in Quaker venues at a time when liberal Quakerism's growth and reputation were at their height. His pamphlet *Art and Faith* (1952) appeared in the "Pendle Hill Pamphlets" series that shaped both outreach and Quaker self-definition.[40] And he provided a frontispiece for the *Hymnal for Friends* in 1955.[41]

Eichenberg's writings on art and spiritual life are themselves artifacts of pacifist culture, matrices of the language and reference points of post-1940 religious pacifism. To begin with, Eichenberg argued for art as the creative expression of the individual human spirit and the individual hand, the antithesis of industrial society's mechanization and imposed uniformity. In this argument he echoed both Ruskinian antimodernism, which influenced pacifist material culture in several directions, and the liberal reverence for individual personality. Second, Eichenberg believed art was profoundly rooted in spiritual life: a manifestation of the image of God, a divine gift, and an act of worship. He refused, however, to identify spiritual life with any one religious commitment. What mattered, he thought, was that the practice of art would integrate "mind, matter, . . . soul," and the soul's connection to God. Such integration was a threat to the industrial order, which profited by compartmentalizing; it would therefore lead inevitably to prophetic suffering. However, integration also offered freedom—freedom from greed, from haste, and from patronage, and freedom to recognize the suffering other. Hence, third, Eichenberg associated the integrated life of the artist with joyful voluntary poverty, "as Christ and

St. Francis and Gandhi knew it." And voluntary poverty was, in his view, "the only way to remove entirely from our lives the causes of strife and frictions." Thus Eichenberg connected faith, art, craft, and peace in a way that echoed pacifist cultural traditions, restating them for his time and his audience.[42]

Since Eichenberg's thought was grounded in the practice of visual art, though, my primary concern is with his visual imagery. Much of it reflected on labor and poverty. Eichenberg also created contemporary images of saints, biblical themes, and scenes from the life and death of Jesus. Among his pictures of saints are at least four of St. Francis, including one of St. Francis receiving the stigmata, which was uncommon in Protestant usage.[43]

Eichenberg's art used familiar icons of peace—a lamb, a dove, a child, a mother—and also moved in fresh directions. Farmers acquired new prominence, in part because of the *Catholic Worker*'s visual and ideological focus on labor. Images of St. Benedict and of the Holy Family, made for the *Worker*, are examples. Eichenberg's St. Benedict wields a shovel vigorously, not just to dig, but to slay a demonic dragon. The white shovel makes a conspicuous, almost vertical line in the mostly dark image. Below Benedict is his motto *Ora et Labora*—pray and work—and above him is the word "Pax," peace. A dove appears to his left, carrying a scroll that bears the title of his Rule.[44] Here the shovel, the most humble of tools, serves as a symbolic and visual link between Catholic tradition and contemporary ideals of peace, manual work, rural life, and communitarianism.

In another image, Eichenberg represented the Holy Family as migrant farm workers. Here Joseph is the central figure, while Mary feeds the baby in the foreground. Joseph is digging in a field, and his shovel, slightly below the center of the image, replicates the angle of Benedict's.[45] Another picture, *Catholic Worker Family*, similarly centers on an embracing paternal figure, here holding a shovel at rest.[46] The centrality of the iconic shovel in all three images serves to link rural families and labor with sanctity.

Eichenberg also made numerous images of Isaiah's vision of the Peaceable Kingdom or Holy Mountain (Is 11:6–9).[47] The passage, in the familiar King James version, reads,

> The wolf also shall dwell with the lamb, and the leopard shall lie down with the kid; and the calf and the young lion and the fatling together; and a little child shall lead them. And the cow and the bear shall feed;

Fritz Eichenberg, St. Francis, Sermon to the Birds, 1952. Image courtesy of Yale University Arts Library. Art © Fritz Eichenberg Trust/Licensed by VAGA, New York, N.Y.

Fritz Eichenberg, St. Benedict, 1953. Image courtesy of Yale University Arts Library. Art © Fritz Eichenberg Trust/Licensed by VAGA, New York, N.Y.

Edward Hicks, The Peaceable Kingdom, ca. 1833, oil on canvas, 44.5 x 60.2 cm. Worcester Art Museum, Worcester, Massachusetts, museum purchase.

their young ones shall lie down together: and the lion shall eat straw like the ox. And the sucking child shall play on the hole of the asp, and the weaned child shall put his hand on the cockatrice' den. They shall not hurt nor destroy in all my holy mountain: for the earth shall be full of the knowledge of the LORD, as the waters cover the sea.

Eichenberg was not the first to draw this text; in fact, he had probably seen other versions of the image. Though never widespread in traditional Western peace iconography, it had appeared in the nineteenth century and had become increasingly familiar during the 1930s and 1940s. The folk-art revival of that period brought into the public eye the naive paintings of the Quaker Edward Hicks (1780–1849), a sign painter by trade, who had produced over one hundred versions of the *Peaceable Kingdom*.[48] His paintings varied in detail, but all represented the text more or less literally: wolves and lambs lay side by side, bears took mouthfuls of corn. In addition, Hicks frequently added a background vignette of William Penn making a treaty with the Indians (see chapters 5 and 10).

The Peaceable Kingdom also appeared in the work of the twentieth-

Fritz Eichenberg, The Peaceable Kingdom, 1950. Image courtesy of Yale University Arts Library. Art © Fritz Eichenberg Trust/Licensed by VAGA, New York, N.Y.

century naive artist Horace Pippin (1888–1946), who made a series of Holy Mountain paintings between 1944 and 1946. Pippin, an African American, was becoming well known at this time through the prominent art dealer Robert Carlen. Carlen also introduced Pippin to Hicks's work. Pippin's paintings, like Hicks's, varied in detail but depicted literally the imagery of the text.[49]

Eichenberg made Peaceable Kingdom woodcuts in 1950 and 1955, and similar imagery appears in his contemporaneous pictures of the Garden of Eden, Noah's Ark, and St. Francis.[50] All include literal representations of some parts of the biblical text, especially the wolf alongside the lamb, the leopard with the kid, and the child with the snake. Other elements of these works, however, suggest a freer interpretation. In one image, the child cuddles a rabbit; in another, lion cubs play together.[51] The 1950 woodcut shows a city in the background, much like the poster from 1920.[52] A later version centers on a mother holding a child in her lap.[53]

What was the appeal of the Peaceable Kingdom image? Unlike the "swords into plowshares" icon, it is not a narrative. It is virtually static, and much of its meaning lies in what is *not* happening: they shall not hurt or destroy; the wolf refrains from eating the lamb; poisonous creatures do

PACIFIST ICONOGRAPHY | 107

not sting. Unlike the energetic action of beating swords into plowshares, this image is strange and dreamlike: a lion eats straw, a baby plays with snakes.

It is also about a different kind of vision of peace: a more universalistic vision than the end of warfare. There is nothing literal in the text about war itself, nor about weapons, although the actors can be (and were) understood metaphorically as nations or as human oppressors and underlings. The image does evoke the Edenic garden, but it is not primarily restorationist. Rather, it is a projection into the future. It suggests a broad conception of peace as a state in which members of unlike categories live in harmony together—the weak with the strong, the helpless with the powerful, predator with prey, and by extension, citizens of different nations, members of different races, and practitioners of different religions.[54] Thus it spoke to the contemporaneous movement of mainline pacifism from narrowly defined opposition to war into an all-encompassing commitment that affected every aspect of individual lives and social structures. This imagery did not, however, displace "swords into plowshares" imagery, but supplemented it.

FROM ROOTS IN MAINLINE Protestant culture, Protestant pacifism developed a new visual language of peace, unprecedented either in church life or in fine art. Initially, peace iconography drew on elements of Protestant culture: the Bible, church design, and the traditions of Christian art. It used media already available in the culture: stained-glass windows, statues, posters. Peace art remained closely tied to the word, as one would expect in this verbally oriented culture.

But peace advocates also made verbal images visual, material, and practical, reflecting their desire to live out biblical directives, to realize the faith as a whole way of life. Peace iconography evoked nature, original innocence, beneficent humanity, growth, and transformation. Peace advocates made alternative saints—at first, saints of progress, technology, and human well-being, and then saints of resistance and counterculture; first of individual initiative, later of communitarianism.

Thus iconography illuminates the ways pacifists negotiated modernity. Ringing affirmations of the modern, as in the Methodist peace poster or the Lindbergh window, subsided after the late 1930s. Yet modern peace heroes were still valorized in the postwar era, Mary Phillips and others retained a progressivist optimism in the 1950s, and physical artifacts have long lives in any case. At the same time, the antimodern imagery of farm and craft and alternative ways of life did not emerge without precedent; it was strongly prefigured in earlier pacifist iconography. The difference between the two paradigms lies not in an abrupt break but in a change of emphasis.

Most remarkably, however, pacifists turned to biblical imagery to create icons of peace that have persisted in American culture, both within and beyond the pacifist community. As late as 2004, an antiwar demonstration at the Democratic National Convention in Boston was to have included a plow made of used bullet shells.[55] The activist image of beating swords into plowshares, and the eschatological vision of wolves lying down with lambs, have become widespread vernacular references, instantly recognizable and endlessly varied.

7 "The Practice of the Presence"

PACIFIST SPIRITUALITY

"I'm a mystic, but I'm a practical mystic."—Anonymous source in "The Way of Contemplation," Peacemaker

Despite the concreteness and materiality of visual images, many pacifists entertained the conviction that true religion was grounded in "mysticism"—direct, experiential contact with the divine. This contact, they argued, would motivate and sustain the actions of pacifist life, both everyday and extraordinary. Thus in 1940 a "plan in the event of war or conscription," drafted by the prominent Christian pacifist A. J. Muste, advised pacifists to face the trials of wartime with "continual practice of the presence of God."[1]

Muste was not alone: in the following year, a Civilian Public Service camp newsletter reported on a lecture by Douglas Steere on "techniques of silent meditation";[2] an imprisoned conscientious objector quoted Muriel Lester on the joy of "practicing the presence";[3] and Jay Holmes Smith, Methodist organizer of the Harlem Ashram, spoke to the Episcopal Pacifist Fellowship on pacifist spiritual "training," also quoting Lester.[4] A 1942 pamphlet from the Fellowship of Reconciliation listed three devotional manuals: *Training for the Life of the Spirit* by Gerald Heard, *Ways of Praying* by Muriel Lester, and *A Testament of Devotion* by Thomas Kelly. These books had in common the beliefs that true faith was inward and experiential and that it manifested itself in action. Indeed they appeared alongside titles typical of the pacifist activist interests of the early 1940s: Muste's *Nonviolence in an Aggressive World*, Harold Gray's *Character "Bad,"* Harold Fey's *Cooperatives and Peace*, and Allan Hunter's *White Corpuscles in Europe*, which I discuss further in chapter 10.

Leigh Eric Schmidt has argued convincingly that spiritual seeking has been allied with social and political progressivism since at least the time of Emerson.[5] Here I focus on the particular interface of mystical spirituality with mainline Protestantism and pacifism, using sources from the 1920s through the 1950s. As we shall see, pacifist leaders offered written guides to mystical practice and accounts of their own experiences. Rank-and-file pacifists, too, left evidence of their efforts to practice mysticism and of its meaning for them. Like the nineteenth- and early-twentieth-century seekers whom Schmidt describes, they favored intellectual and spiritual purity, athleticism, activism, and universalism, broadly construed as a desire to cross religious and social boundaries.

The growth of Protestant pacifist mysticism coincided with the growth of pacifist antimodernism and was in many ways associated with it.[6] As the events of the 1930s challenged both modernist optimism and the churches' commitment to pacifism, and peace activists began to shift their attention from progress and reform to systemic alternatives, interest in spiritual practice also increased. The change in Kirby Page's writing, which I noted earlier, was only one example of many.[7]

The idea and practice of mysticism, which emerged before the paradigm shift, proved crucial to its realization. Mysticism enabled pacifists to sustain the liberal antipathy toward ritual and form, but it also added something new—a way to accommodate a variety of beliefs under the broad umbrella of religious pacifism. As individual and group practice, it promised intense spiritual experience to support the intense ethical commitments of pacifism.

For mainline pacifists, mysticism commonly meant continuous direct communion with God. For some, this communion began in a single transformative experience; for others it required a willed effort to sustain meditation or prayer. Others had both kinds of experience. The practices they used were recollection, disciplined attention, and sometimes surrender, all drawing on physical as well as mental techniques. The results, pacifists claimed, were universal love, social action, and peacemaking, but also strength, resistance, and protest.

As I suggested in chapter 2, liberal Friends often identified themselves as mystics and argued that authentic religion, mysticism, and activism were intimately connected.[8] Interest in mysticism was not limited to Friends, however, nor did it originate solely in Quakerism. Mysticism was widely discussed among mainline Protestants, including some on the evangelical end of the spectrum.[9] Both mainliners and Quakers turned to earlier Christian mystical sources.[10] And, as elsewhere in pacifist culture, there was considerable cross-fertilization between Friends and other liberals. Those interested in mysticism read one another's works, spoke at one another's conferences, and built bridges between denominations. Pendle Hill, a Quaker community and school for adults, offered courses on mysticism regularly, beginning in its first term, and also hosted as faculty or advisers such mainline luminaries as Georgia Harkness, Vida Scudder, Henry Pitney Van Dusen, Herbert Gezork, and Amos Wilder.[11] Quaker pacifists who were former mainline Protestants transferred cultural materials along with their loyalties.

This chapter outlines these connections and surveys the range of Protestant pacifist mystical practices. As a way of mapping the field, I present a historical text that was central to mainline Protestant mystical practice; four spiritual teachers whose thought and practice were well known; and testimony from ordinary practitioners of Protestant pacifist mysticism. The discussion shows how mystical spirituality functioned in part as a religious response to modernity, and how liberal Quakerism offered the primary institutional space for it.

The published works I have relied on represent the shared culture, the common "vernacular references," of Protestant pacifist mysticism.[12] Passed from hand to hand, offered to newcomers, reviewed and advertised in pacifist publications, they were the common coin of this culture. In another sense, of course, they are a distillation, since most of them emerged from oral, informal, and practical contexts that I do not examine here. Muriel Lester, for example, lived in community and lectured widely; Thomas Kelly taught college students and explored mysticism with a small group; Glenn Clark developed his practices in church groups and camps.[13]

It is worth noting, though, how many of these mystical leaders knew one another or one another's work. For example, Rufus Jones taught Thomas Kelly and engaged in common projects with Muriel Lester and Glenn Clark.

Kelly quoted Frank Laubach.¹⁴ Lester and Laubach attended Clark's prayer camps.¹⁵ All looked to common historical models, notably St. Francis of Assisi, Brother Lawrence, and the seventeenth-century European mystics. And all were read and quoted by a range of pacifists in CPS camps, in the FOR, in seminaries, and in cooperatives.

THE TEMPLATE: BROTHER LAWRENCE

It was not only contemporary experience, or, as Schmidt noted, scholarly analysis, that caught Protestants' attention. It was also primary historical sources, albeit in edited versions. One of the favorites of pacifist mystics was *The Practice of the Presence of God*. This was a collection of writings and "conversations" of a seventeenth-century French Carmelite, Nicholas Herman (1611–91), known in monastic life as Lawrence of the Resurrection and in popular literature as Brother Lawrence. After some years of military and domestic service, he became a lay brother in 1666. His letters and "conversations"—a visitor's accounts of private talks—were first collected and published in Paris shortly after his death. They did not find a large following among Catholics, but within twenty years they were well known among European Protestants.¹⁶ The collection was first issued in the United States by the evangelical publishing house Fleming Revell in 1895 and went into four more printings before 1914. By the mid-1950s at least a dozen other British and American publishers had issued English-language editions. A short and portable work, *The Practice of the Presence* reached YMCA members, pacifists in jail, nondenominational spiritual seekers, and many others.

The book presented an unlettered man, assigned to humble work in the kitchen, who was yet able to maintain a "*habitual sense of* GOD's *presence*," a soul in constant "secret conversation" with God. The text offered advice to others, both lay and religious, who sought to attain a similar spiritual state. The practices Lawrence recommended were personal; they did not stem from monastic disciplines, community, or regular times of prayer. He said that "it was a great delusion to think that the times of prayer ought to differ from other times" and that "it [was] not necessary for being with God to be always at church." Rather, his primary concern was the relationship between the individual and God. Christ was mentioned only twice in the book, and the church was defined as simply "the way of faith."¹⁷

The experiences the book recounted had much in common with those of classical mystics. Lawrence began by renouncing "everything that was not [God]." He then strove to keep his thoughts constantly on God, to turn them back to God when they wandered, and to do everything for God's sake rather than for human approval. "I found no small pain in this exercise," he emphasized. For about ten years, he said, he experienced doubts and difficulties. Then he found himself transformed all at once, able to be constantly with God without this strenuous discipline, and the recipient of consolations and guidance. Of this state he wrote, "I have no will but that of GOD."[18]

His conversations and letters advised others on "practicing the presence" as he did. The believer was to renounce all hindrances to communion with God, to endeavor to practice constant recollection, to confess his or her failings, and to trust in God's gracious help. One should do one's work only for God, not for self-satisfaction or human recognition. Lawrence himself, says the text, was "pleased when he could take up a straw from the ground for the love of GOD."[19]

The term "the practice of the presence" became part of the Protestant pacifist vernacular, and this is not surprising. The "practice of the presence" reinforced liberal religion by being noninstitutional, nonritual, and nondoctrinal, while at the same time calling for an all-encompassing, demanding "way of life."[20] It met the particular needs of pacifists by emphasizing love and by being usable in public or communal as well as private situations. And Brother Lawrence's life story reinforced pacifists' desire to identify with common folk.

Still, pacifists appropriated Lawrence on liberal terms. His images of the soul as a "poor criminal" or "dumb and paralytic beggar" were largely absent from pacifist writing; few pacifists seemed to have experienced themselves as miserable sinners.[21] Renunciation of self was central to Lawrence's communion with God, but was a muted and ambivalent theme for pacifists.

FOUR TEACHERS: LESTER, LAUBACH, CLARK, KELLY

Muriel Lester

Lester (1883–1968) was a pacifist icon of the 1930s and beyond, frequently named with Mohandas Gandhi and Toyohiko Kagawa as one of a handful of exemplars of the fully committed life. A longtime pacifist and member of the Fellowship of Reconciliation, she became ambassador-at-large of the

International FOR in 1932 and was its traveling secretary from 1934 until 1956. As a young woman she had founded an urban workers' community, Kingsley Hall, in London; she refused to call it a "settlement," thinking the term condescending. Raised as a Baptist, she led an independent congregation at Kingsley Hall and joined a Christian lay order that shared both spiritual life and money.

Her private rule of spiritual practice attracted widespread attention. Lester developed this practice during a period of crisis and change around 1915. Its sources included Brother Lawrence, St. Francis, and the modern mystic Evelyn Underhill.[22] In 1930 Lester shared some of her practices in a series of lectures offered in the United States to raise funds for Kingsley Hall. Her little book *Ways of Praying* grew out of the lectures.

Lester's approach to "practicing the presence" relied on the patterns of ordinary daily life. "Anyone can live the life of prayer," she wrote. Its habits could be acquired "while you dress, bath, brush your hair, walk to work, or sit on the bus." She recommended daily morning and evening prayer and regular "acts of recollection" triggered by such ordinary activities as washing one's hands. Her use of temporal routine for spiritual purposes recalls the various Christian traditions of praying the hours, but without their connection to formal liturgy.[23]

Ways also recalls contemplative traditions, including Brother Lawrence's work. Upon waking, said Lester, one's first act should be the contemplation of God—a God of "shining beauty, radiant joy, creative power, all-pervading love." Next, in morning prayer, one should seek immersion in God, praying, "Spin me backward or spin me forward, for I desire nothing other than the doing of thy will." Acts of recollection, she wrote, would help to return one to this state throughout the day as one struggled or became distracted. Eventually one would attain "an almost unbroken sense of joy, peace, and harmony with God and our fellow."[24]

These disciplines took on new applications as war approached. Lester's *Training*, published in 1940, joined Richard Gregg's *Training for Peace* and Gerald Heard's *Training for the Life of the Spirit* in focusing on disciplines for the committed pacifist life, as we will see in more depth in chapter 8.[25] The works reflected pacifists' concern with resisting the pressures of militarism and fascism, as well as with building a peaceful society. And they reached beyond Protestantism: the parental God of *Ways* became in *Training* an "Unseen Reality" or a "Creative Spirit."[26]

Training conveys the sense of imminent danger pacifists felt in the early

1940s. "We must out-train the totalitarians," Lester wrote. "[We] must make ourselves spiritually and physically fit to endure torture." She advocated athleticism and physical "wholeness" alongside the "practice of the presence." *Training* sketched the same model of daily prayer as in *Ways* but, again, conveyed a greater sense of urgency. Morning prayer, which previously was to occupy fifteen to thirty minutes, was here reduced to five. Recollection, formerly a mild discipline, now meant that "[we must] *force* ourselves" to return to God many times a day.[27] But this spiritual training, she said, would help the practitioner resist the powers of war and oppression and live with minimal material comforts.

Lester's letters from a British prison camp in Trinidad, where she was held for ten weeks in 1941 pending deportation, recount her spiritual practice in a concrete situation. "Brother Lawrence is a necessity for this sort of life," she wrote. "Awareness of God is our greatest safeguard—our only weapon—our complete joy." This awareness outweighed particular commitments: Lester identified with "other Evangelicals" but kept a "Benedictine silence" in the evenings and reflected on Asian Christianity and Islam.[28]

Lester's disciplines, then, looked back to earlier Christian sources but ultimately crossed religious boundaries. Her early work presented practices of prayer as ways of maintaining awareness of God through the everyday, the domestic. Later she offered these practices as ascetic modes of countercultural resistance.

Frank Laubach

Frank Laubach developed a spiritual discipline for missionary purposes, but his work also reached pacifist circles. Laubach (1884–1970) was a Congregationalist missionary and teacher of literacy. In 1930 he undertook a mission to the "Moros," the Filipino Muslims, on the island of Mindanao. Here he spent some months in isolation, separated from his family and unable to speak the local language. He spent much of this time on spiritual experimentation. Laubach described his experiences in letters to his father between January 1930 and January 1932. Excerpts were published in 1937 as *Letters by a Modern Mystic*.[29]

Like Lawrence and Lester, Laubach began with the practice of recollection. "Two years ago," he wrote early in 1930, "a profound dissatisfaction led me to begin trying to line up my actions with the will of God about every fifteen minutes or every half hour." Laubach agreed with Lawrence that this required a "strenuous" effort of will. But he combined discipline with a sense of "surrender," which was not only spiritual but physical. "I tried to let [God] control my hands while I was shaving and dressing and eating breakfast," he wrote. "Now I am trying to let God control my hands as I pound the typewriter keys."[30]

Laubach reported only intermittent success in the first few months. At times he experienced the "joy of complete hourly, minute by minute" communion, "marvelous experiences of the friendship of God." At other times he recorded contact with God for perhaps half the day, or a third, and at still other times, he recorded near failure.[31]

Finally his efforts broke through to a transcendent experience of union: "The day had been rich but strenuous, so I climbed 'Signal Hill' back of my house talking and listening to God all the way up, all the way back, all the lovely half hour on the top. And God talked back! I let my tongue go loose and from it there flowed poetry far more beautiful than any I ever composed. It flowed without pausing and without ever a failing syllable for a half hour. I listened astonished and full of joy and gratitude. I wanted a dictaphone for I knew that I should not be able to remember it."[32]

Two things are especially interesting here. First, Laubach's breakthrough experience bore a striking resemblance to speaking in tongues. But he and his editors presented the experience as mystical rather than Pentecostal, and as poetry rather than tongues. In keeping with liberal and antimodern sensibilities, then, they located intense experience in art and mysticism.[33] Second, Laubach attributed his interest in God's will to his close contact with Islam, not to any Christian source—a further indication of liberals' willingness to look beyond religious boundaries.[34]

Laubach attributed his most significant work—a method of teaching literacy to adults—to the inspiration of this steady contact with God. He also wrote regularly on the connection between peace and prayer, although he apparently did not make a formal commitment to pacifism until 1956, when he joined the FOR. In 1960 he was a featured speaker at a nonviolent protest against biological warfare.[35] Laubach's writings on spirituality continued to advocate the methods he developed in 1930: frequent recollection, self-surrender, and involvement of the body. As late as 1959, his prayer booklet *The Game with Minutes* advised the reader to think of God for one second in every minute. In England it was published with the subtitle *Practising the Presence of God*.[36]

Glenn Clark

Glenn Clark first came to public notice as a teacher of prayer. Clark (1882–1956) was a professor of English and an athletic coach at Macalester College. Raised as a Congregationalist, he was also active in Presbyterian churches, and he reached out to people of other denominations and religions.[37] Clark claimed to have experienced a spiritual awakening during a time of personal stress in 1919. His article on how to pray, "The Soul's Sincere Desire," was published in the *Atlantic Monthly* in 1924 to an enthusiastic response.[38] Like other liberals, Clark rejected formalism and institutionalism, promising instead to make religion "a part of life." To this end he outlined a method of prayer as spiritual "calisthenics" involving stretching, inhaling, and exhaling. He advised the reader to make spiritual exercise a "continuous habit," for which he used Brother Lawrence's phrase, "practising the presence of God." By this method Clark claimed to have experienced for the previous two years "a continuous stream of answered prayer."[39]

Clark gave increasing attention to his spiritual work after 1930. In that year he established the Camps Farthest Out, which still survive.[40] He also set up a publishing company for his own works. In 1937 Macalester appointed him to a new chair of Creative Religious Living, which he held until his retirement in 1942.[41]

Although Clark was an important figure in Protestant pacifist mysticism, he was also atypical. On the one hand, he made the attainment of peace through prayer a central interest. He associated closely with Rufus Jones, Muriel Lester, Frank Laubach, and others in mystical pacifist circles.[42] He also followed news of Toyohiko Kagawa, a pacifist hero, and edited the English edition of Kagawa's novel *A Grain of Wheat* (1936). Among major influences he named Jones, Evelyn Underhill, and Brother Lawrence. A memorial tribute remembered him as a mystic and an "intense seeker of world peace" and made the requisite comparison to St. Francis.[43]

On the other hand, Clark avoided any formal profession of pacifism. He was more interested in such pursuits as business and sports than most pacifists were.[44] Many of his ideas about prayer and healing were derived from New Thought, which was uncommon among pacifists.[45] And he cultivated a personal following through the Camps Farthest Out.

Clark saw prayer as an almost physical force, subject to the spiritual "laws" of the universe. Most pacifists affirmed the power of love, for example, but for Clark this power was unusually concrete. His young son liked to climb on the roof of their house, and Clark felt sure that the child would not fall so long as Clark and his wife kept up a continuing current of love. When the parents quarreled one day, however, they made the boy come down from the roof until they had reconciled.[46] For Clark, then, love was not a general feeling or undefined power but a force with predictable and observable effects in time and space.

In the Camps Farthest Out, Clark used bodily action and ritual to invoke spiritual power. An early brochure was particularly prescient: headed "A Camp for Training Athletes of the Spirit," it not only recalled the "muscular" element of Protestant prayer but prefigured the spiritual athleticism of pacifist "training" as the war approached.[47] Clark's first aims were to remove obstacles to divine action and to come into harmony with the laws of the universe. This process incorporated prayerful attention, balance, movement, and art. Clark's earlier "spiritual calisthenics" here became plainly physical, as in this intercession for the president of the United States: "While pushing our arms full length out, up, front, down, we can repeat rhythmically: 'Lord . . . use—my body—and my—mind—and my—emotions—to help—the President—to hunger—and thirst—to hear—Thee speak.'"[48]

Frank Laubach described another intercession, this one a "dramatized prayer," or ritual, at the camp: "A hundred or more people form circles, or horseshoes, or a V, like the outstretched arms of Christ, and hold hands while they 'broadcast.' . . . They imagine their circle transferred to Washington, where it encircles the White House, with the President seated in the center. Then the leader says: 'Lord use this circle as a great funnel through which Thy love can flow to the President.'" He added, "Glenn Clark's camps have seen miraculous happenings during and immediately following their prayer broadcasts."[49] Clark made explicit connections between bodily fitness, spiritual openness, and international peace, without abandoning interest in modern society. Indeed his experimental, "scientific" approach was invested in modernity.

Thomas Kelly

Thomas Kelly's *Testament of Devotion* appeared in 1941, on the heels the pacifist works on "training." Like those books, it advised constant contact with the divine, referred to Brother Lawrence and other historical mystics, and sought ways to effect peace and social change. But it was less concerned with method and discipline and closer to "orthodox Christian love mysticism" than most pacifist works.[50]

Kelly (1893–1941) was a lifelong Quaker with connections beyond the Society of Friends. He grew up in the evangelical midwestern branch of Quakerism, but as a young adult embraced a "spiritualized liberalism" influenced by Rufus Jones.[51] Kelly served with the YMCA during World War I and studied at Hartford Seminary and Harvard University. In 1936 he began to teach philosophy at Haverford College. Following a period of crisis and depression, however, he acquired a "new life direction" in late 1937, shifting his focus from philosophy to religious thought and devotion. From 1938 until his death in early 1941 he studied classical and modern mystical writings and lectured and wrote on mystical practice. *Testament* was a posthumous collection of some of these writings.[52] Most were directed to Kelly's fellow Quakers, berating them for lukewarm religion, complacency, and formalism. But it was not long before his work began to reach a wider audience.

Kelly was less interested in methods of spiritual practice than in their results: the transformed lives of individuals and of religious communities. The transformed individual, he wrote, would experience continuous prayer and communion with God simultaneously with everyday activity.[53] The mystical life was one of absolutes, of total devotion, unreserved obedience, and forgetting of self.[54] One lived "in the Presence" or "from the Center," which was "a divine Abyss . . . a Heart, a Life."[55] Transformed individuals, said Kelly, would be free to act and willing to enter into suffering—especially as the prospect of war grew more immediate. And they would recognize others of like spirit across boundaries of class, race, education, and confession.

Kelly wrote about transformative mystical events with an immediacy that suggested personal experience. "It is an overwhelming experience to fall into the hands of the living God," he wrote, "to be invaded to the depths of one's being by His presence, to be, without warning, wholly uprooted from all earth-born securities and assurances, and to be blown by a tempest of unbelievable power which leaves one utterly, utterly defenseless. . . . Then is the soul swept into a Loving Center of ineffable sweetness, where calm and unspeakable peace and ravishing joy steal over one. . . . [One finds that] marks of glory are upon all things, and the marks are cruciform and blood-stained."[56]

Some people, he said, were fortunate enough to enter the mystical life through a singular experience such as this. Most, however, caught the vision of the transformed life at one remove, from others' accounts of it. For them, the mystical life was accessible through discipline, will, and receptivity.

Kelly also described divine speech in language reminiscent of Laubach's. "There come times when prayer pours forth in volumes and originality such as we cannot create," he wrote. "It rolls through us like a mighty tide. . . . Here the autonomy of the inner life becomes complete and we are joyfully *prayed through*." Unlike Laubach, however, Kelly implied that this prayer was internal, not vocal, and he presented it not as a single peak experience but as a manifestation of continuous, "autonomous" divine work. "All we can say is, Prayer is taking place, and I am given to be in the orbit," he concluded.[57]

Kelly was particularly incisive about the means by which the mystical life would sustain activism. Sharply critical of the assumption that religion must "prove its worth" by changing society, he depicted busy activists who take on every project that comes along or feel guilty when they do not, base their plans and decisions on merely human calculations, and finally, as an afterthought, "breathe a prayer" for help in carrying out their agendas. Their condition was constant strain at best, despair at worst. "And religious people think they must work hard and please God and make a good record and bring in the Kingdom!" he exclaimed.[58]

Kelly called instead for simplicity. Although mystical communion would ground one in universal love, he said, it would also make one aware of the particularity of one's calling. One would be free to act on only a few "concerns" with unreserved dedication. "We learn to say *No* as well as *Yes* by attending to the guidance of inner responsibility," he wrote.[59]

Kelly, then, was both with the modernists and against them. With them, he resisted the categories of doctrine and church and questioned Christian exclusivism in favor of universal spiritual experience. Against them, he revived orthodox theological categories and criticized progressive activism, human self-reliance, and complacency. He emphasized divine otherness and transcendence and stressed the primacy of God's initiative, but envisioned that initiative working itself out in pacifist action.

ORDINARY PRACTITIONERS: "PRACTICAL MYSTICS"[60]

The association between mysticism and pacifism was not limited to a few leaders. By the early 1940s it was widespread in pacifist religious culture. While not all practitioners can be identified with certainty as Protestants, their language, ideas, and published sources indicate a substantial degree of connection. Indeed, they suggest that the peace culture developed in an explicitly Protestant context was spreading beyond those bounds.

Visions of the pacifist "way of life" often included mysticism explicitly. For instance, the School of Pacifist Living, an initiative within CPS camps, devoted considerable attention to the skills of personal and group meditation, with the overall aim of living "the Life of the Spirit." Among its resources were works by Heard, Gregg, Laubach, Underhill, and Steere.[61] And the CPS men who prepared a booklet on "A Way of Life" included this nuanced account of mystical practice:

> Most of us who have endeavored to travel this road have sometimes experienced deep discouragement because of a complete failure of inspiration, and absolute barrenness in the inner world of thought. And we have found it extremely difficult to keep on striving under such circumstances. However, such barrenness is well known to every soul who has set out upon this difficult road. . . . This earnest search for truth in spite of unrelieved darkness, this thirsting after God in a "dry and thirsty land," is indeed one of the most creative things we can do. . . . Sooner or later the gift of God's presence is granted.[62]

Postwar religious publishing continued to promote mysticism. Howard Brinton's popular *Guide to True Peace* brought together writings of the seventeenth-century mystics Fénelon, Molinos, and Madame Guyon. New editions of Brother Lawrence's writings appeared, as did several printings of *The Cloud of Unknowing*, an anonymous medieval work. Commercial publishers advertised books by Brinton, Kelly, Heard, Gregg, Steere, Allan Hunter, and the spiritual writer Sarah Cleghorn in pacifist publications. The American Baptist Publication Society offered "religious" and "devotional" books by Heard, Kelly, Clark, and Laubach.[63] Abingdon Press, a Methodist house, issued Thomas Kepler's anthology *The Fellowship of the Saints*: organized around a mystical and socially activistic definition of sainthood, it juxtaposed classical Christian figures with many of the twentieth-century "saints" I have discussed here.[64] In 1946 a group of well-known mainline

Protestant mystics, some of them pacifists, proposed a new model of the Christian church based on their own "Pentecostal" experience. This experience was not speaking in tongues but "unity of life and spirit," an experience of a divine "presence" by whom they were fused together and guided.[65]

A few "lay" mystics—pacifists who did not write specifically on mysticism or instruct others in it—give a window into the meaning of mysticism for ordinary practitioners. Tracy Mygatt, the Episcopalian playwright and activist, described herself as a "throw-back mystic." She associated mysticism with resistance to formal theology, an imaginative relationship with God and church, and a certain antimodern otherworldliness—"Anyone who has ever seen me cross the street without a traffic policeman," she said, "knows that I belong more in the first than in the twentieth century."[66] Sarah Cleghorn, an Episcopalian writer and teacher who later became a Quaker, wrote that her discovery of the mystics introduced "a far better conception of God than any other which I knew"—a God who flowed through all aspects of life and was "readily reached at any time." As Glenn Clark had done, Cleghorn applied this new relationship with God to healing, first for a friend and then for her own chronic sinus trouble.[67] Peace Pilgrim, an unchurched mystic who spent much of her life on solo peace walks, described herself in 1954 as God's "little instrument," happy to walk or to do humble tasks in accordance with God's will. "Do you know what it is to know God—to have his constant guidance—a constant awareness of His presence?" she asked.[68] Letters from anonymous World War II conscientious objectors described their spiritual grounding in similar terms. "Somehow the presence of God, whose Light I have come further to enjoy, seemed to prevent any further harm from befalling my body," said one. Another reflected that becoming "transmitters of Love," an image borrowed from Glenn Clark, could be an effective form of action. "This is, of course, the view of a mystic, but it is logical too," he wrote.[69] And a radical newsletter wrote approvingly, "A Quaker lady was heard to say, 'I'm a mystic, but I'm a practical mystic.'"[70]

The California activist Josephine Whitney Duveneck (1891–1978), in her autobiography *Life on Two Levels* (1978), left an unusually full account of her experimentation with mysticism. Raised as an upper-class Episcopalian, she had accepted a liberal theology based on the teachings of Jesus and the primacy of love. As an adolescent she explored Anglo-Catholicism, Eastern religions, and Theosophy. Some years later, as a mother and activist, she began to study mysticism, reading Underhill, William James, and historical Christian writings.[71] Actual mystical experience, however, eluded her until a breakthrough occurred during a period of deep despondency: "I said to God, 'It's no use. I've tried all I can. I can't do anything more.' All of a sudden I seemed to be swept bodily out of my bed, carried above the trees and held poised in mid-air, surrounded by light. . . . All was ecstasy. I have no idea whether it lasted a minute or several hours. . . . For the rest of the night I lay in a state of peace and indescribable joy."[72]

After this experience, Duveneck began to give intensive attention to "practicing the presence" in the midst of her extensive and varied activity. While solitary meditation was not too difficult, she wrote, maintaining constant awareness of God required of her "a rigorous apprenticeship." She used physical objects as reminders: a large safety pin on the front of her dress, a button in her pocket. She also used "a mantra"—the first line of the prayer attributed to St. Francis: "Lord, make me an instrument of your peace." Like Muriel Lester, she used her regular activities as occasions for recollection: passing through a doorway, for example, or meeting someone. Gradually, she said, the deliberate actions became habitual. "It is like learning to drive a car," she wrote. ". . . Gradually your reactions become automatic . . . [and you] just enjoy the scenery."[73]

Duveneck experimented with Vedanta Hinduism but resisted religious exclusivity. She found local Quaker groups congenial, however, and ultimately became a Friend. "Thomas Kelly's *Testament of Devotion* was echoed word for word in my thoughts," she wrote.[74]

THE INSTITUTIONAL LOCUS: LIBERAL QUAKERISM

From the mid-1930s, silent-worship Quakerism offered the primary institutional space for pacifist mystics. It was not the only space, for, as we have seen, mystical practices flourished in many other settings. But Quakerism offered more stability than such venues as camps and cooperatives, and it differed from other Protestant denominations in the way it made both mysticism and pacifism central to its historical and present identity.

This mystical identity was in part a twentieth-century phenomenon. While Friends had always affirmed the centrality of spiritual experience for authentic Christianity, they did not generally identify themselves as "mystics" until the late nineteenth century, concurrently with wider cultural interest in mysticism.[75] In the United States, Rufus Jones was the primary exponent of this identity, though not its only one.[76] Jones's historical argument for continuity between Continental mysticism and Quakerism, which has since been contested, was seminal for twentieth-century Quaker mysticism, and his teaching, lecturing, reflective writing, and personal example reinforced its influence. From 1930 onward, a second generation of teachers and writers, notably Howard Brinton and Douglas Steere, reinforced and extended Jones's work in the direction of corporate spiritual experience. Institutions such as Pendle Hill (founded 1930) and the Wider Quaker Fellowship (founded 1936), whose histories await scholarly assessment, did much to link social change with mystical worship. While identification of Quakerism with mysticism was not universal or uncontested, it was nonetheless well established by the mid-1930s and grew steadily thereafter.[77]

This emergence of mystical identity coincided with the numerical growth in Friends General Conference. Membership had been declining for nearly a century before 1925, but around that year, it began to hold steady, and it increased after 1940, as I show in chapter 2. There were a number of reasons for this increase.

Testimony such as Duveneck's, however, points to the particular connections between pacifist mysticism and liberal-Quaker growth.[78] Both Quakers and outsiders ultimately came to see Friends as a community of mystics. In 1947, for example, a Pendle Hill evaluation committee, composed of both Friends and prominent mainline Protestants, recommended for its curriculum "a concentration on the mystical dimension of Christianity which made Quakers unique."[79] And the 1955 version of Philadelphia Yearly Meeting's "book of discipline," *Faith and Practice*, said:

> [George Fox] had found the way to communion with God without aid of ritual or clergy . . . This belief in the immediate presence of the light of Christ within the soul . . . has been the vital message of Quakerism wherever it has been effective. It is a faith that does not stand on ritual or creed, but on the experience and practice of the presence of God within the individual heart. It is universal in its scope . . .
>
> Love, the outworking of this Divine Spirit, is the most potent influence that can be applied to the affairs of men. This application of love to the whole of life the Society of Friends conceives to be the core of

> the Christian doctrine.... [W]orship is a personal communion with God and a yielding of our wills to the divine will, for which no form of service nor aid of clergy is necessary.[80]

This is the familiar language of personal communion, practice of the presence, and yielding of the will, together with an emphatic dismissal of ritual, creed, and clergy. The statement drew on material from earlier books of discipline, but foregrounded that material at the beginning of a new section headed "Quaker Faith." In these ways *Faith and Practice* presented Quakerism as a thoroughgoing alternative to churchly institutions, theology, and practice. In their place it offered a structure and an institutional setting for individual and corporate worship focused on experiencing the unmediated presence of God.[81]

HERE, THEN, IS A collection of people who sought to practice mysticism and who testified to mystical experience as defined by mid-twentieth-century mainline Protestants, which can be called "presence mysticism." Its practitioners sought direct communion with God, and their goal was a continuous state of such communion. Presence mysticism might use physical, visual, or verbal aids, but it was not structured by time or place. It looked to Christian roots but was open to crossing religious boundaries.

Presence mysticism assumed the constant availability, beneficence, and effective power of the divine spirit. The principal means of attaining the ideal state of communion were human effort, will, and discipline, although in some schemas, a divine gift might either begin or complete the process. Advocates promised that discipline would be rewarded by internal consolations and by guidance and strength for action. This strength would support both work—for peace and social action—and, sometimes, suffering.

Human subjects being what they are, however, Protestant pacifist mystics refuse to be corralled in any well-defined area. Presence mysticism extended to the boundaries of high contemplation, faith healing, controlling unseen forces, speaking in tongues, and asceticism. Modes of instruction and practice varied, though they all aimed at the same set of spiritual goals. Approaches ranged from the isolated to the public, from domestic to muscular, quietistic to impassioned, everyday to transporting, technical to intuitive. Where Muriel Lester forced herself to return to awareness of the divine, Thomas Kelly was ravished by the divine aggressor. Where Glenn

Clark sought world peace by group exercises, Frank Laubach received divine poetry in solitude.

The balance among mainline Protestantism, "mysticism," and pacifism did not hold. Multiple forces drove them apart: the mainline's renunciation of pacifism, the absence of a strong Protestant tradition of mysticism, the resistance of both liberals and mystics to confessional commitment, the midcentury critiques of Christian triumphalism and exclusivism, and the growing availability of Hindu and Buddhist modes of meditation and religious experience. Another consideration, necessarily more speculative, is the difficulty of maintaining a strenuous spiritual practice and a strenuous mode of life. And a theological critique would surely reveal unresolved tensions in the assumptions behind liberal mysticism.

What did hold was the connection between intense experience and antimodernism. Meditation was a common spiritual practice in peace cells and on cooperative farms, themselves exemplars of antimodern intensity. Quakers similarly connected mysticism with pacifism and simplicity.

Most important, mysticism was integral to the pacifist critique of modernity. Like Frank Laubach's experience, this critique had much in common with Pentecostal religion. In mysticism, as in Pentecostalism, the peak experience was a sense of being taken out of oneself, of being used and directed by a supernatural power. Both movements testified that the peak experience would lead to a transformed life, even if one were challenged by obstacles and subject to backsliding. Both affirmed the empowering quality of submission of the individual's will to the divine will. Joel Carpenter has written that Pentecostals offered "moral and experiential answers to modern secularity's challenge," as opposed to the "cognitive and ideological" claims of fundamentalism.[82] Pacifist mysticism was a different "moral and experiential" response. It offered a way to intense experience and a means of resistance to the secular modernity that was inextricably enmeshed with war.

8 Training for Peace

RICHARD GREGG AND THE REALIGNMENT OF PACIFIST LIFE

The suggestions contained in this pamphlet are intended as an answer to the oft-repeated question, "Yes, we believe in peace but what can we do about it?"
—*Program Suggestions for World Peace, 1934*[1]

We have looked at theological, performative, visual, and spiritual dimensions of mainline Protestant peace culture, and at the ways they built up to a paradigm shift in the years around 1940. This chapter considers another essential aspect of that culture: everyday practice. My concern is not with large-scale public gestures such as marching or performing civil disobedience, but with the ordinary ways pacifists tried to live out their convictions and build peace in the world. The next chapter will examine a committed, all-encompassing mode of living that also emerged from the paradigm shift.

The bedrock of peace activism was discussion, persuasion, and education. Liberals were confident of human reasonableness and educability, and mid-century mainline culture was heavily verbal. When Protestant peace activists asked, "What can we do about it?" their first responses reflected this character above all. The first part of this chapter examines the manifestations and meanings of their practices, both before and after the paradigm shift.

The second section turns to a crucial text that was in many ways a reaction against the verbal character of Protestant activism, even as it retained a measure of confidence in human improvement. Richard Gregg's *Training for Peace* offered a new model for the "way of life" pacifists advocated. In it one sees both traditional sources and the emergence of a new understanding and practice of peacemaking. This section of the chapter summarizes *Training* and attends to its implications for religious thought, the body, folk arts, and ritualization.

WORDS AND ACTION

Persuasion

Mainline Protestant peace action of the interwar period often began with reasoned measures, based on spoken and written words, with the goals of education and political pressure. Pacifists wrote to government officials, produced and handed out leaflets, issued statements, presented speakers, held public forums, circulated petitions, took surveys, recited pledges, and fed the local press information on international affairs and peace work. They published and shared reading lists and donated books to libraries. They joined peace organizations, formed local committees, and urged churches and other organizations to take a stand on peace. Even indirect forms of action such as worship, drama, and storytelling often incorporated information and argument.[2]

A typical approach to action appeared in 1932 in a Presbyterian adult-education booklet that began by posing the rhetorical questions, "What can churches do?" and "What can the individual do?" Its responses to the questions first linked the Presbyterian program with the wider pacifist culture by quoting the well-known peace evangelists Page and Fosdick. Then the booklet suggested, for churches, preaching and conducting worship on the theme of peace, presenting plays, holding "special meetings or forums," circulating petitions, mounting a poster campaign with World Peace Posters as a source, organizing a speakers' bureau, working with national peace organizations, and urging local papers to carry international news. For individuals, the program recommended reading, starting "a group for study and discussion," participating in some peace organization, becoming well-informed, writing to government representatives, working with children on international friendship, and "having frequent discussions at your dinner table."[3]

There is ample evidence that advice such as this was acted upon. For instance, in 1934, the sixty-seven participants in a youth retreat in New Jersey issued a statement in which they promised to perform seven kinds of peace action: taking an individual stand, circulating a petition, reading, "creating community interest" by producing a peace play, planning a Fourth of July peace demonstration, contacting the FOR and the NCPW, and "consistent living." They promised to involve others in these projects; for example, each was to "sign and get five others to sign a statement of personal opposition to war." The group statement was suffused in the language of liberal Protestant peace culture, making reference to "Jesus' method and spirit of love" and to standard reading such as *The World Tomorrow*.[4]

Even gestures that were intended to be innovative incorporated commonly used verbal methods. For example, the American Friends Service Committee sponsored summer "peace caravans" during the 1920s and 1930s. College students, after a period of training, would travel by automobile to as many towns as they could reach in order to spread the peace message. Participants and historians alike have pointed to the caravans as a model of creative peace work.[5]

Still, apart from the fact of their traveling, the caravanners used the same methods as other peace workers: they spoke, hosted discussions, handed out leaflets, and put on plays. And, like members of the NCPW or the YMCA, they worked through existing organizations, speaking to church groups, social clubs, and the like.[6] As late as 1950, the FOR sent out two peace caravans that used these established practices. Although the participants had by then made the epochal transition to Gandhian nonviolent action, they still "saw great value in such techniques as street meetings, leaflet distribution, and other opportunities for presenting the straight pacifist point of view."[7]

Discussion

It is difficult to overstate the extent to which pacifist life in all contexts and periods revolved around talk. The public dissemination of pacifist ideas depended, of course, on word-based media. But even in private, local, or informal settings, pacifist activity was rooted in discussion. Kirby Page's daughter, when asked what her father and his pacifist friends and colleagues did in informal gatherings, said simply, "They talked."[8] A World

War II CO recalled, "Perhaps nothing characterized the spirit of life in a CO camp more than talk—innumerable, often endless, and sometimes heated discussions on matters of ethics and religion."[9]

Discussion was a way of recruiting and enculturating new pacifists. For instance, a 1941 article in *Fellowship*, probably written by FOR youth secretary John Swomley, recommended using discussion to recruit high school students to the pacifist cause: pacifists should "invite the students to [their] homes for recreation, singing and a brief period of discussion."[10] Stephen Cary, a World War II CO and later an AFSC officer, credited discussion with pushing him to a decision for pacifism. Reared as a Quaker, Cary nevertheless said that "my Quakerism in 1940 was still largely subliminal; fortunately, I met Joseph Havens . . . an articulate and convinced pacifist engaged in nightly debates with two Air Force–bound Cornellians. I joined in these proceedings and in two weeks I had debated myself into a pacifist position from which I have never retreated."[11] Cary went on to reiterate pacifist rhetoric and theology. He said he found "reinforcement" of his decision in "the life and teachings of Jesus," especially that "love is the overcoming power in the world."[12]

Careful ethical scrutiny of public and personal issues was characteristic of all these discussions. In a statement reminiscent of Harold Gray, a World War II CPS alumnus wrote, "No issue was too profound or too complex in its moral implications; none was too mundane or petty to be granted a place on the agenda. Issues ranged, for example, from whether or not to go on strike . . . to how much sugar should be put on each camper's breakfast cereal."[13] Participants in the Fast for Peace in Washington, D.C., in 1950, a collaborative effort of several peace groups, made time for discussions of economics, draft registration, and tax refusal. "We as pacifists," they announced, "must continually ask ourselves whether we are doing all that is possible."[14] In the discussions, they defined where consensus lay and where there was latitude for disagreement. Discussion served to clarify or challenge moral positions and to draw tentative boundaries.

There was also an element of entertainment to pacifist discussions, a sense that lively argument was an interesting way for serious people to pass the time. A member of Ahimsa Farm observed that meetings were "long and raucous, and usually fun."[15] In CPS camps, "there was never an idea without its challengers; no beliefs were left undisputed; and we were expected to defend every pronouncement with line, verse, and chapter of authority. Some of us relished the dialogue. . . . A wit observed, 'We split wood all day and hairs all night.'"[16]

AND YET, ALTHOUGH pacifists never abandoned talk or rational persuasion, a 1950 account of these activities has a rueful quality, a sense of ironic self-questioning. In that year *Fellowship* published an imaginary debate between "the Guardian Angel" and "the Pacifist."[17]

In the dialogue, the angel awakens a pacifist who would prefer to remain asleep. The angel lists all the issues to be addressed: the atomic bomb, the draft, children starving overseas. "'I don't care,' [says] the Pacifist desperately. 'I've worked my head off passing out leaflets and worn out three pairs of trousers sitting in meetings, and where did it get me?'"

The angel, however, persuades the pacifist to struggle on. At first reluctantly, and then with growing enthusiasm, the pacifist takes action: he decides to send *Fellowship* to the local library, to make a donation to the FOR, and, most prominently, to catch up on literature, including Tolstoy, Muste, E. Stanley Jones, G. H. C. Macgregor's arguments against neo-orthodoxy, and Herbert Read's book on peace education.[18] Of course, these suggestions advance the FOR's goal of selling more subscriptions and books. But they also reflect the familiar agenda of education and persuasion.

So it is significant that the piece conveys a tinge of uncertainty. "Can't you at least give me some assurance that all this effort will come to something?" asks the pacifist. "No," says the angel, "I promise you nothing except a hard fight." In the face of such weariness, some pacifists were already seeking other weapons than leaflets and meetings for the "hard fight" to come.

A NEW WAY OF LIFE

"Honest and intelligent pacifists are troubled by a sense of ineffectiveness," wrote Richard Gregg in 1936. "Though they are sure of the soundness of their beliefs, they see on all sides the failures of those beliefs in action. Pacifism seems to consist merely of reading books and articles, going to meetings, listening to speeches, urging people who are in high places to do something. . . . It is true that education and definite public opinion are necessary before society can act. Nevertheless for successful pacifism, just as for successful militarism, there must be ways for the individual to translate his beliefs into concrete action."[19]

Thus began Gregg's pamphlet *Training for Peace: A Program for Peace Workers*, a practical manual intended to supplement his well-received *Power of Non-Violence*. Here, in barely forty pages, Gregg drew the outlines of the pacifist culture of the next two generations. The work was synthetic rather than completely original: few of the ideas and practices it recommended were new or unique. Nor was it the sole source of things to come: it never enjoyed the wide circulation of *Power*, and few pacifists cited it as a direct influence. But it marked with particular clarity a synthesis that was beginning to occur throughout pacifist culture, a realignment of assumptions and habits into a fresh ideal of the pacifist "way of life."

Training for Peace proceeded from the assumption that war was an "integral part and inevitable result" of the social, economic, and political structures of society. It was not a "simple excrescence" that could be removed without changing the rest of the social body. It could not therefore be abolished through education, legislation, or even individual pledges not to participate. Rather, pacifists must seek to change society from the inside out, beginning with themselves.[20]

Gregg was not entirely fair to his predecessors in the peace movement. Pacifists had long maintained that economic and political structures generated war; this was why so many of them had turned to socialism. And they had long advocated inner change and whole-life commitment.

But Gregg proposed a fresh and concrete program. Since changing society would be challenging work under great external pressure, at least in its early stages, pacifists must train for peace as rigorously as soldiers did for war.[21] There would be three elements to this training. Its foundations would be intellectual and organizational: pacifists should "get [their] bearings" through reading and discussion and should form "teams" or five to twelve members. Then, individually and together, they should seek to develop appropriate "sentiments," which Gregg defined as "organized systems of feelings, ideas, and impulses to action." The most important sentiments were self-respect, unity, and morale. Gregg's suggestions for cultivating unity were particularly interesting, since they centered on three marks of later pacifist culture: singing, folk dancing, and meditation.[22]

Finally, pacifists should incorporate "deeds" into the program. Working for the good of the world would not only express right sentiment but also feed and reinforce it: "action and sentiment always go together and interact." Possible actions included various forms of social "service" and nonviolent resistance to societal wrongs, but Gregg devoted the most space to a discussion of manual work, including a lengthy excursus on the then pressing problem of unemployment. Gregg's proposal, then, was for a unified, holistic way of living in which process was integrated with result, spirit with body, and individual with community, with the ultimate goal of building peace.[23]

Gregg emphasized that his program was "a method, not a dogma." It was a concrete practice and a process, not an ideal formula or doctrine. It was set in present rather than future time: means would determine ends, and only means were under direct human control. "Only the near goals can be clear goals," Gregg wrote. "Our direction lies mainly in our method." Indeed, the outbreak of war would mean not that the method had failed, but that it had not yet been used enough by enough people. "We merely didn't get started soon enough," he concluded. "The method will still be valid."[24]

Five aspects of *Training* are particularly noteworthy. First, it illustrates an emerging shift in pacifists' religious self-understanding. Second, it gave conscious attention to the work of the body in pacifist daily life and action. Third, it drew close connections between folk dancing, singing, and meditation. Fourth, it provided a rationale for integrating traditional, preindustrial manual work with pacifism. And finally, it marked the introduction of a higher degree of ritualization into pacifist life.

Religion

Training illustrates the growing complexity of the relationship between Protestantism and pacifist culture in the late 1930s. On the one hand, many aspects of Gregg's work lay well within the traditions of the existing Protestant pacifist culture. Despite his critique of talk, he grounded his program in reading and discussion, though he conceded that this first step might seem a little "forced and artificial." He also affirmed the value of reading and discussion in maintaining morale. To that end he recommended as subjects of discussion the usual range of pacifist heroes, including Jesus, St. Francis of Assisi, John Woolman, Toyohiko Kagawa, Jane Addams, and Gandhi. Gregg also cited many of pacifism's standard works and authors: Tolstoy, Cadoux, Harold Gray, Kirby Page, Ernest Louis Meyer's *Hey! Yellowbacks!*, Walter W. Van Kirk's *Religion Renounces War*, Fosdick's sermon "My Account with the Unknown Soldier," and others. In addition, he invoked familiar virtues with familiar terms: pacifists should develop "respect for personality," cultivate "good will," and maintain "faith in the ultimate possibilities of human nature." He did suggest that pacifists replace the "much abused term 'love'" with "interest-affection," but this new term did not take hold.[25]

Beyond texts and terminology, though, Gregg's thought resonated with two liberal Protestant themes. One was human improvability. Gregg assumed that people could learn a new mind-set and a new way to live, not through any converted heart or infusion of grace, but by their own diligent efforts.[26] The effects of their efforts would be something very much like bringing in the Kingdom of God, a modernist as well as a liberal theme. Changed people would change others, a few at a time, by their word and example. Slowly, by a process of organic growth, society would be transformed from within. Those laboring in the present should have confidence in this vision, but could not know the time or manner of its ultimate realization.

On the other hand, Gregg's religious ideas extended well beyond Protestantism. He made frank reference to an eclectic group of non-Christian sources — Rabindranath Tagore, Alice Bailey, anonymous Theosophist works, Buddhism — and also showed the influence of alternative cosmology. "Energy is everywhere," he wrote, "in evil forms and processes as well as in good. If we renounce one of the evil forms [for example, participation in war] but do not replace it with a good one, the energy will promptly find some other mode of action in the situation." Meditation, he said, would connect the pacifist with "intangible moral and spiritual forces, and a realization that each of us shares in those forces."[27]

What Gregg was doing, then, was devising a form of pacifist thought and practice that would be accessible to Protestants and non-Protestants alike. This was explicit in a few places. When he discussed singing, for instance, he conceded that "some groups composed entirely of church members may wish to sing hymns sometimes" — but "if any member of the team prefers not to have hymns, it will be best to stick to folk songs."[28] Likewise, meditation should be practiced by all, but "those who are religious" might gain similar benefits from prayer, and individuals or groups "may choose religious ideas as subjects of meditation." Religious confession, then, was permitted but was subordinated to a common pacifism instead of being the necessary basis of it.[29]

The Body

Training elevated the role of the body in pacifist practice. Although passing out leaflets, caravanning, and putting on plays certainly involved physical actions, Gregg made the body the subject of conscious awareness and argued that it was central to pacifist life. "As long as we have bodies coordinated with our nervous systems . . . we must use our bodies as part of any sound system of education and discipline," he asserted. He drew an analogy with military training, which shaped both mental attitudes and physical actions. He also alluded to progressive-education theory, which elevated the role of the senses, the hands, and physical movement in learning. Hence the body was involved in many aspects of pacifist practice. "Personal cleanness of body," he said, was fundamental to health, self-respect, and positive public opinion. Physical work, whether heavy labor or handwork, should be the first and most constant element in pacifist social action. Dance functioned as creative outlet and discipline; it was "a mode of music in which our own bodies are the instruments and media of expression."[30]

Beyond this, the body offered an alternative mode of thought. "Probably all thinking and some emotion," Gregg reflected, "takes place by means of imagery or symbolism of some sort." Words were one such symbol system, but there were others, such as "kinesthetic and tactile imagery." Pacifists should cultivate these modes of knowing in addition to their accustomed verbal modes. "The imagery of great numbers of inarticulate people . . . is probably largely kinesthetic and tactile," Gregg wrote. "A common form of physical activity, such as folk dancing and knitting, giving a common kinesthetic experience and imagery, will thus enable all who take part in it to reach a closer mutual understanding."[31]

In an important detail, Gregg attended to the spatial arrangement of pacifist meetings, advising that chairs be set in a square or circle rather than in rows. This informal, face-to-face positioning, with no one singled out as hierarch, signified the equality and intimacy that a "peace team" sought to build.[32]

Two further bodily practices are implied, but the text does not dwell on them. One is nonviolent protest, which generally incorporated the physical with the verbal. If dance, for example, fostered discipline, rhythmic coordination, and attunement to others, surely these skills would be put to use in direct-action events. The second, also part of nonviolent protest, is the acceptance of bodily suffering. Gregg makes it clear that pacifists were aware of the possibility of "physical suffering, maybe even death." Protest and suffering remained peripheral, however. The book's primary focus was on the slow, organic growth of a new society, not on sacrifice or martyrdom.[33]

Folklife and Meditation

Training crystallized the implicit association between folk arts, silent meditation, and pacifism. All three practices were already present in liberal Protestant pacifism, but after the paradigm shift their connection with peace activism came to be taken for granted. For Gregg, folksinging, folk dancing, and meditation were ways to cultivate the "sentiment"—the ideas, emotions, and impulses—of unity. This meant both unity within the pacifist fold and unity "with all mankind."[34]

Pacifists were singing folk songs before 1936. In *Training*, however, singing as a practice—rather than as an incidental part of some other activity—became part of the pacifist program. The act of making music would produce effects by itself, said Gregg, and singing, as opposed to instrumental music, had the moral and practical advantage of being free of charge and within the capacity of most people. Gregg recommended folk music partly for practical reasons: folk songs and "Negro spirituals" were easy to sing and emotionally "close to the heart of everyone."[35] But folksinging would also have reinforced pacifists' sense of identity with ordinary people and traditional lifeways.

For the individual, the effects of singing would be integrative, imaginative, and emotional, said Gregg; music expressed feelings "which cannot be put into words or even into acts." In the peace team, group singing would help develop unity, equality, confidence, and "rhythmic coordination"—as soldiers, congregations, college students, and others well knew. Gregg also pointed to the way Danish folk high schools used singing to build community spirit. These schools had served as models for pacifist educational and cooperative enterprises as well.[36]

Folk dancing, said Gregg, had several merits. It was an almost universally known activity, it strengthened community spirit, and it was a means of building civilization. In these functions, as well as in form, it was "completely different from formal society dancing." Gregg particularly affirmed its strong—and implicitly masculine—character. Folk dance, he said, was earthy and vigorous, not "'arty' or affected or namby-pamby" when practiced by "peasants and savages of all countries." Folk dancing, then, was presented as a powerful and morally sound mode of common rhythmic movement for pacifist society.[37]

Meditation was the third practice in the triad. Gregg's description of meditation was free of confessionally specific religious content; indeed, he barely mentioned any power outside the self and the group. Meditation was, he assured the reader, "a valid psychological exercise apart from religion." Gregg offered two ways to meditate. One was the purist approach, the stilling and emptying of the mind. In this context Gregg made no reference to the body. Mental meditation, practiced regularly, would lead to balance, "serenity," and "a unity at a deeper level than that which comes from the other methods mentioned." Gregg struggled to describe these effects: "an inner integration, a reunion between the deeper and more superficial levels of the mind, a silent growth of imagination, of sensibility, of organic emotional relationships, of common apprehension, common sentiment and common purpose."[38] Regular practice of individual and group meditation would strengthen the group for action.

The other method of meditating was to concentrate together upon an exemplar or sentiment of pacifism. This, too, would shape the intention and self-understanding of the group, but it relied on storytelling, mythmaking, and identification with the exemplar. Thus Gregg pointed back to the narrative and iconographic dimensions of pacifist culture. He recommended that thoughts generated by this process be shared with the group after the period of meditation was over.

Only as a sort of afterthought did Gregg mention relationships beyond the group. The sense of unity, he said, might be "widened" by meditating on such topics as "tolerance, the unity of all mankind and love of all people." As proposed here, however, meditation worked primarily within the group to form identity, create bonds, and strengthen resolve, with the ultimate purpose of supporting action.[39]

"Deeds" and Manual Work

"The spindle, knitting needle, loom, pick, shovel, hoe and other hand tools are the creative pacifist's substitute for the soldier's weapons," wrote Gregg.[40] *Training* laid out a way to embody the idea of replacing swords with plowshares. This embodiment was worked out more fully in the cooperative farming movement, as we shall see in the next chapter. But manual work was not merely a substitute for or a moral equivalent of war. It was also a proactive step into a new way of being, just as singing was.

Training recommended manual work of all kinds. Ideally such work would serve the wider community, but any kind of domestic or local activity—sweeping, cooking, making beds, carrying coal—was desirable.

"Men," added Gregg severely, "should get over the foolish idea that it is not fitting or is beneath their dignity to do any of such things." Manual work, said Gregg, would diffuse tension, restrain "mystical or sentimental" tendencies, and help pacifists develop a common "imagery" with the unemployed and undereducated.[41]

The paradigm of manual work in *Training* was knitting, presumably the functional equivalent for the United States of Gandhi's spinning. Knitting was practical, accessible, and morally pure. It produced one of the necessities of life, clothing, from materials that were in principle available outside the industrial economy. Within the pacifist movement, it was a way for everyone to contribute—the elderly and disabled, women caring for small children, children themselves. It offered the gratification of reaching short-term goals in a context where the long-term goals were out of reach. And it was portable and could be done concurrently with mental activities such as discussion. "In the context of this movement," said Gregg, "spinning or knitting would be work for a better order of society. Not everyone can make speeches; and everlasting listening to speeches eventually becomes emotional and intellectual debauchery and gets us nowhere."[42]

Gregg also argued that knitting would be have wider social benefits, particularly for the unemployed. It would provide tangible goods and increase self-reliance and self-esteem. By practicing and teaching handcrafts, social activists would help the unemployed help themselves.[43]

Ritual and Liturgy

Gregg never used the word "ritual," but there is undoubtedly an element of ritual in the way of life he outlined. Gregg thought folk dancing, for example, would alter consciousness, bring group unity to a new level, and empower individuals for action. It engendered "a development of power to receive and act upon suggestions . . . a heightening of emotions, a fusion of sense and spirit, and a feeling of liberation, spontaneity, and joy. . . . [a] strong and enduring sense of unity, of harmony and concord, of mutual coordination, and of the proper subordination of the parts to the whole."[44] This description goes far beyond dance as exercise, recreation, or moral gesture. Here dance is the locus of transcendence and altered awareness.

Training placed such transcendence in the context of a kind of liturgy. Although Gregg confined his liturgical outline to a footnote, it was replicated quite consistently in later years. Unlike church liturgies, it was transmitted by folk processes, a folk group's common knowledge of what one did at a gathering of members.[45] I cannot argue that Gregg created this liturgy; it may have emerged spontaneously in multiple venues. But its appearance in *Training* is significant because it is embedded in Gregg's overall restatement of the pacifist way of life.

Gregg suggested that a team meeting "might be" arranged in the following way:

    I. Singing together, 8 minutes.
    II. Reading aloud from some book, 30 minutes. Members may be doing their manual work while the reading is going on.
    III. Discussion of:
        A. The reading just completed, or
        B. Work planned for the team, or
        C. Some public event related to the team's purposes, 30 minutes.
    IV. A report of work done since last meeting, with discussion, 15 minutes.
    V. Meditation, 15 minutes, or folk dancing or singing for the same time.[46]

Compare this to a "Typical Week-End Program" at Ahimsa Farm in the early 1940s, which included the following Saturday evening schedule, following a full day of farm work.

    6:00 pm—supper
    6:30–7:00—singing at table
    7:00–8:30—Discussion: Non-Violent Direct Action
        or similar pacifist topic
    8:30–9:30 Folk Dancing
    9:30–10:00 semi-silent meditation—sharing of philosophies

On Sunday mornings the residents added a "fully silent meeting": meditation in sacred time.[47]

A similar pattern emerged at the rural outpost of Philadelphia's Fellowship House. In 1951 this urban project acquired a farm as a retreat and study center. The daily schedule there during weekend conferences included "quiet time," work, discussion, singing, and square dancing. "[It] is a proven fact," a 1952 brochure explained, "that we learn thru our hands what we never do thru our heads, so that manual labor is a part of each day. Also, real Fellowship is not dependent upon 'much speaking' but is often strengthened by silence. Silence is kept before meals and at morning and evening periods."⁴⁸

Finally—to look ahead in time—some visitors to Highlander Folk School in 1977 had this to say:

> Early that evening . . . we went down the hill to the center's main building for the evening session of a workshop in progress. . . . We found places in the rocking chairs that ringed the room and listened as Mike Clark [the president and educational director] quietly brought up ideas and raised questions. People talked about their perceptions of the problems, the ways they might be able to solve some of them and about the progress some groups were already making. . . .
>
> Since this was an evening session, there was more than talk. Candie and Guy Canawan and Phyllis Boyans were there to bring people together in song, to get to a place beyond the factual recounting of events and organizing for the future.
>
> Then we all watched a film about the organization of a coal strike, *Harlan County, U.S.A.*, which Highlander had a hand in making. Later everyone got up from their rocking chairs as Mike started a square dance.⁴⁹

Here the main program for a group of nonviolent activists was still discussion. The manner, as well as the content, of discussion signaled nonviolence: chairs were placed in a circle, voices were not raised. And in addition to using their rational faculties, participants sought transcendent unity in song and dance.⁵⁰

After the paradigm shift, pacifism and left-wing social activism were consistently joined with folksinging and folk dancing, with meditation, and with talk. In contrast to traditional mainline church liturgies, silence became central. The evangelical worship structure culminating in personal commitment faded away, and the content of ritual was no longer biblical or traditionally Christian. But the element of continuity in pacifist culture was evident in the use of singing to mark the shift into ritual time, and in the use of verbal expression and reasoning. The habit of using the Bible selectively now implied selection from all sacred or potentially sacred texts.

GREGG'S "LITURGY" IS emblematic of the paradigm shift in Protestant pacifism around the beginning of World War II. Protestant pacifists already embraced peace, equality, the Sermon on the Mount, religion as a way of life, mystical prayer, cooperative economics, and folk arts. Gandhian nonviolent protest and life practice, mediated through Anglo-American pacifist interpreters, acted as a catalyst for a discouraged folk group to incorporate these disparate elements into a new model of pacifist life. Like any such model, it was variously appropriated and adapted. It relativized Protestantism yet retained many of its sensibilities, notably an emphasis on love and a whole way of life, and a sense of building a holy kingdom. Significantly, in light of the verbal emphasis in mainline Protestant and pacifist culture, it placed silence on an equal footing with speech.

Pacifists' use of folk arts suggests a questioning of modernity analogous to the antimodernism of the Protestant mystics. This questioning is apparent in pacifists' skepticism toward technological progress and the industrial economy. And the antimodern tendency was supported by the shift in the pacifist "way of life" toward farming and cooperative living, the subject of the next chapter.[51]

9 Milking Goats for Peace

A NEW PARADIGM

Too many pacifists say, "I want to start a Farm Community," ... though they may not know on what end of the cow to sit down and milk.
—Carl J. Landes, "A Critical Study of the Urge to Pacifist Farming"

The idea of the pacifist cooperative farm caught fire quite suddenly around 1940. Over the next two years there was an unusual proliferation of pacifist cooperatives of all kinds, but especially of subsistence homestead farms. Indeed, in 1942 the FOR Commission on Rural Life asked, "Can it be said, 'Rural life is the pacifist pattern?' Should a rural culture be the foundation of pacifism?"[1]

The cooperative farm was understood as a paradigmatic form of pacifist living—not the only model for such living, but unquestionably an essential and central one. The association of cooperative, self-sufficient life on the land with absolute pacifism became a deeply embedded assumption in pacifist culture, resurfacing in many contexts both within and beyond Protestantism. Because it was an embodied, whole-life commitment, the cooperative-farming movement encompassed most of the expressions of pacifist culture we have discussed.

It was, to begin with, a fresh mode of social organization for post-1940 pacifists. Cooperatives were enclaves of purity, preserving pacifist ideals and practices in difficult times, a type of abeyance structure for a movement under threat. Pacifists, like many homesteaders, also regarded co-ops as laboratories for a new society and as places of retreat for refreshment and learning. In addition, cooperative farms were deeply rooted in the material world, in contrast to the more cerebral exercises of discussion, leafleting, or didactic theater. The iconic image of the farmer emerged alongside the pacifist farming movement itself. Co-ops were also performative, enacting or ritualizing pacifist life.

Many cooperatives claimed to have a spiritual basis. For those who embraced them, the farms seemed to be a natural outgrowth of the religious living they were cultivating. Most of the communities located their spiritual life within the larger framework of liberal pacifist theology — a way of life, progress toward a better world, the Sermon on the Mount, and perfectionism — whether or not they formally professed Protestant faith.

Yet there is no necessary, self-evident, or biblical connection between milking goats or grinding one's own wheat, on the one hand, and world peace on the other hand. This chapter asks why pacifists made that connection beginning in the early 1940s and considers some of its meanings. Pacifists' own sense of history located the connection in early Christian and Anabaptist communalism and in Tolstoyan peasant practices, but I query this sense of history, not because it is false but because it is incomplete. Antecedents of and parallels to cooperative farming can be found in other forms of American communitarianism, in the cooperative movement generally, in liberal Protestant activism, in the Social Gospel, and in "back-to-the-land" homesteading movements. The chapter looks at these histories and at the rise of pacifist cooperatives, both suburban and rural. It then focuses on the rise, fluctuation, and survival of pacifist cooperative farming in the 1940s and 1950s. It considers the nature of life on the farms and its spiritual foundations and expressions. Finally, I return to the question of the meanings of cooperative farms in pacifist life and culture.

HISTORY AND INTERPRETATION

American Alternatives

Intentional communities have been a continuous presence in American life. The communitarian impulse, continuous but flexible and adaptable, has generated settlements with great diversity of intention, purpose, size, and endurance. There is broad scholarly agreement, however, that both communitarian and homesteading experiments have arisen especially frequently during periods of social stress or transition, and that alternative communities are often devoted to social experimentation, purity, and perfection. Indeed, one author has aptly characterized the communitarian model as a "noncoercive path to change."[2] A charismatic leader often serves as a catalyst in the founding and survival of a community.

Timothy Miller, in his works on twentieth-century communities, and Rebecca Kneale Gould, in her work on homesteading, agree that the back-to-the-land communes of the 1960s were not sui generis. Communes were, in Miller's words, part of "a continuous, if not utterly seamless, communal fabric that stretches back for more than three centuries," while the impulse toward rural homesteading can be traced back to the mid-nineteenth century, an expression of unease with modernity on several levels.[3] In the twentieth century, new intentional communities proliferated before World War I, during the 1930s, and during the 1960s and 1970s. This last group was preceded by a gathering wave of communitarianism in the late 1940s and 1950s.[4]

PACIFIST INTENTIONAL COMMUNITIES had precursors in pacifists' long concern for alternative economics and education, as well as in their theological and historical self-understanding. In a general sense, pacifists' movement toward intentional communities resembled that of other American communitarians in that it was a response to social stress and a move toward closer association with like-minded people. That is, the wave of pacifist cooperative farming occurred in the context of the war in Europe, the bombing of Pearl Harbor, and the suspect status of pacifism. But pacifists dealt with these stresses in other ways as well, for instance by forming or joining denominational fellowships, and their socioeconomic concerns had found other forms of expression in the years before 1940. Living in common and farming not only were responses to stress but also had particular meanings for pacifists.

Gould's study of modern homesteading as "meaning-making" has much explanatory power for pacifist farming. She argues that homesteading was a "lived response to problems of meaning," a practice of both "spiritual regeneration and cultural dissent."[5] Its cultural sources lay in the ways Americans since Thoreau had negotiated the relationship of self, nature, and modernity. Homesteading was one response to industrialization, urbanization, and overconsumption, with their attendant anonymity and uniformity. It was not a simplistic answer. Homesteaders, like Protestants, embraced aspects of modernity, albeit in varying ways and on their own terms. And the meanings they assigned to "nature" were not uniform. But the larger values homesteaders affirmed—self-sufficiency, natural cycles, sense of place, craft—signified resistance and reform as well as personal purity and fulfillment. Later, homesteaders embraced the works of Ruskin, Tolstoy, Gandhi, and Richard Gregg.

Homesteading also responded to the challenges posed to Christianity in the nineteenth and twentieth centuries. Many homesteaders rejected conventional or explicit religion yet spoke of their way of life in implicitly spiritual terms. Themes of conversion, rebirth, *imitatio*, sacrifice, self-surrender, and contemplation recur in their stories. The liberalizing of Protestantism, Gould argues, left room for emergent ideas of a God of nature. Most significantly, by focusing on Scott Nearing, she finds in twentieth-century homesteading clear traces of activistic liberal Protestantism, among them perfectionism, exceptionalism, discipline, and mystical tendencies. Scott and Helen Nearing were known in pacifist circles before the publication of *Living the Good Life*, their practical and philosophical guide to homesteading, in 1954. And their many followers after that date undoubtedly absorbed, or had already embraced, their ethics and spirit.

Neither Gould nor Miller, however, addresses pacifist cooperative farming as a particular phenomenon. Miller notes the importance of pacifism in the postwar intentional communities but gives little attention to the multiplication of pacifist communities as World War II began. He recognizes the importance of Arthur E. Morgan, a pacifist and promoter of co-ops whose influence extended from the 1930s into the 1960s.[6] But pacifist communitarianism cannot be attributed to the work of any single leader or theorist. Gould notes in passing the pacifist strain in modern homesteading but does not examine pacifist homesteading as such, nor does she give extended attention to cooperatives. We turn now to those issues.

Protestants and the Cooperative Movement

The cooperative farms of the 1940s emerged after a long period of progressive interest in cooperative economics. Most advocates pointed to the Rochdale cooperative as the origin of the movement: in 1844, industrial workers in Rochdale, England, formed a cooperative store and developed a set of principles for consumers' cooperatives. Petr Kropotkin's 1902 book

Mutual Aid: A Factor in Evolution added a theoretical dimension to the movement. The Cooperative League of the United States, established in 1915, grew rapidly after the First World War. Its primary interests were manufacturing, retailing, and credit unions.

The resurgence of the Social Gospel movement in the 1930s was also important. Mainline Protestant writers and lecturers regularly advocated cooperative economics. For example, in 1930 the sociologist and pacifist Jerome Davis wrote that cooperatives exemplified the "spiritual values of service and sacrifice" consistent with the radical Jesus. Kirby Page, with many others, pointed to the economic sources of war, and he edited a volume called *A New Economic Order*. The Council for Social Action of the Congregational Churches offered a study packet on cooperatives.[7] Toyohiko Kagawa, whose modeling of the committed life was so much admired by American pacifists, also advocated cooperative economics. His 1935 speaking tour of the United States appears to have galvanized many churches and church members into action—although the presence of "packed masses" and "overflows" at his lectures suggests that there had been considerable advance preparation.[8]

A number of cooperatives, pacifist and nonpacifist, were already in place by the time of Kagawa's tour. Harold Gray, for example, founded Saline Valley Farms in 1932, and Upton Sinclair noted the existence of 175 "self-help" co-ops in California in the introduction to his 1936 novel *Co-op*.[9] But significant growth occurred in the late 1930s. Government policy on rural life was one factor: several New Deal agencies sponsored homesteading programs between 1933 and 1943, with the greatest growth occurring from 1935 through 1937. Religious activism was also important: prominent Protestants, including Reinhold Niebuhr and pacifist Sherwood Eddy, organized Delta Cooperative Farm in 1936 and its neighbor, Providence Farm, in 1939, both in southern Mississippi. Clarence Pickett, of the American Friends Service Committee, and Arthur Morgan participated in forming the Celo Community in 1936. Morris Mitchell bought a tract of land in Georgia and founded the Macedonia Cooperative Farm in 1937.[10]

All these cooperatives were intended first of all as aid to struggling rural communities. They aimed to offer instruction in "modern" methods of farming and to increase economic stability through the sharing of property, materials, and labor. Their model was economic cooperation rather than communalism: members might buy shares or pool their knowledge and material resources, but they did not undertake to live together as a community. In some cases, there was a shade of paternalism, as in Harold Gray's "benevolent autocracy" or Morris Mitchell's overpowering personal presence.[11]

A number of educational experiments with close connections to pacifism also fed into the cooperative-living movement. Brookwood Labor College, founded in 1919 in Katonah, New York, aimed to apply "Christian principles to the use of property, community living, and education."[12] Under the leadership of A. J. Muste, from 1921 until 1933, it specialized in the training of labor leaders. Pacifists such as John Nevin Sayre and Sarah Cleghorn, as well as many lesser lights, taught at Brookwood, and a number of similar schools were subsequently established.

Pendle Hill, founded in 1930, sought to combine life in community with spiritual grounding and intellectual growth. Its courses explored social activism, Quaker identity, and non-Christian religions, in addition to mysticism. Among its directors were FOR founder Henry Hodgkin and Richard Gregg. In addition to the mainline Protestants I mentioned earlier, its faculty included at various times prominent Friends such as Rufus Jones and Douglas Steere, the communard Arthur Morgan, and the mystic Gerald Heard. Heard founded Trabuco College, a spiritual-intellectual community, in 1939 in California.[13]

Myles Horton set up the Highlander Folk School, initially called the Southern Mountains School, in 1932 in Monteagle, Tennessee. His supporters included Reinhold Niebuhr, Sherwood Eddy, and Kirby Page. A fund-raising letter noted that the school would be arranged "along the lines of a Danish folk high school" and that the students, all adults, would "live with the teachers on a small farm where all will work, study, and discuss together."[14] Also, beginning in 1933, the AFSC worked with displaced coal miners in folk schools and on government-funded homesteads.

In 1936 Ralph Borsodi established the School of Living, which became an influential center for homesteading movements. Borsodi and his family left New York City for a small upstate farm in 1920, and his account of that experience, *Flight from the City*, first appeared in 1933. The school sought to use progressive-education methods to teach the philosophy and skills of homesteading and small-scale production.[15]

E. Stanley Jones's "Christian ashrams" also deserve mention. Jones was a Methodist missionary to India, a pacifist, and a prolific and influential religious writer. The idea of the Kingdom of God was central to his theology. His work in mediating Indian culture to Protestant North America—in

Protestant terms, but with more than usual sympathy and with receptiveness to what India could teach Christians—helped to prepare the ground for Gandhian nonviolence and community living.[16] Jones, who knew and admired Gandhi, followed his lead by setting up "Christian ashrams." In the United States, these were generally short-term arrangements, more like conference and outreach centers than ongoing intentional communities. Jones's Indian ashrams, however, were settled communities dedicated to simple living, social equality, and "discussing religious problems." Morning worship consisted of a hymn, silent prayer, meditation, and the Lord's Prayer sung in Hindi. A number of advocates of intentional community, such as Ralph Templin and Jay Holmes Smith, had spent time in Jones's Indian and American ashrams, and similar patterns of life and worship appeared in the pacifist cooperatives.[17]

The Pacifist Cooperative Movement

The pacifist cooperatives of the early 1940s drew on the antecedents I have outlined, but they placed particular emphases on egalitarian group living and pacifist commitment. There were several approaches. In home-ownership co-ops such as Skyview Acres in Pomona, New York, and Bryn Gweled, near Philadelphia, people of like mind owned land together and lived in loose community. Interracial co-ops, such as the Harlem Ashram in New York City and Koinonia Farm in Americus, Georgia, worked primarily in race relations. Cooperative farms focused on morally viable subsistence and on mutual support, and some ran subsidiary programs in education, rural aid, or peace work.[18]

The first pacifist co-op to attract widespread attention was Ahimsa Farm. In 1940 a group of Antioch College students, claiming inspiration from the teaching of Indian-born professor Manmatha Chatterjee, set out to establish a center for study and social experimentation, particularly with respect to nonviolence. Antioch's own history of experimentation, and its former president Arthur Morgan, probably also influenced them. The farm began as a summer project, but the arrival of a nonstudent couple in the fall of 1941 made year-round operation possible. The members repaired the farmhouse and chicken coop, grew wheat and vegetables, and raised goats.[19] They read and discussed pacifist authors such as Gregg, Heard, and Krishnalal Shridharani.[20] They also attempted two public projects: a "march to the sea" to call attention to hunger in Europe, and, with other groups, the desegregation of a public swimming pool in Cleveland.

Ahimsa Farm attracted considerable attention among pacifists. Its more prominent supporters included Muriel Lester, A. J. Muste, Allan Knight Chalmers of the Broadway Tabernacle in New York, and James Farmer, later a civil rights activist. Most of its members credited the farm with formative influence on their lives and concerns. The farm broke up in 1942, however, partly for financial reasons and partly because most of the men, faced with conscription, went into CPS.[21]

Also in 1940, many currents in the pacifist cooperative movement came together at the FOR annual conference at Chautauqua, New York. The conference was preceded by a "retreat or training school" led by A. J. Muste and Muriel Lester, at which fifty participants discussed cooperative living, nonviolent civil disobedience, techniques of meditation, and pacifist discipline. The program also included folk dancing and manual work and recommended fasting as a way to raise funds for the hungry of Europe. And the members of Ahimsa Farm gave a presentation. At the general meeting two Mennonites, Donovan Smucker and Carl Landes, proposed that the FOR establish a rural secretaryship. Their purpose was chiefly to forge connections among isolated rural pacifists and to bring them into the FOR, but youth secretary John Swomley also suggested that Ahimsa Farm might serve as a "pattern" for farmers' peace work. This proposal bore some fruit: by 1942 Landes, who by then was the rural secretary, was said to be making "big plans connected with the current trend of pacifists back to the land." At the same time, he attempted subsistence farming himself. Later, in 1946, he made an abortive effort to organize a cooperative farm. As the FOR turned its attention to the war and to conscientious objectors, however, the rural program took a back seat, and in 1946 it was discontinued.[22]

Two other early cooperatives also left deep impressions on pacifist culture. The Harlem Ashram was founded in 1941 at the initiative of Jay Holmes Smith, a former "underworld gang" member who had been converted and had spent some years in India as a Methodist missionary. Following Gandhi and E. Stanley Jones, and with support from the FOR, he and his associates undertook communal living and urban social work with an interracial emphasis. They offered educational programs to pacifists and other activists and were a center for informal study and discussion. Bayard Rustin, a prominent activist and theorist of CORE and the civil rights movement, belonged to the ashram's circle of supporters. The ashram disbanded in 1944 after disagreements over its purposes and religious basis, which were exacerbated by financial problems. In addition, several families decided to leave Harlem for places with better public schools as their children reached school age.[23]

Koinonia Farm, founded in 1942, was an experiment in racial integration in the segregated South. Its founders, Clarence Jordan and Martin English, drew on ideas of primitive Christian community (*koinonia*), cooperative economics, and Danish folk-school education. Both were pacifists and FOR members and, like Smith, had been missionaries. Koinonia resembled the cooperative rural-aid programs of the 1930s in its emphasis on outreach, but unlike them, it worked at developing internal community as a means to that end. As racial tensions increased during the early stages of the civil rights movement, Koinonia offered a witness of nonviolent response to threat and attack.[24]

These well-known co-ops were not alone. Others in the pacifist landscape included the Bryn Gweled housing cooperative, founded in 1940; a "Fellowship 'Farm'" in the Midwest, regularly visited by Muriel Lester; another Fellowship Farm established in June 1941 in Prairie du Sac, Wisconsin, "designed to be a Cooperative Farm, a Folk School and a Refuge"; Hilltop Farm in Jamaica, Vermont, which arose out of a study group at Pendle Hill; and the Newark (New Jersey) Christian Colony, later known as the Newark Ashram, begun in 1940 by longtime activist David Dellinger and others. Dellinger, then in inner-city Protestant ministry, mentioned both Student Christian Associations and the Catholic Worker as resources. Elsewhere, John Swomley recommended that younger pacifists develop Fellowship Farms and urban Fellowship Houses, and the Rural Cooperative Community Conference began publishing its newsletter *The Communiteer* in 1942.[25]

The Conference of Pacifist Farming Communities in February 1942 is a good indicator of the state of pacifist farming and its ideals at that point. It was held at the School of Living and at the Labor Temple in New York.[26] Among its participants were Arthur Morgan, A. J. Muste, Jay Holmes Smith, Ralph Templin, Carl Landes, and Bob Luitweiler of Ahimsa Farm. The conference noted the variety of forms of community—folk schools, training centers, subsistence farms, spiritual centers, decentralized economic bases—and considered their relationship to pacifism and nonviolence, along with some practical matters. The speed with which the idea of farming had taken hold among pacifists is perhaps best indicated by Landes's remark, "Too many pacifists say, 'I want to start a Farm Community,' and wonder why they can't begin next week by buying a 100 acre farm; though they may not know on what end of the cow to sit down and milk."[27] And Muste remarked, "When I told Mrs. Muste I was going to deliver an address on 'farming,' she gave me one of those laughs which she reserves for my *best* jokes."[28]

The War and Afterward

Not all pacifists were free to live on cooperative farms. For many men of draft age, the war years were shaped by the ambiguous experience of Civilian Public Service. The CPS camps for conscientious objectors were envisioned as models of a pacifist way of life: men would live in community with a simple standard of living, would alternate manual labor with socially beneficial service, and would have leisure to study together. The pamphlet *Creative Pioneering*, by CPS director Thomas E. Jones, exemplified the approach of "personal sacrifice and joyous living."[29]

Disillusionment with these high ideals soon set in, but the camps nonetheless did serve as laboratories for cooperative living. Many participants were already acquainted with cooperatives: a number of camps had stores run on "Rochdale principles," and a few small groups held all their goods in common. Wives of CPS men sometimes cooperated with one another in food gardening and shared their housing.[30] Morgan's *Small Community Economics* (1943) was a favorite text for study groups, and speakers on cooperative principles visited the camps. Most important, several camps — notably those at Merom, Indiana; Walhalla, Michigan; and Trenton, North Dakota — ran "schools of pacifist living," which trained members in methods of whole-life commitment to active peacemaking. These methods included the spiritual disciplines advocated by contemporary Protestant mystics such as Muriel Lester, Gerald Heard, and Douglas Steere, and the group practices described by Gregg and others. Morris Mitchell, of Macedonia Farm, and Arthur Morgan taught at these schools. Communication between the camps, and transfer of personnel, was extensive enough that information traveled widely.[31] Outside the camps, cooperatives survived during the war but suffered from an absence of younger men and a diminution of institutional and financial support.

After the war, however, there was a new and sizable movement of pacifists into cooperatives. Part of the attraction was probably economic: CPS men were not eligible for GI Bill tuition support, so they were confronted immediately with problems of work and housing. But cooperative living was also continuous with the ideals of the prewar co-ops and the CPS camps.

Older co-ops such as Macedonia and Koinonia received an influx of new members interested more in communal living than in rural aid. New farms were founded, such as Tuolumne Co-op Farm in Modesto, California, by Methodist ministers George Burcham and Wendell Kramer and their wives, in 1945, and the Glen Gardner homesteads in Hunterdon County, New Jersey, later known as St. Francis Acres, in 1947. Cooperative housing communities such as Skyview Acres in New York, whose founders included FOR luminaries Alfred Hassler and Charles and Margaret Lawrence, also arose. Notices appeared in *Fellowship*: for example, "CPS men wishing to live in a cooperative group . . . will be welcomed by the Fellowship House Association of Kansas City, Mo."; "Kirkridge, an experiment in Christian living, has an opening for one or two CPS men"; and "A small group of pacifists, wishing to start a cooperative subsistence farm by the end of May, would like to correspond at once with any person having a 200-acre farm in the East for sale."[32] The Peacemakers groups practiced cooperation without necessarily living together, and their periodical *The Peacemaker* followed co-op news intently. Borsodi's *Flight from the City* was reprinted.

One other important postwar development was American pacifists' growing awareness of the Bruderhof. This was a radical Christian separatist group, both communitarian and pacifist, founded in 1920 in Germany by Eberhard Arnold. Arnold was ordained to the ministry in a Hutterite community in 1933, and the Bruderhof maintained close ties to Hutterites thereafter. In 1937 the Bruderhof members left Germany for England, and a few years later they moved on to South America. There they came to the attention of American pacifists, particularly after the war. Said one admirer, "None . . . have so clearly seen to the basic principles of Jesus and his first followers, avoiding attachment to non-essentials (form of baptism, communion, etc.) and at the same time so absolutely adhered to them in every single expression of life as these folks." The Bruderhof established its first American community in 1954 at Rifton, New York, and by 1958 had added two more. The Kingwood cooperative, in New Jersey, disbanded to join the Bruderhof en masse, as did most of the members of Macedonia after two collective conversion experiences. Koinonia seriously considered becoming a Bruderhof as well.[33]

The cooperative communities had a substantial, even a disproportionate, influence in postwar pacifism. Pacifist farms held conferences and institutes and received numerous visitors. They fostered discussion and practice of nonviolent direct action. They contributed significant voices to pacifist writing and action and engaged in at least some outreach beyond their own boundaries.³⁴

On the other hand, pacifist cooperatives suffered setbacks in the late 1950s. After the Macedonia community disbanded, the property was sold, ironically, under the capitalist rubric of "the ultimate for investment." Koinonia experienced both racial violence and severe financial loss beginning in 1956. It survived but was remade as an economic and social "partnership" enterprise rather than a community—a model not too different from its origins. Tuolumne Farm closed in 1959. A number of smaller communities gave up the struggle, perhaps because their members enjoyed better material prospects in the prosperous 1950s.³⁵

But this is not really a story of declension. A few new communities formed, such as May Valley in Renton, Washington, in 1957.³⁶ Communities of the 1960s drew on the experiences of their predecessors, then in abeyance. More importantly, as Christopher Clark has observed, the success of a community cannot be measured solely by its longevity. Members of utopian communities, however transient, bring their experiences into their own histories and that of the wider society. This was surely true for pacifists.³⁷

Why Cooperatives?

Why, then, did pacifists make the connection between milking goats and building world peace? In one sense, this connection can easily be located within the trajectory of Protestant pacifist thought. On another level, pacifists, like homesteaders, were engaging in a complex negotiation of cultural forces and internal impulses. Peace-building by means readily available in culture had not worked. Alternative models were essential, but complete withdrawal was not an option. For many pacifist farmers, the mode of living *became* the action for peace; social change inhered in what they did.

As a theoretical matter, it is not surprising that peacemaking as a "way of life" would ultimately be thought to encompass livelihood, housing, food, family life, and community. Pacifists also understood their historical models—Jesus and the disciples, the early church, Franciscans, separatist Anabaptists—to have practiced community of goods and, to some extent, community living. The principles of love and of the Sermon on the Mount seemed well suited to fostering group living. Other religious communities that have tried to reproduce the pattern of the early church, or to follow the Sermon on the Mount literally, have often come to much the same positions.

Yet neither Jesus nor St. Francis was a farmer. Not only ideology, then, but historical and cultural particulars contributed to the emergence of the pacifist farm. Cooperative economics, rural aid, folk and progressive education, and homesteading were all within pacifists' awareness and experience. Pacifist icons such as Francis, Kagawa, Gandhi, and Lester modeled simplicity and poverty. Gandhi associated community with nonviolent action. Gregg and others elevated handwork and folk arts to pacifist essentials. Many sources connected living close to nature with beauty, purity, and spiritual values.[38] All these cultural practices interacted with the Protestant affirmation of a whole "way of life" and the intention of building a better society.

Practice itself was especially important. It is only a short step from gathering in small groups, performing manual work, and learning folk arts to settling on a farm. Indeed, practice was often prior to thought: many pacifists joined in cooperative living and farming first, and then argued about ideology. "As to our principles, we are still in the process of defining them," wrote one cooperator. "Perhaps our only common principle is that of pacifism or nonviolence."[39] Beyond living and working, cooperators joined in the "liturgies" of discussion, folksinging and folk dancing, and meditation.[40]

Pacifists' concern about participation in systems was critical. Co-op farmers were refusing to support a system—economic, political, and social—that produced war. Despite pacifists' hopes, no large-scale system of cooperative economics emerged during the 1930s, and after Stalin, communism no longer appeared to be a reasonable alternative. Thus the small cooperative or commune and the individual homestead were virtually the only alternatives left. Homesteading, wrote one pacifist, "goes far to remove one from the errors of materialistic, exploitive culture." And it "makes it almost possible to secede from the government, too."[41] At the same time, the impulse to withdraw from society was balanced by the desire, common to most communitarian movements, to demonstrate a better way of life.[42] And both perceptions were sharpened in the early 1940s by a sense of urgency. One newsletter said, "We who profess a faith in the way of peace must either go down discredited in the wreck of the old order—or must show the way of the new. Either we commit ourselves to the task of showing, in the small, how we can live together without setting in motion those frictions whose inevitable end is war—or in common honesty we had better forgo our pacifist pretentions [sic] and come to terms with the prevailing disorder."[43] Here, encapsulated, is the rationale for a practice that shaped pacifism from 1940 onward.[44] In the context of pacifists' ambivalence about modernity, the cooperative farms represented a decisive step away.

LIFE ON THE FARMS

Farming and Lived Pacifism

The ideal, and to at least some extent the practice, of pacifist farming included community outreach, study, spiritual life, artistic culture of a homemade kind, and above all the discipline of living in community. Equally attractive was the rural ideal, the vision of life lived close to nature and ordered by seasonal rhythms. In most of the co-ops, though, the greatest share of energy and attention went toward the daily demands of survival: food production, housing, and money. As a religious matter, this was a "way of life" that involved the whole person, necessarily and inescapably. Pacifist homesteaders lived out their convictions by living in peace daily with a very few close associates. And, like the conscientious objector in jail, the homesteader expressed with his or her body the refusal to compromise with war and capitalism.

Ralph Templin of the School of Living, a former Methodist missionary, linked pacifism with farming in precisely this way. "'Total pacifism' takes the soil as 'radical' ('getting at the roots')," he wrote; farming was a way of "opposing centralized, intrenched privilege with its violence." Templin also connected farming with pacifist theology by arguing that decentralized agriculture used a method of "creative, cooperative Love." And he drew on earlier materials of pacifist culture in quoting Jane Addams: "Peace and bread are inseparably connected."[45]

Some pacifists claimed to have come fairly close to an ideal of total pacifist living, integrating farming with intellectual, activist, or creative activities. For instance, at the end of Ahimsa Farm's first season, one member reported:

> A day's WORK AT THE FARM started at seven.... At eight, we each went to whatever work was to be done that day. As for my personal

work, I was from time to time, bookkeeper, electrician, baker, cook, ditch-digger, farmer—including plow-jocky [sic], house-keeper, & plumber, besides the more specialized but less obvious—educator.... After lunch, we spent time in reading, writing, discussing, and planning. This period was followed by preparing for dinner, feeding the chickens, and finishing up odd jobs. The evenings were free for reading, discussing, visiting, and going to meetings.[46]

In addition, an observer noted that the 7:00 A.M. hour included "morning meditation."[47]

Others experienced the idyllic side of farming. Mildred Craig, of the married couple who lived at Ahimsa Farm year-round, wrote, "The goats like carrot tops, potato peelings, etc. The 'book' says it is alright [sic] to give them table scraps of certain kinds. Star is an angel child, she is so eager to take care of the animals she doesn't shun the dirty work.... Do you suppose we could let her have a kid for her very own when they come?"[48] Another pacifist farmer mentioned the efforts of his community to "carry the cultural life with us, as we learned at Trenton [North Dakota]," by counting one member's artistic pursuits toward his share of the community's labor. This farmer also found time to study "psychology, the history of mysticism, and farming."[49]

What the early report from Ahimsa did not mention was that the students relied on a farmer neighbor to teach them how it was done; that they nearly failed at building a brick cottage; and that the main farmhouse needed substantial repairs.[50] Other farms experienced similar stumbling blocks. Tuolumne Co-op Farm struggled with "undercapitalization."[51] Macedonia made several unsuccessful attempts to build a dam for its water supply in 1941 and 1942, and by 1948 still had not finished it.[52]

In 1949 another pacifist farmer, noting that "all of us are aware of a widespread urge among pacifists to 'go rural,'" offered this warning:

> But, you say, it's the simple life for me.... Does it sound simple to you to be able to wake up in the morning and think that, besides getting in 4 or 8 or 10 hours at whatever your remunerative work is, you really should, before you go to bed again, fix that flat tire, fertilize the orchard, clean the chicken house, mow the weeds in the would-be "patio," burn rubbish, dig a new hole for cans, detick the dog, get at those kitchen cupboards you scheduled to build month before last,

stop putting off building a swing for Johnny, and more and more and more?"[53]

For this pacifist farmer, discussion and meditation were not even on the agenda. As to activism, he warned that local people were often reluctant to be treated as "projects" for instruction or enlightenment.[54]

Art Wiser managed to strike a balance between the idyllic and the pragmatic in his 1952 account of Macedonia Farm. He described rising early to milk the cows. Afterward, he wrote, "Mary has breakfast ready... eggs that were laid yesterday, toast from whole wheat bread that Mary baked, coffee, some honey from Koinonia." Wiser had managed to find time for playing the recorder with his wife and for reading and writing in "the cool quiet of our open, stone-walled home." The community held biweekly suppers "with singing and folk dancing." They also managed some local outreach: several members were working with a prisoner who they thought had been wrongly convicted. On the other hand, said Wiser, meetings were "interminable, sometimes, and frustrating." The workshop and office, in an old chicken barn, were "a fire trap." And free time was minimal: "If the hay is on the ground today, then today [not tomorrow] is the time to put it in."[55]

Spiritual Life: From Protestantism to Umbrella

The religious life of the cooperatives showed much the same pattern as *Training for Peace*. A few communities professed explicitly Protestant Christian principles. Most, however, devised common practices and ideologies that were intended to form a sort of umbrella under which all could comfortably gather. Individuals might adhere to an organized religious body, a self-devised spirituality, or no overt religion at all, but such individual beliefs and practices were private.[56] In addition, pacifist culture in the co-ops continued to be highly verbal. Most co-ops and organizations of co-ops struggled repeatedly to articulate who they were and what they believed.

Although the ideological umbrellas of the cooperatives were intended to be interfaith or nonreligious, their statements reflected a good deal of liberal Protestant orientation, both implicit and explicit. Some referred directly to Jesus or to the Kingdom of God. Most, though, echoed the theology of Protestant pacifism at one remove, referring to "a way of life," "love," "working for a better world," inner life, and spiritual unity, while omitting biblical or ecclesial language.

Ahimsa Farm, for example, described itself as "a fellowship farm dedicated to the ideals of a non-violent Christian life," but the members' life together was built around "meditation, manual work, study, and group discussion," not explicitly Christian activities such as Bible study or hymn singing. Tuolumne Co-op Farm, founded by Methodists, defined maturity as "moving from self-centeredness to God-centeredness," but a longtime member said, "There was no attempt to develope [sic] or impose any theology or religious doctrine. . . . All were free to attend church services of their choice in Modesto, 9 miles away." Tuolumne's weekend educational conferences included "work, discussion, singing and recreation." At Macedonia, religion was "of a very liberal variety" and members' "own private business," though most of them came from Protestant backgrounds. Members of The Vale, in Yellow Springs, Ohio, sought to "bring to pass the Kingdom of God" but otherwise professed a general, not explicitly Christian theism. Similarly, the Fellowship of Intentional Communities repeated many pacifist theological terms—"love," "the ultimate worth of personality," "evolv[ing] a way of life"—without professing a particular religion. Perhaps the members of St. Francis Acres in Glen Gardner, New Jersey, went farthest: they drew up a contract naming God the owner of the property and themselves the trustees. They described themselves as "'Universal Citizens' whose nation is Humanity, the Earth their country, and God the only sovereignty they recognize."[57] The common ground for co-op members, then, was not Protestant profession but pacifism itself, usually combined with loosely defined theism or spirituality.

Tensions

Pacifist co-op farms suffered from tensions that went beyond the spiritual. One, of course, was the matter of money. Few of the cooperative farms ever achieved the life of self-sustaining plenty, even at a simple standard of living, that models such as Borsodi's and the Nearings' promised. A number of co-ops relied on benefactors for land and sometimes cash.[58] And there were differences over such issues as control of finances or how much profit to take on cash crops.

Issues of leadership, authority, and decision-making were also sources of tension. The "charismatic leaders" who organized co-ops often had an extra measure of authority despite their egalitarian principles. As one author observed, "Local people still considered [Koinonia] 'Mr. Jordan's farm,' and in differences over policy he usually had his way. . . . Usually, if someone really disagreed with a decision, he or she left." The seniority and financial input of the founders certainly played a part. A number of founders, such as Smith, Mitchell, and in a different context, Borsodi, generated conflict by their forceful personalities and strong opinions.[59]

But other pacifists had strong personalities, too. Indeed their individualism and nonconformity often made cooperation difficult. If CPS men lived by discussion, the co-ops did so even more. "The meetings seemed to be interminable," recalled a former Macedonia member. "At the beginning I enjoyed them—it seemed to be democracy at work. But then when you get [sic] the total group concerned with the littlest minutiae, it got to be wearying." A member of Ahimsa similarly remembered "endless meetings and conferences."[60]

Co-ops also experienced tension between outreach and internal affairs. While the postwar communities, in contrast to the prewar groups, tended to emphasize community life itself as a goal, outreach and community were never considered mutually exclusive. With limited financial and human resources, though, most communities had difficulty maintaining both emphases. This tension could become particularly pointed where children were concerned. There were problems when the principle of neighborhood outreach meant sending children to public schools of poor quality, to say nothing of times when an unpopular witness meant endangering children.[61]

In many co-ops, the basis of community itself was a locus of tension. Harlem Ashram members disagreed over whether to be a "definitely Christian ashram" or "a cooperative fellowship with a minimum of group discipline."[62] Koinonia redefined its identity and purposes several times. At Macedonia, the spiritual basis of the community was never adequately defined or agreed upon.

Pacifist farms, like other utopian communities and individual homesteads, were hopeful, idealistic, and beset with struggle. They existed within a complex social network, providing outsiders with training and respite, receiving from them moral and financial support. They sustained a practiced religion, and their idyllic side fulfilled deeply rooted longings for community and closeness to nature. But they contended with practical and interpersonal pressures that sometimes proved too great to be overcome.

MEANINGS

By 1957 the rural ideal was firmly embedded in pacifist culture. In that year Seymour Eichel, a draft resister in the federal prison at Danbury, Connecticut, undertook a fast for freedom. Richard Fichter, a Pennsylvania dairy farmer, decided after some correspondence with Eichel's family to go to Washington, picket the White House on Eichel's behalf, and try to see President Eisenhower personally. The radical magazine *Liberation* described Fichter's journey and reproduced excerpts from his journal.

Fichter was rooted in pacifist culture in many ways. On his journey he encountered, in various capacities, the WILPF, the NCPW, and the FOR. He defined his faith by the old Social Gospel phrase, "the fatherhood of God and the brotherhood of man . . . Spiritually I belong to no organized church." He spoke in familiar terms of "overcoming hate with love." This farmer had been a tax resister and a Methodist minister. He appears, then, not to have been utterly naive.

But the article presented him as straight from the land. Entitled "Farmer at the Gates," it told how he "left his dairy herd" and impressed observers with his "direct approach." Here the pastoralist ideal is combined with pacifism to make the farmer an image of purity and peace, an image we have also seen in pacifist iconography and in the homesteading impulse.

Indeed, farming had come to function as a sort of pacifist credential, as in this description of a contributor to *Fellowship*: "Henry Little, author of *Minority Report on the Bruderhof*, is a CO, twice imprisoned during the war, now living with his family on a near-subsistence farm in Vermont."[63] Conscientious objection, prison, subsistence farming, religious community: this was an evolving set of cultural markers drawn from familiar roots.

The idea of a credential can be carried further, if somewhat speculatively. I suggest that cooperative farms were in some respects a functional equivalent of monasticism for pacifists. One could make something of the matters of poverty, chastity, and obedience: the communities appear to have practiced chastity in the sense of fidelity in marriage; commitment to community was a form of obedience, and matters of authority were at least important enough to be contested; and there is no question that co-ops were usually poor. But this is not really the main point. The more important qualities that pacifist communitarianism had in common with monasticism were the desire to live a fully committed life and the belief that such a life should be lived in community. Since not everyone had the will or ability to undertake this kind of life, a two-tiered membership emerged in pacifism as in the church: the truly elect who led the "religious" life—including the priesthood of protest and the settled monasticism of cooperation—and the much greater number of ordinary "lay" souls. The communities of the elect then functioned, like monastics, as examples of the committed life, as resources for the "laity," as bearers of an endangered tradition, and as teachers and missioners.[64]

For all their love of Francis—and of Jesus—midcentury pacifists did not propose mendicancy as an escape from "the errors of materialistic culture." Perhaps begging was incompatible with the work ethic, or perhaps pacifists retained enough middle-class sensibility to want the minimal degree of security that came from a settled place and a productive bit of land.[65] Besides, it is likely, though often forgotten, that the early Franciscans worked as much as they begged. Nonetheless, for communal living and farming, the Benedictine tradition would seem to be a better model than the Franciscan. Pacifists did occasionally practice the "Benedictine silence" at night, but Benedictine monasticism as a model of living in community on the land is largely absent from pacifist literature.[66] Possibly the Benedictine model was perceived as too authoritarian, both socially and doctrinally. Undoubtedly the wider culture offered less access to Benedict than to Francis.

A. J. Muste was critical of cooperative farming as the pacifist "way of life" because of its potential to remove participants from activity in the world, a criticism that has also been made of monasticism. But he was also one of the first to see the positive connections. At the 1942 Conference of Pacifist Farming Communities he noted that communal living "offers a vocation and a way of life for those fitted for it." Cooperatives might be "centers of spiritual energy . . . *Lay orders. Send out religious-pacifist missionaries.*"[67]

Yet this loosely defined spiritual energy proved insufficient for many communities. We have seen how many communards were drawn to the Bruderhof as offering a firmer and more coherent foundation for pacifist life. At the same time—during the postwar era and beyond—umbrella theology was challenged by the growth and increasing visibility of the Catholic Worker. Thus, outside mainline Protestantism and Quakerism, there was a revival of pacifist communities with an explicit and demanding Christian basis.

10 "Victories without Violence"

PACIFIST STORIES

> Scrambled eggs and prayers are stronger than guns.
> —Fred Small, "Scrambled Eggs and Prayers," on No Limit

Long after the paradigm shift of the 1940s, the Cambridge, Massachusetts, songwriter Fred Small recorded an original ballad, based on news reports, called "Scrambled Eggs and Prayers." The song tells the story of an elderly woman and an escaped prisoner. The woman is alone when the convict invades her home with a shotgun. She invites him to sit down and firmly orders him to "put that gun away." She then engages him in conversation, asks him about his mother, and talks about prayer and the Bible. She prepares bacon and eggs after he confesses that he hasn't eaten for three days. Eventually the police arrive and he surrenders unarmed. At the end of the story, the song rhetorically alerts the audience that a moral message is coming and then presents the message: "You can tell it to your daughters and teach it to your sons / That scrambled eggs and prayers are stronger than guns."[1]

Small's song, recorded in 1985, is a recent example of a kind of story that had circulated among pacifists in various versions since at least 1920.[2] The story is one of several types of pacifist literature that can be grouped together as "exempla"—stories told within a social group to illustrate a belief, to give moral instruction, or to inspire emulation. Usually they claim to be historically true; at the very least they are presented in a realistic style. But their primary purpose is the construction of meaning.[3]

This chapter explores Protestant pacifist exempla. In contrast to the two preceding chapters, which have focused on a relatively narrow span of time, this one broadens the lens to take in the entire period of this study, returning to larger questions of continuity and change. It also carries forward themes of gender, family, and child rearing, which the next chapter considers in more depth.

Although historians have generally overlooked them, the exempla are among the most revealing of pacifist cultural productions. They define and explore the meaning of peace and what it means to live as a pacifist, and in so doing reveal a worldview, a set of shared assumptions about the nature of reality. We have seen elements of this worldview in other pacifist cultural practices; this chapter explores how it was shaped and sustained by narrative.

These narratives fall into three overlapping genres: brief heroic biographies, often tending in the direction of hagiography; stories that express a commonly held belief, such as the feasibility of international peace; and stories that show how to live a life consistent with pacifist convictions. In addition, pacifist exempla may be either internationalist or interpersonal in orientation. Internationalist narratives treat peace as the absence of war and as friendly relations among nations and their citizens; interpersonal ones regard it as a transaction between individuals, akin to what came to be called active nonviolence. The internationalist stories stand within the broad tradition of peace activism or advocacy, while the interpersonal ones reflect an orientation closer to absolute pacifism.

The reader should be aware, however, that the people who disseminated and used this lore were not divided into mutually exclusive groups of internationalists and absolutists telling mutually exclusive sets of stories. Nor was there any absolute division in time; the types of stories coexisted through at least 1964. There was, however, a shift of emphasis in the late 1930s from internationalist to interpersonal exempla, as pacifist culture moved toward its redefinition as a personal and small-group "way of life," with nonviolence as a major theme.

The theology expressed in the exempla is consistent with that of other pacifist cultural materials. The exempla assume that peace is possible. Those that link peace explicitly with Christianity emphasize Jesus' teachings and "way of love." Most share modernism's confidence in the human capacity for improvement and its focus on the present world. Thus victory over violence is not the otherworldly victory of salvation or of the martyr's crown; it is here and now and concrete.

The familiar themes of love, good will, service, a way of life, and perfectionism recur in the exempla. Verses and book titles refer explicitly to "good will"; hero stories and interpersonal tales illustrate whole ways of life. Love is central. In the internationalist stories it is the means by which commonalities overcome differences and is the basis of international friendship. In the interpersonal stories it is the antithesis of fear and anger. But its most important function is as a powerful force. Like the concrete power of love experienced by some pacifist mystics, love in the exempla has real, this-worldly effects on the course of international and interpersonal events.

The exempla, then, make arguments — by illustration and implication — about what constitutes peace, what it means to be a pacifist, and what the consequences and effects of pacifism are. The stories constitute a lore of pacifist behavior, survival, and victory. They present role models and suggest how pacifist convictions can be lived out. They offer encouragement and hope; despite occasional caveats to the contrary, they generally depict pacifism's successes.

HEROIC TALES

Heroes of Peace

One type of exemplum is the presentation of a model for emulation. This type is particularly visible in the literature of "heroes of peace," which I touched upon in the chapters on iconography and training. Emerging in the late 1920s, this literature included among its more prominent collections *Heroes of Peace* (1929), by the popular author Archer Wallace, and Hermann Hagedorn's *The Book of Courage* (1929), which appeared in seven printings by three different publishers in thirteen years.[4] Hagedorn later wrote *The Bomb that Fell on America* (1946), an influential narrative poem. His 1929 collection included a section on St. Francis, as did many similar works. But he was the only one of the early authors to discuss Gandhi. Within a decade, however, Gandhi came to epitomize the new peace hero, one who practiced peacemaking itself and a way of life consistent with it.[5]

More than any other author or speaker, Allan Hunter distilled this trend into a new set of exempla, aimed at adults rather than children. Hunter was closely involved in many of the pacifist developments of the period. As pastor of a mainline church, he led YMCA and other youth groups, worked closely with the mystic Gerald Heard, and organized a peace team. He wrote several collections of exempla, which he clearly intended as moral models to be followed. "The creative heroism of goodwill does not belong on a pedestal," he wrote. "It is for every man."[6]

Hunter emerged into literary prominence during the period of pacifist transition that began in 1939. Two of his collections of heroic biographies appeared in that year and remained on pacifist booklists through the war. These were *Three Trumpets Sound: Kagawa—Gandhi—Schweitzer*, published by the YMCA's Association Press, and *White Corpuscles in Europe*, issued by the trade publisher Willett, Clark. Hunter followed these in 1943 with the FOR booklet *Heroes of Good Will* (see chapter 6).

Three Trumpets typified the redefined heroic ideal. On the one hand, Albert Schweitzer's story served as a link with earlier peace heroism. On the other, Gandhi represented large-scale pacifist activism, communal living, and voluntary poverty.

The third exemplar, Toyohiko Kagawa (1888–1960), was an internationally recognized Protestant model of the dedicated Christian life.[7] A Japanese convert to Christianity, Kagawa attended the theological seminary at Kobe from 1905 to 1908. He decided to put his beliefs into practice by living with the poor in a notorious Kobe slum, which became his home for fifteen years. Later he founded labor unions, advocated cooperative economics, and proposed improvements in agricultural practice. He was also a street evangelist, and in 1930 he organized the "Kingdom of God Movement" with the dual aim of converting Japan and Christianizing its social order. An active pacifist, Kagawa was jailed in 1940 and in 1943 for his position. He disappointed his international following by expressing loyalty to Japan during the war, but he justified his stance as an expression of care for his people and for the Christian church, not as nationalism. Kagawa was not only a practitioner; he studied at Princeton University and was a prolific writer and lecturer. His reputation among pacifists, however, was based on his social activism and, to a lesser extent, on his mystical spirituality.[8]

As is fitting for exempla, Hunter's account of him was anecdotal and adulatory. He recounted stories of Kagawa's suffering, of his rescuing lost souls and bodies, of his success at building cooperative and evangelistic movements. Most notably, Hunter offered several narratives of would-be attackers turned away by Kagawa's calmly "show[ing] love" and "abiding in God." "Not once," Hunter declared, "has he been frightened nor for any length of time become discouraged." Hunter also compared Kagawa to Father Damien and, more than once, to St. Francis.[9]

White Corpuscles added some European "heroes of peace" to the list.[10] It comprised five short biographies and an epilogue about Kagawa. Three of its subjects were particularly influential among pacifists: Pierre Cérésole, Philippe Vernier, and Muriel Lester, whom Hunter among others called "the Jane Addams of London".[11] Cérésole, a Swiss conscientious objector, founded an organization called the *Service Civile Internationale* (International Civil Service) as an experimental alternative to national military service. The *Service* recruited youth to work in postwar reconstruction, agriculture, forestry, and other labor throughout Europe. Vernier, a French Protestant pacifist and non-ordained pastor, devoted his life to working with the rural poor. He was also an evangelist, and his spiritual writings were popular among American pacifists. Both Cérésole and Vernier spent time in prison for their war resistance.[12] Rufus Jones compared Vernier to St. Francis, whom Vernier himself quoted in his first book of meditations.[13]

Lester was one of three female figures—the other two were Jane Addams and Dorothy Day—whose status as pacifist legends spanned most of the twentieth century. The woman peace activist living among the urban poor was by far the most common model of female hero in the exempla.[14] Less obviously, however, these three female icons reflect the changing religious landscape of pacifism. Addams was ambivalent about organized religion, but she made it easy for others to construe her life as representing Christian living. Lester, of course, was a Protestant with mystical and syncretistic tendencies. Day, on the other hand, as a Roman Catholic signified the end of Protestant hegemony in pacifist culture and was an early harbinger of the Catholic leadership that developed more fully in the Vietnam-era peace movement and afterward.

The new heroic tales, which predominated by 1940, suggest that the hero of peace should be an antihero. Both newer and older types of peace heroes were thought to exercise courage, perseverance, creativity, and in many cases a calling or an insight rejected in their own time. But where earlier literature places the heroes within the flow of an advancing civilization, the later literature represents heroes as resisters. To the extent that they do advance civilization, it is by convicting society of sin or by building alternative structures, not by participating in an inexorable forward march. When the nation is preoccupied with news of war, these heroes are "not in the headlines."[15] Like Harold Gray, they take ironic pride in their "bad character." Thus, as pacifists moved out of the mainstream of American culture and hegemonic Protestantism, they developed narratives of heroic outsiderhood.

INTERNATIONALIST STORIES

A second type of pacifist exempla literature was the internationalist story. The purpose of such stories was not so much to provide models for emulation as to prove a point or reaffirm a belief. They did, however, overlap with heroic narratives by offering characters for emulation—just as the stories about heroes also offered moral lessons.

Here I look at four narratives that were pillars of internationalist storytelling—three accounts of historical events and one parable. The historical narratives, like other exempla, are realistic in style: they refer to public, documented events; take place in public spaces; and address the problems of nations, communities, or officials rather than of private individuals. But they make a moral argument by presenting the events in a particular way—as successful peacemaking arising from moral suasion rather than, say, skillful diplomatic negotiation or economic pressures or complex multifactorial events. The parable is of course primarily a moral tale.

A useful tool with which to identify moral messages embedded in stories is the concept of the topos, as Mark Silk has argued with respect to religious journalism. A topos—from the Greek *koinos topos*, literally "common place"—is a rhetorical convention or theme expressing a moral principle or judgment familiar to both the speaker or writer and the audience. In short, it is a commonplace, or in Silk's phrase, a "moral least common denominator."[16] Most peace stories convey topoi. For example, the topos of most "international friendship" materials is something like "People are all the same under the skin" or "Our similarity is greater than our difference." Sometimes this message is stated explicitly; other times it remains implicit. But the topos is shared and familiar, and the story that expresses or illustrates it affirms a common worldview. Such affirmation has emotional, as well as intellectual and ethical, power.

The Christ of the Andes

The flagship of the internationalist stories is "The Christ of the Andes." This was the common name of a statue raised in 1904 on the border between Argentina and Chile, in honor of the peaceful settlement of a long-simmering boundary dispute between the two nations. The statue shows Christ standing on a globe with his feet on the map of South America, his right hand gesturing upward, his left holding a tall, narrow cross, like a processional cross. A plaque, added in 1937, shows the words of a pledge made at the dedication of the statue: an English rendition is "These mountains will crumble into dust before the people of Argentina and Chile break the peace which at the feet of Christ, the Redeemer, they have given their word to keep."

The outline of the story is clear. Chile and Argentina were on the brink of war in 1900. At Easter of that year, an Argentine bishop, Marcolino Benavente, preached a homily opposing military action and subsequently worked to stir up popular sentiment for peace. A Chilean bishop soon mounted a parallel effort. Both traversed their countries on foot, preaching against war. At length the two governments agreed to arbitration by King Edward VII of the United Kingdom. When his decision was accepted and peace concluded, in 1902, Benavente proposed melting down unused cannon to make a statue of Christ on a border mountain. People — one version specifies "women" — of both countries raised funds for this project. The statue was installed amid much ceremony; most noted was cross-border camping, with Argentines on the Chilean side and Chileans on the Argentine side.[17] Retellings of the story customarily ended by quoting the pledge.

"Christ of the Andes" makes a point of connecting peace with Christianity. The Christ figure and the pledge, of course, are the most obvious manifestations of this. A few versions, however, add suggestions of a supernatural aura around the events. For example, one version draws implicit parallels between the two bishops and the Christ of the Gospels: the bishops traveled on foot, and "at first only a few listened but finally they were followed about by crowds."[18] Two versions add cosmic drama: the statue is unveiled at sunrise, or the people kneel for the dedication at sunset.[19] The primary topos of the story is "international disputes can be settled by peaceful means." A secondary topos, more conspicuous in some versions than in others, says that Christian profession impels peaceful settlements.

Historically, this story formed a connecting link between the pre–World

Marie Louise Rochon Hoover, Christ of the Andes, Christmas card, 1922, Records of the National Council for Prevention of War, Swarthmore College Peace Collection. Image courtesy of SCPC.

War I peace societies and postwar peace culture. It was first written and published by Frederick Lynch of the American Peace Society in 1905. After the war it appeared in the well-known peace-education collections of the 1920s and was also picked up by missionary-education publications.[20] Sunday schools dramatized the story, sometimes affirming the pledge as well; exhibits, lecture illustrations, and Christmas cards featured pictures of the statue.[21] By 1933 educator Paul Limbert could observe that most of the children in a study of sixth- to tenth-graders "identified correctly the Christ of the Andes," and in 1935 John Leslie Lobingier claimed that "every high-school boy and girl knows its inscription."[22] The story continued to appear in well-known peace literature through the late 1930s and reappeared in a 1964 peace-education collection.[23] The persistent use of this story, then, shows that reasoned internationalism and political alternatives to war, flavored with Christian references, continued to appeal to pacifists.

The Rush-Bagot Agreement

A similar, though less dramatic, story concerns the boundary between the United States and Canada. It recounts the genesis of an 1817 agreement negotiated by acting U.S. secretary of state Richard Rush and Sir Charles Bagot, the British minister to the United States. Although the agreement dealt only with limiting naval armament on the Great Lakes, the story presents the issue as the full disarmament of the entire border and ascribes the resolution of the issue to the private moral decisions of the two diplomats. The topos is the effectiveness of trust between nations.[24]

The centennial of the ratification of the agreement, in the same year as the end of World War I, had generated a number of peace monuments. The earliest and best known of these was the "peace portal" built by a private committee at Blaine, Washington.[25] It stood, and still stands, on the boundary line between the United States and Canada and was embellished with quotations affirming peace. Most remarkably, it incorporated physical relics: a fragment of the *Mayflower* on the west side and one of the Hudson Bay explorer *Beaver* on the east.[26] In this way it embodied both the common British-colonial past of both nations and their separate identities.

The open border, like the heroic figure of Lindbergh, served as a symbol for many causes, some with only tenuous ties to the peace movement. For example, Kiwanis International put up "Boundary Peace Tablets" at twelve border crossings between 1935 and 1937, and a group of Rotary Clubs built a park and a garden spanning the border. But, as with Lindbergh, pacifists appropriated the symbol in particular ways. Verbal accounts of the Rush-Bagot Agreement invoke an ideal of trust; the topos is that nations can live in peace if they trust one another. A second topos of the narratives is the moral force of the individual. The monuments complement these topoi with an image of endurance: peaceful agreements can last. Topoi and images further imply, realistically or not, that the United States and Canada may serve as a model of international relations. Zonia Baber summarized the topoi in wording that recalls "Scrambled Eggs and Prayers": "This long unarmed boundary is convincing evidence that international goodwill is a more powerful defence than forts and guns."[27]

Penn and the Indians

The third example in this group concerns a colonial rather than an international treaty: William Penn's agreement with the Lenni Lenape Indians. No contemporaneous documentation of the treaty survives. According to the story, however, when Charles II deeded Penn the tract of North American land that would become Pennsylvania, Penn determined to treat the native people fairly.[28] Upon arriving in the new colony in 1682, he met with Indian representatives unarmed under the "Treaty Elm" at Shackamaxon, now a part of Philadelphia, and paid them a fair price for the land. Both parties then agreed that their respective peoples would live side by side without harming each other. The story maintains that the peace between Indians and Quakers—not necessarily other Pennsylvania colonists—survived until the Quakers lost control of Pennsylvania's government in 1755 during the French and Indian War.[29] The topoi here include the exemplary qualities of Quakers, the importance of keeping one's word, the practicability of preventing war by honorable agreement, and, occasionally, racial harmony.[30]

Although Penn, as a major figure in American colonial and religious history, never sank into obscurity, the anniversaries of his first landing and of his birth occasioned unusual attention to his memory. These anniversaries were observed in 1932 and 1944, respectively. In addition to various official and popular commemorations, seven full-length biographies were published in the United States (and several more in Britain) between 1929 and 1938, with shorter pieces and assessments appearing through the 1930s and 1940s. Another biography appeared in 1957.[31]

The extent of the literature corresponds to Penn's popularity as an exemplar of the peaceful life. His name appeared in most lists and collections of peace heroes. His example was also invoked in support of particular causes, such as the League of Nations in 1919 and improvement of race relations in 1944.[32] The importance of his myth is implicit in the introduction to a liberal Quaker curriculum of 1953, which began, "It is assumed that children of the fourth or fifth grade level . . . will have some knowledge of the life and teachings of Jesus and of the work of William Penn."[33]

The story of Penn's treaty with the Indians and the continued peace in Pennsylvania was, like "Christ of the Andes," one that most schoolchildren of the 1930s could repeat.[34] Dramatized versions of the story were numerous, and some had even been composed by children.[35] And, as we have seen, the image of Penn and the Indians was a part of visual iconography. Penn's agreement with the Indians, then, was a durable exemplum that appeared in unusually diverse contexts, and, like other Protestant imagery, linked word and image.

The Parable of the Shoe

Florence Brewer Boeckel's parable "A Shoe, a League of Nations" provides a point of transition between the internationalist and interpersonal stories. Its content and message were clearly internationalist, but it was a kind of domestic internationalism, concerned with everyday objects rather than with treaties. It resembled the interpersonal stories in the way it participated in a folk process: since the central point of the parable was not tied to historical events, those who retold it were free to vary the settings and symbols of the story while reiterating the same topoi. Some published versions also credited Boeckel directly.

The point of the parable was that an ordinary object such as a shoe was made of materials that came from many countries. Stories of this type generated a number of topoi, often placed in the mouths of characters in the stories: "If the people of the world did not work together, you could not have shoes"; "The nations must learn how to be friendly"; "Each one has something to contribute"; "They [other nations] need us, just as we need them"; and, by implication, "Domestic comfort depends upon peaceful international relations."[36]

Boeckel's parable was retold in several media: pamphlets, stories, plays, and pageants. Variant versions also appeared. One of these described the materials in a telephone rather than in a shoe, thus adding communication as a symbolic dimension of the object in question. Others extended the motif from material objects to human beings. For example, a 1930 pageant depicted a succession of immigrants bearing symbols of their respective contributions to American life. An inversion of this idea appeared in a play in which, instead of immigrants bringing gifts, "foreigners" were forced to leave America for their places of origin, taking their contributions with them. In this play, even the protagonists were ultimately revealed as "foreigners" by the arrival of a group of Indians.[37] While the shoe as motif seems to have disappeared after World War II, similar ideas surfaced as late as 1960, when a peace newsletter for children and youth reflected on the international sources of several common objects and ideas.[38]

A children's song of the 1930s aptly summarizes domestic internationalism. Familiar themes and watchwords—technology and transportation, international friendship, Christianity, love, good will—support the overall message. There is also a disturbing self-centeredness, appropriate, perhaps, for young children, but also suggesting a current of unreflective nationalism beneath liberal internationalism.

> The world came to my home today
> To spread a wondrous feast;
> The ships and planes in bright array
> Brought gifts from west and east;
> From India, spice; from China, tea,
> My table high to fill;
> Each nation sent in peace to me
> A token of good will.[39]

The internationalist exempla were primarily concerned with affirming belief in the possibility of peace among nations and, somewhat ambivalently, with developing a broader outlook than nationalism. To a lesser extent they presented heroes or saints for emulation: the bishops, the diplomats, Penn. The folklore of interpersonal nonviolence, by contrast, turns the lens from international affairs to the smallest unit of peacemaking: the individual pacifist life.

INTERPERSONAL STORIES:
THE FOLKLORE OF NONVIOLENCE

Folklore, History, and Worldview

The interpersonal stories are the most distinctive of the pacifist exempla. Their messages are counterintuitive: while the heroic models measured themselves against an accepted cultural category, and the internationalist stories were capable of appealing to a broad audience, the interpersonal stories present characters who act in a manner contrary to accepted notions of common sense. In all their variations these stories describe people who, confronted with grave danger, do not defend themselves; that is, they neither fight nor run away. Most of the characters claim, moreover, that they are in fact using the best defense, which is love. And this is the underlying topos: love is stronger than violence; love overcomes violence. Scrambled eggs and prayers are not merely not guns but are stronger than guns.

Even more than the internationalist stories, these accounts function like folktales: one encounters many examples of a given narrative or plot, but the narratives are told through different characters and placed in different settings, with details and smaller elements added, subtracted, and exchanged. Like all exempla, the interpersonal tales claim to be based on real events, but because of their form, I believe they are best understood as folklore. The concepts of "tale types" and "motifs," which folklorists developed early in this century, are useful for describing pacifist folktales.[40] A "tale type" is a general narrative plot; "Scrambled Eggs and Prayers," for instance, can be classified with similar stories as belonging to the pacifist tale type "intruder disarmed by friendliness." Particular tales within a given type will vary by setting, characters, and so on. "Motifs" are smaller elements of content: objects, episodes, settings, and so on. The occurrence of particular motifs within the tales will also vary.[41]

Since the purpose of an exemplum is to convey a moral message, the stories also incorporate or illustrate topoi. Mark Silk hints at the close relationship between folk narrative and topoi when he mentions the conventional, "ritual" nature of many news stories: both the moral commonplace and the story's plot and structure follow conventional lines.[42] In peace stories the message is "Love overcomes violence" or "Nonviolence works." In all such stories—intruders disarmed by friendliness, soldiers in opposing armies making friends, hostile Indians declining to attack trustful white settlers—the question of violence is raised, the tension is heightened, and the topos of the peaceful solution is repeated once more time.

Pacifists would argue that we should understand these stories as history. Is there validity to this claim? Is it possible that similar narratives recur because they are true, because the types of events the stories recount have happened more than once? While it is not possible here to trace the documentation of every tale, it does seem probable that some of them had a genesis in historical fact. There is nothing inherently implausible in a chance meeting of enemy soldiers, or in sensitive boys' rejecting wanton cruelty to animals.[43] Contact across enemy lines during World War I has been well documented. The events behind "Scrambled Eggs and Prayers" are also documented, though with some variations. And at least two published stories have the kind of incomplete resolution that suggests historicity insofar as they decline to conform to a topos.[44]

On the other hand, it is also clear that some stories were extensively elaborated from minimal historical documentation or were altered to fit a topos.[45] In others, contextual details were altered to suit modern sensibilities.[46] This evidence suggests that meaning, rather than precise accuracy, was foremost in at least some editors' minds.[47] Those stories that cite unnamed friends or friends of friends as the sources of several stories raise further suspicion, since this claim is a characteristic of the urban legends of our own time. To make such a claim does not, of course, prove that the story is a legend, but the claim is suggestive when taken together with the conventional nature of the story's narrative shape.[48]

In the end, however, my aim is not to determine whether the stories were or were not true, and by extension whether nonviolence does or does not work. Rather, it is to describe the persistent and characteristic forms of the folktales about interpersonal nonviolence. What is important is that the stories were circulated and received as legitimate models of behavior at least, and as literally true at most. As such, they, along with other texts and lore, shaped a distinctive pacifist worldview.

A brief note on the sources: Most of the stories are found in story collections compiled by Quakers and directed at children, beginning in 1917; collections in several genres by non-Quaker educators, most of them in mainline Protestant denominations, beginning in 1926; and story collections directed at adults, beginning about 1936. Some of the stories also appear in other formats such as plays and worship services. As in twentieth-century mysticism, the Quaker strain in this literature occurs in a context of exchange and transmission across theological and organizational lines. The Quaker books began as in-house explorations of identity, moved on to issues of "human progress and Christian living," and ended as "education for peace."[49] Together with Friends' curricula, they borrowed eclectically from various religious and secular sources. Other denominations and organizations used Quaker material freely.[50]

The stories circulated in more ephemeral sources as well. For instance, a 1929 FOR pamphlet on youth education advised teachers to "collect peace stories," suggesting as sources the Quaker stories, Rufus Jones's memoirs, and Laurence Housman's *Little Plays of St. Francis*.[51] A Methodist teaching guide from about 1939, "Children Learn Peace," recommended books by Quakers Griscom and Broomell, educators McPherson and Lobingier, and activists Gregg and Page. It also included a poster of *Christ of the Andes*. The nonviolence stories, then, existed in the matrix of the pacifist culture alongside other cultural markers, and their use was not restricted to any one subgroup.

"VICTORIES WITHOUT VIOLENCE": THE STORIES

The tales of interpersonal nonviolence fall into three principal groups or tale types, with one subtype. I designate the tale types "intruder disarmed by friendliness," "group of attackers deflected by friendliness," and "soldiers make friends across enemy lines." In the "group of attackers" tales the invaders are often soldiers, and these tales have a subtype: "attackers deflected by children." Within the tale types numerous common motifs occur. The most frequently appearing motifs are the threatening figures of robbers, soldiers, and invading armies; children representing innocence; food; and restoration, as when a robber is restored to social respectability.

Soldiers Make Friends Across Enemy Lines

These tales are set in wartime, with men, of course, as the actors.[52] Typically, two soldiers from opposing sides meet each other while separated from their military units, for instance while carrying water or on late-night patrols. Both are armed but decline to use their weapons; usually one takes a peaceable initiative to which the other responds. They make a gesture of friendship, such as a wave of the hand or an exchange of amicable phrases, and separate. Their action has no effect on the course of war but is shown to serve a larger moral purpose. The topoi are "friendship crosses national boundaries," "love is stronger than hate," "the individual transcends the state," "love overcomes violence," "above all nations is humanity."[53]

One widely circulated story was set in summer during World War I. In this story French and German army units face each other across a no-man's-land through which a stream flows. They arrive at a tacit agreement by which the two sides take turns fetching water from the stream. A new German unit arrives without knowing of this custom and thus poses a threat to the French. One night a Frenchman and a German accidentally meet at the stream. They draw their guns, but after a moment the German lowers his and goes on getting water. The surprised Frenchman does the same; they wave and depart. Later, they meet by chance at a peace conference and "clasp hands" or, in another version, "fall into each other's arms."[54]

Another story describes a young man, identified as a Canadian, who arrives at a position of conscientious objection while in the middle of his military service. He and his commanding officer come to a casuistical understanding by which he will follow all orders except actually to shoot at anyone.[55] The encounter with the enemy soldier occurs when the Canadian is alone in a German trench during "mopping-up operations." There he meets a German soldier who is ready to bayonet him. The Canadian greets him with outstretched hands and tries to express friendship with the words "*Mann*" and "*Liebe*" ("man" and "love") or "*Liebe alles mannen* [sic]." Eventually the German joins him in comradeship. In one version they then shake hands and sit together in silence; in another they converse, "mostly by gestures," for twenty minutes.

The Intruder Disarmed by Friendliness[56]

In this tale type, an armed intruder enters a home or a temporary dwelling such as a room at an inn. The occupant shows no fear and does not fight back, sometimes because of conscious choice and effort, sometimes by pure unconscious innocent goodness, and occasionally crediting Jesus. She or he welcomes the intruder as a guest, and they share a meal or some food. Usually the intruder is found to be unemployed but proud and desperate; the occupant puts him in the way of honest work.[57] The intruder then goes his way without causing any harm.

Allan Hunter used a version of this tale to summarize the message of *Courage in Both Hands*. For its back cover he wrote: "Two friends of mine have had their houses entered at night while they slept," he wrote. "One friend was afraid and . . . shot and nearly killed the thief. . . . The other friend was unafraid . . . and in the face of a gun in the hand of his would be robber refused to tell where his money was kept until the fellow sat down and had a bite to eat and listened to an offer of a night's lodging and help in finding a job."[58] The author adduced several topoi: anger does not pay, creative action is good, and love casts out fear.

Unlike Hunter's friends, however, the protagonists of most intruder stories were women.[59] Variants of the story were told, for example, about Jane Addams, about the Quaker prison reformer Elizabeth Fry, about ordinary or anonymous women, and even about a nine-year-old girl.[60]

A typical tale is "The Old Lady of Purchase," which first appeared in *The Children's Story Caravan*. In this story an elderly woman is at home alone on a stormy night. Hearing a noise at the door, she opens it to a strange man, whom she invites in without question. She lends him a garment of her late husband's to wear while she lays his clothes out to dry. While her back is turned, he approaches the corner cupboard where she keeps her silver. She then asks his forgiveness for not offering him food and prepares eggs and bacon for him. The man sleeps on her sofa and, the next day, goes to her brother for work as a farm hand. Before leaving, he confesses that his intention the previous night had been to steal, "but something about you made me change my mind." "No, it was Jesus Christ who changed thy mind," she replies.[61]

"The Silver Tankard" adds the motif of childhood innocence to the tale. Here a nine-year-old girl, Hetty, is left alone in a Maine farmhouse while her parents attend a distant Quaker meeting. They know that a gang of notorious thieves is nearby, but Hetty's father does not want to "teach her fear," so he tells her nothing. When the thieves arrive, she welcomes them and gives them a meal. Their leader is deflected from robbery by the sight of "Hetty's trusting little upturned face."[62]

Group of Attackers Disarmed by Friendliness

This tale type is similar to the first, but the threat is posed by organized groups of attackers, such as soldiers or hostile Indians, and those threatened are families or communities. As in the first tale type, the protagonists neither fight nor flee, and in many of the stories they positively welcome the attackers.

In "The Invincible Leader," the residents of a Tyrolean village invaded by the Austrian army offer no resistance but instead greet the invaders and then go about their business. They have no soldiers, the mayor explains, because "we have chosen Christ for our leader, and he taught men another way." Confronted with the effects of this "invincible leader," the commander of the unit finds it impossible to do anything but march on without taking over the village. Later, he comes to "hate [his] business."[63]

In other versions, the invaders are Indians and the invaded are white, usually Quakers, a motif that recalls the heroic figure of William Penn. In these tales, white settlers, surrounded by Indians with hostile intentions, make it clear that they pose no threat. The Indians respond by doing no harm and sometimes by leaving a permanent sign of truce. The motif of the shared meal appears in some stories as well. The topoi, then, are "We are all alike under the skin," "human beings respond to friendliness with friendliness," and of course, "love overcomes violence."

An example of this genre is "Fierce Feathers," which is set in Easton, New York, during the War for Independence. Quakers are gathered in worship when Indians, who are in the pay of the British army, approach the meetinghouse. The unarmed Friends continue worshipping in silence; in some versions a Quaker leader conveys love to the Indians through a steady, kindly gaze. The Indians, instead of attacking, put down their weapons and join in the silence. Afterward a Friend gives them a meal and they depart quietly.

The earliest historical reference to this event says simply that the Indians arrived "just as [the meeting] was breaking up," and when they "understood that Friends were at a Religious Meeting, they went to one of their Houses, got some Victuals . . . and then quietly departed." The rest, including narrative details and topoi, appears to be a later elaboration. In this case it has even taken on a ritual dimension, since the event is commemorated annually in Easton.[64]

In a variant version of the story, Quaker settlers under threat from Indians go about their business unharmed until, out of fear, they begin to carry guns, whereupon the Indians attack them. A character in one such story states its topos, "Fear begets fear." "Hetty's" father would have agreed.[65]

A third version of the intruder motif occurs in the genre of robber stories. The characters are all men. In these tales, the intended victim or his proxy first chases the robbers away, but later pursues them and gives them the spoils they seek, whereupon the robbers repent. The topoi are the virtue of nonresistance to evil and the humanity of the evildoer.

For example, in "St. Francis and the Robbers," bandits approach a Franciscan hermitage. One of the brothers drives them away. On hearing of this, Francis rebukes the brother, since he counts the robbers among the poor, who are beloved of Christ. Francis sends the brother after them with a supply of food and an offer to provide for them if they will give up their wickedness. The robbers are moved to repentance. In the *Little Flowers*, where this story first appeared, they then join his order. In a twentieth-century version, though, they ask Francis for help in "living like honest folk." This change renders the story Protestant, of course, and in the present context it also suggests the motif of the offer of work found in the "intruder" stories.[66]

Group of Invaders Disarmed by Children

"The Invincible Leader" used the topos of childhood innocence in passing—a "golden-haired tot" reminded an old soldier of his granddaughter, for example. But the power of innocence is the central topos of "The Cherries of Hamburg," or, variously, of "Naumburg." Printed versions of these stories circulated through, among others, the Women's Christian Temperance Union, the NCPW, the FOR, and the Friends' Peace Committee.[67]

In the Hamburg version, a sixteenth-century siege of the city is broken when the children of the city, dressed in white and carrying boughs of cherries, go out to meet the besiegers, whose hearts are thereby warmed. Peace is then concluded: "What the warriors of the town could not do the peaceful children in white did." In the Naumburg version, the children in white leave the besieged city in procession, but it is the besiegers who give cherries to the children, "whose bright eyes met their gaze / With innocence and courage all / Unversed in war's dread ways." As in "The Silver Tankard," the message of the story is that innocence wards off violence, whether by brigands or by armies.

The power of innocence was of course a favorite nineteenth-century theme, and the existing versions of the "Cherries" stories clearly emerge from that era. But the topos was repeated in very different form as late as 1952. In her collection *Victories without Violence*, Ruth Fry recounted a story, heard at several removes, of a 1944 protest against the Nazi occupation of Aarhus, Denmark. A growing crowd of children, "from two to fifteen years old," "surged" through the streets tearing down German road signs. Both local police and occupying army "were said to have been helpless against this demonstration of unarmed children." Since we know that Nazis were not in fact helpless against unarmed children, this story suggests the power of pacifists' will to believe in their moral exempla.[68]

THIS ELEMENT OF BELIEF is a key to understanding how distinctive the worldview of pacifist culture was. Read without the cultural assumptions that informed them—faith in the direct, this-worldly, applicable power of love and nonviolence—these stories are barely credible, even dangerous. Their nearest analogy is the literature of martyrdom, inspiring to those who have accepted its presuppositions, but strange and frightening to those who have not. Read without faith, tales of martyrdom seem only to recommend violent death. Stories of pacifism, read without pacifist faith, seem to recommend that women welcome invaders into their homes and that children be sent to fend off military invasion. Only by the logic of pacifist assumptions do these stories make any sense at all.

As constructed in pacifist narratives, the meanings of peace covered a wide range. Peace could mean international treaties, economic interdependence, cultural exchange, social justice, refusal to fight, resolution of conflicts without violence, and even winning miscreants from their evil ways. To live as a pacifist might mean engaging in the moral equivalent of war, seeking nonmilitary forms of heroic action, or being an antihero; it might mean personal commitment, consistent living, or exercising the power of love in risky situations. All of these meanings are present throughout the period this study covers, even though emphases shifted from international and culture-affirming actions to outsiderhood and interpersonal nonviolence.

In the moral universe of the exempla, peace is possible. Commonalities among human beings are greater than differences. Peace depends upon courageous individual action, friendship, trust, honesty, and good will. All of these initiatives evoke equivalent responses: friendliness begets friendliness, trust fosters trust. Love is antithetical to fear and anger as well as to hate and indifference. Above all, love, enacted in nonviolence, is the ultimate power, an effective force that works in real-world situations. It overcomes violence, it gives "victory."

This moral universe rests upon two characteristically liberal religious assumptions. The first is that humans are able to do good; its corollary is that they respond in kind to goodness. The second is the present availability of the Kingdom of God. In the exempla, following "Jesus' way of love" brings power and success, albeit of a paradoxical and antiheroic kind. Outside this moral universe it is not self-evident that the way of love should be successful. One can, for example, imagine a story in which an intruder kills a welcoming, nonresisting householder; the topos of such a story might be that love is morally right even when it is not effective in this world. But such topoi are notably absent from pacifist narrative.

This fact recalls another quality of pacifism and of liberal Protestantism more generally: its ambivalence about crucifixion. On the one hand, the idea of crucifixion—undeserved suffering as the outcome of love—is not absent from pacifist culture. Harold Gray found joy in such suffering; significant peace plays revolved around crucifixion metaphors; Richard Gregg warned pacifists to expect resistance. Yet the exempla suggest an unwavering belief in the power and triumph of love in the present world, and in the ultimate abolition of war—whether through peace treaties, or through persuasion, or through interpersonal nonviolence. They reflect a confident and optimistic vision that rejects the Niebuhrian critique of pacifism and minimizes the theology of the cross.

The exempla, then, present a self-contained and essentially religious worldview. If the pacifist accepts their premises—that peace is possible, that individual action matters, that love is effective, and that nonviolence works — it makes sense to forgo national enmities and, equally, to welcome intruders. Without such premises — for instance, if one assumes instead that inevitable human evil cannot be overcome but must be contained — these are illogical and unreasonable actions.

In addition, the exempla suggest some pacifist ambivalence about gender. The heroic exempla offered active countercultural models to women yet also affirmed the culturally entrenched virtue of female self-abnegation. And the interpersonal stories are paradoxically culture-affirming. The idea that love is stronger than violence is profoundly countercultural, yet it leads back to the familiar, questionable idea that female love is the antidote to male aggression.

These are the limitations of narrative thinking. The arguments in the exempla are powerful but indirect and implicit. The exempla do not use the careful theological reasoning of an A. J. Muste or a Georgia Harkness, nor do they rely on the closely reasoned ethical hairsplitting to which pacifist discussions were prone. But, precisely for those reasons, they tell us as much about pacifism's heart as about its mind.

11 "Bad Mother"

MARJORIE SWANN

Someday it may be a disgrace for a pacifist not to be in jail.
—Rosalie Regen, "Bad Mother"

In the summer of 1959 Marjorie Swann, a mother with four children at home, participated in a civil-disobedience action at a nuclear-weapons site near Omaha, Nebraska. She was tried and sentenced to six months in federal prison. The judge who sentenced her said, among other things, "You are a bad mother." An article in a national magazine, and later a play for children and youth, took up the "bad mother" comment as a way to explore the role of women in pacifist activism. Considered alongside Harold Gray's account of his "bad character" forty years earlier, Marjorie Swann's "bad" motherhood illustrates continuities and discontinuities in Protestant pacifist religious culture and raises new questions about it.[1]

Swann's story takes the discussion of pacifist culture in several directions.[2] First, her life, from her late teens on, was immersed in this culture and embodied many of its characteristics. She came from a liberal Protestant background, became a committed pacifist through a youth group, and participated in the whole-life pacifism of cell groups and co-ops. She affirmed a theology of love. Observers drew parallels between her imprisonment and that of conscientious objectors. She participated in the rituals of nonviolent action, and her story was used in pacifist drama.

Second, her action was historically important. It signified the opening of radical protest to women and mothers. At the same time, it anticipated the respectable maternalist pacifism of Women Strike for Peace (WSP) and Another Mother for Peace; maternalist pacifism assumes that women's greater sensitivity, gentleness, and especially their urge to protect their children make them more "naturally" peace-loving than men.[3] Swann's action also prompted conversation about motherhood among pacifists.

Third, Swann's story offers a particularly clear illustration of the ways narratives can be developed and used for particular ends. The magazine article emphasized the theme of family and used the "bad mother" question to raise social issues for a general audience. The play simplified the story with alterations and omissions, partly for dramatic effect but also to generate moral lessons, transforming an event in recent history into a drama and an exemplum.

A Pacifist Life

Marjorie Swann was born in 1921 near Cedar Rapids, Iowa, and spent her early years on the family farm, which was prosperous when her "beloved" grandfather worked it, but was less successful under her father's care.[4] Ultimately the family left the farm for Chicago, where Marjorie entered high school at the age of twelve. Her mother held jobs outside the home in both Iowa and Chicago, leaving Marjorie responsible for much of the housework and care of her younger siblings. She was a superior student, however, and at sixteen won a scholarship to Northwestern University.

She recalled as formative several aspects of those early years. The first was her experience of domestic violence, which she came to associate with international violence early on. Some of her strong reaction against war came from these personal roots.[5] Another source of her reaction was the American Legion. Her father was a member, and she recalled the legionnaires' engaging in a sort of "pseudo-pacifism," in which they denounced war and affirmed that their sons should not have to suffer its horrors.[6] They changed their rhetoric, however, as World War II approached. Meanwhile her mother, as an officer of the women's auxiliary of the Legion, visited veterans' hospitals for the severely disabled. Marjorie, accompanying her, experienced shock and trauma at seeing these effects of war. The final formative influence was more positive: a Methodist Sunday school teacher whose role I discuss more fully later on.

Swann's 1959 summary of these early influences suggests some of the ways the interwar Protestant peace culture—its rhetoric, theology, institutions, practices—could shape a particular life:

> As I grew up, I was taught in Sunday School that God is Love, that *all* men are brothers, that we should love our enemy as ourselves. In school I was taught the futility of World War I, and my high school principal organized an international relations club for high school students which emphasized understanding and good will among the people of all nations, and the necessity of settling international conflict without war. I heard my father and his fellow Legionnaires say many times, "Never will *my* son go to war!" I believed all these things and took them seriously. About the age of 17, I came to understand that the anti-war attitudes of the twenties and thirties was [sic] not sufficient.[7]

Swann embraced the interwar peace movement's ideals of love, good will, and international friendship. Yet, as she matured and historical circumstances shifted, she also came to see their inadequacies. This experience was, of course, common to many interwar peace advocates. But unlike those who qualified or moderated their advocacy, Swann moved into a more fully realized commitment.

Conversion to absolute pacifism was not the earthshaking event for Marjorie Swann that it was for Harold Gray. While at Northwestern, she began attending a youth group at the First Methodist Church of Evanston, Illinois, where the well-known pacifist Ernest Fremont Tittle was pastor. There she discovered that "there was a philosophy that fit my feelings, and then I found out there were organizations that went with the philosophy, and I was just right in it from the first few months that I was in college."[8] Here she found a name and a shape for her experiences and beliefs.[9] Her conviction was rooted in Protestantism but reached beyond it; the 150 to 175 students who belonged to Tittle's group included non-Methodist Protestants, Catholics, and Jews. Of the men, who constituted half the group, thirty-five became conscientious objectors.

Marjorie left Northwestern to work in Washington for the National Committee for Conscientious Objectors. There she met and married Robert Swann, who had served a prison term for refusing military service after his application for legal CO status had been denied. Robert was a builder who devoted much of his work to designing and constructing cooperative and "open housing" (interracial) communities. Barbara, the Swanns' first child, was born in 1945. Over the next fifteen years the family lived in Yellow Springs, Ohio, in southwestern Michigan, in Chicago, and in Trevose, Pennsylvania. In the early 1960s they organized a well-known pacifist community in Voluntown, Connecticut: the New England Committee for Nonviolent Action (NECNVA). As construction work was not steady, Marjorie worked at various jobs during the course of marriage and child-rearing.

The Swanns' life together resembled that of many postwar pacifists: liberal religious beliefs, cooperative living, nonviolent protest, and antiindustrial practices such as "natural" food production. The Swanns were active and committed members of the informal organization Peacemakers, whose public practices of tax resistance and nonviolent direct action took place in a matrix of mutual material aid, broadly bounded theology, mystical practice, and, often, homesteading and folk arts. When they went to Yellow Springs, a center of antiwar and cooperative activity, it was at the invitation of Arthur Morgan, the advocate of decentralized communities. Marjorie worked with Morgan on fund-raising for his Small Communities, Inc., and both Swanns were active in a group connected with the Congress of Racial Equality. Coretta Scott, later King, was a good friend and helped care for the Swanns' children.

In Michigan the Swanns continued to practice their convictions. They lived in a cooperative camp dating from the 1930s, Circle Pines Center, without indoor plumbing but with "a magnificent garden." Marjorie and several friends at one point formed a bakery cooperative, selling wholegrain breads and cereals locally and nationally, with the goal of making healthful food available at a low price. Perhaps it is not surprising that they were unable to make a profit on those terms. The Swanns also performed nonviolent direct action in several causes: they picketed the uraniumprocessing plant at Oak Ridge, Tennessee, and, nearer home, lay down in front of trucks that were spraying DDT, several years before Rachel Carson's *Silent Spring* brought the question of pesticides to public attention.

In 1956 the Swanns moved to the Philadelphia area, where they settled in Concord Park, an open-housing community in Trevose. It was from Concord Park that Marjorie went to the Omaha protest where she was arrested. After her release from prison the Swanns continued their close association with pacifist communities: the family took a six-week trip across the country that included visits to the Celo and Koinonia co-ops and to the Vigil at

Fort Detrick. Following the Polaris Action in Groton, Connecticut, in late 1960, the Swanns moved to Connecticut and founded NECNVA. One visitor, according to Marjorie, said the Voluntown community was "more like a Gandhian ashram than any place I've ever seen." It survived into the 1990s as a loose organization and base for activism, though the Swanns left for other projects in 1971. Robert and Marjorie were divorced ten years later.

Marjorie continued to be active in various phases of the peace movement. During the Vietnam era she was executive secretary of the American Friends Service Committee for New England, raised funds to aid Vietnamese orphans, tried to organize a women's exchange to Vietnam, called on members of the peace delegations in Paris, and fasted, consuming only liquids, for nearly two years. At the time of our interview in 1998 she was, among other things, a member of the executive committee of the AFSC and had just returned from a pacifist conference in Florida. She still maintained firmly that nonviolence "works. I've seen it work."

Religious and Spiritual Life

Many aspects of Marjorie Swann's religious life follow the larger contours of Protestant pacifist culture. She grew up in a Methodist church that was "imbued," she said, with Social Gospel principles. Her nascent pacifism became a strong conviction while she was a student. The university-based Methodism of her young adulthood was not only socially active but theologically broad. It provided a shape and language for her inchoate but strongly intuited pacifism. By the time of the Omaha Action in 1959, she and Robert had become Unitarians and Quaker "fellow travelers"; Marjorie made the latter affiliation official only when she entered the employment of the AFSC. Nor did formal membership mean exclusive commitment for Swann: in 1998 she understood herself to be both a Quaker and a Methodist. Her affiliation, however, was no longer with liberal white Methodism but with an African Methodist Episcopal church. She described her marriage to the Ghanaian Methodist bishop John Edwin as "the first Methodist Quaker African wedding ever." This is, then, a religious life that began, as for so many pacifists, in Social Gospel Protestantism and that moved toward an "umbrella theology" without entirely abandoning Protestantism. It identified with a community less by denomination or confession than by action and compatibility.

Such flexible identification did not exclude a strong and consistent spiritual life. Swann described in retrospect a deeply felt religious basis to her pacifism, going back to the Sunday school of her youth. The teacher who most influenced her was physically deformed, yet "her face radiated love and joy. And she taught us over and over again, 'Jesus loves *everyone*.' She just taught us about love, and about Jesus, and she was really teaching us pacifism, whether she knew it or not." Swann understood the basis of her adult activism to be a continuation of this early experience. She described that basis as follows: "What keeps me going is faith—it's faith in the Holy Spirit who is in *every* one of us *all* over the world. And it's also faith in the human spirit. . . . I believe that though there's the potential for both good and evil in every human being, nonviolence appeals to and evokes the good, and that's why I believe in it, because I've seen it in action."[10] From a foundational emphasis on Jesus and love, Swann came to believe in a universal Holy Spirit. This Spirit complemented and perhaps supported the human ability to do good, but Swann's confidence in human goodness was more qualified than that of earlier Protestant liberals. She affirmed, however, that nonviolence was not only morally right but effective.

Her sensibility of universal connectedness also applied to Swann's embrace of various causes. Over the course of her life these causes included not only long-standing pacifist concerns such as world peace, interracial harmony, and alternative economics, but also issues characteristic of the final third of the century: the environment, land conservation, women's equality, and support of domestic-violence survivors. "I think that all of these things go together," she said. "There's a wholeness about this—that you need to live in that spirit of the earth, the universe, humanity, as a whole, and we need to take care of all of it, we need to serve all of it."[11]

This is a spirituality that seeks to embrace and include. Although, as we will see, radical pacifists did not abandon the habits of scrupulosity and hairsplitting, there is no evidence of this in Swann's religious sensibility. Hers is, however, a spirituality of complete conviction. Even though she expressed some doubts over her choices at Omaha, and spoke generously of those who adopted forms of activism different from hers, her moral stance and life commitment were constant.

Omaha Action

Omaha Action was one of a series of protests organized by the CNVA, the organizational center of radical antinuclear action in the late 1950s.[12] CNVA used Gandhian techniques of nonviolent resistance, including civil disobedience, to call attention to the dangers of nuclear weapons and to try to stop their development. CNVA's actions derived their impact from bodily and dramatic action as well as from reasoned argument.

CNVA's first action, on Hiroshima Day in 1957, was to trespass at Camp Mercury, near Las Vegas, Nevada, where the Department of Defense was conducting atmospheric tests of atomic bombs. In 1958, two private boats, the ketch *Golden Rule* and the yacht *Phoenix*, attracted national attention when they attempted to disrupt nuclear testing in the South Pacific by sailing into the designated area. That summer there were small-scale actions at missile sites in Wyoming, where the first intercontinental ballistic missiles (ICBMs) were to be built, and in Nebraska.

Omaha Action was a more sustained effort to call attention to, and protest against, the construction of ICBMs. Its steering committee planned a five-week project of education and vigils, to begin in mid-June. Whether the action would include civil disobedience was initially an open question, but participants did perform civil disobedience beginning on July 1, and individuals continued such acts after the termination of the original project on July 21.[13]

CNVA struggled with issues of goals, tactics, and leadership. Some of its dilemmas reflected the same kind of scrupulous attention to ethical legitimacy and symbolic meaning that we encountered in the story of Harold Gray. In 1959, for example, CNVA divided over the matter of civil disobedience: should it be a tactic of last resort in a context of peace education and public relations, or was it the sole method drastic enough to address the urgency of the nuclear situation? Further controversies occurred over the legitimacy of nonviolent coercion, as opposed to noncoercive protest and witness; over whether to oppose nuclear testing alone or all manifestations of militarism; and over the relative desirability of acting by group consensus or individual leadings.[14] The prominent radical-pacifist magazines *Liberation* and *Peacemaker* discussed these and other distinctions frequently. For instance, Arthur Harvey, who, like Swann, served a prison term after the Omaha Action, devoted a lengthy article in *Peacemaker* to the distinctions between "cooperating with arrest," "accepting arrest," "not actively resisting arrest," and "noncooperation."[15] Marjorie Swann mentioned, as an example of noncooperation, a woman who was arrested while at home and "refused to get dressed. . . . They finally took her off to jail in her pajamas." Swann herself was unwilling to go that far in 1959.[16]

Marjorie Swann felt impelled to go to Omaha because of the ICBMs.

In her view they constituted "a quantum leap into the nuclear arms race because they made it possible to deliver nuclear weapons . . . all over the world, farther than an airplane could." Her stated intention was to stay in the background, to help with daily chores and press releases, and to return to her family within a few weeks. Once she was there, however, she was increasingly inclined to join in civil disobedience with others who were "crossing the fence." On July 20, she planted some zinnia seeds, walked through the gate, and was arrested. As she anticipated, she spent a few days in the county jail and was then released on probation. Her husband approved of this gesture, and her children tolerated it.[17]

The crucial decision for Swann, as for most participants in the action, was whether to enter the base a second time, thus violating her probation and leaving herself open to a federal prison sentence. She discussed this question with her husband, children, and close friends, and their uncertainty was such that they accumulated some $300 in phone bills in the process. Ultimately Robert expressed support on the family's behalf.

Apparently Marjorie herself continued to feel some uncertainty. On August 6, Hiroshima Day, she began to fast, abstaining from all nourishment. After a period of inner turmoil, she attained on the fourth day a state of "peace of mind [and] moral certainty." "Suddenly I knew what I was there for. . . . I had to continue to protest nuclear armament as often as I could, as strongly as I could, until they stopped me."[18] The next morning, she put on her best dress and hat, which she had brought along for such occasions as church services and speaking engagements. She repeated her trespass until she was arrested again. Later that day she was sentenced to six months in the federal prison for women at Alderson, West Virginia. The main building there was called, ironically, "Jane Addams House." She was released in mid-January with time off for good behavior.[19]

Like Harold Gray, Swann entered upon a course of action that she knew would end in imprisonment. For both, issues of freedom and obedience were worked out in bodily action. When Gray disobeyed orders, his physical freedom was already limited by his position as a conscript. His freedom was moral or internal; he exercised it by choosing whether or not to obey human authority, while at the same time citing obedience to divine authority. Swann and her fellow protesters, on the other hand, were physically free, but felt themselves to be in bondage to the threat of nuclear war. Like Gray, they showed their obedience to higher authority by disobedience to human authority. But, since the human authorities did not recognize the nuclear threat as a form of bondage, Swann and others had to initiate the action of disobedience. Thus Swann's and Gray's actions were parallel, but they arose from differing circumstances and depended upon differing assumptions.

Swann described the rite that preceded and surrounded acts of civil disobedience as a "Greek drama." Each morning would begin with a silent meeting on the hillside below the pacifists' campsite. Then the two or three people—men, except for Swann—who were to go "over the fence" that day would stand up, read statements they had prepared, and walk toward the missile base. The pacifists would line up on one side of the road to support the protesters with cheers, posters, and leaflets. A group of counterprotesters usually took the opposite side of the road. "We invited them to come and sit in the circle with us [at the meeting]," said Swann, "but they never would." The military guards also took part in the drama: they gathered in a group, allowed the protesters to cross the fence, issued a formal warning, and escorted them out. When the protesters crossed the fence again, the guards arrested them. By the tenth of August these daily rites had been attracting local news media and curious onlookers for several weeks, particularly as word of women participants got out.

In Harold Gray's story, ritualization was only hinted at, in such gestures as crossing and not crossing the arms. By Swann's time pacifists had developed public rituals—though they would not have used that term—for initiating and responding to protest. In future years pacifists elaborated on these rituals and developed others.

Arguments about Motherhood

Harold Gray was a young single man when he was imprisoned. Marjorie Swann was a mature married woman and a mother. When her turn came to issue a statement at Omaha, Swann addressed, among other concerns, the matter of her motherhood:

> I know many of you ask why I take this action . . . [p]articularly, why a mother who has the responsibility of raising four children? Do I not feel guilty in disgracing them by going to prison, and in leaving them without my care for a number of months? I can only say that the guilt I feel now, and the pain at leaving my husband and children, is nothing compared to the guilt and pain I will feel—if I am still alive—at seeing my children blasted to death by an H-bomb; die slowly of radiation

sickness; wander starving and in rags down a cratered road as did the children of Korea; or become robots in a militarized and totalitarian state which must obliterate freedom in order to survive.[20]

Robert Swann issued a supporting statement that expanded on these arguments. He argued that, while children might suffer from the absence of their mother, they also suffered harm from the effects of nuclear testing, from anxiety about nuclear war, and from desensitization to the prospect of war, which he called "mass murder." "Perhaps a mother, because she is a mother, may understand and sense more deeply the real meaning of this kind of suffering in a child than any of the rest of us who do not quite share this close sympathy with children," he suggested.[21]

The federal judge who presided at Marjorie Swann's trial and sentencing questioned her particularly closely about her family responsibilities. In the formalized questioning of the court, he asked the ages of her children and whether they were with their father. He asked whether she felt, as he put it, "constrained to spend time in jail when your children are very much in need of your counsel, advice and affection," and she stated that what she did in Omaha was itself "for my children and for your grandchildren." From there the judge's questioning took on a more argumentative tone; he pressed her particularly on her obligation to her two-year-old. Swann remained firm: she knew that her children would miss her, she said, but she was fulfilling an obligation to their "life and freedom in the future" and hoped that they would "understand some day."[22]

Judge Robinson's penultimate question was the crux of the matter for many observers: what would happen if all mothers followed her example? Swann replied as she typically did to this question: "If all mothers would do the same thing as I am doing, which I have called upon all mothers to do, I think that we would have a world based on understanding and love and peace."[23] The judge's remarks typified the opposing argument: that mothers concerned about their children should exercise that concern directly by staying home with them. In the end he observed that he had no choice under the law but to sentence her to prison, even though, he added, "as far as you are personally concerned, Mrs. Swann, my plain duty would be to send you back to those who need you, and need you now." Earlier, Swann and some other protesters had met with Judge Robinson in chambers and tried to explain their concerns and purposes. At that time he made remarks that were later reported as follows: "You are an irresponsible, irrational, stubborn, foolish woman. You are a mother, but you are a bad mother."[24]

Under other circumstances Swann expressed more ambivalence than this courtroom drama would suggest. She readily conceded that not everyone felt able to take such radical action as she did, since individual circumstances and commitments varied. And she admitted to some uncertainty about whether she had in fact done the right thing by leaving her children.[25] But the courtroom drama called for the opposition of two unambiguous positions. In this it prefigured a later dramatic narrative.

The Pacifist Reaction

Later narratives tended to depict the Swanns as a nuclear family coping with a crisis largely alone. In fact, they received considerable support from fellow Peacemakers, and other radical pacifists followed their situation closely. One Peacemaker, Juanita Nelson, moved in with the Swann family to help with housework and child care; others assisted Nelson occasionally. The organization set up a fund to aid the helpers and the family. Unnamed friends maintained a mailing list of some 200 supporters. Numerous encouraging letters were either published or circulated privately. *Peacemaker* reported extensively on the action.[26]

Swann's status as a mother was central to the publicity and discussion among radical pacifists. *Peacemaker* issued offprints of her piece "A Mother at the Gate," with a photograph of her children appended and a sidebar reporting her comments to the judge about motherhood. At least one denominational peace fellowship distributed these to its membership. One woman who had been at Omaha praised Swann for enduring the "cruel separation" from her children for the sake of other children.[27] Another preceded a thoughtful discussion of mothers' responsibility for peace with the observation that Swann had "made many members of her sex stop and consider. . . . Women try to promote the ways of peace among the members of their families, yet remain silent" in public demonstrations.[28] A third recognized "the criticism you must bear from people who feel a woman must forsake her duties as a citizen when she becomes a mother."[29]

On the other hand, few observers outside radical circles took any notice of Swann at all. The *Omaha World-Herald* ceased substantive coverage of the action after July.[30] Neither the *New York Times* nor the *Christian Century* mentioned her in their reports on Omaha. *Fellowship* published bulletins on Omaha in its news section but gave more attention to a mother's letter-writing campaign against war toys in cereal boxes than to Swann's action.³¹

National Exposure

In August 1960 an article titled "You Are a Bad Mother" appeared in *Redbook*, a magazine for young middle-class adults that interspersed serious fiction and commentary with household advice. *Redbook* at that time claimed a circulation of three million. The article carried the discussion of Swann's action beyond pacifist circles to a wider public already concerned about nuclear testing and fallout. Its authors were the socially progressive reporters Jhan and June Robbins, who used the family theme in Marjorie Swann's story to raise, gently, the issues of nuclear weapons, peace, and protest. Their narrative was the source of the later, more one-sided use of Swann's story as an exemplum.

The Robbinses began by emphasizing the Swanns' modest suburban respectability and the judicial system's integrity. They told enough about Marjorie's and Robert's early years to explain their pacifist commitments. They then skipped over the intervening period of activism to focus on a detailed account of Marjorie's experience at Omaha with a sympathetic explanation of her actions.

Unlike the pacifist press, however, the Robbinses also dwelt at some length on the children's distress. The two older daughters—Barbara, who was thirteen at the time, and Judy, who was eleven—were concerned at first with their standing among their peers. Later, under the pressure of coping with housework along with their schoolwork, they grew sullen and uncooperative. Carol, who was six, acted out her distress at home with tears, fights, and nightmares, and made little progress in school. Her father took her to see her mother, hoping that would ease her anxiety, but the trip did not go as planned: the child was carsick all the way, and the family was permitted to see Marjorie only for two short periods totaling an hour and a half.³²

But the Robbinses' conclusions were gently positive. The children's problems, they said, had been addressed successfully, and the Swanns had been strengthened as a family. Marjorie's action had raised others' consciousness and had provoked discussions of the issues. The article concluded with the question the judge had raised: Did Marjorie Swann think that every mother should "protest as radically as she did"? The authors reported her usual reply: "If they did . . . we would have peace. But," she adds in this version, "not everyone is able to do it. There are many ways to work for peace. This is my way." Thus this article—sympathetic toward Swann without being doctrinaire, balanced with respect to the children, alert to fears of nuclear weapons and concerns of family life and citizenship—leaves the audience of parents pondering whether Swann was in fact a "bad mother." Responses in subsequent letters, selected of course by *Redbook* editors, represented a range of positions from full support to complete disagreement.

Drama, Hero, and Exemplum

The *Redbook* article was written for a thoughtful but uncommitted audience. In 1962 elements of the article's narrative were made into a play intended to teach pacifism to children and youth.[33] "Peace plays" were no longer the widespread phenomenon that they had been, but the method of using drama for instruction had survived. This one, not surprisingly, was published by a Quaker religious-education agency.

While the play was not particularly influential, it does offer a revealing snapshot of how and what pacifists were teaching their children in the early 1960s. It brings together several modes of pacifist instruction and cultural transmission—drama, heroic narrative, exemplum—and its content refers to the practical and ritual world of resistance, civil disobedience, and prison.

In the opening scene, the audience encounters an ordinary family in a "cheerfully shabby" home. "Marj" explains her motives for going to Omaha in a dialogue with her rebellious teenage daughter "Barbara." Soon afterward, three pacifist men, including A. J. Muste, arrive to pick up Marj. While waiting for her they discuss the horrors of war and the need for protest. At the conclusion of the scene, the three men and Marj depart, singing, "We ain't gonna study war no more." In the second scene, a disorderly and discouraged household awaits the imminent return of mother and housewife. The telephone rings. The audience then hears "Bob"'s end of a frantic dialogue: "What happened? Oh, no! . . . Don't go, Marjorie. . . . Your place is here. Marj, Marj! . . . She's hung up. She's gone!" He then tells the children that Marj is going to prison rather than coming home, and he describes the actions leading up to this conclusion. The two younger children are upset; the older ones are inclined to disagree with their mother, express a fear of ostracism, and foresee practical problems with housekeeping and child care. However, neighbors appear with casseroles and offers of help. The third scene shows a bedraggled Christmas tree as the family awaits Marj's return home in January. "Carol" expresses a fear that her mother is dead, but is quickly reassured. Marj then arrives to a happy reunion followed by moral discussion. She expresses gratitude to her family and wonders aloud whether she did the right thing to leave them. There is no explicit resolution on this point. Bob poses the question of what would happen if all mothers protested as radically as Marj had done. Her response is hedged with qualifications: the strength of her protest depended on family support, but if others would "sacrifice their comforts" and "protest . . . in whatever way they could," peace would have "a much better chance." The play concludes with Christmas celebrations.

Like other peace plays, this one raises and refutes arguments against Marj's activism. Some objections are fairly readily disposed of. "Can't you find something to protest against around here?" asks Barbara. "Suddenly this seems more important," Marj replies. Judy says after Marj's arrest, "We were afraid nobody would speak to us any more." A neighbor responds, "I don't exactly agree with her, but I admire her courage."

But the central moral questions of the play are treated with more subtlety than those in prewar works. In Scene 2 Bob says, "[The judge] called her an irresponsible, stubborn, foolish woman, and a '*bad mother.*'. . . She told him she loved her children dearly, but that . . . goodnight kisses are less important right now than stopping the H-bomb." A little later he quotes her as saying, "Pretty soon it may be a disgrace for a pacifist *not* to be in jail." The children, however, are never fully reconciled to this point of view, and, as we have seen, Marj herself expresses some ambivalence in the concluding scene. As a teaching device, then, the drama leaves some room for discussion. As ritual it suggests the sober sensibility of the nuclear age. In place of elaborated symbolism it offers domestic realism; in place of triumphalism, a note of cautious ambivalence, even while it celebrates an act of courage.

As an exemplum—a model of the pacifist life—it raises new issues. According to this model the children of pacifists would have to be reconciled to the prospect of sudden parental abandonment, even if temporary, and to the prospect of their own imprisonment if they adhere to their parents' values. That is, it appears that a group of ordinary suburban children lose contact with their mother through an act that is essentially impulsive, even if morally informed. Moreover, they themselves face the prospect of being "disgraced" if they do not follow her path.[34] The exemplum also asks both children and adults to consider which view of motherhood—giving "goodnight kisses" or stopping the bomb—is more valid for a pacifist. In the context of a social and religious group already committed to pacifism, it would be difficult to argue for goodnight kisses.

Like the children of sectarians, who have historically been taught to expect forms of social exclusion up to and including martyrdom, pacifists' children were taught to expect consequences of "nonconformity" that might include early self-reliance and peer-group rejection.[35] We know little so far about the effects of such teachings—and actions—on real children, but anecdotal evidence suggests that this consciousness of difference strengthened some and devastated others. Carol Swann, who showed signs of trouble as a child, as an adult fully supports her parents' choices. She said, "I consider my parents heroes. I was given an incredible gift, brought up in a political action center. I thrived. [I] was included, adored, I had a blast."[36] Judy Kaplan and Linn Shapiro's insightful work on "red diaper babies" has noted the variety of children's responses to growing up in an alternative political community. Some throve, others were traumatized; some families offered warmth and support while others used political rhetoric to mask dysfunction.[37] Children from communities of religious outsiders similarly report complex interactions between exceptionalism, family dynamics, fear, and strength.[38]

As a heroic narrative, the play places Marjorie Swann among antiheroic heroes of peace such as those in Allan Hunter's exempla, and it adds new comments on gender and motherhood. It differs from the magazine article—and from the historical incident—in being cast as a traditionally "female" narrative, in which a woman who becomes active in the public sphere justifies her action by invoking something outside her control, such as an overwhelming impulse, an unforeseen opportunity, or the importunities of others.[39] The play treats Swann's decision to risk prison in this way: her decision arises unexpectedly and in isolation out of her fast, with no prior action or arrest, without consultation with her husband and friends, and without previous thought.[40]

In keeping with this narrative framework, the play bends over backward to show that Swann was in every way a "good" mother by conventional standards. In this respect it insists more strongly on conventional gender roles than did the article or the Swanns themselves. As it opens, "Marj" is darning her husband's socks. Indeed, the play depicts this as her last act before leaving for Omaha. In the accompanying dialogue, she differentiates her own role from "the men's"—not from "the more active members" or "the committee" or "the unencumbered"—and describes her intention to be an inconspicuous, modest helper. After her return from prison, the family presents her with the incongruous Christmas gift of a negligee—which, the stage directions add, "transforms her into a queenly woman."[41] Thus this character conforms in every way to female stereotypes and traditional narratives. As a pacifist she expresses some ambivalence, but as a woman she is unambiguous.[42]

The play's suggestions about pacifism and gender arise from this conformity. Women should be, or at least can be, both good activists and good mothers, or, to put it another way, good and bad mothers at the same time. Just as the male-gendered "hero of peace" is both heroic and antiheroic, the pacifist mother is both a traditional mother and an antimother: she darns socks, loves her children, and goes to jail. Potential tension between these two roles is resolved by the female-gendered shape of the narrative and by the maternalist nature of the woman's concern for the wider world—solutions with long precedent in American women's activism.

A Harbinger of Things to Come

Shortly after Swann's action, an admirer called her "the first woman conscientious objector to go to federal prison."[43] This statement marks a significant moment in the widening of the definition of conscientious objection between World War I and the Vietnam period. Harold Gray and his generation argued for conscientious objection as a cross-denominational Christian position, not merely the particular witness of a few sects. Other men and organizations argued for a still broader definition that would require no formal religious basis at all. Marjorie Swann's action extended the definition of conscientious objection, decisively and pivotally, to include women.[44]

Women had already been involved in all phases of peace work, of course, from the relative ease of letter-writing to the hard work of homesteading. Some pacifist women during World War II went further, seeking to express and live out their conscientious objection by working with Civilian Public Service. Others, like Swann herself, worked closely with released COs. But these women's actions were voluntary and finally indirect. Since the government did not demand their direct participation in military service, they did not have the option of direct refusal, disobedience, or interference with conscription or war. Direct resistance as part of pacifism for women awaited the development of nonviolent direct action tactics.[45]

Nonviolent direct action offered a method of witnessing to nonviolence in which women were not mere auxiliaries. It was available not only to women, of course, but to men who were beyond draft age or were otherwise exempt from conscription. In addition, it was independent of the nation's involvement in any given war or conflict. This was appropriate as the nature of war began to change from formally declared, exclusively military engagements to "total war" and continuous low-level threat. Going to prison, which pacifists continued to regard as a high spiritual calling, now became, in theory, equally possible for women and men.

Swann was not the first pacifist woman to be imprisoned: Dorothy Day and others were jailed for resisting civil-defense drills in the 1950s, and at Omaha Action, Erica Enzer served a term in Douglas County Jail for obstructing a truck on its way to Fort Mead. Swann's term in federal prison, however, more directly paralleled the experience of male COs and was a clearer symbol of resistance at the national level.

Swann also prefigured a different kind of women's activism. In 1961 the new movement Women Strike for Peace began to harness both the real and the symbolic power of suburban housewives in public action against nuclear weapons and war. The image of the respectable housewife was part of the larger maternalist ideology that WSP invoked. Maternalist pacifists argued that there was a natural association between motherhood and peace, and they sought to extend this association into the public realm.[46] Amy Swerdlow summarized this position with the words "we had to leave the home in order to save it"[47] — exactly the argument Swann had used. Both claimed to be unaware that the maternalist argument had been invoked before on behalf of peace and other social causes.[48]

Like Swann, many members of WSP had histories of political involvement. After World War II, as marriage and motherhood were idealized, they had turned away from public activism. By 1961, however, many were growing restless, especially as their children grew older.[49] The rise of antinuclear activism thus coincided with the gradual emergence of a generation of educated, politically aware women from the most intense period of their child-rearing. Swann was the first public figure to exemplify this trend.

As Swerdlow put it, "The image projected by WSP of respectable middle-class, middle-aged ladies, wearing white gloves and flowered hats, picketing the White House and protesting to the Kremlin to save their children ... helped to legitimize a radical critique of the Cold War and U.S. militarism."⁵⁰ Swann sensed the effectiveness of similar imagery in 1959. Before her second trespass she put on her best dress and a hat. She chose to walk through the gate instead of climbing the fence as the men did. She made these gestures, she said, because "I thought of myself as a mother who was representing the children. And I knew that the photographers and TV cameras were going to be there; and in those days we mostly wore dresses. . . . I just felt that that would symbolize what *I* was there for: as a mother, and concerned about children."⁵¹

Marjorie Swann's action anticipated the innovations of WSP by two years. An educated woman from an activist background, as well as a wife and a mother, Swann used a maternalist argument to justify leaving her own children, temporarily, for public action. She deliberately invoked the symbolism of suburban maternal respectability, and the legend that followed her highlighted that respectability even more.

MARJORIE SWANN OPENED UP to women a realm of witness previously available only to men. At the same time, she called on an image and ethic unique to women. Her life departed from standard female narrative, yet her story was eventually told precisely in the rhetoric of such narratives. Her action fed existing discussions, within and outside pacifism, of the relationship of motherhood to peace and to action outside the home. She also stood at the beginning of a revival of maternalist pacifism.

Like the members of cooperative farms, Marjorie Swann negotiated a lived radical dissent with the varied and sometimes conflicting calls of family, society, and religion. Her story unfolds in many layers: the place in pacifism of women, of mothers, and of gender constructs; the effects of activism on the children of activists, and the effects on them of teaching activism; and the development of pacifist narratives and the purposes for which they can be used.⁵² It proceeds through layers of ritual: the "Greek drama," the courtroom, the dramatic reenactment. It calls on the imagery of the farm, the prison, and the mother.

From Harold Gray to Marjorie Swann there is an arc of continuity amid discontinuities. The two have in common a flexible theology deeply rooted in mainline Protestant Christianity, a worldview fully oriented to pacifism, careful attention to ethical and tactical detail, and a willingness to associate other forms of social action with pacifism. They are separated, however, by the turning point of pacifism around 1940. After World War I, Gray participated in a broadly based, optimistic, largely antiwar movement; Swann saw the end of that movement and joined a minority focused on complete nonviolence and a dedicated mode of living. Swann, unlike Gray, participated in the development of nonviolent direct action after Gandhi. Both were shaped by modernity, but Swann's life questioned it as Gray's did not. Since Gray and Swann differed in age and sex, they faced different opportunities and limitations.

Swann's story also raises questions about the consequences of activism for children, questions too far-reaching to answer here. Maternalist pacifism, of course, insisted that there was no conflict between mothers' and children's interests, and pacifist folktales declined even to raise the questions. But life stories suggest somewhat more ambiguity. The experimental psychologist Steven Pinker has argued that the biological, evolutionary interests of parents and offspring can diverge, and he has suggested that such conflict is "unacknowledged in our public discourse about children."[53] It would be useful, at least heuristically, to extend the idea of natural conflict into the social realm — to acknowledge, for the sake of children, that a mother's actions may have painful consequences for them, and yet not to assess the mother's actions by those consequences alone.

Epilogue

Within a few years of Marjorie Swann's action, American pacifism moved from abeyance structures into a large-scale movement reacting against the Vietnam War. That movement invoked an ideology of love, a spiritual practice of meditation, a folk aesthetic, and, later, a renewed back-to-the-land movement. It insisted on consistency of word and action, and its members were confident of basic human goodness and human improvability. The peace movement of the 1960s had many sources, of course, but it undoubtedly drew on the abeyance structures of post–paradigm shift pacifism—the older pacifist organizations like the FOR and the AFSC; the earlier generation of pacifists like Gregg, Swann, and Muste; the comprehensive alternatives embodied in places like the Highlander Folk School, Koinonia Farm, and Pendle Hill; the print community that circulated not only Tolstoy's and Gandhi's works but also those of Brother Lawrence and Thomas Kelly; nonviolent protest groups like CNVA; and the religious resources of modernized "peace churches." Quakers emerged as a strong force in the peace movement and an essential resource for conscientious objectors. Mainline Protestants like William Sloane Coffin became strong public voices in the antiwar movement. Many individuals and congregations worked at the grassroots level. Their history remains to be recovered.

In this book, I have sought to show that pacifism between World War I and the Vietnam era was a multidimensional culture rooted in the particulars of its time and context. I have also sought to lay out some particulars of that culture in all their overlapping complexity. I have argued that cross-denominational mainline Protestantism was the center of religious pacifism after World War I, and that this Protestant pacifist culture underwent a paradigm shift around the beginning of World War II, primarily between 1939 and 1942. The paradigm shift carried forward many elements of the existing culture, but realigned them and added newer cultural materials. I have also argued that new-paradigm pacifism moved from a mainstream position to a sectarian and marginal one; from an embrace of modernity to skepticism about it; and from a Christian center to a pacifist one.

PACIFISM WAS NOT ONLY an ethical stance, but a culture. To become a pacifist was to embrace a social world with an array of assumptions, texts, artifacts, and practices—a folk group with its own vernacular. Midcentury Protestant pacifists shared reading and discussion, ritualized and bonded, trained for peace, theologized, sought spiritual sustenance, acted out their commitment, developed a visual language out of biblical imagery, told stories that produced a religious worldview, created their own heroes, first with and then against the majority culture, lived in protest, lived apart, lived as examples, and sought to live with integrity.

Historians of pacifism have tended to systematize or schematize their subject in order to construct coherent narratives, but it is important to remember that lived pacifism was not schematized. The elements of pacifist culture overlapped like circles in a Venn diagram. David Dellinger's urban co-op called on both the Student Christian Movement and the Catholic Worker for help. Quakers made free use of mainline Protestant literature and hymnody, mainliners studied mysticism, and peace stories were passed around in both groups. The image of swords beaten into plowshares appeared in hymns and parade floats, sculptures and cooperative farms. The religious ideal of a "way of life" manifested itself in theological discussion, conscientious objection, and material culture.

Pacifism also illustrates the way cultural formation occurred in mainline Protestantism. The cultural particulars of the mainline are only beginning to be understood, largely because its normative status has tended to render them invisible. Pacifism provides both a cultural case study and a window into mainline "piety"—affective, interior religiosity, and religiosity as practiced, especially by everyday people in everyday life. The most ordinary Protestant materials—Bible texts, worship services, hymns, church architecture, mission drama—became the vehicles of a very particular language, full of allusions and internal references that meant peace, pacifism, and commitment to those who used and heard that language.

But pacifism was not only a microcosm of the mainline. Pacifists sought greater spiritual intensity, whole-life practices, and witness that involved the body as well as the soul. The mainline—indeed any mainstream church—necessarily lives with a degree of compromise and paradox, but the all-consuming commitments of pacifism, of Jesus' way of life as they saw it, could not compromise.

WHILE IT IS NOT surprising that Protestant pacifism changed in response to the onset of war, the traditional assessment that pacifism "turned inward" is not entirely accurate.[1] Certainly circumstances muted pacifism's public voice. But the changes in thought, practice, and social organization that occurred between 1939 and 1942 had authentic inner trajectories; much in the new face of pacifism was continuous with earlier ideas and practices. This is why the change is best seen as a paradigm shift, a reordering of existing cultural materials in a new pattern.

The widespread post–World War I peace movement derived most of its religious ideas and language from hegemonic mainline Protestantism. The mainline was not monolithic, however: pacifists built on long liberal and evangelical traditions, turn-of-the-century modernism, and the Social Gospel's blend of confidence and critique. They also drew on the history and practices of Protestant missions, often with personal connections.

For a host of reasons, however, the mainline ultimately turned away from absolute pacifism. Critics either have attributed this change to Niebuhrian "Christian realism" or have questioned the depth of mainliners' commitment to peace. In reality there was probably more moral ambivalence than either narrative would suggest. The Great Depression and the increasing pace of international conflict through the 1930s generated unease about modernist progressivism. Genuine revulsion at fascism, differences in applying scriptural norms to present circumstances, and concerns for institutional viability also played a part. Neo-orthodox theology provided the intellectual justification for change, but was not its only source.

The pacifist culture already formed in mainline Protestantism then began to find its own way. In some aspects this development resembled the historical process of sect formation. Pacifists developed separate institutions and communities, stringent expectations about ethics and behavior, internal rituals and ways of bolstering group solidarity, and material culture. There was a moral center—pacifism itself—and an underlying element of pure faith.

Yet the pacifist community, marginalized though it was, did not quite fit the pattern of a sect. It allowed multiple belonging: mainline pacifists survived in denominational fellowships and college Christian associations, and among the clergy, as well as among individuals located under the broad theological umbrellas of pacifist groups. In addition, many members blended into an existing religious structure—liberal Quakerism—rather than inventing their own.

This suggests that other models for the formation of new religious groups may be in order. I have suggested that the emergent fundamentalism of the early twentieth century is one such model. I would also like to return to the concept of the folk group. In this context, "a demonstration of belonging lies in the expression of shared tradition as much as it does in intellectual pronouncements of philosophy and personal opinion."[2] It is likely that subcultures like this abound within established religious bodies, and they deserve further attention from historians.

The pacifist response to the pressures of the 1930s was not only structural. It also reflected a struggle with modernity. This struggle was not unique to pacifism: Americans' unease with the modern world has manifested itself, at various times, in such diverse forms as Craftsman architecture and nostalgia for European Catholicism, wilderness camps and recurring back-to-the-land movements. Mainline Protestantism's modulation of modernist theology also partook of this impulse. As the mainline adjusted its course in the direction of pragmatic engagement with the world, however, pacifists moved decisively toward resisting that world.

Pacifist culture enacted this differentiation in many dimensions: in intimate communities, in a sense of outsiderhood, in an imagery of the poor and the humble. Alternatives appeared in production and labor, in ritual dance and song, in experiential rather than rational spirituality, and in the symbolic and practical value ascribed to farmers, land, and nature. Resistance did not, however, mean rejection: pacifists created their alternatives with the aim of changing and saving the world, not of withdrawing from it.

In the early 1940s, the evangelical sensibility that had been taken for granted in interwar mainline pacifism largely disappeared, except for an interest in making and keeping converts. It seems likely that this disappearance reflects the growing separation between evangelicals and liberals associated with the resurgence of fundamentalism. The founding of the National Association of Evangelicals in 1942–43 was a landmark in this process, a staking out of conservative territory separate from the mainline.

Pacifists, meanwhile, who were already theologically flexible, were moving in the opposite direction, toward "umbrella" rather than specifically Christian theology. The influence of Hinduism and Buddhism on American pacifist spirituality is well-documented, but Protestant liberalism was a homegrown source of this spirituality. Its emphases on the humanity of Jesus, the importance of the present world, and the value of every person led naturally toward theological and institutional openness.

Quakerism was particularly significant in the pacifist paradigm shift. Here was a denomination with a tradition of absolute pacifism, and a distinctive "way of life," that nonetheless spoke the language of liberal and modernist Protestant theology. This interdenominational cross-fertilization was central to its success. By the 1930s, Quakers' theological conversation with liberal Protestantism had already been going on for a generation. A new group of spokesmen, following in the path of Rufus Jones and accompanied by the flowering of new institutions, including independent meetings and the Wider Quaker Fellowship, brought an influx of liberal converts while consolidating a separate Quaker identity as pacifists and mystics. Liberal Quakers' emphasis on divine immanence, inward spiritual experience, and activism left room to modulate Christian doctrinal language and belief without abandoning Christian identity—although the question of Christianity versus "universalism" has since become a pressing one in Quakerism.

As mainline Protestantism ceased to identify broadly with pacifism, the "historic peace churches"—Quakers, Mennonites, and Brethren, who had always maintained testimonies against bearing arms—became a classification separate from the "mainstream churches." Where prewar pacifists had argued that pacifism was the only true Christian attitude to war, after about 1940 pacifism came to be identified in the public mind with particular denominations rather than with all Christians. Protestant pacifism, however, was not coterminous with any one denomination, either before or after the paradigm shift.

What, then, did pacifism retain of Protestantism? Much in the culture carried with it an essentially Protestant shape. It relied on the word in the sense of particular biblical texts, and also in the sense of extensive verbal discourse. It privileged the Gospels and the person of Jesus over doctrine and ecclesial tradition. It located authority in a community of believers, rather than in historical or hierarchical institutions. It was modernist in its progressivism and its openness to new information, but was ambivalent about technological and nationalistic expressions of modernity. More broadly, it reflected the optimism, practical this-worldliness, sense of mission, and often strenuous perfectionism that are common in American Protestantism, along with a detailed self-scrutiny familiar from Puritanism and its offshoots. And it reflected characteristic tensions—the vision of the good society from which the present world has strayed; the incorporation of both conversion and nurture; and the critique of contemporary conditions by both reasoned and experiential means.

Pacifism maintained a particularly strong tension around voluntary suffering, or in Christian terms, crucifixion. Suffering was implied in *imitatio Christi*, and some pacifists embraced or least accepted it—the CO in military prison, the cell group preparing for persecution, the would-be mystic crucifying the self. Crucifixion was also familiar as an image for the suffering other—the soldier, the war victim, the laborer. Yet at the same time, many pacifist cultural expressions minimized suffering, insisting that peace was possible, love was a force, nonviolence was effective, and good will would prevail. This tension, usually unspoken, is perhaps the deepest unresolved contradiction in Protestant pacifism.

And there remained, it seems, a felt need for a more explicitly Christian pacifism. In the 1950s some pacifist communards and individuals joined the Bruderhof, long a subject of interest among pacifists. In later years, the Catholic Worker gradually displaced liberal Quakerism as the icon of lived pacifism; at this writing, the pacifist and liberal press routinely refer to its founder, Dorothy Day, alongside Gandhi and Martin Luther King as a model of the committed life. Both the Bruderhof and the Worker are communities of theological as well as ethical "high demand," contrasting with the flexibility of liberal belief.

The distinctive nature of pacifist culture became more apparent with the paradigm shift. But pacifism had always had an element of exceptionalism, in that it required a change in world view in order to be understood. As Muriel Lester put it, "Once you see it, you can't unsee it."[3] It was as impossible for Harold Gray's father to understand why his son would not take an army desk job as it was for Marjorie Swann's judge to understand why she would leave her children. Tales of deflected armies and of intruders rendered harmless by love required a leap of faith to be taken seriously. However compelling the reasoned arguments, pacifist commitment had an intuitive and even mysterious element that in theological language might be called vocation.

SO MUCH FOR WHAT we have done. But any work of this kind necessarily leaves many interesting avenues of inquiry unexplored. I want to suggest a few areas that seem particularly promising for extending our understanding of pacifist cultures.

To begin with, there are many suggestive parallels between Roman Catholic and Protestant pacifism. Historians of the pacifist Catholic Worker movement have tended to treat the movement as an isolated and spontaneous phenomenon, and historians of pacifism have tended to notice Catholic peacemakers' public actions but not their ethos. Yet it is likely that there were common sources to both movements and that they had common interests. It is clear, for example, that Dorothy Day was acquainted with Protestant activism through the FOR, Pendle Hill, and other sources, and that at least some Protestant communards were acquainted with the Catholic Worker. At the same time, genuine differences between Catholic and Protestant pacifisms support the argument that pacifist cultures are historically contingent. For example, Roman Catholic ethicists and activists have argued since the 1980s for a "consistent ethic of life," which associates war with abortion as moral evils. It was, and is, rare for liberal Protestant pacifists to draw this connection.[4]

A large pacifist literature deserves recognition as a force in shaping twentieth-century peace culture. Some works, of course, are still well known and popular, especially those of Thoreau, Tolstoy, and Gandhi. Others circulated widely but are now forgotten—*Religion Renounces War*; *Hey! Yellowbacks!*; *Halt! Cry the Dead*; *I'm an Ill-Adjusted Veteran*. Cadoux and Macgregor were foundational in pacifist theological thinking. I have given only marginal attention to A. J. Muste, one of the most eloquent and elegant apologists for Christian nonviolence. The texts I name at the beginning of chapter 7—on mysticism, stories, cooperatives, and training for peace—crystallize a historical moment. *Speak Truth to Power* articulated a theology and politics of nonviolence for the 1950s and 1960s.

Many of the figures I have mentioned would make rewarding subjects of biographical study. Colorful personalities all, they should also be integrated into narratives of reform, dissent, religion, popular iconography, and gender studies. Muriel Lester's life calls for attention alongside those of Jane Addams and Dorothy Day. Kirby Page's life illuminates a forgotten practice of liberal social evangelism. Richard Gregg was a pivotal figure in twentieth-century pacifism. Toyohiko Kagawa's life touches on mission history, liberal piety and mysticism, and the tension between peace and justice. Pierre Cérésole, André Trocmé, and Philippe Vernier were pacifist icons of the 1940s and 1950s. The tireless and influential Florence Brewer Boeckel, of whom little is known; women like Sarah Cleghorn, who defy simple assessment; educators like Imogene McPherson and John and Elizabeth Lobingier; communards such as Arthur Morgan and Morris Mitchell; and the creative and original Protestant mystics offer further opportunities. We might also inquire more deeply into the way social groups like families and congregations have negotiated pacifism.

Many questions about gender and Protestant pacifism remain to be addressed. Very basic information about the numbers of women in mixed-sex peace organizations, and their function and work there, has not yet been compiled. Religious life in women's peace organizations—including unofficial "sacred" narratives, hagiographic stories, iconography, and ritual—also warrants attention. Marjorie Swann's story raises questions about whether scrupulosity was a preoccupation of men more than women.

Nor have gender issues been fully explored in relation to pacifist men. Their refusal to fight was, of course, a major transgression against ideals of masculinity. While some embraced the transgression, the more common response seems to have been to identify pacifism with male-gendered virtues like courage and strength. Despite Richard Gregg's encouragement of knitting, there was little overt questioning of gender ideology or gender roles in pacifist circles. Indeed, recent scholarship has suggested that, after World War II, the movement itself was increasingly gendered male.[5] This idea should be evaluated in light of earlier phases of the movement as well as later ones.

More work remains to be done on pacifist visual imagery. What pictures might a pacifist minister display in his study? What adorned the dining rooms of pacifist cooperative farms? How were word and image connected on picket signs and posters, and did their relationship change over time? What was the nature of the viewer's imaginative engagement in the image—did the image offer inspiration, signify the presence of peace, constitute action against war? It would be well worth asking how visual art functioned in Protestant pacifist spirituality, and how the culture appropriated, generated, and assigned meanings to pictures.

The extensive and varied ritual enactments of pacifism also call for further study. At least as far back as World War I, pacifists were developing formalized performances and symbolic gestures. Walking, food, and food deprivation accumulated many layers of meaning in the decades following.

Particularly important are the ritual aspects of going to jail. Again, pacifist protest that risked imprisonment went back at least to World War I, but jail took on increasing importance with the rise of nonviolent direct action. The playwright Rosalie Regen's comment that "someday it [might] be a disgrace for a pacifist *not* to be in jail" was prophetic: at this writing imprisonment seems to be a necessary part of almost any left-wing social protest. Staughton Lynd makes "breaking the law for conscience' sake" part of the very definition of nonviolence; an antinuclear activist writes frankly about "going to jail on purpose"; a gay-rights group disrupts Protestant denominational conventions with the aim of getting arrested; even activist bicyclists expect to be arrested on "car-free day" in Boston.[6] The central importance of ritual imprisonment indicates that a long history and a complex body of ritual await unfolding.

A DIFFERENT KIND OF question also remains. Does an academic study such as this one have anything to say to practitioners and activists? In part, of course, the answer must be left to activists themselves. Still, I would like to offer a few reflections from the perspective of a historian and an observer.

In the very earliest stages of this work, one of the questions that led me toward the idea of culture was why pacifism seemed to be associated with a host of other commitments. In the rhetoric and practice of the 1960s and 1970s, absolute pacifism also implied fighting racism, working to abolish poverty, assisting the poor, and, often, making particular choices of dress and lifestyle. At this writing, liberal peace activists tend also to support gay and lesbian rights, free immigration, and environmentalist action. The meaning of nonviolence has expanded over time as well—from personal behavior, to political tactics, to resisting all social and economic inequities. Thus a commitment to nonviolence now reaches into almost every action of daily living. My intention here is not to judge the value or importance of these issues, but to ask why the meaning of pacifism seems to extend so far.

To some degree, of course, the reasons are historical. In the 1920s, and indeed before, pacifists were concerned with economic relations. In the early 1940s they added race to their leading concerns; the FOR was instrumental in fostering nonviolent action for civil rights. Pacifists' relationship to the natural world, in Protestant liberalism and in rural cooperatives, also has a long history. Concern with gay rights, on the other hand, is a substantial change from the 1940s and 1950s, as the cases of Bayard Rustin and Gerald Heard make clear.

There is also an inner logic to the extension of meaning, as we saw in the case of cooperatives. Whether the pacifist is seeking to follow Jesus in every aspect of life, or to eradicate the causes of war and violence, or to treat all humanity as brothers and sisters, he or she soon becomes unable to see war as an isolated problem or pacifism as an isolated commitment. Personal decision then seems inextricably tied to human relations, social systems, and global politics and economics. This is perhaps one reason why mainline churches and freestanding peace organizations, at this writing, often define their concern as "peace and justice" rather than simply peace or pacifism.

But all this has created some problems of its own. The first is that the cluster of issues now associated with pacifism comes very close to general left-wing politics, and naïve or inexperienced activists might find it easy to confuse the two—to assume that being a pacifist means belonging to a particular political party, for example, or supporting the liberal cause célèbre of the moment. The second is that advocates of "peace and justice" very often seem to overlook the possibility of conflict between these two goals. This conflict was a crucial issue during World War II, as it had been a decade earlier in the FOR. Third, embracing a cluster of issues can diffuse energy; any focus on peace as such can get lost amid the need to change the world on so many fronts. Some admirable people can, like Kirby Page, sustain this kind of energy. But many would do well to heed Thomas Kelly's warning about trying to do too much and ending in strain and despair.

Above all, the extension of meaning tends to create a set of unexamined assumptions. In one sense, of course, these assumptions are the very fabric of pacifist culture. But any culture is selective; its cultural filters obscure as much as they illuminate. For all the depth and richness with which a culture sustains its particular constellation of beliefs and practices, there are others it will not see. Peace and nonviolence organizations, for example, have rarely attended closely to domestic violence, or to urban gang warfare, or to the violent imagery in video games, movies, television, and pornography. I do not want to suggest that generous activists should add even more issues to their already full agendas. I would, however, invite pacifists to be aware of their presuppositions and priorities—to think anew about what conduces to violence, what threatens human safety, and what transgresses against human dignity.

I would also caution against reflexive calls to "keep religion out of politics." This admonition surfaced with increasing frequency as the religious right gained political influence in the early twenty-first century. But I have sometimes wondered whether liberals in the conversation remembered earlier ways of connecting religion with politics. Religious conviction has in other times been directed against the hasty turn to war as a solution and against nuclear weapons. It has vigorously supported the right of conscience and has insisted on care for the poor and weak. Religious conviction has even meant the plain righteousness that does not require extraordinary sacrifice—telling the truth, charging fair prices, allowing rest. It is not at all clear that these convictions belong outside the realm of government.

Finally, I would ask activists to consider the consequences of parents' moral commitments for children. Since there is no consensus about the effects of parents' choices on children in such instances as the employment of both parents or the absence of a parent, there is not likely to be any more consensus on the effects of parents' moral conformity or nonconformity. Nor do I mean to suggest that parents should refrain from acting on moral commitments while their children are young. But the issue should at least be articulated and the interests of children weighed in the balance, as indeed the church has done for many years in considering whether religious activists such as priests and missionaries ought to have families. More specifically, the consequences of this particular set of moral commitments—pacifism and nonviolence—for children deserve careful consideration. A related question is the extent to which children should be expected to take risks for social change. One such child, Ruby Bridges, is already well on the way to becoming a myth.[7]

IT IS SAID THAT generals are always fighting the last war, and it is worth asking whether the same observation is true of pacifists. Reasoned internationalism was not an adequate response to Hitler. Nonviolent protest did not stop the United States' involvement in Vietnam. Experience with antinuclear activism left pacifists baffled over "humanitarian" intervention in Somalia.

And Richard Gregg's comment that "honest and intelligent pacifists are troubled by a sense of ineffectiveness" remains timely. This sense, I think, recurs over and over in pacifist history, and it is the ground of both attrition and innovation. Some erstwhile pacifists ultimately turn to other causes or methods, as did the labor activists who left the FOR in 1934 and the Black Power advocates who grew impatient with the nonviolent civil rights movement in the late 1960s. Others evolve new modes of action, as when the Berrigan brothers and the Plowshares group moved from marches and demonstrations to symbolic destruction of weapons. The limits of reasoned discourse in the 1980s generated responses as different as the meditative visualizations of Beyond War and the embodied risk-taking of Witness for Peace.

It is too soon to draw any conclusions about the U.S. involvement in the Middle East, despite some suggestive historical parallels. Although opposition to the Iraq war is widespread at this writing, the peace movement remains diffuse and decentralized, and no popular antiwar movement has yet appeared. Pacifism seems to be awaiting a creative gesture, a prophetic figure, or a new set of tactics. There is no lack of suggestions: David Cortright, Scott Ritter, Glen Stassen, and many others have offered proposals, while Stanley Hauerwas, Walter Wink, and others provide theological arguments.[8] For ways into activist cultures, one need look no further than *Fellowship* or *Sojourners* magazines. Many small-scale programs—from Christian Peacemakers, placing their bodies in war zones, to the weekly vigilers on my local town common—continue their efforts. But none of these sparks has yet caught fire. Thus far, the most conspicuous iconic figure of opposition to the war has been Cindy Sheehan, who once again invoked the maternal ideal. Yet her protest arose, not from any conviction of pacifism, nor from any opposition to war in general, but out of a personal and immediate situation.

Some years ago the Bread and Puppet Theater reinvented the pageant.[9] Masks and symbolic figures were created out of found materials which themselves carried symbolic weight. Ordinary people, "garbagemen" and "washerwomen," also played important roles. The pageants enacted suffering, rescue, and redemption, on a cosmic scale. Afterward, the audience shared bread; in the early years it was passed around from hand to hand like communion. None of this was churchly religion: indeed the theater often satirized religious institutions. Nor was it tactical action; it was a ritual of encouragement and belonging.

But, as in the Peaceable Kingdom images, the achievement of peace was here moved out of the realm of work, striving, struggle, information, and practical matters and into the realm of transcendence. The effort of peacemaking is always worth making, yet it remains, so far, unfulfilled. Perhaps its best hope lies in the eschatological vision — the confidence that the ultimate disposition of human affairs, however arrived at, really will resemble the improbable companionship of wolves and lambs.

Appendix   HYMN TEXTS

THE SON OF GOD GOES FORTH FOR PEACE

The Son of God goes forth for Peace
Our Father's love to show;
From war and woe He brings release,
O, who with Him will go?
He strikes the fetters from the slave,
Man's mind and heart makes free;
And sends His messengers to save
O'er ev'ry land and sea!

The Son of God goes forth for Peace,
That men like brothers live,
And all desire the other's good,
And other's sin forgive.
He turns our spears to pruning hooks,
Our swords to ploughshares warm,
And war no more its death-blast brings,
Nor men their brothers harm!

The Son of God goes forth for Peace,
Nor lands nor pow'r to gain;
He seeks to serve, to love, to lift,—
Who follows in his train?
A glorious band, in ev'ry age,
In spite of scorn and pain,

True sons of God, His peace have made;
Who follows in their train?

Now let the world to Peace be won,
And ev'ry hatred slain;
Let force and greed be overcome
And love supreme remain!
Let justice rule in all the earth,
And mercy, while we live,
Lest we — forgiven much — forget
Our brother to forgive!

We send our love to ev'ry land —
True neighbors would we be;
And pray God's Peace to reign in them,
Where'er their homeland be!
O God, to us may grace be giv'n
Who bear the dear Christ's name,
To live at peace with ev'ry man,
And thus our Christ acclaim!

PEACE HYMN OF THE WORLD

Mine eyes have seen the splendor of the promise of the Lord,
Men are beating swords to plowshares in accordance with His word,
The music of His footsteps by the nations now is heard,
His peace is marching on!

(Chorus)
Peace and friendliness forever,
Peace and friendliness forever,
Peace and friendliness forever,
Good Will and Peace to men.

Lift high the shining banners with Good Will in every fold,
Let the angels sing it over as they did in days of old,
To every land in sorrow the glad story shall be told,
Good Will and Peace to men!

(Chorus)

Let all men live as brothers in the friendliest accord,
Let them know the peace and power that true loving will afford,
Let them put their trust in honor, not in cannon or the sword,
For Peace is come to reign!

(Chorus)

Let thoughts of hatred perish, and let friendship take their place,
Let all men know they are kindred in one common human race,
That all are of one Father and must meet Him face to face,
When these short days are done!

O HEAR THEM MARCHING, MARCHING

O, hear them marching, marching,
The legions of good will,
The men of peace who seek not
To bomb and maim and kill;
They march not to their conquest
With battle-flags unfurled;
But with their gentle spirit
They shall subdue the world.

Through all the bloodstained ages
Their numbers have increased,
The spirit struggling upward
To overcome the beast;
The meek who shall inherit
And rule the warring earth,
With patient faith are bringing
The new regime to birth.

The men of war oppose them,
And seek to bar the way,
The powers of darkness striving
To thwart the coming day;
But, led by unseen forces,
Their hosts are marching still,
To build for future ages
The kingdom of good will.

A mighty captain leads them,
The valiant Prince of Peace;
They shall possess the future,
And ancient wrongs shall cease;
O men of good will, marching
To bloodless victory,
We join your hosts in building
The kingdom that shall be.

Notes

ABBREVIATIONS USED IN NOTES

ABHMS American Baptist Home Mission Society
CSC   Broomell, ed., *Children's Story Caravan*
FOR   Fellowship of Reconciliation
FSC   Broomell, ed., *Friendly Story Caravan*
SCPC   Swarthmore College Peace Collection, Swarthmore, Pa.
SF   Subject file
TIC   *The Intentional Communities*

INTRODUCTION

1. Kirby Page, "Total Allegiance to the Prince of Peace," in Page, *Light Is Still Shining*, 76–79.
2. *By an Unknown Disciple*. The book, published anonymously, was written by Cecily Spencer-Smith Phillimore.
3. Because the song entered the folk process early in its life, it has been known by various names, including "Ain't [or: I Ain't] Gonna Study War No More," "Study War No More," "War No More," "Gonna [or: Gwine] Lay Down My Burden," "Gonna Lay Down My Sword and Shield," and "Down by the Riverside." The word "gwine," an attempt to reproduce black dialect, was common in the early twentieth century but is considered offensive today. For the song's publication history, see note 16; for recent versions see Blood and Patterson, *Rise Up Singing*, 163; and *Worship in Song*, 295.
4. Lynd and Lynd, *Nonviolence in America*.
5. On the seminal idea of the paradigm shift, see Kuhn, *Structure of Scientific Revolutions*.
6. Wittner, *Rebels against War*, 213.

7 Hutchison, "Protestantism as Establishment," 4.
8 Hamm, *Transformation of American Quakerism*, 172.
9 For example, Fitzgerald, "Losing Their Religion"; Prothero, *American Jesus*; and Stowe, *How Sweet the Sound*.
10 Toelken, *Dynamics of Folklore*, 37, 56–58.
11 Marini, *Sacred Song*, 302.
12 Hutchison, *Modernist Impulse*, 2–4 and passim.
13 Dorrien, *Making of American Liberal Theology*, 2:11.
14 "Conscientious Objectors in World War II," 9.
15 The watershed was Paul Sabatier's *Vie de Saint François d'Assise* (1893), published in the United States as *Life of St. Francis of Assisi*.
16 Rodeheaver, *Golden Bells*, no. 111; Boeckel, *Across Borderlines*, 142–43; Sandburg, *American Songbag*, 480–81.
17 The best discussion of the prayer's origins is in three articles in *Greyfriars Review*: Schulz, "So-Called Prayer of St. Francis"; van Dyck, "Prayer in Search of an Author"; and Poulenc, "Modern Inspiration for the Prayer." The earliest English-language sources (cited by Schulz) are British. The earliest American source I have located is *Prayers for the Church Service League*, 117. Many earlier devotional books quote Francis's "Canticle of the Sun," but not the peace prayer.
18 For early sources see Marsh, *Story of the Jubilee Singers*, no. 84, p. 204; *National Jubilee Melodies*, 152; and Jackson, *White and Negro Spirituals*, 192–93. For the 1920s, see note 16; Deas, *Gems of Love*; and H. Augustine Smith, ed., *American Student Hymnal*, no. 322, p. 291. A 1926 source said it had heard it sung by the Fisk Jubilee Singers "a few years ago, when the Great War was still in every one's mind" (Fisher, *Seventy Negro Spirituals*, 60). The Cleveland Public Library's *Index to Negro Spirituals*, 5, cites as a source Burleigh's *Negro Spirituals* (London: G. Ricordi, 1917–19), which I have been unable to locate, but Anne Key Simpson's catalog of Burleigh's music first lists it in 1922 (see *Hard Trials*, 391). Boeckel also credits a 1922 Burleigh arrangement. However, Rodeheaver, in *Golden Bells*, gave the copyright date 1918 for his entire section on spirituals (preceding no. 110). I am indebted to Mary Louise VanDyke of the Hymn Society's Dictionary of American Hymnology Project and to Judith A. Gray of the American Folklife Center, Library of Congress, for assistance with this research. My relative was William L. Holladay (1901–2000) of Altadena, California.

CHAPTER ONE

1 Heywood Hale Broun, quoted in "W. Colston Leigh Presents Vera Brittain" (New York: W. Colston Leigh, Inc., 193?, brochure), Papers of Vera Brittain, SCPC.

2 On use and recommendations see, for example, "When War Passions were Inflamed" (review), *The World Tomorrow*, Jan. 26, 1934, 381–82; *Pacifist Handbook*, 13, 27, and 47; "Books Recommended for Conscientious Objectors," which "may be ordered from any depository of the Methodist Publishing House," *World Peace Newsletter*, Oct. 14, 1940, 5; Armstrong, *How Peace Grows*, 29; Syracuse Peace Council, *Peace Education in Public Schools*; *Christian Youth Peace Demonstration*, 26; and "This is Your Job" (New York: FOR, [1942]), SF Conscientious Objection, SCPC.
3 Among similar titles are Meyer, *Hey! Yellowbacks!*, and Randall, *Improper Bostonian*.
4 Kenneth Irving Brown, the editor of Gray's letters, described the family circumstances as "modest" (Gray, *Character "Bad,"* 3), but Gray's fellow objector Howard Moore said Gray's father was Ford's second-largest stockholder and "owned half of Detroit" (Moore, *Plowing My Own Furrow*, 113). See also Page, *Social Evangelist*, 25.
5 Harold Gray, *Character "Bad,"* 3–4.
6 Conscientious objectors were at this time under the jurisdiction of the military and were expected to provide noncombatant support services. Those who refused were subject to court-martial and imprisonment. Alternative service outside the military became a legal option only in June 1918, and Gray refused it.
7 Gray, *Character "Bad,"* 255.
8 Ibid., 256; "These Said No to Conscription," *Fellowship*, May 1942, 72; Chatfield, introduction to *Character "Bad,"* 8. The farm, which incorporated canning and marketing operations, was evidently organized on the earlier cooperative model, that is, as assistance to the rural poor rather than committed group living. A visitor in 1946 described it as "very lacking in the cooperative principles" (Clara Wray to Morris Mitchell, April 30, 1946, Records of Macedonia Cooperative Community, Box 1, SCPC).
9 "These Said No"; Hassler, *Conscripts of Conscience*, 27–30.
10 Gray, *Character "Bad,"* 100, 104, 118–19, 184, 190–94, 215, 236.
11 Hutchison, "Protestantism as Establishment," 4.
12 Shattuck, "Christian Church (Disciples of Christ)."
13 Brown, in Gray, *Character "Bad,"* 4; Chatfield, *For Peace*, 44.
14 Gray, *Character "Bad,"* 17, 38–45; Dorrien, *Making of American Liberal Theology*, 2:105–8.
15 Caldwell, *Puritan Conversion Narrative*, 2 and passim; Lambert, *Inventing the "Great Awakening,"* 50–51, 72–73; Brereton, *From Sin to Salvation*, xi, 3–13.
16 Gray, *Character "Bad,"* 3, 9–10.
17 Ibid., 31.
18 Ibid., 23–24, 31–32.

19 Ibid., 10–11, 32–36.
20 Ibid., 34, 36–37, 57, 60–61, 72; Page, *Social Evangelist*, 26. Orchard was by that time well known as a modernist religious writer and poet. Harry Emerson Fosdick drew on his work in *The Meaning of Faith*. Hodgkin, an evangelical Quaker, was the moving spirit behind the FOR and one of its founders. Royden was a settlement-house worker, speaker, and until World War II, a pacifist.
21 Gray, *Character "Bad,"* 53–54.
22 Ibid., 48, 54, 57, 59–60, 63. Throughout, Gray uses simplified spellings such as "tho," "thru," etc.
23 Ibid., 54, 60.
24 Some years later, Georgia Harkness wrote in the *Christian Century* that there were more pacifist preachers than theologians, because of the Social Gospel–oriented training they received in seminary. See Georgia Harkness, "The Christian's Dilemma," *Christian Century*, Aug. 6, 1941, 977.
25 Gray, *Character "Bad,"* 22, 59, 107, 124, 204, 211, 217.
26 "By temperament, I am an evangelist" (Page, *Social Evangelist*, 109). Cf. Eddy, *Pilgrimage of Ideas*, 64.
27 The book also describes but does not quote a statement to the examining board in military camp. See Gray, *Character "Bad,"* 118.
28 Ibid., 180–86.
29 Ibid., 69, 73, 183.
30 This is not the only possible approach to the Christian life; Christians have held a variety of views on how such a life is best lived.
31 Sheldon, *In His Steps*.
32 Gray, *Character "Bad,"* 185.
33 Ibid., 73, 175.
34 Ibid., 104.
35 Ibid., 48.
36 Ibid., 18, 57, 121.
37 Ibid., 24, 47, 52–53, 57.
38 See Chapter 3; Dorrien, *Making of American Liberal Theology*, 3:9–57; Fosdick, *Adventurous Religion*, 37, and *Spiritual Values and Eternal Life*, 32; and Page, *Jesus or Christianity*, 273.
39 Gray, *Character "Bad,"* 69, 73.
40 Ibid., 24, 56, 213.
41 Ibid., 38, 55, 181–82.
42 Ibid., 90, 120, 203.
43 Ibid., 116–17, 214–15, 224.
44 Ibid., 134.
45 Ibid., 93–95.
46 Ibid., 104.

47 Ibid., 126.
48 Ibid., 104, 107, 110.
49 Ibid., 105, 116. It is perhaps worth noting that Gray's battalion, as he later learned, was called out because of "a mutiny in a Negro labor battalion." "The feeling among the Negroes is very bitter," Gray wrote. "They are up at five every morning and driven like slaves all day in labor gangs. They can't see this war-game for dust" (ibid., 116).
50 Ibid., 120, 124–25.
51 Ibid., 129.
52 Evan Thomas, brother of the socialist Norman Thomas, had been one of Gray's fellow YMCA secretaries in London. Both he and Moore became prominent peace activists. The three men reached their decision during a walk into town, where they had planned to have lunch. They abandoned this plan upon concluding that the government should feed them. "Accordingly," Gray reports innocently, "we had only some ice cream which we felt we would have had in any case" (ibid., 132).
53 Ibid., 130–32.
54 Ibid., 127.
55 Ibid., 134, 139–40.
56 Ibid., 138, 152.
57 Ibid., 196–97, 202, 213. Gray had also agonized over whether to work in prison. He ultimately made a distinction between working under conscription and working under compulsion. He also saw "opportunity for Christian service" in his prison work. He refused, however, any work directly connected with the military (see ibid., 202).
58 Ibid., 228. Gray's instincts were not completely off the mark. In 1943, *Fellowship* quoted an army chaplain who argued that since all authority was from God, the military officer represented "God for you" to the soldier. "In a very real sense you're saluting God Himself" (Edward Trower, *Hospital Church Bulletin*, quoted in *Fellowship*, July 1943, 134).
59 Gray, Character "Bad," 229–32.

CHAPTER TWO

1 Van Kirk, *Religion Renounces War*, 33, 36; Chatfield, *For Peace*, 124–35; Wittner, *Rebels against War*, 5–6.
2 Chatfield used this image with a different meaning in *For Peace*, 129.
3 Others included Henry Cadbury and Willard Sperry, Harvard Divinity School; Roland Bainton, Jerome Davis, Halford Luccock, Kenneth Scott Latourette, and H. Richard Niebuhr, Yale Divinity School; Paul Limbert, Adelaide Case, and George Coe, Columbia University; Edgar S. Brightman and Walter

Muelder, Boston University; Dorr Diefendorf, Drew University; Walter Marshall Horton, Oberlin College; A. Burns Chalmers and Ralph Harlow, Smith College; Georgia Harkness, Mt. Holyoke College and Garrett Biblical Institute; Bruce Curry, Daniel Fleming, Mary Ely Lyman, Arthur L. Swift, Harry Ward, Union Seminary; Nels Ferré, John Woolman Brush, Norman Gottwald, and Elizabeth Lobingier, Andover Seminary or Andover Newton Theological School; Ozora Davis, Arthur Holt, Charles Gilkey, and Albert W. Palmer, Chicago Theological Seminary; and John Bennett, Pacific School of Religion. This list was compiled from Chatfield, *For Peace*, 129; Nelson, *Peace Prophets*, 23; Dorrien, *Making of American Liberal Theology*, 2:316; "Affirmation of Christian Pacifist Faith," *Fellowship*, Mar. 1939, 6–7. The presence of pacifist faculty did not necessarily signify institutional support; cf. Dellinger, *From Yale to Jail*, 61–65, on Union Seminary.

4 "Dear Brother Ministers," May 1, 1941, circular letter, and "Statistical Report," [June] 1941, Records of Churchmen's Committee for a Christian Peace, SCPC. See also "A Christmas Manifesto 1942," pamphlet, Records of Churchmen's Committee; and "Affirmation of Christian Pacifist Faith," including a list of "the first 100 signers," *Fellowship*, Mar. 1939, 6–7.

5 Knox, "Re-examining Pacifism," 33.

6 Kirby Page, "20,870 Clergymen on War and Economic Injustice," *The World Tomorrow*, May 10, 1934, 222–56; offprint, n.d., SF Religion, War, and Peace, SCPC. Page polled approximately 100,000 Protestant ministers and Jewish rabbis, and 20 percent responded. The survey results probably reflect self-selection by those sympathetic to the cause; see Chatfield, *For Peace*, 128.

7 Hutchison, "Protestantism as Establishment," 6–7; King, "Reform Establishment," 122.

8 Boeckel, *Through the Gateway* and *Across Borderlines*.

9 Frederick L. Redefer, "Child Education: A Corrective of the Adult's War Spirit" (New York: World Peaceways, [1934]), SF Children and War and Peace, SCPC. Redefer was executive secretary of the Progressive Education Association.

10 At times pacifism conflicted with social justice; for an extended discussion see Chatfield, *For Peace*, 191–202.

11 "An Interpretation and Forecast," *The New World*, Jan. 1918, 5.

12 Lynn, *Progressive Women*, 28–29.

13 David Levine, *American College and the Culture of Aspiration*, 206; Chatfield, *For Peace*, 260, 295–96.

14 "Conscientious Objectors and the R.O.T.C.," [1].

15 "Thousands . . . made no distinction between the Student YM-YWCAs and the SVM," wrote Hopkins in *John R. Mott* (568). After 1950 some regional umbrella organizations took "Student Christian Movement" as an official

name. See also Dean K. Thompson, "A Pre-eminent Generation of Protestant Leaders," *Christian Century*, Jan. 7–14, 1976, 13–14.

16 Parker Rossman, "Seeking a Dynamic Student Christian Movement: An Interview with Fern Babcock Grant," *Christian Century*, April 20, 1983, 374.

17 Sherwood Eddy used evangelical language to describe this trend, writing of "glorious conversions" to social Christianity and "missionary" fervor for the social gospel. See Eddy, *I Have Seen God Do It*, 43; and Eddy, *Pilgrimage of Ideas*, 64. See also Hopkins, *History of the Y.M.C.A.*, 643.

18 Burkhardt, "Drawing Strength from the Past," 505.

19 Curry, "Purpose and Hope of This Conference," 2–4, 6–8; E. Raymond Wilson, *Thus Far on My Journey*, 14. Wilson was a founder and the first executive secretary of the Friends Committee on National Legislation. Reared in the Reformed Presbyterian Church, he served in the navy in World War I, was active in the YMCA for many years, joined the Society of Friends in 1936 after long acquaintance, and lived at the cooperative Bryn Gweled Homesteads after 1942.

20 Hopkins, *History of the Y.M.C.A.*, 643; Hopkins, *John R. Mott*, 627.

21 Some of the community YWCAs also dealt with social issues, particularly labor problems. Since the community Ys were autonomous, however, it is difficult to generalize about them. See Lynn, *Progressive Women*, 25–27.

22 Rossman, "Seeking," 373; Lynn, *Progressive Women*, 29–31, 69.

23 On SVM see, for example, Hopkins, *John R. Mott*, 567–68; and E. Raymond Wilson, *Thus Far on My Journey*, 21–24; on other youth movements and fellowships see Van Kirk, *Religion Renounces War*, 14; and Page, *Religious Resources*, [v].

24 James P. Mullin, in "W.W. II Civilian Public Service," Papers of Robert Horton, SCPC.

25 *Friends in Civilian Public Service*, 215–16, 224.

26 This "print community" evolved alongside the growth of religious publishing as a commercial venture after World War I. Many religious books of the 1920s focused on Christian activism and on controversial issues, while "inspirational" and devotional reading was prominent after 1930, alongside a market for left-wing writing. See Tebbel, *Golden Age*, 237–41, 485.

27 Holmes, *I Speak for Myself*, 166.

28 Lippincott was founded and managed by Philadelphia Quakers but was primarily a commercial, not a religious, publishing house.

29 Two of *The Christian Century*'s editors, Charles Clayton Morrison, from 1908 through 1947, and Harold E. Fey, from 1956 through 1964, were Disciples of Christ pacifists, though Morrison abjured pacifism as World War II approached.

30 See Nelson, *Peace Prophets*, 35; and Roberts, *American Peace Writers*, 295–328.

31 Eddy, *Pilgrimage of Ideas*, 94. The traveling speaker has a long and complex history in American culture. The institution of itinerant speech has served preachers and pastors, revivalists, healers, salesmen, social reformers, and others. During the nineteenth century the lecture circuit developed as a means of social betterment for communities, encompassing education, social reform, and entertainment. It also offered a means of earning a living, particularly for those whose opportunities were otherwise limited, such as women and African Americans. The traveling Chautauqua, from the early twentieth century until its demise in 1924, combined edification, entertainment, and inspiration on a rural and small-town lecture circuit.

32 For example, Boeckel, *Between War and Peace*, 420–22.

33 Report of the World Peace Commission, *Journal of the 31st Delegated Conference*, 1637–42.

34 John Nevin Sayre, "In Memoriam: Kirby Page," *Fellowship*, Mar. 1, 1958, 31; "On the Pacific Coast," *Fellowship*, Sept. 1940, 114.

35 "Speaking Schedule A. J. Muste, Co-Secretary F.O.R.," Sept. 12–Dec. 12, 1940, Records of FOR, Section II, Series A-2, Box 2, SCPC. Muste was soon afterward named executive secretary.

36 Burkhardt, "Drawing Strength from the Past," 506.

37 Women's American Baptist Home Mission Society, Report, in *Annual of the Northern Baptist Convention* (1928), 408.

38 E. Raymond Wilson, *Thus Far on My Journey*, 23; "8,000 Miles for the Fellowship," *Fellowship*, Sept. 1940, 114.

39 While the institutes of international relations were undoubtedly influential, Chatfield is incorrect in treating them as a spontaneous Quaker development in 1930; the Methodists' Epworth League had been holding "institutes" for study and social bonding since at least 1915. See, for example, George S. Butters, "New England Epworth League Institute," *Zion's Herald* 93 (July 7, 1915): 856; "New England Young People Training for Service," *Zion's Herald* 96 (July 10, 1918), 886–87; and P. G. B., "Enthusiasm Marks Lasell Institute," *Zion's Herald* 103 (July 8, 1925): 856. On Congregational-Quaker institutes, see Minutes, International Relations Committee, April 20, 1935, Records of Congregational Christian Churches of the United States, Council for Social Action, Records, 1934–56, Series 9, Congregational Library, Boston, Mass.

40 A fine survey of the social history of youth camping appears in Van Slyck, *Manufactured Wilderness*, xix–xxxvii. On Christian camping, see Bowman, *Spiritual Values in Camping*, and Clifford Anderson, "Camping History." Many camps had a rich and intentional ritual life, with fictionalized Native American elements, "alternative" styles of Protestant worship, and rituals related to

everyday camp life. See Van Slyck, *Manufactured Wilderness*, 169-213; Hofer, *Camp Recreations and Pageants*; and Webb and Webb, *Summer Magic*.

41 Frazer and O'Sullivan, "We Have Just Begun to Not Fight," 127.
42 "Eliot," quoted in Richard Anderson, *Peace Was in Their Hearts*, 126-27.
43 "William L. Richards," Papers of Robert Horton, SCPC.
44 Chatfield, *For Peace*, 127; Muelder, *Methodism and Society*, 148.
45 Goossen, *Women Against the Good War*, 97.
46 Clarence Klingensmith, in "W.W. II Civilian Public Service," Papers of Robert Horton, SCPC.
47 On conversion see Page, *Social Evangelist*, 26; and John Nevin Sayre, "Instrument of Peace," unpublished memoir, ca. 1975, item 7, pp. [12-14], Papers of John Nevin Sayre, Series H, Box 1, SCPC.
48 Taylor, "Social Movement Continuity." I am indebted to Mark Chaves for bringing this to my attention.
49 Thomas Moore, interview.
50 "Pacifist Youth in Action," *Fellowship*, Oct. 1938, 13-14.
51 Balch wrote, "I stop being nonresistant when it is a question of offering my neighbor's cheek for the blow" (Emily Greene Balch to Alice Hamilton, Feb. 20, 1941, Papers of Emily Greene Balch, SCPC, reproduced in Solomon, "Dilemmas of Pacifist Women," 152-55). See also Eddy, *I Have Seen God Do It*, 206-18.
52 For an extended discussion of organizational changes see Wittner, *Rebels against War*, 34-61.
53 Wittner, *Rebels against War*, 32, 152. FOR membership rose from 8,000 in 1940 to 12,000 in the next year, eventually reaching a wartime peak of 15,000 members, compared with 4,300 in 1935. As for other groups, secondary sources agree that the War Resisters League also grew during this period but give wildly conflicting figures. Brock reports 12,000 members in 1942 (*Twentieth-Century Pacifism*, 108; *Pacifism in the 20th Century*, 100), DeBenedetti, 19,000 (*Peace Reform*, 115), and Wittner, only 2,300 in 1945, up from 900 in 1939 (*Rebels against War*, 54). WILPF, on the other hand, experienced a precipitous decline, perhaps because of its nonabsolutist stance (Wittner, *Rebels against War*, 33) or its reliance on education (Foster, *Women and the Warriors*, 346-47).
54 The Episcopal Pacifist Fellowship, led by longtime FOR leader John Nevin Sayre, was founded in 1939, followed by Baptist and Unitarian fellowships in 1940, Lutheran in 1941, and, further from the mainstream, Christian Science, also in 1941. The FOR encouraged the formation of such groups after 1935 as part of a strategy of decentralization, but their proliferation around 1940 is noticeable. See Chatfield, *For Peace*, 299-302; Pierce and Ward, *Voice of Conscience*, 8; and "Jottings," *Fellowship*, Sept. 1946, 153.

55 Pierce and Ward, *Voice of Conscience*, 9.
56 "Being in the Marine Corps in the South Pacific in 1943–44 made a pacifist out of me," commented one such person (Alfred E. Kuenzli to Frances Witherspoon, June 6, 1969, Papers of Mygatt and Witherspoon, Series B, Box 6, SCPC). Edgar L. Jones enjoyed a brief period of fame among pacifists in the late 1940s as an "ill-adjusted veteran" who turned to pacifism. Some had encountered pacifist ideas before or during the war but had not come to a decision before they were called up for military service ("Letter from a Soldier," *Fellowship*, June 1943, 119; Edgar L. Jones, *I'm an Ill-Adjusted Veteran*; Edgar Jones, "The Veteran and the Peace Movement," *Fellowship*, Feb. 1947, 28–29; Thomas Moore, interview).
57 Van Kirk, in *Religion Renounces War*, did not use it, referring instead to the three denominations as "long-time pacifist bodies" (vi). A. J. Muste, in a FOR communiqué, Oct. 1940, used it in quotation marks (see A. J. Muste, "Last Minute News and Suggestions Regarding Registration Day," Oct. 10, 1940, SF Conscientious Objection, SCPC). *Pacifist Handbook* used it without quotation marks (22, 45–46); Thomas E. Jones's *Creative Pioneering*, a CPS booklet, used it freely, and it was taken for granted in the CPS literature. On the founding of CPS see Wittner, *Rebels against War*, 70.
58 *San Dimas Rattler* (CPS Camp 2), Mar. 17, 1943, [1], quoting Charles F. Boss, chair of the Methodist Commission World Peace.
59 Keim, *CPS Story*, 81; Kniss, *Disquiet in the Land*, 70; Frazer and O'Sullivan, "We Have Just Begun to Not Fight," xviii.
60 This was John Thomas, secretary of the Department of Cities for the American Baptist Home Mission Society (Records of the ABHMS, American Baptist Historical Society, Valley Forge, Pa.).
61 Jones wrote in *Creative Pioneering*: "It is true that many young men poorly express their own convictions. Instinctively they feel that they cannot render military service, but they lack words and experience" ([1]). Cynthia Eller noted that many could not articulate why they were pacifists (*Conscientious Objectors*, 3). Some concise examples of the transmission of existing peace culture are the titles of camp newsletters: "Plowshare," "A Way of Life," "Service for Peace," "The Second Mile," and several called "Action," supplemented after 1943 by titles such as "The Alarmist" and "High Time" (Records of American Friends Service Committee, CPS, Series A, SCPC).
62 Morgan was the director of the Merom Institute for Congregationalist rural studies; Mitchell founded Macedonia Coop Farm. The camps at Walhalla, Michigan; and Trenton, North Dakota, ran the best-known but not the only schools. Traveling speakers also advocated cooperative living.
63 Lester, *Training*, 13–15. Cf. Gregg, *Training for Peace*: "I agree heartily with

Gerald Heard, who says five to twelve are enough" (8). Gregg used the word "team" for a small training group.

64 Gregg, *Training for Peace*, 8.
65 Chatfield, *For Peace*, 299–301; "Pacifist Preparedness," *Fellowship*, Feb. 1937, 8. Examples of reports on local groups are "Yale Fellowship Meets" and "Philadelphia Group Meets," *Fellowship*, Dec. 1937, 2; and Laurence T. Hosie, "News of the Fellowship," *Fellowship*, April 1939, 10–11.
66 E. Stanley Jones used the term "cells" in 1935 in *Christ's Alternative to Communism*, 276, but it did not come into general use until around 1940.
67 Both were published by the FOR. The first was undated, but *Pacifist Handbook* gave 1938 as its publication date (p. 48), and a 1938 article referred to it (see "Pacifist Youth in Action," *Fellowship*, Oct. 1938, 13–14). Participants in the FOR national conference of 1947 met in "cell groups" for discussion (see "National Conference Draws 300 Registrants," *Fellowship*, Oct. 1947, 160).
68 A. J. Muste, "The Direction of Growth," *Fellowship*, Sept. 1944, 158–59.
69 "The Disciplines," *Peacemaker*, June 1949, 5. For a description of life with a peace team, see "Where Life Is Changed," *Fellowship*, May 1937, 4–5, about a group named after Muriel Lester and convened by minister and writer Allan Hunter. For an extended description of the ideal see *Pacifist Living—Today and Tomorrow*, 62–71, and "Building the Cell" [advertisement], *Fellowship*, Oct. 1947, back cover.
70 Hamm, *Transformation of American Quakerism*, 172.
71 Ibid., 149. Jones came from an evangelical Quaker background in New England, and there were Friends, especially in the Midwest, who accepted modern knowledge but preserved "programmed" worship and a stronger sense of biblical authority than did silent-worship liberals.
72 For a fuller discussion see Chapter 7.
73 See, for example, Swayne, *Observance of Easter*, passim; and *A Hymnal for Friends*, passim.
74 As noted above, many Quaker men did in fact serve in the military, and some CPS men criticized the AFSC for collusion with the government in its management of CPS; see, for example, Curtis Watson, "Our Leaders Criticized: The Failure of CPS, or Is It?," *Action* (CPS Camp 32, Campton, N.H.), April 5, 1943, 3, 5. But as a body the Society remained opposed to war.
75 This calculation represents growth unrelated to the large increases from two mergers—with the Orthodox Yearly Meeting of Philadelphia, and with Pacific Yearly Meeting—during this period. Note that Five Years Meeting, later Friends United Meeting, the moderate-evangelical Midwestern body, recorded generally stable numbers during these years. See *Yearbook of American Churches*, 1949–60, and Barbour and Frost, *Quakers*, 234–35. Two devel-

opments prepared the ground for this movement: the growth of modernist-minded independent meetings during the 1930s and the creation of the Wider Quaker Fellowship for sympathetic non-Friends. Some of the increase in numbers probably came from the independent meetings' movement into denominational connection. See Allen Smith, "Renewal Movement," 3–4; Cazden, "Modernist Reinvention of Quakerism," passim; and Eleanor Slater, "I Became a Quaker," *Christian Century*, Sept. 21, 1938, 1125–28.

76 Thomas Moore, interview.
77 Whitfield Cobb, "Reader Types in C.P.S.," *Service* (Duke Hospital, Durham, N.C.), April 1944, 12. The comment about signs is an allusion to the Anglican definition of a sacrament, "an outward and visible sign of an inward and spiritual grace."
78 *Friends in Civilian Public Service*, 246–47. This book includes a section titled "The Legacy of CPS," on objectors after World War II.
79 "This Summer for Service," *Fellowship*, May 1943, back cover; cf. Jacob, *Peace to End Wars?*, and Rosenhaupt, *How to Wage Peace*, 151–55. An illuminating account of FOR conferences is found in "Regional Fall Conferences Mark Year of Progress," *Fellowship*, Dec. 1944, 210.
80 See, for example, "Background of the Printed Bulletin," *Peacemaker*, June 5, 1949; "Peacemakers Continuation Committee Holds Inspiring Meeting at Koinonia," *Peacemaker*, Sept. 24, 1956.
81 For this discussion I have relied on Ahlstrom, *Religious History of the American People*, 473–74, 230; and Finke and Stark, *Churching of America*, 42.
82 Chang, "Sect"; Albanese, *America, Religions and Religion*, 137–38; Bryan Wilson, *Social Dimensions*, 1–2, 10–11, 47–61, 106–7.
83 Bryan Wilson, *Social Dimensions*, 106.
84 The following discussion is drawn from Carpenter, *Revive Us Again*, xi–35.

CHAPTER THREE

1 Dorrien, *Making of American Liberal Theology*, 3:4.
2 Hutchison, *Modernist Impulse*, 3.
3 Evidence about the early church is scattered and can be interpreted in divergent ways. See, for example, Cadoux, *Early Christian Attitude To War*, first published in 1919 and in print as late as 1982; Horsley, *Jesus and the Spiral of Violence*, 149–51; and Lampe, *From Paul to Valentinus*, 134–35 and notes.
4 For a thorough discussion of nineteenth-century nonresistant theology see Ziegler, *Advocates of Peace in Antebellum America*.
5 Beecher, "Love, the Fulfilling of the Law" (1859), 162.
6 Dorrien, *Making of American Liberal Theology*, 1:xiii–xiv, xviii, xxiii; 2:1–3, 9; Hutchison, *Modernist Impulse*, 4.

7 Macintosh, *Social Religion*, 72.
8 Bowne, *Essence of Religion*, 39.
9 Mathews, *Faith of Modernism*, 147.
10 Fosdick, *Modern Use*, 8, 15, 209, 223–24.
11 Niebuhr, *Moral Man*.
12 Chatfield, *For Peace*, 191–97; Fox, *Niebuhr*, 136–41; Dorrien, *Making of American Liberal Theology* 2:449–51, 457–64; Hutchison, *Modernist Impulse*, 288–98.
13 Hutchison, *Modernist Impulse*, 303–10; Dorrien, *Making of American Liberal Theology*, 2:9–10, 435–83. Dorrien further argues that Niebuhr should be regarded as a "neoliberal."
14 For example, Raven, *Theological Basis of Christian Pacifism*; Church Peace Mission, *Christian Conscience and War*; A. J. Muste, "Theology of Despair: An Open Letter to Reinhold Niebuhr," *Fellowship*, April 21, 1948, reprinted in A. J. Muste, *Essays*, 302–7; Muste, "Saints for This Age," Wallingford, Pa.: Pendle Hill, 1962, reprinted in Muste, *Essays*, 410–25.
15 John Nevin Sayre, "Now is the Time," review of *Now Is the Time to Prevent a Third World War*, by Kirby Page, *Fellowship*, Sept. 1946, 154; Sayre, "In Memoriam: Kirby Page," *Fellowship*, Mar. 1, 1958, 30–33.
16 Page, *War*, 74.
17 Sayre, "In Memoriam," 31–32; Page, *Social Evangelist*; "Kirby Page Dies; Peace Evangelist," *New York Times*, Dec. 18, 1957, 35.
18 Page was sole author of twenty-five books and editor or co-editor of three. For a bibliography see Chatfield and DeBenedetti, eds., *Kirby Page and the Social Gospel*, 37–38.
19 Page, *Jesus or Christianity*, 38; Page, *Personality of Jesus*, 118–19; Page, *Living Triumphantly*, 93.
20 Page, *Personality of Jesus*, ix–x, in part quoting Joseph Klausner, *Jesus of Nazareth: His Life, Times, and Teaching*, trans. Herbert Danby (New York: Macmillan, 1926), 20; Page, *Personality of Jesus*, 139; Fosdick, introduction to Page, *War*, [iii]. Page was also concerned to show that religious life was not incompatible with science; see, for example, *Living Triumphantly*, 1–21.
21 Page, *Personality of Jesus*, 53; Page, *Living Triumphantly*, 97–98.
22 Page, *Living Creatively*, 65; Page, *Personality of Jesus*, 39; Page, *Living Triumphantly*, 87.
23 Page, *Living Triumphantly*, 97; Page, *Jesus or Christianity*, 42.
24 See *Living Creatively*, *Living Triumphantly*, *Living Courageously*, *Living Prayerfully*, *Living Abundantly*, and *Religious Resources for Personal Living and Social Action*. Similar methods, less fully developed, appear in *War* and in *Personality of Jesus*.
25 Page, *Living Triumphantly*, 103.
26 Compare Mary Farrell Bednarowski's observation on new American religions:

while all those she described sought some balance between past and present, individual and community, she noted, "In regard to the grace-works polarity, there is almost no tension at all. 'Works' and responsibility will save us" (Bednarowski, *New Religions*, 138–39). "Creativity" was another favorite theme of pacifist conversation. See Bays, *Worship Services for Youth*, 76; Lieberman, *Creative Camping*; and Eddy and Page, *Creative Pioneers*. Page's *Living Creatively* was available through such sources as *Church and Sunday School Builder*, the catalog of the American Baptist Publication Society, 1939 (29). The Harlem Ashram included "creative living" in its statement of intention (see "The Harlem Ashram," [1944?], mimeographed brochure, Records of the FOR, Series II, A-3, Box 3, SCPC).

27 Page, *Living Creatively*, v.
28 Ibid., 92.
29 Congregationalist educator John Leslie Lobingier offered a similar chart in *Is War the Way?*, 13: "Do I care to the extent of making sacrifices for . . ." myself, my family, international justice and good will, etc. The pacifist mystic Gerald Heard also provided a chart and referred often to "ladders" and levels (Heard, *Preface to Prayer*, facing p. 96; Heard, *Creed of Christ*, 33; Heard, *Code of Christ*, 4–5 and elsewhere.)
30 For more on Protestants and fine art, see Chapter 6.
31 For fuller discussion see Blumhofer and Noll, eds., *Singing the Lord's Song in a Strange Land*; Marini, *Sacred Song in America*; and Hobbs, *I Sing for I Cannot Be Silent*.
32 Benson, *English Hymn*, 585. "Where Cross the Crowded Ways" has proved remarkably durable: first published in 1903, it has appeared in virtually every mainline hymnal up to the 1990s.
33 Ibid., 590. A collection called *Hymns of Service* did in fact appear in 1924, edited by H. Augustine Smith and Grace Widney Mabee.
34 *The Hymnal*, iii.
35 *A Hymnal for Friends*. These collections were intended primarily for use in schools, Sunday schools, and informal gatherings, rather than in formal worship. Other branches of the Society of Friends had adopted hymn-singing and other evangelical practices in worship during the nineteenth century.
36 For example, *The Hymnal* (Presbyterian) classified its hymns under adoration and worship, the persons of the Trinity, the scriptures, prayer and inner life, church and sacraments, mission and social action, and eternal life; then children's hymns and "Special Seasons and Services." The Congregationalist *Pilgrim Hymnal* of 1935 used headings of public worship, the life of Jesus, the "Divine Being," the "Christian Way of Life," mission and social service, and the church, which last included special occasions, holidays, and children's hymns. The responsive readings in *Christian Worship* began with the New Year and

ended with Christmas, including along the way Mother's Day, Memorial Day, and reflections on patriotism, race relations, Pentecost, and heaven.

37 These were *The New Hymnal for American Youth* (1930) and the *Pilgrim Hymnal* (1935). Pacifist and Social Gospel emphases did not preclude the inclusion of some national or patriotic selections in most hymnals.

38 Under the heading "World Friendship and Peace," this hymnal included fifteen hymn texts and sixteen settings—as compared, for instance, with fourteen texts in *A Hymnal for Friends* (1942 and 1955) and eleven in the *Pilgrim Hymnal*. (The Quaker hymnals grouped peace hymns with hymns that appeared under the heading "Brotherhood" in *Christian Worship*.) Two of these were not, as far as I can determine, published anywhere else, and several others were uncommon. Nos. 559, "The Son of God Goes Forth for Peace," and 564, "O Hear Them Marching, Marching," were otherwise unpublished. Nos. 552, "God of Our Fathers, Whose Almighty Hand," 553; "To All the Nations, Lord"; and 554, "The Prince of Peace His Banner Spreads," were uncommon.

39 Quakers of this tradition did object to trinitarian and much christological language: in *A Hymnal for Friends* (1955), many existing hymns were altered in a unitarian direction. See, for example, "Holy, Holy, Holy," no. 41; "Now Thank We All Our God," no. 62; and "Hark! The Herald Angels Sing," no. 144.

40 Mussey intended the hymns for interfaith use, but her use of hymn-singing itself suggests a Protestant bias. See Mussey, *Social Hymns of Brotherhood and Aspiration*, [v]; Mabel Hay Barrows Mussey, "How the Hundred Hymns Were Brought Together," *The Survey*, Jan. 3, 1914, 383; and Benson, *English Hymn*, 586.

41 *World Citizenship and the Religious Program*, [1], SF Education and Peace, Box 33, SCPC.

42 See, for example, H. Augustine Smith, ed., *Hymnal for American Youth, American Student Hymnal*, and *New Hymnal for American Youth*; *Hymns for Worship*, prepared for the Council of North American Student Christian Movements; and *Hymns for Christian Youth*. From denominational presses came *The Beacon Hymnal*, *The Church School Hymnal for Youth*, and *Hymns for Creative Living*.

43 H. Augustine Smith, ed., *New Hymnal for Christian Youth*, iii. On the needs of youth see also Page, *Religious Resources*, [v], and *Light Is Still Shining*, [iii]; *Beacon Hymnal*, t.p.; and David R. Porter, *Worship Resources for Youth*, 174, 176.

44 For spirituals see H. Augustine Smith, ed., *American Student Hymnal*, nos. 316–23, pp. 286–92; and Alexander and Goslin, *Worship Through Drama*, 322.

45 I do not discuss here the hymns' musical settings, but some settings did comment on the texts, as when *A Hymnal for Friends* used Diademata, a tune written for the high-christological "Crown Him with Many Crowns," for "Peace in Our Time, O Lord" (1942, no. 95; 1955, no. 114).

46 "O God of Love! O King of Peace" appeared in *The Hymnal*, no. 421; in *The*

Methodist Hymnal, no. 511; in *The Hymnal of the Protestant Episcopal Church*, no. 528; and in *A Hymnal for Friends* (1942, no. 22; 1955, no. 113). "Lead Us, O Father, in the Paths of Peace" was in *The Pilgrim Hymnal* (1935), no. 281; in *The Hymnal*, no. 262; in *The Methodist Hymnal* (1935), no. 271; in *Hymnal of the Protestant Episcopal Church*, no. 433; in *A Hymnal for Friends* (1942), no. 22; and in H. Augustine Smith, ed., *New Church Hymnal*, no. 230. "God of Our Fathers, Known of Old" was in *Pilgrim Hymnal*, no. 383; in *Methodist Hymnal*, no. 497; in *Hymnal of the Protestant Episcopal Church*, no. 147; and in H. Augustine Smith, ed., *New Church Hymnal*, no. 442.

47 "The Prince of Peace His Banner Spreads" appeared in H. Augustine Smith, ed., *New Church Hymnal*, no. 357, and in *Christian Worship*, no. 553. "God of the Nations, Near and Far" was in *Pilgrim Hymnal*, no. 380; in H. Augustine Smith, ed., *New Church Hymnal*, no. 351; in *Christian Worship*, no. 556; and in *A Hymnal for Friends* (1942, no. 104; 1955, no. 107). "Peace in Our Time, O Lord" was in *Hymnal of the Protestant Episcopal Church*, no. 527, and in *A Hymnal for Friends*, no. 114.

48 The text of the hymn was also an epigraph to "Leader's Guide—Young People's Institutes," [1], SF Education and Peace, Box 33, SCPC.

49 Ernest Bourner Allen, "The Son of God Goes Forth for Peace," in *Christian Worship*, no. 559. Sherwood Eddy and Kirby Page used the same wording in their *Abolition of War*, 76. For "The Son of God Goes Forth to War" see, for example, *Hymnal of the Protestant Episcopal Church*, no. 549.

50 The question of the effect of language and imagery on behavior was central to the debates of the 1980s and 1990s over gendered language and metaphor in worship. See, for example, Emswiler, *Women and Worship*, and Wren, *What Language Shall I Borrow?*.

51 Howard Arnold Walter, "I Would Be True," in *Church School Hymnal*, no. 225, p. 193; H. Augustine Smith, ed., *Hymnal for American Youth*, no. 170, p. 141; Smith, ed., *American Student Hymnal*, no. 180, p. 166.

52 The text appears in Boeckel, *Across Borderlines* (1926), 145.

53 For full text and sources see Blood and Patterson, eds., *Rise Up Singing*, 218.

54 Here the text seems to comment on the tune; see note 45.

55 Emphasis in the quotation is mine. It is not possible to review all such hymns here, but I would call attention also to Earl Marlatt's rewriting of "The Strife Is O'er, the Battle Won" in H. Augustine Smith, ed., *New Hymnal for American Youth*, no. 132, p. 113. It includes the line, "No longer, Lord, thy sons shall sow / Hatred and death where poppies blow," an allusion to the famous World War I poem "In Flanders Fields." Among recent efforts, Miriam Therese Winter's revision of "America the Beautiful" (*New Century Hymnal*, no. 594) goes so far as to include "nonviolence."

56 Marion Franklin Ham, "O Hear Them Marching, Marching," in *Christian Wor-*

ship, no. 564. Ham (1867–1956) was a Unitarian minister who published a number of hymns and poems.

CHAPTER FOUR

1 Lansbury, *My Pilgrimage for Peace*, 46–47.
2 *International Problems and the Christian Way of Life*, 21. By way of comparison, the group asked, "Would it, or would it not, be more profitable to study the life and teachings of some modern, high-minded international statesman?"
3 E. Raymond Wilson, quoted on back cover of Page, *Social Evangelist*. See also Eddy and Page, *Abolition of War*, 67–68: "Jesus' teaching and example were understood as opposed to war by his followers and the early Church."
4 A. J. Muste and John Nevin Sayre, "Dear Fellow-members" (New York: FOR, 1940, pamphlet), SF Conscientious Objection, SCPC, on eight Union Seminary students who refused draft registration.
5 "We Must Draw the Line—Now," [1950], brochure, Records of Fast for Peace Committee, SCPC.
6 Bible Study Packet, 195?, Records, Council for Social Action, Series 22, SP-1, Congregational Library, Boston, Mass.
7 This was true for the Old Testament and the Pauline epistles alike. In biblical quotations I use the King James Version because it was most familiar to Protestants of this period. Some pacifists also used the American Standard Version (1901), the Moffatt translation (1922–35), the American or Chicago translation (1939), or the Revised Standard Version (New Testament, 1946; Old Testament, 1952), but the KJV form was most often quoted. Romans 13, on obeying government authority, was the archetypal text for moderate peace advocates in the mid-nineteenth century (Ziegler, *Advocates of Peace*, 37) but was much less prominent in twentieth-century discussions.
8 Fosdick, *Modern Use*, 30.
9 Holmes, *New Wars for Old*, 161–72; "A Syllabus of Topics, Problems, and Suggestions for the National Study Conference on the Churches and World Peace," 1925, printed draft, 5, 18, SF Religion, War, and Peace, SCPC. See also *Christian Attitude toward War*.
10 Macgregor, *New Testament Basis* (1936), 17, 67, 117.
11 See, for example, "A New Year, a New Era," *Fellowship*, Jan. 1950, inside back cover.
12 Macgregor, *New Testament Basis*, 9. "Though due weight," he added, "must, of course, be given to those sayings in the context of Jesus' whole teaching."
13 *Peace Study Outline*, 13–14. For similar juxtapositions, see, for example, "A Christmas Greeting to the People of Frederick," [Dec. 1959], Records of Appeal at Fort Detrick, SCPC.

14 In most Protestant usage this was the sixth commandment; in Lutheran and in Roman Catholic, it was the seventh.

15 Current scholarly opinion concurs generally, but not universally, with the Moffatt interpretation. For commentary see Childs, *Book of Exodus*, 419–21.

16 Pacifists did not advocate breaking the other commandments but gave them less attention. Erling Lunde, a former Lutheran-turned-"independent Christian thinker," read the commandment against killing as Christ's own statement—a characteristically Lutheran interpretation. See "Defense of Erling H. Lunde" (Chicago: American Industrial Co., [1918], pamphlet), 15, SF Conscientious Objection, SCPC.

17 Without a doubt the Sermon on the Mount is a central Christian text, but its background and interpretation are more complex than pacifists have liked to make them. For recent interpretive work see Betz, *The Sermon on the Mount*, and Horsley, *Jesus and the Spiral of Violence*.

18 "Syllabus of Topics," 5; Hennacy, "An Open Letter to the United States District Attorney regarding the Selective Service Act and Myself," Dec. 19, 1941, SF Conscientious Objection, Box 10a, SCPC.

19 "Report of Conference on Pacifist Farming Communities," 1942, mimeograph, 7, SF Conscientious Objection, SCPC. For more on Morgan, see Chapter 9.

20 Swayne, *Sermon on the Mount*, 3.

21 In Britain, the pacifist and urban activist Muriel Lester began her school for workers in London's Bow district with study of the Sermon on the Mount. "It took us months to get through those three chapters, so modern and revolutionary did they prove to be," she wrote. See Lester, *It Occurred to Me*, 52.

22 Cf. Rauschenbusch, *Christianity and the Social Crisis*, 1–43, and his *Christianizing the Social Order*, 50–53.

23 Pacifists sometimes shifted this text into the declarative or imperative voice. But it originally referred to the future reign of God in the Israelite nation, not to peacemaking per se. For commentary see Clements, *Isaiah 1–39*, 39–42; and Wildberger, *Isaiah 1–12*, 82–96.

24 For example, Cranston, *Swords or Plowshares?*; Mary Hoxie Jones, *Swords into Ploughshares*; Arthur Chew, *Plowshares into Swords*; and Claude, *Swords into Plowshares*. Compare Ingrid Rogers, ed., *Swords into Plowshares*; and Laffin and Montgomery, eds., *Swords into Plowshares*.

25 Kate Devereux Blake, "To the Children of America," [1915], printed circular letter, Records of Children's Peace Petition Committee, SCPC; "Litany of Peace," [1933], printed sheet, Records of Fellowship of Peace, Meadville, Pa., SCPC; "Leader's Guide—Young People's Institutes: Youth Marches On!! Toward Peace?—War?," Chicago, General Conference Commission on World Peace, Methodist Episcopal Church, 1939, mimeograph, [1], SF Education and Peace, Box 33, SCPC.

26 Kite, *When Friends Sing*, 41. Emphasis mine.
27 W. E. Orchard, "The Kingdom of God Is at Hand," *New World*, Jan. 1918, 20–21. *New World* changed its name to *The World Tomorrow* in July 1918.
28 *International Problems and the Christian Way of Life*, ii (emphasis mine). Cf. John D. Rockefeller, "The Christian Church: What of Its Future?" *Saturday Evening Post*, Feb. 9, 1918, quoted in Hutchison, *Errand to the World*, 150.
29 "Proposed Summer Ashram Training Course," [1941], typescript, Records of the FOR, Series II, A-3, Box 13, SCPC.
30 A growing literature on mysticism and spiritual practice, often linked with pacifism, had appeared during the 1930s. See Chapter 7.
31 Brenda Brasher argues that emergent religious groups typically attract adherents by claiming to be doing something new while affirming connection to tradition; the Pentecostal women she studied insisted they were not doing "religion" but "relationship" (Brasher, *Godly Women*, 91, 201 n).
32 "Christmas Greeting," Records of Appeal at Fort Detrick, SCPC.
33 Of course love is by any standard foundational to the Christian faith (see, e.g., Jn 15:13, 1 Cor 13), but Christians in other historical periods or cultural settings have privileged ideas of salvation, the Last Judgment, or holiness, to take just a few examples. On the emergence of love as a liberal theme see, among others, William Ellery Channing, "Unitarian Christianity," in Robinson, ed., *William Ellery Channing*, 88, 94–97; Robinson, introduction to *William Ellery Channing*, 6; McLoughlin, *Meaning of Henry Ward Beecher*, 81–82, 85–89; and Fox, *Jesus in America*, 251–52.
34 Page, *Living Creatively*, 63, 66.
35 Reinhold Niebuhr, "Would Jesus Be a Modernist Today?," *The World Tomorrow*, Mar. 1929, 122–24.
36 FOR statement of principles, quoted in back matter of Page, *War*.
37 Tentative Statement of Purpose, ca. 1935, typescript, Records of Disciples Peace Fellowship, SCPC; cf. "The Harlem Ashram," [1944?], mimeographed brochure, Records of FOR, Series II, A-3, Box 13, SCPC.
38 Letter to Marjorie Swann, reproduced without attribution in "To Friends of Marj Swann and Sympathizers with her Concerns," mimeographed newsletter, [autumn 1959], 2, Papers of Horace Champney, Series B, Box 4, SCPC.
39 Broomell, ed., *Friendly Story Caravan*, 153. The story went on to tell of supernatural manifestations at the underground bunker where the two had met (153–54). On stories, see Chapter 10.
40 See, for example, A. J. Muste, "The Doctrine of Perfection—I," *Fellowship*, Mar. 1950, 7–10. Allan Brick addressed similar issues in "The Sermon on the Mount for Today," *Fellowship*, Mar. 1, 1960, 14–15.
41 "Good Will, the Magician" was reproduced in Boeckel, *Through the Gateway* (1928), 53–59. Boeckel credited the Woman's Press, the publishing arm of the

YWCA. Goodwill Day, May 18, was a celebration invented in 1899, abandoned during World War I, and revived by the 1920s peace movement. See Boeckel, *Through the Gateway*, 106–8.

42 Evans and Thomas, eds., *Pioneers of Good Will*; Griscom, ed., *Peace Crusaders*. Other examples include Walter W. Van Kirk, *Highways to International Good Will*, and Brooks, *Adventuring in Peace and Goodwill*.

43 Reinhold Niebuhr did use the term during the 1940s to mean that which is "intrinsically good" (Niebuhr, *Moral Man*, 173, 247).

44 "This Summer for Service," *Fellowship*, May 1942, back cover; "Summer Service," *Fellowship*, June 1949, 29. On service, see Benson, *English Hymn*, 584–90; Fosdick, *Meaning of Service*; and Rufus M. Jones, *Service of Love in War Time*. The women in CPS who spoke of their urge to "service" thus were not only affirming a personal calling but also using well-established rhetoric. See Goossen, "Pacifist Professional Women," 335. One World War II–era source suggested that overemphasizing service might be a "heresy in pacifism" and urged pacifists to substitute "soul force" for "service" (*High Time*, CPS Camp 41, July 23, 1945, 3).

45 On the question, see Hutchison, *Modernist Impulse*, 111.

CHAPTER FIVE

1 Glassberg, *American Historical Pageantry*, 285.
2 Ibid., 284.
3 Toelken, *Dynamics of Folklore*, 37–43.
4 David Morgan, introduction to *Icons of American Protestantism*, 17.
5 Methodists were an exception here, as their communion rite was explicitly called "the ritual" (*Methodist Hymnal*, 521).
6 There are exceptions, notably Anglicans (particularly on the high-church end of the spectrum) and the Methodist liturgical-renewal movement of the 1950s, but the general observation still holds.
7 Responsive readings were intended to be read antiphonally, a verse or half-verse at a time, for example by minister and congregation.
8 *Methodist Hymnal*, 561–623, 627–43.
9 Also incorporated were parts of Isaiah 55 and 65, Luke 10, and Matthew 16 and 26. Denomination is not a factor in selectivity: the Methodists' reading on temperance used nine different texts.
10 See White, "The Missing Jewel of the Evangelical Church," 104–5. The Christian Church (Disciples of Christ) continued with a brief service of the Lord's Supper every Sunday, unlike most churches, which served communion less frequently. The Disciples nonetheless held the sermon in high regard.
11 See *Beacon Hymnal*; Bays, *Worship Services for Youth*; Page, *Religious Resources*

and *Light Is Still Shining*; Porter, *Worship Resources for Youth*; *Hymns for Creative Living*; and works on camping in Chapter 2. For intended audiences, see Page, *Religious Resources*, foreword; Page, *Light Is Still Shining*, foreword; *Beacon Hymnal*, t.p.; and Porter, *Worship Resources for Youth*, 174, 176.

12 See, for example, Bays, *Worship Services for Youth*, 10, 76, 90, 110; and the use of outdoor settings in Mattoon and Bragdon, *Services for the Open*, passim.

13 H. Augustine Smith, ed., *New Hymnal for American Youth*, 367.

14 The Kellogg-Briand Pact outlawed war as an instrument of international policy. Peace organizations and churches responded with enthusiasm; indeed, said Walter Van Kirk, "preachers are taking the Kellogg-Briand Pact much more seriously than are the politicians and diplomats" (Van Kirk, *Religion Renounces War*, 64).

15 Ibid., 16–18; Chatfield, *For Peace*, 260. The history of public pledging itself went back at least to the temperance movement.

16 Tracy D. Mygatt and Frances M. Witherspoon, "An Office of Commemoration for the Dead Who Died in the Great War and of the War Resisters' Pledge of Brotherhood to All Mankind," *The Pilgrim Highroad*, Nov. 1935, 1–2, Papers of Mygatt and Witherspoon, Series C, Box 8, SCPC. An introductory note states that this work appeared first in *Unity* in 1932, had later been revised by the authors, and was available from the WRL. "Office" is a term in common use among Roman Catholics and Episcopalians for public prayer.

17 Page, *Light Is Still Shining*, foreword and 120 n.

18 The texts were Mark 8:34–35; Matthew 5:29–30; Matthew 10:37–38; Mark 13:12–13; Luke 10:3; John 16:12.

19 [Phillimore], *By an Unknown Disciple*, 61; see also ibid., 49, 58–62.

20 Kennedy, *Terrible Meek*; Mygatt, *Good Friday*; Holmes and Lawrence, *If This Be Treason*. Mygatt, an Episcopalian, was a cofounder of the War Resisters League and was active in several peace organizations. Holmes, a Unitarian minister, was a leader in the FOR and a cofounder of the ACLU. Kennedy was an Episcopalian and a pacifist until 1941. See *American National Biography*, 12:565–67. The title "The Terrible Meek" was borrowed for two later works: a peace pamphlet by the Methodist Albert Edward Day in 1939, noted in *World Peace Newsletter* (Commission on World Peace of the Methodist Church), Oct. 14, 1940, 5, and reprinted in *Fellowship*, Jan. 1940, 3–5; and a 1948 essay on Gandhi (Manshardt, *The Terrible Meek*).

21 But see Rogers, *Swords into Plowshares*. Rogers's introduction seems to indicate that drama as a medium was a fresh discovery for her. However, many of the plays, written during the 1970s and early 1980s, repeat familiar topoi and are as self-consciously didactic as some of their earlier counterparts.

22 See, for example, Sanford, ed., *Peace Plays*; Lobingier and Lobingier, *Educating for Peace*, 141–80; *Program Suggestions for World Peace*, 24–27; *World Citizen-*

ship and the Religious Program, [3–4]; *Young People and a New World* (New York: FOR, ca. 1929), [3], [5], SF Education and Peace, Box 30, SCPC; and E. Vesta Haines, "Good Will Around the World." SCPC holds eight manuscript boxes of peace plays. It is difficult to know what proportion of these plays were actually performed and how they were received. I assume that writing and publication would not have continued at the rate they did if a substantial number had not actually been produced.

23 See Orsi, "Everyday Miracles," 7.

24 H. Augustine Smith, ed., *Hymnal for American Youth*, title page; Bendroth, *School of the Church*; Elizabeth Miller, *Dramatization of Bible Stories*; Corinne Bowers, "Peace Plays," *Fellowship*, July 1941, 127. The article also mentions the Religious Drama Council of the Greater New York Federation of Churches; cf. "'The New Star,' by Tracy D. Mygatt," clipping, no source given, Papers of Mygatt and Witherspoon, Series A, Box 3, SCPC. See also Alexander and Goslin, *Worship Through Drama*.

25 Pohl, *Gas*; Dix, *Where War Comes*.

26 Boeckel, *World's Christmas Tree*; MacKaye, *Good Will*, in Boeckel, *Through the Gateway* (1928), 53–59. On international friendship, see Robert, *American Women in Mission*, 272–92; Elizabeth Miller Lobingier, *Ship East*; and Committee for World Friendship among Children, "Doll Messengers," 1927, brochure, SF Children and War and Peace, SCPC.

27 The cast of characters, still eerily familiar, included officials of Electric Boat in Groton, Connecticut. Although the Fellowship was an umbrella group of representatives from religious and secular women's organizations, all the performers in this production were men. See "A Repeat Hearing of the United States Senate Munitions Investigation," Feb. 1935, printed program, Records of Fellowship of Peace, Meadville, Pa., SCPC.

28 Rockwell, *All We Like Sheep*, 28.

29 Tracy D. Mygatt, "The New Star," typescript, p. 10, Papers of Mygatt and Witherspoon, Series A, Box 3, SCPC.

30 Addams, *Peace and Bread*, 126; Norman Thomas, *Conscientious Objector in America*, 197–200. See also Brock, *Twentieth-Century Pacifism*, 58; see Chatfield, *For Peace*, 385 n. 34, for a discussion of the confusion in this story.

31 Sanford, ed., *Peace Plays*, 1–12.

32 For a fuller discussion of repeated patterns in familiar narratives, see Chapter 10. For dramatized stories see, for example, *With Children Leading*, 7–14, 50–53.

33 Douglas, "To the Unknown Soldier," 223–27; Agnes K. Winkler, "The Unknown Soldier Speaks," adapted from the sermon by John Haynes Holmes (New York: Community Church, n.d), cited in *World Citizenship and the Religious Program*, [3], and in *Program Suggestions for World Peace*, 26, which men-

tioned that the (Methodist) Epworth League offered copies for sale; Bruce Barton, "Unknown," 15; Losey, *And the World Forgot*.
34 *Program Suggestions for World Peace*, 22.
35 Dorothy Clarke Wilson, *Friendly Kingdom*.
36 Louis Wilson, *Testing Hour*.
37 Davol, *Handbook of American Pageantry*, 22, 62, 102; see also Beegle and Crawford, *Community Drama and Pageantry*, and Glassberg, *American Historical Pageantry*. On a post-1960, antiwar and anticapitalist revival of pageantry, see John Bell, *Landscape and Desire*; Simon and Estrin, *Rehearsing with Gods*; and Brecht, *Peter Schumann's Bread and Puppet Theatre*.
38 It is likely that they were organized mainly by women, although many of the performers were men (Davol, *Handbook of American Pageantry*, 62).
39 As late as 1930, one local study mentioned a historical pageant with 2,000 participants, presumably adults, and an audience of over 75,000. The state provided part of the funding. See Paul W. Penningroth, "Cityville: 'Cityville for World Friendship': A Study of Public Opinion on International Affairs," 1930, typescript, 46, SF Education and Peace, SCPC.
40 Crum, *Guide to Religious Pageantry*, 2.
41 Grace Darling Phillips, *Far Peoples*, xix. Phillips added that missionary drama "often is written in a pious or patronizing style which is resented by the people concerned." See also Crum, *Guide to Religious Pageantry*, 5–7.
42 McPherson, *Educating Children for Peace*, 138. The unnamed girl was a participant in a 1935 Vacation Bible School program of the Department of Religious Education, Greater New York Federation of Churches, sponsored by the Carnegie Endowment for International Peace.
43 See, for example, Davis-DuBois, *Education in Worldmindedness*, SF Education and Peace, SCPC, 46. Davis-DuBois was active with the FOR. The feminine, angelic image and the dove and olive branch were common in visual representations of peace in this period.
44 See, for example, McPherson, "The Shoe, a League of Nations," in her *Educating Children for Peace*, 104–6; Katharine Sherer Cronk, "America for Americans" (Philadelphia: Women's Missionary Society of the United Lutheran Church, n.d.), in Lobingier and Lobingier, *Educating for Peace*, 165–66.
45 These figures also appeared in iconography and in storytelling; see Chapters 6 and 10.
46 Summary of Beulah Marie Dix, "A Pageant of Peace" (Boston: American School Citizenship League, 1915), in Lobingier and Lobingier, *Educating for Peace*, 172–73.
47 The human races and the personified virtues seem to be allusions to Tennyson's "Vision of the Future," a mildly eschatological poem that concludes the pageant. See Davis-DuBois, *Education in Worldmindedness*, 46.

48 Georgina Johnston, "Building for Peace," presented by Metropolitan Federation of Daily Vacation Bible Schools, July 25, 1939 (SF Religion, War, and Peace, SCPC).

49 The program, funded by the Carnegie Endowment, is described in detail in McPherson's *Educating Children for Peace*.

50 Written in only 1936, this hymn later appeared in *Christian Worship* (no. 489) and *A Hymnal for Friends* (1942, no. 86; 1955, no. 117), and was popular in the YMCA (see Bunting, "YMCA," 89).

51 Holmes, *I Speak for Myself*, 219. Nor were *The Terrible Meek* or *Good Friday* commercial successes.

52 McPherson, *Learning about War and Peace*, 27.

53 Paul Limbert, "What Children Think about War," offprint from *Progressive Education*, Feb. 1933. Limbert was also a pacifist.

54 For more on liberal churches, theater, and ritual, see Driver, *Magic of Ritual*, 82–83.

55 Catherine Bell, *Ritual Theory*, 88–93, 204.

56 Davol, *Handbook of American Pageantry*, 92. The author assumes that everyone takes an active part "either in preparation or participation" (91).

57 Crum, *Guide to Religious Pageantry*, 34.

58 Toelken, *Dynamics of Folklore*, 37, 56–59, 316.

59 Compare Driver's analysis of prayer (*Magic of Ritual*, 96), which, he says, may "have not only, and not mainly, the function of conveying information, but rather that of establishing or consolidating relationship . . ." through thought, speech, and physical action.

60 Wittner, *Rebels against War*, 67–69, 160–61, 247–50.

CHAPTER SIX

1 Armistice Day poster, n.d., source unknown, Poster Collection, Box P7A, SCPC.

2 Progressive churches drew on the history of art and began to develop contemporary iconography. The Riverside Church in New York mounted an "elaborate iconographical program" in 1931 (see David Morgan, *Protestants and Pictures*, 321); Church of the Messiah, later Community Church of New York, had installed "up-to-date iconography" in stained glass by 1919 (see Holmes, *I Speak for Myself*, 87–88). Trinity Methodist Church, Springfield, Mass., which I discuss below, is another example. Grace Cathedral in San Francisco, constructed between 1928 and 1964, and the National Cathedral in Washington, D.C., built between 1907 and 1990, deserve further study in this regard. On missionary artifacts see Robert, *American Women in Mission*, 272–92; Crum, *Guide to Religious Pageantry*, 72; Elizabeth Miller Lobingier, *Ship East*, 81–82;

Committee for World Friendship among Children, "Doll Messengers," 1927, brochure, Records of Committee on World Friendship among Children, SCPC; and Boeckel, *Between War and Peace*, 451. The American Baptist Historical Society in Valley Forge, Pa., maintains a collection of missionary dolls.

3. David Morgan, *Protestants and Pictures*, 318–19, citing Lawrence Levine, *Highbrow Lowbrow: The Emergence of Cultural Hierarchy in America* (Cambridge: Harvard University Press, 1988).

4. There are also some suggestive links between iconography and progressive education, which advocated visual as well as verbal learning, and which interested many pacifists. See, for example, Zonia Baber, *Peace Symbols* (offprint from *Chicago Schools Journal*), 4; and Redefer, "Child Education," SF Children and War and Peace, SCPC.

5. Doves appear with saints, in depictions of Pentecost, and on tombs, signifying the soul flying to heaven (Murray and Murray, *Oxford Companion to Christian Art*, 144, 356).

6. The cartoon is reproduced on a poster titled *Sermon on the Mount*, [192?], World Peace Posters, Poster Collection, SCPC.

7. See Eddy and Page, *Abolition of War*, 41–45; Gibbs, *Now It Can Be Told*; and Ponsonby, *Falsehood in War Time*. The manual *Christian Youth Peace Demonstration* recommended as a peace slogan a quote from Harold Gray: "The first casualty of war is truth" (19).

8. *Sermon on the Mount*, poster, 1931, NCPW, Poster Collection, Box P2a, SCPC.

9. Florence Brewer Boeckel, *Disarmament Poster Program* (Washington, D.C.: National Council for Prevention of War, 1931), 5–11, SF Art in War and Peace, SCPC. For copies of the posters see *Sermon on the Mount*, poster, 1931, NCPW, Poster Collection, Box P2a, SCPC; and *Sermon on the Mount*, poster, n.d., World Peace Posters, Poster Collection, Box P2, SCPC.

10. "Sermon on the Mount" poster, Peace House, [193?], Poster Collection, Box P2, SCPC.

11. "The Sermon on the Mount," illustration, in Barber, ed., *Halt! Cry the Dead*, 46.

12. It appears in none of the standard art-historical dictionaries of symbolism or iconography. Samuel Chew (*Virtues Reconciled*, 128) notes its existence in the sixteenth century, but it was apparently uncommon, while doves, olive branches, and truncated or blunted swords were standard symbols of peace. Peace was historically represented as eschatological, as a classical virtue, or in homage to a powerful ruler, not as a Christian way of life or a democratic political condition. Cf. Cheney, "Peace," 701–5.

13. *L F N A: Do You Want Peace?*, poster, [1919], League of Free Nations Association, Poster Collection, Box P8, SCPC.

14 "They Shall Beat Their Swords into Plowshares" poster, [193?], Methodist Peace Fellowship, Poster Collection, Box P11a, SCPC.

15 The church window was one of eleven in the First Methodist Episcopal Church of Meadville, Pennsylvania, built in 1928. See Lobingier and Lobingier, *Educating for Peace*, 55–56. The child perhaps recalls the "Holy Mountain" or "Peaceable Kingdom" passage of Isaiah 11; see below.

16 "The Ministers' Corner," [1958], clipping, SF Peace Monuments, SCPC. An image of the statue appeared on the home page of the church's website in 2007 (<www.ccny.org>).

17 Artillery-shell lamp, [192?], provenance unknown, Memorabilia, SCPC.

18 The plow itself was housed in Geneva, Switzerland. See Peace Symbols, Media Kit 11, SCPC; Peace Monuments, Photo Collection, Records of WILPF, SCPC; Baber, *Peace Symbols* (1937), 1; Baber, "Build Monuments to Goodwill," *Fellowship*, Jan. 1938, 7; Baber, *Peace Symbols* ([1948]), 18–19; and "Pamphlet Parade," *Fellowship*, Feb. 1950, 31. Baber was a professor of geography and a member of the WILPF. Several other material explorations of peace were the projects of WILPF members, notably the Peace Gardens (1951–63) and Art for World Friendship (1946–69).

19 *Christian Youth Peace Demonstration*, 17, SF Religion, War, and Peace, SCPC; cf. Dorothy Clarke Wilson, *Friendly Kingdom* (see Chapter 5).

20 Early in his career, Gandhi experimented with cooperative subsistence farming, following the ideology of John Ruskin in *Unto This Last* (Gandhi, *Autobiography*, 298–310). And "Plowshares" was, of course, the name of a radical movement that used nonviolent, self-sacrificing ritual gestures to protest nuclear-weapons programs during the 1980s.

21 For example, the Nye Commission report on munitions manufacturers' profiteering during World War I, or the 1939 pageant in which craftspeople's work is turned to purposes of war, described in Chapter 5.

22 It is not entirely clear why Sermon on the Mount imagery proved less popular. Perhaps the images—blessed are the peacemakers, resist not evil—were harder to visualize, the only possible exception being the image of a person turning the other cheek. This would have the drawback of being interpersonal instead of public—but in that case one would expect the imagery to reappear after 1940, in concert with stories of interpersonal pacifism. That it did not suggests that the metaphor slipped entirely into language and not at all into the visual realm. In today's context there is an incentive to use an Old Testament image because it belongs to Jews as well as Christians, but this was not a pressing issue in the 1930s.

23 Trinity Methodist Church was designed, in part, to express a socially progressive religious sensibility. The building is Gothic in style, and its stained-glass windows use medieval symbolic conventions to express modern ideals.

The figures depicted include Galileo, Pasteur, Livingstone, Frances Willard, Shakespeare, and St. Francis. I am grateful to Trinity Methodist Church for allowing me to see and photograph the Lindbergh window and others in its sanctuary.

24 In addition to the biblical text cited, the eagle called to mind St. John the Evangelist, and hence the Gospel of John, in Christian iconography, and the United States in national iconography. Other examples of Lindbergh as symbol include his appearance in the pageant described in Chapter 5, and the use of his 1927 flight to Mexico City as the entrée to a four-week Sunday school course on Mexico, which was in turn connected to a peace organization's project with that country. See Lobingier and Lobingier, *Educating for Peace*, 70–78.

25 For more on "peace heroes" literature, see Chapter 10. Lindbergh himself did not last long as a hero of peace, largely because of his support of Nazism in the early 1930s. For recent reflections, see Philip Roth's novel *The Plot Against America*.

26 Favorite subjects included scientists Galileo, Pasteur, Schweitzer, and Curie; inventors Bell, Edison, Carver, and the Wright brothers; explorers Lindbergh, Scott, and Drake; artists Leonardo, Beethoven, and Jenny Lind; social reformers and experimenters Penn, Wilberforce, Addams, and Elizabeth Fry; missionaries Livingstone, Grenfell, and Father Damien; and, of course, Francis of Assisi. Damien (1840–89) was a missionary to the Hawaiian Islands who was best known for his single-handed service to a colony of lepers on Molokai from 1873 until his death. *Paths of Peace*, Book II, compared him to St. Francis (148).

27 Lotz, ed., *Women Leaders*, published by the YMCA's Association Press, was not specifically about peace but had much in common with the "peace heroes" literature. It included "heroes" Addams and Curie, and peace advocates Muriel Lester and Mary Woolley. "Study questions" appended to each chapter raised questions about war, peace, and pacifist commitment. The biographical sketches emphasized independence, courage, perseverance, and achievement, as well as compassion and self-sacrifice.

28 Fletcher, *Pioneers in Peace*, 9–13, 27–29. Others, such as Galileo, Beethoven, and Lind, survived as part of the literature of "creative living" fostered by pacifists such as Kirby Page. Two longtime activists, reared as Methodists, recalled that prewar pastors regularly mentioned Kagawa, Schweitzer, Grenfell, Lester, and Addams, "always in groups" (Doris Hartman and Justin Hartman, interview).

29 Hunter, *Heroes*; Hunter, *Courage*.

30 In addition, there were murals of Mme. Chiang Kai-shek and of James Aggrey, an advocate of racial harmony in Africa. See "Guide to Fellowship House," n.d., mimeograph, Records of Fellowship House, Philadelphia, Pa., SCPC.

31 Baber, *Peace Symbols* (1937), 8–10; Elizabeth Miller Lobingier, *Ship East*, 1–18. As late as 1958, the radical pacifist Peace Pilgrim made a point of visiting a Canadian Peace Garden ("1958 Progress Report to Peace Gardeners and Other Friends," mimeographed newsletter, 3, Papers of Mary Phillips, SCPC).

32 The Rush-Bagot Agreement of 1812, which issued in the removal of U.S. and British warships from the Great Lakes, was another favorite subject of peace narratives; see Chapter 10. The story appeared in Boeckel, *Through the Gateway*, 17–19; Brainerd, *Broken Guns*, 84; Lobingier and Lobingier, *Educating for Peace*, 37; Elizabeth Miller Lobingier, *Ship East*, 4–6; and Brinton, McWhirter, and Schroeder, *Candles*, 94–97. See also Anna D. White, "The Rush-Bagot Agreement," in Griscom, ed., *Peace Crusaders*, 74–75.

33 Mary Phillips, *How to Grow a Peace Garden*, [5], [12], Papers of Mary Phillips, SCPC.

34 Ibid., [5]; "Peace Gardening in 1955," mimeographed newsletter, 5, Papers of Mary Phillips, SCPC; compare the putative prayer of Dutch children in *All Children Pray* (Minneapolis: Children's Plea for Peace, 1958), [4]. Compare also the "flower children" of the 1960s. The 1920s Peace Gardens sometimes grew plants from famous worldwide locations and gave away seeds, especially to children (see Baber, *Peace Symbols*, 8–10). Phillips's Peace Gardens generated a particularly noteworthy doll: a representation of Jane Addams, founder and icon of WILPF, made from gourds. Together with half a dozen smaller dolls representing children of various races, it was exhibited at the Gourd Society of America in a display titled "Gourds for World Friendship," along with two books—Addams's *Peace and Bread in Time of War* (1922) and Philip Noel-Baker's *The Arms Race: A Programme for World Disarmament* (1958). See Papers of Mary Phillips, SCPC, and Memorabilia, SCPC.

35 See, for example, Peace Garden newsletters for 1955, 1956, and 1958; and Phillips to "Dear friend," Sept. 23, 1961, mimeographed circular letter, in Papers of Mary Phillips, SCPC.

36 The fullest discussion of the religious and spiritual meanings of homesteading is found in Gould, *At Home in Nature*.

37 *Who Was Who in America*, vol. 10, p. 101; C. Gerald Fraser, "Fritz Eichenberg, A Book Illustrator and Educator, 89," *New York Times*, December 4, 1990, B21; Forest, "Fritz Eichenberg," 13–25; Eichenberg, *Wood and Graver*, 199. A useful bibliography up to 1977 may be found in *Wood and Graver*, 192–95.

38 Eichenberg's wife died in 1937, leaving their two children, and he fell into severe depression. A friend introduced him to Zen practice; this helped to resolve the depression, but Eichenberg ultimately found it philosophically alien and settled on Quakerism. See Ellsberg, "Revealing the Inner Light," 57–58.

39 For more on Pendle Hill, see Chapters 7 and 9.

40 Eichenberg, *Art and Faith*.

41 *A Hymnal for Friends* (1955), [ii]. Liberal Quakers' exploration of art and music suggests a further broadening of their conversation with the world. Eichenberg assumed that early Friends had forbidden art not for its own sake but because it served worldly purposes, and that later generations "forgot to rescind the old ordinance" (*Art and Faith*, 6–7).

42 Eichenberg, *Art and Faith*, 18, 21, and passim. Compare Ellsberg's comment on "the synthesis of artistic vision, social conscience, and nondogmatic faith that epitomized [Eichenberg's] own personal stance" (preface to Eichenberg, *Works of Mercy*, 12). Many of the same ideas recurred in Eichenberg's *Artist on the Witness Stand*.

43 *Sermon to the Birds* (1952) in Eichenberg, *Works of Mercy*, 66 (originally a Christmas card); untitled image of St. Francis from *The Long Loneliness* (1952) in ibid., 88; *St. Francis Receiving the Stigmata* (1973) in ibid., 71; *St. Francis* (1979) in ibid., 101. Eichenberg also produced three images of St. Francis in 1935–36, when he was working for the WPA (see *Wood and Graver*, 24–25, 195). His 1973 image of St. Francis receiving the stigmata departs from the usual iconography in that a ragged and rough-hewn St. Francis faces the viewer as he kneels.

44 *St. Benedict* (1953) in Eichenberg, *Works of Mercy*, 67.

45 *Holy Family, Farmworkers* (1954) in Eichenberg, *Works of Mercy*, 83.

46 *Catholic Worker Family* (1955) in Eichenberg, *Works of Mercy*, 84. Compare also the *Labor Cross*, a much-reproduced image, in which laborers are arranged around a large rough-grained wooden cross. In the conspicuous upper right position, a farmer hoes a row of corn. Images of a fisherman, a black carpenter, and a Navajo mother herding sheep allude to Christian symbols as well as to labor and race. A miner and a lumberjack also appear (see in ibid., 86).

47 Part of the text is repeated in Isaiah 65:25.

48 Hicks's paintings were exhibited at the seminal Newark Museum show in 1931, and the influential folk-art advocate Abby Aldrich Rockefeller collected and exhibited his work. See Weekley, *Kingdoms of Edward Hicks*, 2, 4, 51, 180–81.

49 Powell, "Biblical and Spiritual Motifs," 128–34. Pippin placed his peaceable kingdom in front of dark woods where images of war and lynching were visible (*The Holy Mountain I*, 1944; *The Holy Mountain II*, 1944; *The Holy Mountain III*, 1945; *The Holy Mountain IV*, 1946).

50 *The First Seven Days* and *And Their Eyes Were Opened*, from *Ten Wood Engravings to the Old Testament* (portfolio, artist published, 1955, reprinted in Eichenberg, *Works of Mercy*, 26, 27); *And in Her Mouth Was an Olive Leaf* (ibid., 28); *Sermon to the Birds* (1952), untitled image of St. Francis (1952), and *St. Francis* (1979). Eichenberg connects St. Francis with peace most explicitly in the last-named print.

51 *The Peaceable Kingdom* (1950) in Eichenberg, *Works of Mercy*, 99; *Peaceable Kingdom* (1955) in ibid., 105.
52 *The Peaceable Kingdom* (1950), in Eichenberg, *Works of Mercy*, 99.
53 Eichenberg also made *Peaceable Kingdom* images after the period under study here, and they became even more experimental. *Pax Lunar* (1964) places the scene on the moon and subverts military imagery of the U.S. moon landing (*Wood and Graver*, 155); *The Peaceable Tree* (1977) groups the animals around a tree with a human form, perhaps a Christ figure (*Wood and Graver*, 13); *The Peaceable Kingdom* (1978) is centered on a mother and child, bathed in light, while a soldier peers from semidarkness behind a tree (Eichenberg, *Works of Mercy*, 103). *Total Disarmament* (1980) reverses the usual imagery. Here a dismayed-looking sheep attempts to preside at a table around which are seated two lions, a snake, a bear, a wolf, a panther, and a crocodile, who all bare their teeth aggressively (*Total Disarmament* from *Fables with a Twist*, portfolio, Gehenna Press, 1976, reprinted in Eichenberg, *Works of Mercy*, 97).
54 A recent work on race relations suggests that "Hicks could locate interracial harmony only in a utopian realm where lion lies down with lamb" (Pencak and Richter, *Friends and Enemies in Penn's Woods*, ix).
55 Jonathan Saltzman, "Dozens Granted Protest Permits," *Boston Globe*, July 13, 2004, B1, B4.

CHAPTER SEVEN

1 Muste also suggested that members have a "spiritual, intellectual, and physical discipline" and recommended books by Gerald Heard, Allan Hunter, and others. See A. J. Muste, "Plan in the Event of War or Conscription," [1940], mimeograph, [1]–[5], SF Conscientious Objection, SCPC.
2 "The Techniques of Silent Meditation," *Days of Our Year* (CPS Camp 9, Petersham, Mass.), Nov. 9, 1941, [1]. "Reader Types in C.P.S.," *Service* (CPS Unit 61, Duke Hospital and Highland Hospital, N.C.), Apr. 1944, 12, mentioned the reader who "may begin a self-imposed regimen of meditation and reading as part of his 'training for the life of the spirit.'"
3 "Letters from Three Prisons," *Fellowship*, Sept. 1941, 156. See below for more on Lester.
4 *Report of the Second Annual Conference of the Episcopal Pacifist Fellowship*, 1941, p. 3, Records of the Episcopal Pacifist Fellowship, Box 3, SCPC.
5 Schmidt, "Making of Modern 'Mysticism,'" 273–302; Schmidt, *Restless Souls*.
6 On mysticism and antimodernism, see Lears, *No Place of Grace*, 174–79, 212–15.
7 Among Page's many works on spiritual matters, his *Living Prayerfully* (1941)

was particularly concerned with "practicing the presence." The work cited Rufus Jones, Muriel Lester, and Glenn Clark; for more on Clark, see below.

8 A recent summary of this point of view is found in Benefiel and Phipps, "Practical Mysticism," 129–30.

9 See below on the evangelical publishing house Fleming Revell; see the material on worship in Chapter 5. Patricia A. Ward has traced Pentecostals' interest in Madame Guyon's work, which Howard Brinton presented in a Quaker context. See Ward, "Madame Guyon and Experiential Theology in America," and Brinton, ed., *Guide to True Peace*.

10 On mainline Protestants, see below. Among Friends, Rufus Jones, Howard Brinton, and Douglas Steere are the best-known exemplars, but see also, for example, Hornell Hart, "Meditation for Liberals," *Friends Intelligencer*, 2nd Month 15, 1936, 101–3; and Howard J. Conn, "Brother Lawrence and the Gale of the Holy Spirit," *The Friend*, 12th Month 12, 1940, 206–9.

11 Mather, *Pendle Hill*, 9, 42, 52; "Summer at Pendle Hill," *The Friend*, 7th Month 14, 1938, 12; "Pendle Hill Notes," *Friends Intelligencer*, 4th Month 12, 1941, 239–40.

12 Toelken, *Dynamics of Folklore*, 37.

13 Frank Laubach is perhaps the exception here, since his experience of transcendence occurred in the context of enforced solitude. But even here, the published account of it was drawn from letters.

14 Rachel R. Cadbury, "Practice of Interior Prayer: Notes Taken from a Talk by Thomas R. Kelly, April 24, 1940," *Friends Intelligencer*, 10th Month 9, 1954, 556–57.

15 Others who deserve mention: Gerald Heard's extensive writing on peace and prayer, and his personal practice, reflected the influence of Vedanta, but he also worked closely with the Congregationalist minister and writer Allan Hunter and taught at Pendle Hill (see his *Quaker Mutation*). E. Stanley Jones, a Methodist missionary who did much to introduce Indian culture and spirituality to the West, wrote several guides to daily prayer that were popular with pacifists and others. He joined the FOR in 1940. The Methodist theologian and prominent pacifist Georgia Harkness described in *The Dark Night of the Soul* (1945) her rediscovery of classical mental prayer following a period of severe depression. Aldous Huxley's *The Perennial Philosophy*, which sought to extract the essentials of truth from the particulars of world religions, gave some attention to spiritual disciplines. The Quaker Howard Brinton followed Jones as an interpreter of mysticism and Quakerism. His work emphasized the communal aspect of emergent Quaker mysticism, and he was particularly influential as director of Pendle Hill. Douglas Steere, a convert to Quakerism, taught at Haverford College with Jones and reached a wide audience through

the YMCA, CPS, the FOR, and his numerous publications. Lester's memoir, *It Occurred to Me* (1937), was a "Pendle Hill Selection" in 1939 See *The Friend*, 8th Month 24, 1939, 56.

16 Joseph de Beaufort, vicar-general (assistant) to the cardinal-bishop of Paris, assembled the collection of "spiritual notes, letters, and many unwritten sayings" (Rodriguez, "Lawrence of the Resurrection," 569; Lawrence, *Practice*, unsigned preface). It seems likely that the cardinal had an anti-Jansenist agenda; in this connection see Lawrence, *Practice*, 23. Two other editions followed in 1693; the relationship of the various versions to the American editions is unclear. Apparently the book fell out of favor with French Catholics because of its use by the mystic Madame Guyon, another favorite of American Protestants. See Rodriguez, "Lawrence of the Resurrection," 569. The edition of *Practice* used for the present work is dated 1895 on the title page and includes an introduction by the evangelical Quaker Hannah Whitall Smith dated 1897. An edition for a Roman Catholic audience appeared in 1974.

17 Lawrence, *Practice*, 8, 11, 15, 16, 21, 25, 34.

18 Ibid., 21–22, 24–25.

19 Ibid., 9, 31; cf. 19, 23, 25.

20 See Chapter 4 for a fuller discussion of this phrase.

21 Lawrence, *Practice*, 21, 25, 33, 35. Muriel Lester is an exception here; her *Ways of Praying* shows a constant awareness of sins and failings and a need for confession, though without Lawrence's vivid self-abasement.

22 Wallis, *Mother of World Peace*, 41–42; Lester, *It Occurred to Me*, 63–68; Lester, *Ways of Praying*, 20–22. See also Underhill, *Mysticism*.

23 Lester, *Ways of Praying*, 3, 15, 16.

24 Ibid., 7, 13, 16.

25 Gregg, *Training for Peace*; Heard, *Training for the Life of the Spirit*; Lester, *Training*. See also Allan Hunter, "Training Now," in his *Say Yes to the Light*.

26 Lester, *Training*, 8–9. Gregg and Heard also addressed themselves to both Protestants and non-Christians.

27 Ibid., 5, 7–8, 10–11; emphasis mine.

28 "Muriel Lester Writes," *Fellowship*, Oct. 1941, 164.

29 Laubach, *Letters by a Modern Mystic*. The book reached its seventh printing in 1940. The editor of the collection compared Laubach to St. Francis of Assisi (Alden H. Clark, foreword to *Letters by a Modern Mystic*, 5).

30 Laubach, *Letters by a Modern Mystic*, 10, 14, 16, 21–22, 24, 26, 43.

31 Ibid., 9, 13, 22–23, 25–26.

32 Ibid., 23. Subsequently, Laubach recorded similar experiences (ibid., 38–40).

33 The emphasis on poetry may also have been a function of social class or edu-

cation. Also, the motif of speech is psychologically significant for a person struggling alone with an unfamiliar language.

34 Laubach, *Letters by a Modern Mystic*, 9–10, 15.
35 See, for example, his *Prayer*, *Wake Up or Blow Up!*, and *Channels of Spiritual Power*. On his joining the FOR see John R. Yungblut, "A Message from our Vice-Chairman," [Apr. 30, 1956], circular letter, Records of Episcopal Pacifist Fellowship, Box 7, SCPC. On speaking, see "Conference on Christian Alternatives to Germ Warfare," 1960, mimeographed program, Records of Appeal at Fort Detrick, SCPC.
36 Laubach, *Game with Minutes* (1956); *Game with Minutes* (1959).
37 His camps (see below) were attended by people "from all denominations, some Jews, a few Catholics, and many who had lost sight of their religious beginnings but wanted a spiritual home" (Miles Clark, *Glenn Clark*, 43).
38 Glenn Clark, *Man's Reach*, 151–55; Tebbel, *Golden Age Between Two Wars*, 237–41; Glenn Clark, "The Soul's Sincere Desire," *Atlantic Monthly*, Aug. 1924, 167–72. Clark later expanded the article into a book with the same title (Boston: Atlantic Monthly Press, 1925).
39 Glenn Clark, "Soul's Sincere Desire," passim.
40 The camps were named for Monhegan Island in Maine, which Clark thought of as the "island farthest out" (Miles Clark, *Glenn Clark*, 42).
41 "Events of Glenn's Life, Given in the Seven Year Pattern He Describes," *Fellowship Messenger*, Sept.–Oct. 1956, 8.
42 For evidence of this close association see, for example, George Washington Carver, Glenn Clark, Rufus M. Jones, and Muriel Lester, "Prayer that Prevails," *Christian Century*, May 8, 1940, 603–4, one of a series of articles calling for "minute men" of prayer against war; D. C. Trapp, "Dear Christian Citizen," Dec. 27, 1944, circular letter, Records of Christian Peace Committee, SCPC; and Rufus M. Jones et al., *Together*, a book proposing a new way of organizing the church.
43 Glenn Clark, *Man's Reach*, 58; Forrest L. Richeson, "Memorial Tribute to Dr. Glenn Clark," *Fellowship Messenger*, Sept.–Oct. 1956, 3–6.
44 Douglas Steere criticized Clark on this count and for his minimizing suffering (Steere, "The Promises of God," review of *A Man's Reach*, *Fellowship*, Oct. 1950, 29–32).
45 New Thought is a diffuse movement related to Christian Science, dating from the mid-nineteenth century. It emphasizes the power of the mind, continuity between the divine and the human, theological openness, and optimism. Norman Vincent Peale credited both Clark and New Thought with shaping his own work. See Melton, *Religious Leaders of America*, 430–31.
46 Glenn Clark, *How to Find Health Through Prayer*, 31–32.

47 "The Camp Farthest Out, under the direction of Glenn Clark," 1931, brochure, Macalester College Archives, St. Paul, Minn.
48 Laubach, *Prayer*, 66.
49 Ibid., 53–54.
50 Dupré, "Mysticism," 6342.
51 Schmidt, *Restless Souls*, 245.
52 Steere, "Biographical Memoir," 1–28; Schmidt, *Restless Souls*, 238–52. Jones, Kelly's Haverford mentor, had retired from teaching in 1934 but was still active with the American Friends Service Committee in the Philadelphia area.
53 To describe this simultaneity Kelly coined the term "life on two levels," another phrase that recurs elsewhere in pacifist writing. See Duveneck, *Life on Two Levels*, and Gerald Heard, "The Practice of the Presence," *Christian Century*, Apr. 29, 1942, 558.
54 Kelly, *Testament*, 35–37, 69–72, 92.
55 Ibid., 98, 116, 124.
56 Ibid., 56–57.
57 Ibid., 44–46.
58 Ibid., 89, 93, 102, 115.
59 Ibid., 106–10.
60 Underhill, *Practical Mysticism*; "The Way of Contemplation," *Peacemaker*, July 20, 1953, 3.
61 "Disciplines Necessary for Pacifist Living" (School of Pacifist Living, CPS Camp 21, Cascade Locks, Ore., Jan. 26, 1944), Records of American Friends Service Committee, Civilian Public Service, SCPC.
62 "A Way of Life: A Group Statement," pamphlet, 9–10, Camp 23 (Coshocton, Md.), Records of American Friends Service Committee, Civilian Public Service, SCPC.
63 Brinton, ed., *Guide to True Peace*. For advertisements see, for example, "Harper and Brothers calls your especial attention to these new books," *Fellowship*, Oct. 1946, back cover; and "Important New Books" and "Building the Cell," *Fellowship*, Oct. 1947, inside back cover; for American Baptist Publication Society, see *Builder* 1947, 40, 43, 52; and *Builder* 1954, 90.
64 Kepler's *Fellowship of the Saints* (1948) included excerpts from works of Underhill, Kelly, Fosdick, Harkness, Hunter, Steere, Lester, Laubach, Heard, Rufus Jones, and Stanley Jones, as well as of Karl Barth, Reinhold Niebuhr, Rudolf Otto, Jacques Maritain, and others.
65 Rufus M. Jones, introduction to Jones et al., *Together*, 7–11 (see note 42, above). Glenn Clark was probably editor (*Fellowship Messenger*, Sept.–Oct. 1956, 9); the twelve contributors included Clark, E. Stanley Jones, Laubach, Howard Thurman, and Clark's protégés Rufus Moseley, Starr Daily, and Glenn Harding.

66 "Descriptive matter for jacket of *The Glorious Company*," 1928, typescript, Papers of Mygatt and Witherspoon, Series C, Box 9, SCPC; Jane Corby, "New Old Christmas Legend," 1928, clipping from *Brooklyn Daily Eagle*, Dec. 20, 1928, Papers of Mygatt and Witherspoon, Series C, Box 9, SCPC.
67 Cleghorn, *Threescore*, 136–37. Cleghorn also made reference to Boston's Emmanuel Movement, an "Episcopalian form of Christian Science" (ibid., 138).
68 "Peace Pilgrim Fasts, Prays for World Disarmament," *Peacemaker*, Aug. 16, 1954, 3.
69 "Thoughts in Prison: Selections from the Letters of Five Imprisoned Conscientious Objectors," *Fellowship*, Jan. 1946, 8–9.
70 "The Way of Contemplation," *Peacemaker*, July 20, 1953, 3, reprinted from *Seeker*, Kingwood, N.J.
71 James, *Varieties of Religious Experience*, was an important source for many twentieth-century mystics.
72 Duveneck, *Life on Two Levels*, 163–66.
73 Ibid., 329–30.
74 Ibid., 218–19, 282–86. The text does not give the date of her membership but refers only to her "middle years."
75 Elizabeth Isichei, *Victorian Quakers* (London: Oxford University Press, 1970), 39, and Caroline Stephen, *Quaker Strongholds* (London: K. Paul, Trench, Trubner, 1890), 30–33, cited in Barbour et al., "Liberal Pastors and New Intellectual Meetings, 1900–1945," 224.
76 Hamm, *Transformation of American Quakerism*, 149–50.
77 For example, Edward B. Rawson thought that nonmystical Friends outnumbered mystics but were put off by the notion that "meetings [for worship] are for mystics only" (letter to the editor, *Friends Intelligencer*, 10th Month 6, 1934, 642). Brand Blanshard, chair of Swarthmore's philosophy department, argued vehemently against mystical perception as a basis for pacifism. See his "Mysticism and Pacifism," *The Friend*, 9th Month 5, 1940, 72–73. Chuck Fager has suggested that Orthodox Friends adopted mysticism earlier than Hicksites did, perhaps because of Jones's closeness to Orthodox institutions; see Fager, "Liberal Friends (Re) Discover Fox," *Quaker History* 93:1 (Spring 2004): 48. My own reading of *The Friend*, *Friends Intelligencer*, and the books of discipline tends to support his hypothesis.
78 Prominent converts such as Muste, Steere, and Cleghorn offer further evidence, as noted earlier in this chapter. During the 1950 Fast for Peace, Muste described his "devotional reading" of the seventeenth-century mystic Fénelon (circular letter, A. J. Muste to FOR E.C. Members and Staff, April 3, 1950, Records of Fast for Peace Committee, SCPC). The Quaker educator George A. Walton argued that converts were drawn primarily to "spiritual religion" and

made reference to Evelyn Underhill. See Walton, "The Forward Look," *Friends Intelligencer*, 10th Month 20, 1934, 665–66). Barbour and Frost (*Quakers*, 242) have noted the influence of Rufus Jones's writing and visitation in the formation of the generally liberal independent and college meetings.

79 Mather, *Pendle Hill*, 52; Leslie D. Shaffer, "Fellowship Council Annual Meeting," *Friends Intelligencer*, 2nd Month 15, 1941, 102–3; Shaffer, "The Wider Quaker Fellowship," *Friends Intelligencer*, 11th Month 14, 1942, 741–42.

80 *Faith and Practice of the Philadelphia Yearly Meeting* (1955), 7–8. The earlier texts are Orthodox (*Faith and Practice of the Religious Society of Friends* [1926], viii, x, xi) and Hicksite (*Book of Discipline of the Religious Society of Friends* [1927], 7). The Orthodox and Hicksite yearly meetings of Philadelphia, which had separated in 1827–28, reunited in 1955 and issued *Faith and Practice of the Philadelphia Yearly Meeting*.

81 I have argued this more fully in "Protestant Mysticism."

82 Carpenter, *Revive Us Again*, 5. See also Griffith, *God's Daughters*, and Poloma, *Main Street Mystics*.

CHAPTER EIGHT

1 *Program Suggestions for World Peace*, inside front cover. Compare Greene, "What Can Christians Do for Peace?"; and John Swomley, "Youth News and Plans," *Fellowship*, Feb. 1941, 31: "Frequently, young people ask, 'What can we do in our own community to create peace?'" Boeckel's *Between War and Peace* included a chapter titled "What You Can Do for Peace" (415–508).

2 See, for example, Boeckel, *Between War and Peace*, 416–42, 494–508; Barber, *Halt! Cry the Dead*, 98; Page, *Religious Resources*, 65–87; "Leader's Guide—Young People's Institutes," Chicago, General Conference Commission on World Peace, Methodist Episcopal Church, 1939, mimeograph, 6–12, SF Education and Peace, Box 33, SCPC; John M. Swomley, "Pacifist Youth News and Plans," *Fellowship*, Nov. 1940, 147; "Pacifists Are Told of Special Responsibilities" [recommendations of Syracuse Peace Council], *Fellowship*, Dec. 1946, 200; and *Report of the Bucksteep Conference of the Episcopal Pacifist Fellowship*, 1947, [6–8], Records of the Episcopal Pacifist Fellowship, Box 9, SCPC. "Hydrogen Bomb Tests Must Be Stopped," *Peacemaker*, July 1957, 5, omits plays and adds picketing and fasting, but devotes most of its space to advice on meetings, letter-writing, leafleting, petitions, etc.

3 *Beyond War*, 20–22.

4 John Leslie Lobingier, *Is War the Way?*, 38–40.

5 Chatfield, *For Peace*, 136–37; Boeckel, *Between War and Peace*, 434; Mary Hoxie Jones, *Swords into Ploughshares*, 174–77.

6 One pair of caravanners is said to have persuaded a traveling evangelist that

they were sent by God to speak to that evening's meeting, but this account is not entirely reliable (see Mary Hoxie Jones, *Swords into Ploughshares*, xvii, 187, 192–93, 200). Chatfield described caravanning as an AFSC project only, but there is evidence that other organizations adopted the caravan idea, such as WILPF in 1931 and the Emergency Peace Campaign in 1936–37. See Chatfield, *For Peace*, 269–73; Curti, *Peace or War*, 172; Alonso, *Peace as a Women's Issue*, 121; and "Speakers' Instructions," Oct. 13, 1936, mimeograph; "Enlist for Peace," mimeograph; "No-Foreign-War Crusade," printed flyer; and "Supplement to the Printed Outline of No-Foreign-War Crusade," mimeograph, Records of Fellowship of Peace, Meadville, Pa., SCPC.

7 Constance Muste, "Soap-Boxes," 32.
8 Mary Page Raitt, telephone interview.
9 Van Dyck, *Exercise of Conscience*, 61.
10 "Pacifism and High School Groups," *Fellowship*, Oct. 1941, 174. Swomley was a Methodist.
11 Stephen G. Cary, in "W.W. II Civilian Public Service," Papers of Robert Horton, SCPC.
12 It is also worth noting that one of the participants in the FOR caravan described earlier was "trying to orient himself in the fairly new atmosphere of pacifism" (Constance Muste, "Soap-Boxes," 9).
13 Van Dyck, *Exercise of Conscience*, 62.
14 "Summary of Discussions on Economics, and Civil Disobedience during Peace Fast," [1951], typescript, Records of Fast for Peace Committee, SCPC. The range of the participants' interests included race relations, "the spiritual interpretation of life," and cooperation in prayer with nonpacifists.
15 Allen Bacon, "Recollections of Ahimsa Farm," May 4, 1989, typescript, Records of Ahimsa Farm, SCPC. See Chapter 9.
16 Richard Anderson, *Peace Was in Their Hearts*, 127–28.
17 "The Return of the Guardian Angel," *Fellowship*, Mar. 1950, back cover.
18 Macgregor, *Relevance of the Impossible*; Read, *Education for Peace*.
19 Gregg, *Training for Peace*, 1.
20 Ibid., 2–3, 35–36.
21 Cf. Lester, *Training*, and Heard, *Training for the Life of the Spirit*.
22 Gregg, *Training for Peace*, 5, 8, 9, 20–21.
23 Ibid., 23, 33.
24 Ibid., 39–40. Compare the common statement among midcentury pacifists that "Christianity has not failed, it hasn't been tried." Sr. Anne McCarthy, of the Catholic pacifist group Pax Christi, discussing the conflicts in Somalia and Yugoslavia, "lamented that large contingents of pacifists were not already well trained in nonviolence" (Peter Steinfels, "Reshaping Pacifism to Fight Anguish in Reshaped World," *New York Times*, Dec. 21, 1992, A1).

25 Gregg, *Training for Peace*, 6–9, 19–20, 27, 33.
26 On human nature he noted, "Human nature even when at first sight repellant [sic], is always interesting if it is closely and intelligently observed" (ibid., 19).
27 Ibid., 2, 11, 18, 21.
28 In keeping with the assumption of human capacity, Gregg advised, the lyrics of the hymns should meet the rather daunting requirement of being "free from doubt, fear, trouble, pride, or warlike connotations" (Ibid., 14).
29 Ibid., 14, 18, 21.
30 Ibid., 10, 15, 21–22, 24–25, 28. On progressive education Gregg cited Peterson, *Creative Re-education*.
31 Ibid., 25.
32 Ibid., 9. Cf. Gould, *At Home in Nature*, on the use of round buildings to encourage "consensus and equality" at one homestead (15).
33 Gregg, *Training for Peace*, 1.
34 Ibid., 13. Compare Crum, *Guide to Religious Pageantry*, 34, on the "broader sympathy" and "more extended vision" fostered by participation in theater.
35 Gregg, *Training for Peace*, 14.
36 Ibid., 13. Gregg does not discuss singing as a bodily event: the use of breath, for example, or the possibility of an altered mental state. The folk high schools, founded by the Lutheran bishop and theologian Nikolai Grundtvig, sought to develop self-reliance and national identity through programs of adult education that incorporated local crafts and skills.
37 Ibid., 15.
38 Ibid., 16–17, 18n.
39 Ibid., 18.
40 Ibid., 33.
41 Ibid., 24–26.
42 Ibid., 23–25.
43 Ibid., 26–27. The folk schools used a similar rationale.
44 Ibid., 14–15.
45 Cf. Toelken, *Dynamics of Folklore*, 39–40, on the "twin laws" of conservatism and dynamism; and Catherine Bell, *Ritual Theory*, on the "construction of tradition," 118–24.
46 Gregg, *Training for Peace*, 26n.
47 "Typical Week-End Program" in "Ahimsa Notes," [1940?], envelope of loose sheets, Records of Ahimsa Farm, SCPC. The Ahimsa Farm community used the Quaker term "meeting" and claimed to hold discussions "after the manner of Friends," but there is no evidence of a common denominational or religious commitment apart from FOR membership. It is unclear from the evidence, an anonymous handwritten document, whether the weekend routine was

"typical" of programs that had actually occurred or was only an ideal or proposal.

48 "So You're Going to Fellowship House Farm!," 1952, brochure, Records of Fellowship House, Philadelphia, Pa., SCPC.

49 Kohl and Kohl, "How This Book Came About," xv.

50 See also the account of a "peace school" in Petzen, Germany, influenced by the International FOR and the (U.S.) Episcopal Peace Fellowship (George Hogel, "A Ton of Old Shoes," *Fellowship*, Feb. 1949, 6–7); and "Kingwood Holds Seminars on 'The Life of Prayer,'" *Peacemaker*, July 20, 1953, 3.

51 In this connection see, for example, the posthumous collection of Gandhi's comments on industrialism, farming, and handwork, *Man v. Machine*.

CHAPTER NINE

1 Draft report, FOR Commission on Rural Life, 1942, p. [2], SF Conscientious Objection, SCPC.

2 Maffly-Kipp, "Communitarianism," 155.

3 Timothy Miller, *Quest for Utopia in Twentieth-Century America*, xiv; Gould, *At Home in Nature*, 8, 190.

4 Few historians have given adequate attention to this period. Kanter argued for three waves of communitarian movements: religious before 1845, "politico-economic" from 1820 through 1930, and "psycho-social" from 1946 through the 1970s. See Kanter, *Commitment and Community*, 8; and Kanter, introduction to *Communes*, xii–xiii. Fogarty's introduction refers to the 1920s and 1930s as a "decentralist-survival" period but then skips to the 1960s (*Dictionary of American Communal and Utopian History*, xxv). Both Lippy ("Communitarianism," 861) and Maffly-Kipp ("Communitarianism") mention the emergence of communities during times of social transition but give little attention to the mid-twentieth century. Berry's correlation of waves of communitarian movements with economic downturns does not account for the 1940s. See Berry, *America's Utopian Experiments*, passim. Timothy Miller's work is most useful here, since it identifies the strands and patterns of communitarianism particular to the twentieth century, together with historical accounts of many communities.

5 Gould, *At Home in Nature*, xvii, 4.

6 Timothy Miller, *Quest for Utopia*, 163–65. Morgan was president of Antioch College from 1921 until 1933, when he became the first director of the Tennessee Valley Authority, a noted experiment in regional planning. In 1943 he published *Small Community Economics*, a popular text among pacifists. Yellow Springs, Ohio, where Antioch is based, was home to a number of pacifist and communitarian ventures. Morgan taught in CPS camps and at pacifist schools

such as Pendle Hill. Raised a Baptist, he became a Quaker in his thirties. A complex and ambiguous figure, he seems to have been charismatic but difficult to work with. See Segal, "Morgan, Arthur Ernest," 820–22.

7 Davis, *Contemporary Social Movements*, 542; Page, *A New Economic Order*; Study Packet on Cooperatives, [1937?], Records of Congregational Christian Churches of the United States, Council for Social Action, Series 22, SP-4, Congregational Library, Boston, Mass.; E. R. Bowen, "A New Pacifist Technique," *Fellowship*, Apr. 1935, 11–12. Davis provides a good general history and description of the cooperative movement to 1930 (*Contemporary Social Movements*, 527–79). The study packet cites Page, Kagawa, E. S. Jones, and Rauschenbusch, among others.

8 George H. Tichenor, "Are the Co-ops Getting Anywhere?," *Christian Century*, Oct. 9, 1940, 1247–49.

9 Sinclair, *Co-op*, xi.

10 *The Intentional Communities*, 20–33; Timothy Miller, *Quest for Utopia*, 133–38, 156–60; Pitzer, "Appendix," 449–94; Carl J. Landes, "Cooperative Farming Communities," *Fellowship*, Dec. 1942, 204.

11 Report of Rural Secretary, Feb. 15–Mar. 14, 1946, Records of FOR, Section II, Series A-1, Box 4, SCPC.

12 Chatfield, *For Peace*, 178.

13 Brinton, *Pendle Hill Idea*, 17, 32; Murphy, *Roots of Pendle Hill*, 18–29; Greenwood, *Henry Hodgkin*; Mather, *Pendle Hill*, 9, 31, 42, 52; "Summer at Pendle Hill," *The Friend*, 7th Month 14, 1938, 12; Heard, *Quaker Mutation*; "Pendle Hill Notes," *Friends Intelligencer*, 4th Month 12, 1941, 239–40.

14 Niebuhr, circular letter, May 27, 1932, reproduced in Myles Horton, *Long Haul*, 61–62. Cf. Chatfield, *For Peace*, 178–79. Highlander later became an important training center for the civil rights movement. Horton (*Long Haul*, 47–50, 52–53) counted Jane Addams and the settlement movement among important influences and connected folk-school practices with the Danish cooperative movement.

15 *Flight from the City* was reissued in 1947, was popular among postwar homesteaders, and was reprinted in 1972 for the next back-to-the-land movement. There is some confusion about the fate of the School of Living. Borsodi resigned amid controversy in 1941. Methodist pacifists Ralph and Lila Templin apparently ran the school until 1945. According to Timothy Miller (*Quest for Utopia*, 132, 156), in that year Mildred Loomis, of Lane's End Homestead in Brookville, Ohio, claimed to be opening a new School of Living. Gould (*At Home in Nature*, 186) regards Loomis as Borsodi's successor. However, in 1949 the Templins were running a School of Community Living near Yellow Springs, Ohio, which also claimed continuity with Borsodi's institution. See "School of Community Living," *Peacemaker*, June 28, 1949, 3; and "These Said

No to Conscription," *Fellowship*, May 1946, 72–74. On education, see also Miller's discussion of earlier experiments: Ruskin, Commonwealth, and Black Mountain Colleges (*Quest for Utopia*, 122–27).

16 Jones's work also supported Protestants' practice of mysticism; see Chapter 7.

17 Tweed and Prothero, *Asian Religions in America*, 209; "School of Community Living," *Peacemaker*, June 28, 1949; Jay Holmes Smith, "A memorandum concerning a New York Ashram," [1940?], typescript, Records of FOR, Series II, A-3, Box 13, SCPC. Jones also wrote on cooperative economics and cooperative cell groups in *Christ's Alternative to Communism*. Catholic Worker urban cooperatives and cooperative farms also arose during these years; the first farm was founded in 1935. See William Miller, *Harsh and Dreadful Love*, 100–101, 121–26, 130–32, 202, 204, 210; and Roberts, *Dorothy Day and the Catholic Worker*, 14, 77–78.

18 Draft report, FOR Commission on Rural Life, [2], SF Conscientious Objection, SCPC. *Fellowship* referred often to new and older cooperative communities during these years. Miller (*Quest for Utopia*, 160–66) and Pitzer ("Appendix," 449–94) provide useful summaries, though they disagree on some details. With respect to the early 1940s, Miller places the founding of Bryn Gweled in 1939, Pitzer and *TIC* in 1940. See Miller, *Quest for Utopia*, 166; Pitzer, "Appendix," 455; and *TIC*, 30.

19 On goats, cf. Borsodi, *Flight*, 34–35. Landes referred to "the famous Landes goats" (Carl Landes, Report to National and Regional Offices, Oct. 8, 1941, typescript, Records of FOR, Series II, A-3, Box 3, SCPC). Cf. Gould, *At Home in Nature*, 21, 135.

20 Shridharani was best known for his *War without Violence* (1939).

21 This account is drawn from Larry Gara and Lenna Mae Gara, "Ahimsa Farm: A Gandhian Experiment in Ohio," *Fellowship*, May–June 1996, 20–21; and from Records of Ahimsa Farm, SCPC.

22 "The Chautauqua Retreat and Conference," *Fellowship*, Oct. 1940, 128; "With Nothing to Keep Them Alive," ibid., back cover; "Mid-West and Rural Work Moving Forward," *Fellowship*, May 1942, 86; "Rural Program Planned," *Fellowship*, June 1942, 106; Carl Landes to John M. Swomley Jr., Aug. 6, 1946, carbon, and Landes to Swomley, Aug. 16, 1946, carbon, Records of FOR, Series II, A-3, Box 3. Landes was appointed field worker for a trial period; the FOR agreed to support the secretaryship in early 1941 and set up an office at Merom, Indiana, where the Congregational Christian Churches also operated a rural-aid school, the Merom Institute. Much of Landes's work consisted of traveling and speaking.

23 A collection of documents concerning the Harlem Ashram is found in the FOR records, Series II, A-3, 13, SCPC. See also Jay Holmes Smith, "Our New

York Ashram," *Fellowship*, Jan. 1941, 2; Jervis Anderson, *Bayard Rustin*, 70–71; and Daniel Levine, *Bayard Rustin*, 29. On the conflicts, see especially "A Proposal Regarding the Future of the Ashram," unsigned and undated but apparently written by Smith, in the FOR records, Series II, A-3, 13, SCPC; and A. J. Muste to E. Stanley Jones, July 3, 1942, carbon, Records of FOR, Series II, A-3, Box 4, SCPC. On influence, see Lightfoot, *Balm in Gilead*, 227–28.

24 K'Meyer, *Interracialism and Christian Community*, 31–52. On Jordan and Koinonia, see also Lee, *Cotton Patch Evidence*, and Fuller, *Briars in the Cotton Patch*.

25 TIC, 30; *Fellowship*, Nov. 1940, 146; *Fellowship*, Feb. 1941, 31; *Fellowship*, Jan. 1942, 18; *Fellowship*, Feb. 1942, 26; Dellinger, *From Yale to Jail*, 66–67.

26 This Presbyterian enterprise, a workingmen's church, was a center of progressive Protestant activity. A. J. Muste was pastor there from 1937 until 1940. See Jo Ann Ooiman Robinson, *Abraham Went Out*, 76, and Lightfoot, *Balm in Gilead*, 227. Regional conferences on pacifist farming were planned for New England, Apr. 11–12, 1942, and for the Midwest at an indeterminate date. See "Pacifist Farm Enthusiasts Discuss Possibilities," *Fellowship*, Aug. 1942, 64.

27 Carl J. Landes, "A Critical Study of the Urge to Pacifist Farming," in "Report of Conference on Pacifist Farming Communities," 1942, 2–3, SF Conscientious Objection, SCPC.

28 Ibid., 4.

29 Thomas E. Jones, *Creative Pioneering*.

30 "Gladys Gray" in *Friends in Civilian Public Service*, 213; "Rosalie Wilson" in ibid., 228.

31 For a good overview of this history, see Orser, *Searching for a Viable Alternative*. Many CPS documents refer to co-ops or to Schools of Living; for example, see "Coop refunds surplus" (on Camp Coshocton's Rochdale-style cooperative store), *Seed*, Aug. 1942, 3; *Pocomoke Opinion*, Feb. 1944, [1], on the "School of Non-Violence" led by Muste, Gregg, Rustin, Douglas Steere, and others; *Pacifist Study Exchange*, a periodical issued at the Merom, Indiana, camp for general circulation "to other camps, ashrams, and all pacifist groups" ("A Restatement of Aims," *Pacifist Study Exchange*, Mar. 1942, [1]); and many others.

32 All from *Fellowship*: May 1946, 84; July 1946, 135; Sept. 1946, 153.

33 K'Meyer, *Interracialism and Christian Community*, 74–75; Pitzer, *America's Communal Utopias*, 487; Orser, "Macedonia Cooperative Community," 379–81; Art Wiser, "A brief, more personal note," [Mar. 25, 1954], Records of Macedonia Cooperative Community, Box 4, SCPC.

34 On the matter of the far-reaching influence of the farm communities, I am indebted to the insights and experience of my husband, William L. Holladay (1926–), who visited Tuolumne Co-op Farm (TCF) many times between 1947 and 1951 and spent the summer of 1949 there while a seminary student. He has emphasized the function of TCF and other pacifist farms as idealized

models of true Christian life for liberal-minded young adults, many of whom undertook visits and short-term residencies. Histories of other communities also recall visitors and seekers, though it is unclear how many there were. Thomas Moore recalled visits and participation at TCF as essential to his formation (Thomas Moore, interview). Cf. Art Dole to "Ginny & Happy" [Virginia and Paul Smith], Jan. 9. 1989: "[In 1941] Ahimsa played host to a flow of pacifists, socialists, Antiochians, oddballs and saints" (Records of Ahimsa Farm, SCPC). See also *Report of Sixth Annual Conference of the Episcopal Pacifist Fellowship*, 1945, 2–3, Records of the Episcopal Pacifist Fellowship, Box 3, SCPC, on cells, cooperatives, and monastic communities as "leaven."

35 Auction notice, [1958], Records of Macedonia Cooperative Community, Box 4, SCPC; K'Meyer, *Interracialism and Christian Community*, 81–98, 172–82; Tuolumne Farm in Transition," *Creative Living* [mimeographed newsletter], Spring–Summer 1959, 1, 4, in author's possession; "T.C.F.—Retrospect, Prospect," *Creative Living*, Fall–Winter 1959, 1, 5. Concerning TCF, a surviving former member recalled the date as 1958 but expressed uncertainty. See Ted Klaseen to author. The farm was listed in *TIC* in 1959, but without recent news.

36 May Valley had been in the planning stages since 1949, and some of its members took an interest in the Bruderhof. See Timothy Miller, *Quest for Utopia*, 168–69.

37 Ibid.; "Oregon [sic] Co-op Community Formed," *Peacemaker*, Apr. 9, 1956, 3; Christopher Clark, *Communitarian Moment*, 5–7. On declension, cf. Gould, *At Home in Nature*, 189–90.

38 See, for example, Page, *Living Creatively*, 42–44, and *Living Prayerfully*, 51; "Job Report, Ahimsa Farm," 1940, Records of Ahimsa Farm, SCPC; and Gould, *At Home in Nature*, 3–4.

39 David Newton to Nicolai Scheierman, July 18, 1948, Records of Macedonia Cooperative Community, SCPC.

40 Here my own conclusions parallel Gould's on the centrality of practice and the presence of "liturgies" of rural life and work. See Gould, *At Home in Nature*, 3–4, 35, and passim.

41 Bob Reynolds, letter, "Says Homesteading Is Valuable," in *Peacemaker*, Aug. 27, 1956, 3. Cf. "Brief for Community," *Communiteer*, Jan. 1944, 1–2.

42 Maffly-Kipp, "Communitarianism," 155.

43 *Communiteer* no. 3, quoted in *Communiteer*, Jan. 1944, 1.

44 In some ways this rationale is not a new argument; compare the eighteenth-century Quaker John Woolman's admonition to "try whether the seeds of war have any nourishment in these our possessions" (Woolman, *Plea for the Poor*, 255). But both the practice and the rationale respond to a particular set of historical circumstances and create a practice to address them.

45 Ralph Templin, "Total Pacifism and Farm Communities," in "Report of Conference on Pacifist Farming Communities," 1942, 5–6, SF Conscientious Objection, SCPC.
46 "Job report," 1940, Records of Ahimsa Farm, SCPC. This report may have been written for the work-study program at Antioch College; see Allen Bacon, "Recollections of Ahimsa Farm," May 4, 1989, typescript, Records of Ahimsa Farm, SCPC.
47 Dorothy Burgeson, "Ahimsa," *Mather Record*, Jan. 17, 1941, 4.
48 [Craig letter (circular letter)], Mar. 19, 1941, mimeograph, Records of Ahimsa Farm, SCPC.
49 David Salstrom to Mary Wiser and Morris Mitchell, Apr. 7, 1946, Records of Macedonia Cooperative Community, Box 1, SCPC.
50 Bryn Hammarstrom to Lee Stern, May 25, 1989, photocopy, Records of Ahimsa Farm, SCPC; caption to undated photograph of neighbor Ralph Dimmick, Records of Ahimsa Farm, SCPC; Gara and Gara, "Gandhian Experiment," 4.
51 Ted Klaseen to author.
52 All from Records of Macedonia Cooperative Community, SCPC: Edward R. Miller for American Friends Service Committee to Morris Mitchell, Sept. 2, 1941, Box 1; Mitchell to Miller, Sept. 15, 1941, carbon copy, Box 1; Mitchell to "Tommy," Sept. 16, 1941, carbon copy, Box 2; Harold Garfinckel to "Art" [Wiser?], July 11, 1947, Box 1; "Articles of incorporation, history and purpose," [1948], p. [1], Box 2. In 1941 Mitchell enlisted the help of an AFSC work camp, but the AFSC refused to give a second year's assistance. See Miller to Mitchell, Nov. 18, 1941, Box 1.
53 Stanley Gould, "Advice to the Landlorn," *Fellowship*, Sept. 1949, 9.
54 A hopeful couple, farming in South Carolina in 1947, wrote, "Most of our neighbors have not yet accepted diversified farming as the answer to their problems" (Wilmer and Mildred Young, circular letter, Dec. 31, 1947, mimeograph, Records of Macedonia Cooperative Community, Box 1, SCPC). Wilmer Young later participated in CNVA's Omaha Action.
55 Art Wiser, "Morning at Macedonia," *Fellowship*, Nov. 1952, 13–17, 32. It was undoubtedly intentional anti-industrial irony that led them to name one of the cows "Velveeta."
56 Cf. Gould, *At Home in Nature*, 228.
57 "Ahimsa Farm, Aurora, Ohio: Leaflet No. 2," n.d., Records of Ahimsa Farm, SCPC; "Tuolumne Co-op Farm," in *TIC* (32–33), which cited FIC Newsletter, Apr. 1956; "Intentional Community Principles and Membership," in *TIC*, 2–3, statement developed in 1953; "Terms of Trusteeship and Non-Ownership for the Workers' Community of the Universal Citizens at St. Francis Acres," *TIC*, 22–24; Klaseen to author; Orser, *Searching for a Viable Alternative*, 122, 187; Dellinger, *From Yale to Jail*, 150–51. See also David Newton to Nicolai Scheier-

man, July 18, 1948, Records of Macedonia Cooperative Community, SCPC; "The Harlem Ashram," [1944?], mimeographed brochure, Records of the FOR, Series II, A-3, Box 3, SCPC; and Wendell Thomas, *There Is but One Individual*. Compare also "The Religious Fellowship of Fellowship House" (n.d., brochure, Records of Fellowship House, SCPC).

58 Ahimsa rented its land and houses from the mother of one of the members and relied on Professor Chatterjee for cash; Tuolumne leased its land; Macedonia's land came from one individual, Mitchell. Carl Landes expected to develop a community on ten acres that a woman had purchased "for just such a program as [this]" (Landes to Swomley, Aug. 6, 1946, Records of FOR, Series II, Box A-3, SCPC). On the Nearings, see their *Living the Good Life*.

59 K'Meyer, *Interracialism and Christian Community*, 54; Orser, *Searching for a Viable Alternative*, 132–35; A. J. Muste to E. Stanley Jones, July 3, 1942, carbon, Records of FOR, Series II, A-3, Box 4, SCPC; Timothy Miller, *Quest for Utopia*, 129–32. At TCF, the founding members were regarded with some deference (Klaseen to author, 1998).

60 Orser, *Searching for a Viable Alternative*, 186; Allen Bacon, "Recollections of Ahimsa Farm."

61 There is evidence that education was a problem at Harlem, Koinonia, and Macedonia. Racial conflicts sometimes placed Koinonia's children in danger.

62 "A Proposal Regarding the Future of the Ashram," an unusually full description of conflicts over religious basis, activity, leadership, and money.

63 Richard Fichter, "Farmer at the Gates," *Liberation*, Oct. 1957, 9–11; "This Month," *Fellowship*, Mar. 1949, inside front cover.

64 This two-tiered life is common in what anthropologist Mary Douglas calls "the culture of the enclave," a model that, like sectarianism, resembles but does not fully explain postparadigm-shift pacifism. See Appleby, "Fundamentalism of the Enclave," 251, and Sivan, "Enclave Culture," 16–17.

65 This might also have been a factor in Protestant pacifists' turn to Quakerism from the late 1930s onward: the opportunity to reject excess without abandoning a minimal level of stability. While I have found no evidence of conscious interest in mendicancy among pacifists, there were a few who apparently practiced it, traveling from one community to another for visitation, with the expectation of being fed and housed (Holladay [see note 34, above]). Arthur Morgan ("Report of Conference on Pacifist Farming Communities," 1942, 7, SF Conscientious Objection, SCPC) mentioned "community tramps" in constant search of perfection.

66 The exception was Howard Brinton (*Pendle Hill Idea*, 9), who applied his thinking primarily to Pendle Hill.

67 A. J. Muste, *Not By Might*, 212; A. J. Muste, "Relation of the Rural Movement to

Total Pacifism," in "Report of Conference on Pacifist Farming Communities," 1942, 5, SF Conscientious Objection, SCPC (emphasis in original). The report was derived in part from lecture notes, hence the telegraphic statements. Gould describes the Nearings' farm as a "seminary in the woods" where they were "first acolytes and then spiritual leaders" (*At Home in Nature*, 164).

CHAPTER TEN

1 Fred Small, "Scrambled Eggs and Prayers," on *No Limit*, Rounder Records 4018, ©1985, Pine Barrens Music (BMI), used by permission; Sue Allison, "Grandmother Who Captured Fugitive Gets Ovation from Senate," UPI, April 15, 1985; Louise Degrafinried as Told to Jeffrey Japinga, "The Woman who Wasn't Afraid," *Reader's Digest*, Feb. 1985, 105–8, condensed from *Guideposts*, Oct. 1984; William H. Willimon, "Bless You, Mrs. Degrafinried," *Christian Century*, Mar. 14, 1984, 269–70.
2 Cf. "The Silver Tankard," in *Children's Story Garden*, 167–70.
3 Exempla have a long history in Near Eastern and European thought. The term comes from classical Latin rhetoric, and specimens appear in Jewish, Christian, and folk literature. See Gottwald, *Hebrew Bible*, 560, 564–66; Dan, "Exemplum," 1020–21; Jülicher, *Die Gleichnisreden Jesu*; Mosher, *Exemplum*; and Lyons, *Exemplum*.
4 Wallace, *Heroes of Peace*; Hagedorn, *Book of Courage*. See also Chamberlin, *Heroes of Peace*, and *Paths of Peace*, Books I–IV. One of the more startling "paths to peace" in Book IV of that title was the invention of the spinning jenny and the subsequent development of the Lancashire textile mills, which, the author argued, enabled England to resist Napoleon's advance and to become prosperous. See *Paths of Peace*, IV:55.
5 Hagedorn, *Bomb that Fell on America*. Hagedorn, an American Lutheran of German descent, regretted his support of World War I and dabbled in Quakerism but was not an absolute pacifist. In 1933 he joined the conversionary and highly moralistic Oxford Group. See Keller, *States of Belonging*, 243–49; and "Hermann Hagedorn, Biographer of Theodore Roosevelt, Is Dead," *New York Times*, July 28, 1964, 29.
6 Hunter, "You Can Hold a Hand Uplifted over Hate," in his *Heroes*, [iv].
7 Kagawa was already well known to Americans by 1939. William Axling's adulatory 1932 biography (*Kagawa*) placed Kagawa firmly in the context of Protestant social activism and mysticism. A new edition appeared in 1946. Kagawa's own spiritual writings, which appeared in English as *Songs from the Slums*, with an introduction by Sherwood Eddy, and *Meditations on the Cross*, were also popular, and his Rauschenbusch Lectures at Colgate-Rochester Seminary were published as *Brotherhood Economics* in 1936.

8 Kagawa was at Princeton from 1914 to 1917. Major influences on his thought and practice were Tolstoy, Kant, and Christian mystical writers.

9 Hunter, *Three Trumpets*, 4, 12–14, 28, 38–39. See below for discussion of the "intruder disarmed" tale type. On Father Damien, see Chapter 6, note 26. A personal experience offers suggestive evidence of his fame in Protestant culture: my late father-in-law and I, who differed in age by over fifty years, recalled hearing identical anecdotes about the moment Father Damien realized he had leprosy—my father-in-law in the YMCA in California, I in public school in New Jersey.

10 Hunter (*White Corpuscles*, 49) said that its title came from Gerald Heard: "The white corpuscles, observes Gerald Heard, are most active where the wounds are deepest." After Hunter, other pacifists borrowed the idea of "white corpuscles"; for example, "Pacifist Action Program, Suggested by Don Baldwin and Chicago F.O.R." (*Fellowship*, June 1941, back cover) said, "Love is working ... in the heroic living of the 'white corpuscles' of Europe." Arthur Holt, social activist and president of Chicago Seminary, referred to the "microbe hunters of social conflict" (Memorial issue, *CTS Register*, Mar. 1942). The language of "creative living" and "heroic living" echoed the Protestant pacifist rhetoric of the 1920s and 1930s.

11 The other two subjects were the English Socialist George Lansbury and the German pastor Friedrich Siegmund-Schultze.

12 One should also mention in this connection a "hero" who was not on Hunter's list—André Trocmé of Le Chambon-sur-Lignon, a village in Vichy, France. Trocmé, a Protestant pastor and pacifist, led the villagers in sheltering Jews. He was arrested, but he survived and was later an unusually thoughtful writer on pacifism and social action. See André Trocmé, "Non-Violence Is Not Enough," *Fellowship*, Jan. 1946, 6–8; and Hallie, *Lest Innocent Blood Be Shed*.

13 Rufus M. Jones, foreword to Vernier, *With the Master*, 5–6; Vernier, *With the Master*, 7. Vernier's translator referred to St. Francis in her foreword to his *Not as the World Giveth*, 8.

14 Other types of exempla had ordinary women as their central characters. For a discussion of the hagiography of Addams see Allen F. Davis, *American Heroine*, 293. Lotz, ed., *Women Leaders*, 8, quoted a public figure who ranked Addams with the Virgin Mary in historical importance.

15 The preface to Hunter, *White Corpuscles*, is titled "Not in the Headlines" ([ix]), a phrase that also appears in the preface to Hunter, *Heroes*, [iv]. The FOR youth periodical *Forerunner* took up the phrase as the heading for a regular feature.

16 Silk, *Unsecular Media*, 53.

17 The work of the folk process is evident in some retellings of this story. One version has "soldiers" of each nation camping on the side of the opposing na-

tion (see Berg, *Story Worship Services*, 60–62), while most versions say it was the "people" who did this.

18 "Christ of the Andes," postcard-sized lecture illustration with text, NCPW, n.d., author's collection; cf. "Toward Peace" set, 1930, Records of NCPW, Postcards, SCPC.

19 "Christ of the Andes" postcard; Mary Esther McWhirter, "Christ of the Andes," in Brinton, McWhirter, and Schroeder, *Candles*, 102.

20 Boeckel, *Through the Gateway*, 23–25; Anna D. White, "Christ of the Andes," in Griscom, ed., *Peace Crusaders*, 68–70; *Educating for Peace*, 81. Boeckel's *Across Borderlines* included a photograph of the statue, facing p. 56. Berg, *Story Worship Services*, 60, gives as her source a pamphlet from the "Missionary Education Movement."

21 Lobingier and Lobingier, *Educating for Peace*, 156–61; *Program Suggestions for World Peace*, 23; *The Exhibit on Friendship Between Nations, Sesquicentennial Exhibition, Philadelphia, 1926* (Philadelphia: Edward Stern, 1927), 26, SF Art in War and Peace, SCPC; Baber, *Peace Symbols*, 4–5; NCPW Christmas card, 1922, Records of NCPW, Postcards, SCPC.

22 Limbert, "What Children Think About War," [2]; John Leslie Lobingier, *Is War the Way?*, 3.

23 Brainerd, *Broken Guns*, 78–83; Elizabeth Miller Lobingier, *Ship East*, 53–59; McPherson, *Educating Children for Peace*, 178; *The Teacher Patriot*, no. 2 (1938), 6–7; *With Children Leading*, 50–53; Brinton, McWhirter, and Schroeder, *Candles*, 98–102, and others.

24 The story appeared in Boeckel, *Through the Gateway*, 17–19; Brainerd, *Broken Guns*, 84; Lobingier and Lobingier, *Educating for Peace*, 37; Elizabeth Miller Lobingier, *Ship East*, 4–6; and Brinton, McWhirter, and Schroeder, *Candles*, 94–97. See also Anna D. White, "The Rush-Bagot Agreement," in Griscom, ed., *Peace Crusaders*, 74–75.

25 Zonia Baber (*Peace Symbols*, 5) notes that the original plan, proposed by a coalition of peace groups, was to celebrate a "Century of Peace" in 1914. For obvious reasons it was postponed. It seems likely that the story began to be told as an exemplum at about the same time, but I have been unable to document this.

26 Baber counted many more monuments—her text says there were seventeen, but she names at least twenty—to peace along the border, including the International Peace Bridge from Buffalo to Fort Erie, Ontario, a fountain in Chicago, and a Good Will Memorial named for Warren G. Harding and erected by the Kiwanis. See Baber, *Peace Symbols*, 7. Inscriptions and dedications of such monuments made familiar general statements about peace and good will, but only the narrative exempla emphasize the moral lessons of trust and individual initiative.

27 Ibid., 5.
28 The story takes for granted the legitimacy of colonization, as did Penn himself. There is, however, good evidence of his efforts to deal justly with the Indians. For further discussion see Soderlund, ed., *William Penn and the Founding of Pennsylvania*, 84–88, 307–17; and Spady, "Colonialism and the Discursive Antecedents," 19, 275 n. 2.
29 Allan Hunter, *Heroes* (27), says that this was a period of thirty years.
30 Among others, this was an explicit meaning of the Fellowship House mural (see Chapter 6): "Penn built his city as a refuge where people of every race and color might be welcome. His Pact with the Indians was one of 'Friendship'" ("Guide to Fellowship House," Records of Fellowship House, Philadelphia, Pa., SCPC).
31 Of these, note especially Gray's *Penn*, published in 1938 and reprinted in 1944, 1947, and 1986; and Henry Joel Cadbury, "Penn the Pioneer," *Christian Century*, Dec. 6, 1944, 1412–13.
32 Hull, ed., *William Penn's Plan for a League of Nations*; Drake, "William Penn's Experiment in Race Relations," 372–87.
33 Fletcher, *Pioneers in Peace*, 3.
34 Limbert, "What Children Think about War," 1–2.
35 Fletcher, *Pioneers in Peace*, 3, 10–13; *With Children Leading*, 7–14 and 28–31; Lobingier and Lobingier, *Educating for Peace*, 155–58; Jacobs and DeBoer, eds., *Educating for Peace*, 259, 263–64; S. Lucia Keim, "Quakers and Indians," cited in *World Citizenship and the Religious Program*, [5]. There is also a record of a Philadelphia pageant in 1908 that included Penn's treaty among "many scenes related to Quakers"—surely not the only pageant to have done so. See Oberholtzer, *Book of the Pageant*.
36 McPherson, *Educating Children for Peace*, 106; "A Boot Is a League of Nations," in *CSC*, 220–25. See also Armstrong, *How Peace Grows*, 37.
37 The Indians do not retain possession of the land; the protagonists repent, offer hasty assurances to the Natives, and invite everyone back. The first pageant script, "A Shoe—A League of Nations," appears in McPherson, *Educating Children for Peace*, 104–6. McPherson cited a Friends Peace Committee leaflet as her source. See also "A Boot Is a League of Nations," *CSC*, 220–24; the editor of *CSC* cited an "idea suggested by" the NCPW (see *CSC*, 320). Another pageant was part of a high school program for Goodwill Day (May 18); see Davis-DuBois, *Contribution of Racial Elements*, 14–15. The play, "America for Americans," in McPherson, *Educating Children for Peace*, 107–13, came from a Lutheran body (Education Dept., Women's Missionary Society, United Lutheran Church in America); it connected the peace movement and Lutherans' long-standing concern with immigration issues. The Vacation Church School programs whose work McPherson describes combined these plays and

pageants with numerous other favorite motifs and texts of the peace movement, for example, the Christ of the Andes story, the song "Ain't Gonna Study War No More," and the example of Jane Addams. See McPherson, *Educating Children for Peace*, 93, 114, 131.

38 *Silver Lining* 8:13 (1960), back page, Records of Children's Plea for Peace, SCPC.

39 Harry Webb Farrington, *Valleys and Visions* (New York: Farrington Memorial Association, 1932), cited in McPherson, *Educating Children for Peace*, 22, 24, 29, 113. Subsequent stanzas of the song bring the world to "my school" and to "church."

40 Aarne, *Verzeichnis der Märchentypen*; Thompson, *Folktale*; Thompson, *Motif-Index of Folk-Literature*. Folklorists now use structuralist and poststructuralist methods of narrative analysis as well, but for my purposes the classical model is useful and sufficient.

41 Compare Toelken on conservatism and dynamism (*Dynamics of Folklore*, 39–40).

42 It seems likely that the ritual nature of the stories would be manifested also in their effect on the audience, even an audience distanced by print — an effect of tension, release, and reassurance, as in some forms of ritual performance.

43 There is good evidence of numerous informal truces between French and German army units at Christmas 1914 and 1915 See Heineman, ed., *Readings in European History*, 206–8. Stories of the truces have become another modern folk song, John McCutcheon's "Christmas in the Trenches." Brinton, McWhirter, and Schroeder, *Candles*, includes three stories about boys — John Woolman, Albert Schweitzer, and George Washington Carver — who forswore violence out of remorse after killing birds (see "Birds and Boys," 51–53; and "The Man who Couldn't Be Defeated," 144–49). A similar anecdote appears in Dellinger's *From Yale to Jail*, 449–50.

44 Richards, "Test of Faith," 617–27; Mrs. St. Clare Stobart, "How to Treat Burglars," from *Miracles and Adventures* (London: Rider, 1935), in Fry, *Victories*, 55–58.

45 See L. Violet Hodgkin, "Fierce Feathers," adapted by Mary Esther McWhirter from Hodgkin's *Book of Quaker Saints*, in Brinton, McWhirter, and Schroeder, *Candles*, 190–93; and historical discussion by Bassett in "Migration of Friends," 31–32. See also "The Missionary's Wife in China," altered from Pearl S. Buck's fictionalized biography of her mother, *The Exile* (New York: Reynal & Hitchcock, 1936), 154–62, in Fry, *Victories*, 69–71, and in Brinton, McWhirter, and Schroeder, *Candles*, 28–33; and Allan Hunter's alterations of Richards' "Test of Faith" in Hunter, *Heroes*, 1–5, and Hunter, *Courage*, 37–40.

46 See "St. Francis and the Robbers" in *With Children Leading*, 78–81. In the story known variously as "The Highwayman" or "Leonard Fell and the Highway-

man," Fell, an early Quaker, submits quietly to robbery. In the earliest account, Fell feels "the power of Truth rise in him" and preaches to the robber to "turn from his evil ways" (George Fox, *Journal*, quoted in Fry, "Leonard Fell and the Highwayman," in *Victories*, 81). A twentieth-century version makes the story a parable of reaching out fearlessly in love and "the holy Light" ("The Highwayman," in *FSC*). Versions of the story also appear in Hodgkin, *Book of Quaker Saints*, and in *Children's Story Garden*, 146–49. Compare "Preaching to Nobody" in Hodgkin, *Book of Quaker Saints*, 511–19, and "The Sermon in the Wilderness" in *FSC*, 239–44, for similar evidence of changed sensibilities.

47 Cf. the preface to *CSC* (13), referring to its predecessor, *Children's Story Garden*: "When selection had failed to offer enough material to cover all the points they [the editors] wished to emphasize, they were forced to supply the deficiency by adapting, rewriting, and inventing."

48 On urban legends see Toelken, *Dynamics of Folklore*, 316–19. For examples, see Allan Hunter's stories about "Mike" or "Michael" in *Heroes*, 24–25, 34–39; *Courage*, 33–37; and *Secretly Armed*, 11–18. A version of these stories, "The Canadian Soldier Who Could Not Kill," also appears in Fry, *Victories*, 82–83.

49 Anna Pettit Broomell, "The Children's Story Caravan: A Quaker Committee at Work," typescript "reprinted from the Friends' Quarterly (British)," ca. 1950, shelf, Friends' Historical Library, Swarthmore, Pa.; Broomell, preface to *FSC*, ix; Janet E. Schroeder, preface to Brinton, McWhirter, and Schroeder, *Candles*, [iii].

50 For example, Quaker religious-education curricula used Rauschenbusch, Fosdick, Page, Heard, Lester, and Hunter, as well as the Quakers Gregg and Jones. See "Reconstructing our World," *First-day School Lessons* (Friends General Conference), 1st Month 1941, 1–68; and "An Evaluation of Bible Material," *First-day School Bulletin* (Friends General Conference), 4th Month 1939, 4. Vesta Haines wrote curricula for both Presbyterians and Friends, using among others McPherson, Boeckel, and Hunter. See E. Vesta Haines, "Good Will Around the World," in *First-day School Lessons*, 4th Month 1940, 1–51, revised from Junior Westminster Departmental Graded Material, Board of Christian Education, PCUSA, 1938. Methodist peace-education material included Boeckel, McPherson, the Lobingiers, Griscom, and Broomell, as well as Kirby Page, Muriel Lester, and Richard Gregg. See *Children Learn Peace*.

51 *Young People and a New World*, 3–5; *Children Learn Peace*.

52 A recent variant concerns a U.S. officer and an Iraqi civilian who are both women. The officer, momentarily alone, is prepared to shoot the civilian but stops herself. They exchange gestures of respect and laugh together. Later the officer advocates peace. See Susan Ives, part 1 of "The Spirit of Nonviolence: Twelve Stories from the Journey," *Peace Notes*, winter 2000, 1. (*Peace Notes* is issued by the Lutheran Peace Fellowship.)

53 *Above All Nations*, compiled by Vera Brittain and others, was entirely devoted to "acts of kindness done to enemies, in the present war, by men of many nations" (dust jacket). It appeared during World War II and was similar in format to the Fry and Hunter books. The stories covered a wide range of "acts of kindness," from medical assistance to sermons. None conformed to the folkloric tale type of friendship between soldiers. The title, according to the authors, came from an "inscription on the campus of Cornell University, U.S.A." E. Raymond Wilson (*Thus Far on my Journey*, 27) quoted the same phrase as "used around International House" at Cornell.

54 Lobingier and Lobingier, *Educating for Peace*, 163; Joseph Folliet, "Not Enemies, but Friends," in Brinton, McWhirter, and Schroeder, *Candles*, 121. The Lobingiers' version was a dramatization (see *Educating for Peace*, 161–63); Griscom, ed., *Peace Crusaders*, included a narrative version by Joseph Folliet called "The Meeting" (57–60), and credited the Junior Red Cross publication *High School Service*. "Not Enemies, but Friends" was an edited version of "The Meeting" (see Brinton, McWhirter, and Schroeder, *Candles*, 118–21). A variant of this tale type is Grete Paquin-Gallwitz, "Holy Ground," *FSC*, 147–54.

55 These are the stories about "Mike" or "Michael" in "The Canadian Soldier Who Could Not Kill," in Fry, *Victories*, 82–83; and in Hunter, *Heroes* (34–39), *Courage* (34–37), and *Secretly Armed* (13–19). The versions agree that the young man thereafter manages a near-miraculous escape from harm; for example, he returns from a raid with only one minor injury despite the many bullet holes in his uniform—in one version sixteen, in another twenty. See "Canadian Soldier Who Could Not Kill," in Fry, *Victories*, 83; and Hunter, *Secretly Armed*, 16.

56 "Friendliness" is of course very close to "love"; I have chosen the former term as descriptive of the gestures and actions rather than of the inner motivation of the characters.

57 The intruder is almost invariably male. The one exception is a story in which Muriel Lester, when threatened by a neighborhood woman, wards off attack by means of calmness and prayer. See Hunter, *Heroes*, 4–5, and *White Corpuscles*, 47–48. This story diverges from the type in that there is no shared meal and no offer of restoration.

58 Charles Mackintosh, "Creative Solutions," in Hunter, *Courage*, back cover.

59 On men, see the tales of Edward Richards and hostile Kurds (Richards, "Test of Faith"), of Toyohiko Kagawa and intruders in Kobe (Hunter, *Heroes*, 5–7), and of Allan Hunter's pseudonymous Canadian "Mike" and a burglar (Hunter, *Secretly Armed*, 12–13, and *Courage*, 33–34). A related story included theft, food, and restoration, but not intrusion (see "The Thief in the Tanyard," in Hodgkin, *Book of Quaker Saints*, 479–88, and "Advertising for a Thief," in *FSC*, 75–78).

60 For example, "Jane Addams's Burglars" in *CSC*, 67–68, and *FSC*, 61–62 (*CSC* credited Addams's nephew James Weber Linn by way of the children's author Marjorie Hill Allee, 318); "Elizabeth Fry and the Burglar," in Fry, *Victories*, 23, which credits *Howard Journal*, 1925; and "Elizabeth Fry and the Boot" in Brinton, McWhirter, and Schroeder, *Candles*, 20–23, which credits *Victories*.

61 Of the source, *CSC* says, "Members of Anna White's family feel sure that this story was based on historical fact but they have not been able to find the source" (317).

62 "The Silver Tankard," in *Children's Story Garden*, 167–70, and *FSC*, 173–76.

63 In *Children's Story Garden*, 56–59; *FSC*, 193–96; reprinted by NCPW; in Rex, *We Worship*, 262–68; in McPherson, *Educating Children for Peace*, 53, and *Learning about War and Peace*, 88, giving *Children's Story Garden* as the source. In 1930 the pacifist journalist Devere Allen (*The Fight for Peace*, 624) said of this story—which by then had appeared in at least three published sources—"This yarn appears to have started with Mrs. Lydia Maria Child . . . [and] has never been proved as fact." The story continued to circulate until at least 1981, with the last reprinting of *FSC*. For other tales of this type see, for example, "Willing to be Plundered" and "Abby Greene and the Soldiers" in Fry, *Victories*, 19–20; "An Ill Wind" in *CSC*, 25–30, and *FSC*, 17–22; "Savages Too Can Become Peacemakers" and "Light in Russia that Overcomes Darkness" in Hunter, *Heroes*, 17–18, 32–34; and "Invite the Aggressor to Tea" and "Can You Fight Fire with Fire?" in Hunter, *Courage*, 72–73, 77.

64 Information on the source of the story is from Bassett, "Migration of Friends," 31–32. The commemoration is not a reenactment (telephone interview with clerk of Easton Monthly Meeting, Feb. 3, 2000). The story appears in Hodgkin, *Book of Quaker Saints*, 465–78; Fry, *Victories*, 18; and Brinton, McWhirter, and Schroeder, *Candles*, 190–93. For others of the type see "The White Feather" in *Children's Story Garden*, 13–18; in *FSC*, 126–31; and in *Pilgrim Elementary Teacher* 14 (Nov. 1930): 489–91; "The Latchstring" in *Children's Story Garden*, 177–79, and in *FSC*, 142–44; "High Tea" in *CSC*, 53–60; and "The 'Holy Experiment' of William Penn" in Fry, *Victories*, 14–15. Boeckel, *Through the Gateway* (1928), incorporates the motifs of the white feather and the latchstring into one tale (15–17).

65 "Faint Heart Failed" in *CSC*, 61–66, and in *FSC*, 183–88; Hunter, *Heroes*, 27, and *Courage*, 94; "'Holy Experiment,'" 14–15. In another variant, Indians decline to fight with Indiana Shakers in 1812 (see Allen, *Fight for Peace*, 622–23). As with the Penn stories, the tales involving Indians assumed that Native and European Americans could and should live side by side, and did not question the legitimacy of colonization.

66 *With Children Leading*, 78–81, which cites Jewett, *God's Troubadour*, and "Brother Angelo and the Robbers," in Caroline M. Duncan Jones, *Lord's Min-*

strel; *Young People and a New World*, 5; "St. Francis and the Robbers," n.d., reprint issued by NCPW, SF Education and Peace, SCPC. The original story is in chapter 26 of the *Little Flowers*, which exists in many editions; see, for example, *Little Flowers of St. Francis*, 100–103. For variant versions see Clarence E. Pickett, "William Pickett Meets the Robbers," in Brinton, McWhirter, and Schroeder, *Candles*, 45–46; "The Highwayman" in *FSC*, 189–92; "Leonard Fell and the Highwayman" in Fry, *Victories*, 81; and "Advertising for a Thief" in *FSC*, 75–78. A similar story, but without the nonviolence topos, appears in chapter 20 of Louisa May Alcott's *Little Men*.

67 "Cherries of Hamburg," Education Dept., NCPW, n.d., typescript; and "Cherries of Hamburg" (Philadelphia: Friends' Peace Committee, 1930), printed leaflet, both in SF Education and Peace, Box 30, SCPC. The NCPW document included a prose version credited to *Messenger of Peace*, Aug. 1922, and a verse version, "The Cherry Festival at Naumburg," credited to the Twentieth Century Medal Contest, National Women's Christian Temperance Union Publishing House. Both versions appeared in Griscom, ed., *Peace Crusaders* ("Cherries of Hamburg," 76–78; "The Cherry Festival at Naumburg," 95–96). *Scattered Seeds*, supplement and final issue, Dec. 1935, reprinted a verse version from vol. 15, 1883. For a variant see "Hospitality that Is Not Appeasement," in Hunter, *Courage*, 56–58.

68 "A Children's Army" in Fry, *Victories*, 84–85.

CHAPTER ELEVEN

1 The article was Jhan Robbins and June Robbins, "You Are a Bad Mother," in *Redbook: The Magazine for Young Adults*, Aug. 1960, 38–39, 97–99. The play was Regen, "Bad Mother." Anxiety about "bad mothers" is a recurrent theme in late-twentieth-century America; see, for example, Ladd-Taylor and Umansky, eds., *"Bad" Mothers*, and Roz Chast's popular cartoon "Bad Mom Cards: Collect Them All!," frontispiece in Chast, *Childproof*.

2 This chapter refers to her throughout by the surname "Swann" for the sake of consistency. At this writing she is married to the Rev. John F. Edwin Jr., a bishop in the Methodist Church of Ghana, and uses his surname.

3 Amy Swerdlow offers a useful summary of maternalist thought in her *Women Strike*, 27–40; see also Ruddick, *Maternal Thinking*.

4 Marjorie Swann, interview.

5 Her family of origin attributed her father's abusive behavior to his having been gassed and shell-shocked during World War I, but she learned as an adult that his father and grandfather had also been abusers (Marjorie Swann, interview).

6 Ibid. Like the Kiwanis and Rotary peace monuments at the U.S.-Canada border, this is an example of the widespread reaction against World War I.
7 "Statement by Marjorie Swann, Participant in Omaha Action," July 21, 1959 (Papers of Marjorie Swann, SCPC).
8 Marjorie Swann, interview.
9 The *Redbook* article describes a particular moment of decision: her brother joined the army amid the congratulations of their father's fellow Legionnaires, and at the next youth group meeting Marjorie declared, "I'm a pacifist too!" (Robbins and Robbins, "You Are a Bad Mother," 98). Neither this story nor Swann's later recollection, however, suggests the kind of wrestling and agonizing that Gray described.
10 Marjorie Swann, interview.
11 Ibid.
12 Its moderate counterpart was the National Committee for a Sane Nuclear Policy (SANE), a broad-based organization of "nuclear pacifists"—opponents or critics of nuclear weapons who did not necessarily oppose all war. SANE used conventional tactics, primarily lobbying and public pressure, in a single-issue campaign to ban atmospheric testing. SANE foundered under allegations of communist infiltration in 1960, and the subsequent "purge" damaged its credibility with many pacifists.
13 Historians differ on the original goals of the project and the reason for the shift in tactics. Neil H. Katz's discussion of the conflicts within CNVA from the beginning of the planning process and their consequences offers the most nuanced explanation; see his "Radical Pacifism," 78–89. See also Chatfield, *American Peace Movement*, 103; Wittner, *Rebels against War*, 262; and DeBenedetti, *Peace Reform*, 161.
14 For a fuller treatment of these controversies, see Katz, "Radical Pacifism," 73–78; DeBenedetti, *Peace Reform*, 61; and Chatfield, *American Peace Movement*, 104.
15 Arthur Harvey, "Noncooperation with Arrest," *Peacemaker*, Aug. 1, 1959, 4–5.
16 Robbins and Robbins, "You Are a Bad Mother," 93. The circumstances of this arrest are unclear. Swann did consider noncooperation while in prison but evidently decided against it. See Marion Bromley, "Visit to Alderson," *Peacemaker*, Nov. 21, 1959, 4. She had changed her views by 1967. See Marjorie Swann, "Noncooperation," *Win*, June 1967, 3–4, reprinted in Lynd and Lynd, *Nonviolence in America*, 272–74. Was scrupulosity a preoccupation of men more than of women? Alongside Arthur Harvey's articles, Margaret von Selle's "Letter from Omaha" described the "wonderful spirit of unity" in the group and minimized differences. See *Peacemaker*, Aug. 1, 1959, 5.
17 It is unclear what her children thought, but the evidence suggests that they

continued to support her work in general and that they were primarily affected by her absence, not by her brief local incarceration.

18 Swann, quoted in Robbins and Robbins, "You Are a Bad Mother," 99.
19 Swann was modest about this sentence: the judge, she said, gave her the minimum sentence in federal prison rather than a shorter sentence in the county jail because he thought conditions in the former were more decent. (For a sentence of fewer than six months, federal marshals had the option, under certain circumstances, of placing a convict in a local jail. A six-month sentence meant that federal prison was the only option.) "Well, I don't think we particularly appreciated his solicitous attitude," she commented (Marjorie Swann, interview).
20 "Statement by Marjorie Swann," 1959, Papers of Marjorie Swann, SCPC.
21 "Statement by Robert Swann in Support of his Wife, Marjorie Swann, Participant in Omaha Action," Papers of Marjorie Swann, SCPC.
22 Transcribed notes of official federal reporter, *United States of America v. Marjorie Swann*, Criminal no. 0444, U.S. District Court, District of Nebraska, filed Aug. 26, 1959.
23 Cf. Robbins and Robbins, "You Are a Bad Mother," 100; "A Mother at the Gate to the Missile Site in Omaha," offprint from *Peacemaker*, n.d. (ca. autumn 1959), 2, Papers of Marjorie Swann, SCPC.
24 There is no written documentation of this remark; the quote appears in Robbins and Robbins, "You Are a Bad Mother," 39, and is similarly recalled by Swann. Judge Robinson's comment on his "plain duty" appears in the court transcript cited above.
25 Robbins and Robbins, "You Are a Bad Mother," 100; Marjorie Swann, interview.
26 "To Friends of Marj Swann and Sympathizers with her Concerns," [autumn 1959], 2, Papers of Marjorie Swann, SCPC; "A Mother at the Gate"; Margaret von Selle, "Copy of a Letter," *Peacemaker*, Oct. 10, 1959, 4; "Swann Family Carries On," *Peacemaker*, Nov. 21, 1959, 1, 3.
27 Margaret von Selle, "A Letter to Marj Swann," *Peacemaker*, Sept. 12, 1959. This letter mentions a meeting of the Episcopal Pacifist Conference led by Albert Bigelow of the *Phoenix* and by Dorothy Day.
28 She also made the prescient suggestion, "Perhaps it is time for an organization of *Mothers Against War*, or a *Mothers' March to the White House*" (Jean Putnam, "A Mothers' March on the White House?," *Peacemaker*, Aug. 22, 1959, 3).
29 Anonymous excerpt in "To Friends of Marj Swann," 2. See also "15 Arrested, 6 Jailed in Omaha Protest," *Peacemaker*, Aug. 1, 1959, 1, which referred to "Marj Swann, mother of four children"; Margaret von Selle, "Copy of a Letter [to the Swann daughters]," *Peacemaker*, Oct. 10, 1959; and "Swann Family Carries On."

30 The *World-Herald* published an editorial critical of the pacifists after the arrest of Karl Meyer, son of Vermont congressman William J. Meyer (see "No-Nonsense Judge," July 16, 1959). Occasional short press releases appeared in August.

31 "Another Conscience Speaks at Omaha," *Christian Century*, July 29, 1959, 868–69; "Pacifist Mother Deals with Cereal Company," *Fellowship*, Peace Information Edition, Nov. 1, 1959, front cover; "News from the Peace Front," *Fellowship*, Peace Information Edition, Nov. 1, 1959, [3]. The *Times* published no reports on Omaha Action between July 15 and Nov. 19 (see *New York Times Index*, New York: New York Times Co., 1960).

32 Marjorie believed that Carol's distress that autumn was due to other causes, largely school-related. Carol remembers little of it. See Marjorie Swann, interview; and Carol Swann, telephone interview.

33 The author of the play credited the *Redbook* article, the narrative is largely extracted from it, and many of the lines are verbatim or nearly verbatim quotes from it. See Rosalie Regen, "Bad Mother."

34 This idea had occasionally been introduced in earlier materials for children. See, for example, Yarnall, "People Who Went to Prison Because They Were Good," in *Changing Swords into Plowshares*, an ecumenical collection of church-school units on peace; Yarnall was a Quaker. Her third- and fourth-grade pupils wrote reports on such "heroes" as Socrates, Eugene Debs, Harold Gray, and Gandhi, and mentioned in passing first Penn, then Jesus, then Galileo, St. Francis, Kagawa, Lester, and others.

35 Materials on pacifist child-rearing from the 1950s bear this out. One branch of WILPF addressed "the problems that face the children of non-conformist parents" and "the mother's dilemma—home and community responsibility" (Marie Lyons and Betty Lindemann to "Dear Mothers," Oct. 23, 1957, circular letter, WILPF, Newton-Wellesley, Mass., Branch; "Resume—Discussion of Dec. 5, 1957," WILPF, Newton-Wellesley Branch, in Records of WILPF, 1919–59, Wilmington, Del.: Scholarly Resources, [1988], microfilm, reel 30). The Family Institutes of Friends General Conference, first held in 1947, gathered parents to discuss common concerns, e.g., "Should a young mother who feels called to a concern leave her family frequently to work on it?"; "How do we help our children maintain our testimonies in the world?"; and "the problem of non-conformity" ("Report of the Family Institute," 1951, mimeographed report, [1], 3; "Summary of the addresses, discussion groups, and family conversations," Friends General Conference Family Institute, 1955, mimeographed report, 6–7; both in Records of Friends General Conference, Friends Historical Library, Swarthmore, Pa.). See also Charles and Margaret Lawrence, "The Child's Own World," *Fellowship*, July 1953, 5–10; and D. D. and R. F. [David Dellinger and Roy Finch], "In Our Own Image," *Liberation*, Sept. 1956,

3–5. As early as 1947, religious educator and mystic Margueritte Harmon Bro addressed this topic in "Children Up a Tree: How to Be a Successful Pacifist Parent," *Fellowship*, July 1947, 111–12, 116.

36 Carol Swann, interview.

37 Kaplan and Shapiro, *Red Diapers*, 4–11 and passim; cf. their "Growing Up Red."

38 There is a large literature on this subject, particularly in the genre of memoir. Examples include Barnes, *In the Wilderness*; Gordon, *Shadow Man*; Simmons, *Unseen Shore*; and Ulstein, *Growing Up Fundamentalist*.

39 Jill Ker Conway, "Convention versus Self-Revelation: Five Types of Autobiography by Women of the Progressive Era," Project on Women and Social Change, Smith College, June 13, 1983, cited in Heilbrun, *Writing a Woman's Life*, 24–25.

40 There is, of course, a larger and finally unanswerable question of prior intentionality. Although Marjorie Swann Edwin has always maintained that she did not go to Omaha intending to perform civil disobedience, one can perhaps wonder whether she felt some unconscious pull or calling. It would not be surprising in an experienced and committed pacifist. But this is speculation.

41 It is unclear whether this episode reflected reality or was a dramatic device; Swann does not recall whether the family in fact gave her a negligee.

42 See Heilbrun, *Writing a Woman's Life*, 20–21, 31, on the "unambiguous" or "ambiguous" woman. The play also affirms traditional gender roles by placing all the responsibility for housework and cleaning on the daughters, where in reality the father took a share of it.

43 "Swann Family Carries On," 1.

44 Another important context was the masculinization of the peace movement. Timothy Stewart-Winter ("Not a Soldier, Not a Slacker," 535 and passim) has shown how, after the Selective Service Act of 1940, pacifism became more tightly identified with conscientious objection than ever before, and was thus increasingly gendered male, despite the large numbers of women in the movement. Marjorie Swann's action accepted this identity, but also offered a corrective to it.

45 Women in other causes, such as women's suffrage, had, of course, engaged in direct-action tactics earlier. Note also Susan Lynn's observation that "just as war privileged men as actors, opposition to war privileged the men who resisted" (Lynn, *Progressive Women*, 95).

46 Swerdlow, *Women Strike*, 27–40; Alonso, *Peace as a Women's Issue*, 164–66, 190–92.

47 Swerdlow, *Women Strike*, 8.

48 Ibid., 27–40; cf. Epstein, *Politics of Domesticity*.

49 However, Swerdlow also cites a 1962 survey indicating that 43 percent of the

married members, who constituted 95 percent of the whole, had up to four children under the age of six. Children in strollers were a common feature of WSP demonstrations. See Swerdlow, *Women Strike*, 66–68.

50 Ibid., 3, 73, and passim.

51 As the quote makes clear, this was not a mere public-relations gesture. Swann was presenting an image that she also accepted for herself. For later treatments, see also Mary McGrory, "3 Mild Mothers Try White House Walk-in," *Boston Globe*, Evening Ed., Mar. 17, 1962, 3.

52 Fathers' activism was rarely questioned.

53 Pinker quotes psychologist Shari Thurer on the "denial of maternal ambivalence": "There's a real silence about the ambivalent feelings . . . it's tantamount to being a *bad mother*." Thurer refers here to a mother's relationship with her children, not to her activity outside the family, but the societal assessment of ambivalence as "bad" motherhood is worth noting. Interview with Thurer by D. C. Denison, *Boston Globe Magazine*, May 14, 1995, quoted in Pinker, *How the Mind Works*, 450–51; see also Thurer's *Myths of Motherhood*.

EPILOGUE

1 See, for example, Chatfield, *For Peace*, 116, 301; and DeBenedetti, *Peace Reform*, 133.

2 Toelken, *Dynamics of Folklore*, 316.

3 Lester, *It Occurred to Me*, 13.

4 McNeal, *Harder Than War*, 223–25, 244–57.

5 Lynn, *Progressive Women*, 95, 139; Goossen, *Women Against the Good War*, 10; Stewart-Winter, "Not a Soldier, Not a Slacker," 527, 529, 535; Sara Evans, *Personal Politics: the Roots of Women's Liberation in the Civil Rights Movement and the New Left* (New York: Knopf, 1979), 179, cited in Stewart-Winter.

6 Lynd and Lynd, *Nonviolence in America*, xii; Samuel H. Day Jr., *Prisoners on Purpose*; "Ecclesial protest," *Christian Century*, May 24–30, 2000, 589; Raphael Lewis, "Pedal power," *Boston Sunday Globe*, Sept. 17, 2000, section B, page 1.

7 See Coles, *Children of Crisis*; Coles, *Story of Ruby Bridges*; Ruby Bridges, *Through My Eyes*; and Marshall et al., *Ruby Bridges Story*.

8 All have published and lectured widely. Useful recent works include the following: Cortright, *Gandhi and Beyond*; Ritter, *Waging Peace*; Stassen, *Just Peacemaking* and *Living the Sermon on the Mount*; Hauerwas, *Hauerwas Reader* and *Performing the Faith*; Wink, *Jesus and Nonviolence* and the *Powers* series.

9 For more on Bread and Puppet Theater, see John Bell, *Landscape and Desire*, and Simon and Estrin, *Rehearsing with Gods*.

Bibliography

ARCHIVAL SOURCES

Boston, Mass.
   Congregational Library
      Records of Congregational Christian Churches of the United States,
          Council for Social Action, 1934–56
St. Paul, Minn.
   Macalester College Archives
Swarthmore, Pa.
   Friends Historical Library
      Records of Friends General Conference
   Swarthmore College Peace Collection
      Papers of Emily Greene Balch
      Papers of Vera Brittain
      Papers of Horace Champney
      Papers of Robert Horton
      Papers of Tracy D. Mygatt and Frances Witherspoon
      Papers of Mary Phillips
      Papers of John Nevin Sayre
      Papers of Marjorie Swann
      Records of Ahimsa Farm
      Records of American Friends Service Committee, Civilian Public Service
      Records of Appeal at Fort Detrick
      Records of Children's Peace Petition Committee
      Records of Children's Plea for Peace
      Records of Christian Peace Committee
      Records of Churchmen's Committee for a Christian Peace

> Records of Committee on World Friendship among Children
> Records of Disciples Peace Fellowship
> Records of Episcopal Pacifist Fellowship
> Records of Fast for Peace Committee
> Records of Fellowship House, Philadelphia, Pa.
> Records of Fellowship of Peace, Meadville, Pa.
> Records of Fellowship of Reconciliation
> Records of Macedonia Cooperative Community
> Records of National Council for Prevention of War
> Records of Women's International League of Peace and Freedom
> Subject Files
>> Art in War and Peace
>> Children and War and Peace
>> Conscientious Objection
>> Education and Peace
>> Peace Monuments
>> Religion, War, and Peace
> Non-Document Collections
>> Memorabilia
>> Peace Symbols
>> Poster Collection

Valley Forge, Pa.
> American Baptist Historical Society
>> Records of the American Baptist Home Mission Society

INTERVIEWS AND CORRESPONDENCE

Hartman, Doris, and Justin Hartman. Interview with author. Tape recording. Amherst, Mass., July 26, 2000.

Klaseen, Theodore A. Personal correspondence with author. Dec. 8, 1998.

Moore, Thomas W., and Anne Moore. Interview with author. Tape recording. Amherst, Mass., May 18, 2000.

Raitt, Mary Page. Telephone interview with author. Transcribed notes. Stockton, Calif.; Newton, Mass., May 5, 1998.

Swann, Carol. Telephone interview with author. May 14, 1998.

Swann, Marjorie. Interview with author. Tape recording. Newton, Mass., May 22, 1998.

PUBLISHED PRIMARY SOURCES

Addams, Jane. *Peace and Bread in Time of War*. New York: Macmillan, 1922.
Alcott, Louisa May. *Little Men*. The Library of America. New York: Literary Classics of the United States, 2005.
Alexander, Ryllis Clair, and Omar Pancoast Goslin. *Worship Through Drama*. New York: Harper, 1930.
All Children Pray. Minneapolis: Children's Plea for Peace, 1958.
Allen, Devere. *The Fight for Peace*. New York: Macmillan, 1930.
Armstrong, Marion C. *How Peace Grows: A World Friendship Unit for Junior Boys and Girls*. Nashville: Cokesbury, 1935.
Axling, William. *Kagawa*. New York: Harper, 1932.
Baber, Zonia. *Peace Symbols*. Offprint from *Chicago Schools Journal*, Mar.–June 1937.
———. *Peace Symbols*. N.p.: WILPF and Society for Visual Education, n.d. [after 1948].
Barber, Frederick A., ed. *Halt! Cry the Dead: A Pictorial Primer on War and Some Ways of Working for Peace*. New York: Association Press, 1935.
Barnes, Kim. *In the Wilderness: Coming of Age in Unknown Country*. Garden City: Doubleday, 1996.
Barton, Bruce. "Let's Advertise This Hell!" *The American Magazine*, May 1932, 15.
———. *The Man Nobody Knows: A Discovery of Jesus*. Indianapolis: Bobbs-Merrill, 1925.
———. "Unknown." In *Beyond War: A Study in Internationalism*. Philadelphia: Presbyterian Board of Christian Education, 1932.
Bays, Alice Anderson. *Worship Services for Youth*. New York: Abingdon-Cokesbury, 1946.
The Beacon Hymnal: For Church Schools, Young People's Services, Day Schools, and the Home. Boston: Beacon, 1924.
Beecher, Henry Ward. "Love, the Fulfilling of the Law." *Sermons*. Vol. 2. New York: Harper and Bros., 1868, 135–64.
Beegle, Mary Porter, and Jack Randall Crawford. *Community Drama and Pageantry*. New Haven: Yale University Press, 1916.
Berg, Mary Kirkpatrick. *Story Worship Services for the Junior Church*. New York: George H. Doran, 1927.
Beyond War: A Study in Internationalism. Philadelphia: Presbyterian Board of Christian Education, 1932.
Blood, Peter, and Annie Patterson, eds., *Rise Up Singing: The Group Singing Songbook*. Bethlehem, Pa.: Sing Out Corp., 1992.
Boeckel, Florence Brewer. *Across Borderlines*. Books of Goodwill, 2. Washington, D.C.: National Council for Prevention of War, 1926.

———. *Between War and Peace: A Handbook for Peace Workers*. New York: Macmillan, 1928.

———. *Through the Gateway*. Books of Goodwill, 1. Washington, D.C.: National Council for Prevention of War, 1926.

———. *Through the Gateway*. New York: Macmillan, 1928.

———. *The Turn Toward Peace*. New York: Friendship, 1931.

———. *The World's Christmas Tree*. Washington, D.C.: National Council for Prevention of War, 1926.

The Book of Discipline of the Religious Society of Friends. [Philadelphia]: Philadelphia Yearly Meeting, 1927.

Borsodi, Ralph. *Flight from the City*. New York: Harper, 1933. Reprint, 1947; Harper & Row, 1972.

Bowman, Clarice. *Spiritual Values in Camping*. New York: Association Press, 1954.

Bowne, Borden Parker. *The Essence of Religion*. Boston: Houghton Mifflin, 1910.

Brainerd, Eleanor Holston. *Broken Guns*. New York: Friendship, 1937.

Bridges, Ruby. *Through My Eyes*. New York: Scholastic, 1999.

Brinton, Howard. *Friends for 300 Years*. New York: Harper, 1952.

———. *The Peace Testimony of the Society of Friends*. Philadelphia: American Friends Service Committee, 1958.

———. *The Pendle Hill Idea*. Pendle Hill Pamphlet 55. Wallingford, Pa.: Pendle Hill, 1950.

Brinton, Howard, ed. *A Guide to True Peace*. New York: Published in association with Pendle Hill by Harper and Bros., 1946.

Brinton, Margaret Cooper, Mary Esther McWhirter, and Janet E. Schroeder, eds. *Candles in the Dark: An Anthology of Stories to be Used in Education for Peace*. Philadelphia: Religious Education Committee, Philadelphia Yearly Meeting, 1964.

Brittain, Vera. *Humiliation with Honor*. New York: Fellowship, 1943.

———. *Testament of Youth: An Autobiographical Study of the Years 1900–1925*. New York: Macmillan, 1934.

Brittain, Vera, George Catlin, and Sheila Hodges, eds. *Above All Nations: An Anthology*. London: Victor Gollancz, 1945.

Bro, Margueritte Harmon. *More Than We Are*. New York: Harper, 1948.

Brooks, Annie Sills. *Adventuring in Peace and Goodwill: A Junior Vacation School*. Boston: Pilgrim, 1930.

Broomell, Anna Pettit, ed. *The Children's Story Caravan*. Philadelphia: Lippincott, 1935.

———. *The Friendly Story Caravan*. Philadelphia: Lippincott, 1949. Reprint, Wallingford, Pa.: Pendle Hill, 1981.

Buck, Pearl S. *The Exile*. New York: Reynal and Hitchcock, 1936.

Challenge to Peacemaking. Chicago: Commission on World Peace, Methodist Church, 1951.

Chamberlin, Ethel Clere. *Heroes of Peace*. New York: G. Sully & Co., 1929.

Changing Swords into Plowshares: Four Units of Work for Junior Children on the Problems of Peace and War. Boston: Pilgrim, 1937.

Chast, Roz. *Childproof*. New York: Hyperion, 1997.

Chatfield, Charles, and Charles DeBenedetti, eds. *Kirby Page and the Social Gospel: An Anthology*. New York: Garland, 1976.

Chew, Arthur Percy, *Plowshares into Swords: Agriculture in the World War Age*. New York: Harper, 1948.

Children Learn Peace: Suggested Plans and Materials. Chicago: General Conference Commission on World Peace, Methodist Episcopal Church, 1939.

The Children's Story Garden. Collected by a committee of the Philadelphia Yearly Meeting of Friends, Anna Pettit Broomell, chairman. Philadelphia: Lippincott, 1920.

The Christian Attitude toward War: The Words of Christ Commonly Quoted for or against War: A Compendium Prepared for Study Groups. New York: [Presbytery of New York City], 1928.

Christian Worship: A Hymnal. Philadelphia: Judson, 1941.

Christian Youth Peace Demonstration: A Handbook of Information and Suggestions. Chicago: Joint Committee on United Youth Program, 1935.

Church Peace Mission. *The Christian Conscience and War*. The Statement of a Commission of Theologians and Religious Leaders Appointed by the Church Peace Mission. New York: Church Peace Mission, [1953?].

The Church School Hymnal for Youth. Philadelphia: Westminster, 1935.

Clark, Glenn. *How to Find Health Through Prayer*. New York: Harper, 1940.

———. *I Will Lift Up Mine Eyes*. New York: Harper, 1937.

———. *A Man's Reach: The Autobiography of Glenn Clark*. New York: Harper, 1949.

———. *The Soul's Sincere Desire*. Boston: Atlantic Monthly Press, 1925.

Clark, Thomas Curtis. *One Hundred Poems of Peace*. Chicago: Willett, Clark, 1934.

Claude, Inis L. *Swords into Plowshares: The Problems and Progress of International Organization*. New York: Random House, 1956.

Cleghorn, Sarah N. "Planting Peace among the Children." In *Pacifism in the Modern World*, edited by Devere Allen, 231–37. Garden City, N.Y.: Doubleday Doran, 1929.

———. *The Seamless Robe: The Religion of Lovingkindness*. New York: Macmillan, 1945.

———. *Threescore: The Autobiography of Sarah N. Cleghorn*. With an introduction by Robert Frost. New York: Harrison Smith & Robert Haas, 1936.

Coles, Robert. *Children of Crisis*. Boston: Little, Brown, 1967.

———. *The Story of Ruby Bridges*. New York: Scholastic, 1995.

"Conscientious Objectors and the R.O.T.C." *Information Service*. Department of Research and Education, Federal Council of the Churches of Christ in America, March 31, 1934.

"Conscientious Objectors in World War II." Supplement to *Fellowship*, Jan. 1949.

Cortright, David. *Gandhi and Beyond: Nonviolence for an Age of Terrorism*. Boulder, Colo.: Paradigm, 2006.

Cranston, Earl. *Swords or Plowshares?* New York: Abingdon, 1937.

Crum, Mason. *A Guide to Religious Pageantry*. New York: Macmillan, 1923.

Curry, Bruce. "The Purpose and Hope of This Conference." In *Religion on the Campus: The Report of the National Student Conference, Milwaukee, December 28, 1926, to January 1, 1927*, edited by Francis P. Miller, 1–8. New York: Association Press, 1927.

Davis, Jerome. *Contemporary Social Movements*. New York: Century, 1930.

Davis-DuBois, Rachel. *The Contribution of Racial Elements to American Life*, 2nd printing, rev. Philadelphia: Women's International League for Peace and Freedom, 1930.

———. *Education in Worldmindedness: A Series of Assembly Programs Given by Students of Woodbury High School*. Philadelphia: American Friends Service Committee, 1928.

Davol, Ralph. *A Handbook of American Pageantry*, 2nd ed. Taunton, Mass.: Davol Publishing Co., 1914.

Day, Albert Edward. *The Terrible Meek*. Pasadena, Calif.: 1939, reprinted in *Fellowship*, Jan. 1940.

Day, Dorothy. *The Long Loneliness*. Garden City, N.Y.: Image, 1952.

———. *The Long Loneliness*. With an introduction by Daniel Berrigan. New York: Harper & Row, 1981.

Day, Samuel H., Jr., ed. *Prisoners on Purpose: A Peacemakers' Guide to Jails and Prisons*. Madison, Wis.: Nukewatch, 1989.

Deas, Edward C. *Gems of Love*. Chicago: Edward C. Deas, 1924.

Dellinger, David. *From Yale to Jail: The Life Story of a Moral Dissenter*. New York: Pantheon, 1993.

Detzer, Dorothy. *Appointment on the Hill*. New York: Henry Holt, 1940.

Dix, Beulah Marie. *Where War Comes*. N.p.: American School Citizenship League, 1916.

Douglas, Margaret. "To the Unknown Soldier: A Brief Miracle Play." In *Educating for Peace*, edited by Ida T. Jacobs and John J. DeBoer, 223–27. New York: D. Appleton-Century for National Council of Teachers of English, 1940.

Drake, Thomas Edward. "William Penn's Experiment in Race Relations." Offprint from *Pennsylvania Magazine of History and Biography*, Oct. 1944, 372–87.

Duveneck, Josephine Whitney. *Life on Two Levels: An Autobiography*. Los Altos, Calif.: William Kaufman, 1978.
Eddy, Sherwood. *I Have Seen God Do It*. New York: Harper, 1940.
———. *A Pilgrimage of Ideas, or the Re-education of Sherwood Eddy*. New York: Farrar and Rinehart, 1934.
Eddy, Sherwood, and Kirby Page. *The Abolition of War: The Case Against War and Questions and Answers Concerning War*. New York: George H. Doran, 1924.
———. *Creative Pioneers: Building a New Society through Adventurous Vocations and Avocations on the Frontiers of Industrial Relations, the Political Movement, the Co-operative Movement, Race Relations, and Socialized Religion*. New York: Association Press, 1937.
Educating for Peace: A Book of Facts and Opinions. New York: Foreign Missions Conference of North America, 1926.
Eichenberg, Fritz. *Art and Faith*. Pendle Hill Pamphlet 68, Wallingford, Pa.: Pendle Hill, 1952.
———. *Artist on the Witness Stand*. Pendle Hill Pamphlet 257. Wallingford, Pa.: Pendle Hill, 1984.
Ellsberg, Robert. "Revealing the Inner Light: An Interview with Fritz Eichenberg." *Catholic Worker*, Oct.–Nov. 1981, reprinted in Eichenberg, *Works of Mercy*, 57–58.
Emswiler, Sharon Neufer. *Women and Worship: A Guide to Nonsexist Hymns, Prayers and Liturgies*, rev. and expanded ed. San Francisco: Harper & Row, 1984.
Evans, Edward W., and Norman M. Thomas, eds. *Pioneers of Good Will: Statements of English Conscientious Objectors in Prison*. New York: Fellowship of Reconciliation, n.d.
Faith and Practice of the Philadelphia Yearly Meeting of the Religious Society of Friends: A Book of Discipline. Philadelphia: [Philadelphia Yearly Meeting], 1955.
Faith and Practice of the Religious Society of Friends of Philadelphia and Vicinity. Philadelphia: Friends' Book Store, 1926.
Fey, Harold E. *Cooperatives and Peace*. New York: Co-operative League of the U.S.A., n.d.
———. *How I Read the Riddle: An Autobiography*. St. Louis: Bethany Press for the Council of Christian Unity of the Christian Church (Disciples of Christ), 1982.
Fisher, William Arms. *Seventy Negro Spirituals*. Boston: Oliver Ditson Co., 1926.
Fletcher, Wanda. *Pioneers in Peace*. Philadelphia: Religious Education Committee, Friends General Conference, 1953.
Fosdick, Harry Emerson. *Adventurous Religion*. New York: Association Press, 1926.

———. *A Guide to Understanding the Bible: The Development of Ideas Within the Old and New Testaments.* New York: Harper, 1938.

———. *The Living of These Days.* New York: Harper, 1956.

———. *The Manhood of the Master.* New York: Association Press, 1913.

———. *The Meaning of Faith.* New York: Association Press, 1917.

———. *The Meaning of Prayer.* New York: Association Press, 1915.

———. *The Meaning of Service.* New York: Association Press, 1920.

———. *The Modern Use of the Bible.* New York: Macmillan, 1924.

———. *Spiritual Values and Eternal Life.* Cambridge, Mass.: Harvard University Press, 1927.

Friends in Civilian Public Service. Wallingford, Pa.: Pendle Hill, 1998.

Fry, A. Ruth. *Victories Without Violence.* 4th ed. London: privately printed, 1952. Reprint, Santa Fe: Ocean Tree Books, 1986.

Gandhi, Mohandas K. *An Autobiography: The Story of My Experiments with Truth.* Translated by Mahadev Desai. Boston: Beacon, 1957.

———. *Man v. Machine.* Edited by Anand T. Hingorani. Pocket Gandhi Series. Bombay: Bharatiya Vidya Bhavan, 1966.

Gibbs, Philip H. *Now It Can Be Told.* New York: Harper, 1920.

Gill, D. M., and A. M. Pullen. *Victories of Peace: Stories of Friendship in Action.* New York: Friendship Press, 1936.

Gordon, Mary. *The Shadow Man: A Daughter's Search for Her Father.* New York: Random House, 1996.

Gray, Elizabeth Janet. *Penn.* New York: Viking, 1938. Reprint 1944, 1947, 1986.

Gray, Harold Studley. *Character "Bad": The Story of a Conscientious Objector, as Told in the Letters of Harold Studley Gray.* Edited by Kenneth Irving Brown. New York: Harper, 1934.

Greene, Theodore Ainsworth. "What Can Christians Do for Peace?" [pamphlet], Boston: Pilgrim, [1935?]

Greenwood, John Ormerod. *Henry Hodgkin: The Road to Pendle Hill.* Pendle Hill Pamphlet 229. Wallingford, Pa.: Pendle Hill, 1980.

Gregg, Richard B. *The Power of Non-Violence.* Introduction by Rufus M. Jones. Philadelphia: Lippincott, 1934.

———. *Training for Peace: A Program for Peace Workers.* Philadelphia: Lippincott, 1937.

Griscom, Anna Bassett, ed. *Peace Crusaders: Adventures in Goodwill: A Book of Recitations for Children.* Philadelphia: Lippincott, 1928.

A Guide to "A Hymnal for Friends". Philadelphia: Religious Education Committee, Friends General Conference, 1955.

Hagedorn, Hermann. *The Bomb that Fell on America.* Santa Barbara, Calif.: Pacific Coast Publishing, 1946.

———. *The Book of Courage.* Philadelphia: John C. Winston Co., 1929.

Haines, E. Vesta. "Good Will Around the World." *First-Day School Lessons*, Fourth Month 1940, 1–51.

Harkness, Georgia. *The Dark Night of the Soul*. Nashville: Abingdon-Cokesbury, 1945.

Hassler, Alfred. *Conscripts of Conscience: The Story of Sixteen Objectors to Conscription*. New York: Fellowship of Reconciliation, 1942.

Hauerwas, Stanley. *The Hauerwas Reader*. Durham, N.C.: Duke University Press, 2001.

———. *Performing the Faith: Bonhoeffer and the Practice of Nonviolence*. Grand Rapids: Brazos, 2004.

Heard, Gerald. *The Code of Christ: An Interpretation of the Beatitudes*. London: Cassell, 1943.

———. *The Creed of Christ: An Interpretation of the Lord's Prayer*. New York: Harper, 1940.

———. *A Preface to Prayer*. London: Cassell, 1945.

———. *A Quaker Mutation*. Pendle Hill Pamphlet 7. Wallingford, Pa.: Pendle Hill, 1939.

———. *Training for the Life of the Spirit*. New York: Harper, 1942.

Hodgkin, Lucy Violet. *A Book of Quaker Saints*. London: T. N. Foulis, 1917.

Hofer, Mari Ruef. *Camp Recreations and Pageants*. New York: Association Press, 1927.

Holmes, John Haynes. *I Speak for Myself: The Autobiography of John Haynes Holmes*. New York: Harper, 1959.

———. *New Wars for Old*. New York: Dodd, Mead, 1916.

Holmes, John Haynes, and Reginald Lawrence. *If This Be Treason*. New York: Macmillan, 1935.

Horton, Myles. *The Long Haul: An Autobiography*. With Judith Kohl and Herbert Kohl. New York: Doubleday, 1990.

Housman, Laurence. *The Little Plays of St. Francis: A Dramatic Cycle from the Life and Legend of St. Francis of Assisi*. London: Sidgwick and Jackson, 1922.

Hull, William I., ed. *William Penn's Plan for a League of Nations*. Philadelphia: American Friends Service Committee, 1919.

Hunter, Allan A. *Courage in Both Hands*. New York: Fellowship of Reconciliation; Los Angeles: New Century Foundation Press, 1951.

———. *Heroes of Good Will: Thirty-Five Stories of Valor in Creative Living*. New York: Fellowship of Reconciliation, [1943].

———. *Say Yes to the Light*. New York: Harper, 1944.

———. *Secretly Armed*. New York: Harper, 1941.

———. *Three Trumpets Sound: Kagawa—Gandhi—Schweitzer*. New York: Association Press, 1939.

———. *White Corpuscles in Europe*. Chicago: Willett, Clark, 1939.

Huxley, Aldous. *The Perennial Philosophy*. New York: Harper, 1945.
The Hymnal. Philadelphia: Presbyterian Board of Christian Education, 1933.
A Hymnal for Friends. Philadelphia: Friends General Conference, 1942.
———. Philadelphia: Friends General Conference, 1955.
The Hymnal of the Protestant Episcopal Church in the U.S.A. New York: Church Pension Fund, 1940.
Hymns for Christian Youth. Boston: International Society of Christian Endeavor, 1927.
Hymns for Creative Living. Philadelphia: Judson, 1935.
Hymns for Worship. New York: Association for the Council of North American Student Christian Movements, 1939.
Hymns of the Rural Spirit. New York: Commission on Worship, Federal Council of the Churches of Christ in America, 1947.
The Intentional Communities: 1959 Yearbook of the Fellowship of Intentional Communities. Yellow Springs, Ohio: Fellowship of Intentional Communities, 1959.
International Problems and the Christian Way of Life. New York: Association for the National Conference on the Christian Way of Life, 1923.
Jack, Homer. *Homer's Odyssey*. Becket, Mass.: One Peaceful World Press, 1996.
Jackson, George Pullen. *White and Negro Spirituals: Their Life Span and Kinship*. New York: J. J. Augustin, 1943.
Jacob, Betty Muther. *A Peace to End Wars? A Study and Action Manual for High School Young People*. Washington: High School Civilian Service, [1944].
Jacobs, Ida T., and John J. DeBoer, eds. *Educating for Peace*. New York: D. Appleton-Century for the National Council of Teachers of English, 1940.
James, William. *The Varieties of Religious Experience: A Study in Human Nature; Being the Gifford Lectures on Natural Religion Delivered in Edinburgh in 1901-1902*. New York: Longmans, Green, 1902.
Jewett, Sophie. *God's Troubadour*. New York: Thomas Y. Crowell, 1910.
Johnsen, Julia E., ed. *Selected Articles on War—Cause and Cure*. The Handbook Series. New York: H. W. Wilson, 1926.
Joint Committee on the Conscientious Objector of the Peace Section of the American Friends Service Committee and the Women's International League for Peace and Freedom. *What About the Conscientious Objector? A Supplement to the Pacifist Handbook*. [Philadelphia: Peace Section, American Friends Service Committee], 1940.
Jones, Caroline M. Duncan. *The Lord's Minstrel*. Cambridge: W. Heffer, 1927.
Jones, E. Stanley. *Christ's Alternative to Communism*. New York: Abingdon, 1935.
Jones, Edgar L. *I'm an Ill-Adjusted Veteran*. New York: Fellowship of Reconciliation, [1947].

Jones, Mary Hoxie. *Swords Into Ploughshares: An Account of the American Friends Service Committee, 1917–1937*. New York: Macmillan, 1937.
Jones, Rufus M. *A Boy's Religion from Memory*. Philadelphia: Ferris & Leach, 1902.
———. *Finding the Trail of Life*. New York: Macmillan, 1926.
———. Foreword to Philippe Vernier, *With the Master: A Book of Meditations*, translated by Edith Lovejoy Pierce. New York: Fellowship Publications, 1943.
———. *The Later Periods of Quakerism*. London: Macmillan, 1921.
———. *Pathways to the Reality of God*. New York: Macmillan, 1921.
———. *A Service of Love in War Time*. New York: Macmillan, 1921.
———. *A Small-Town Boy*. New York: Macmillan, 1941.
———. *Social Law in the Spiritual World: Studies in Human and Divine Inter-Relationship*. Philadelphia: John Winston, 1904.
———. *Studies in Mystical Religion*. London: Macmillan, 1909.
———. *The Trail of Life in College*. New York: Macmillan, 1929.
———. *The Trail of Life in the Middle Years*. New York: Macmillan, 1934.
———. "Why I Enroll with the Mystics." In *Contemporary American Theology*, edited by Vergilius Ferm, Vol. 1, 191–215. New York: Round Table Press, 1932.
Jones, Rufus M., Frank Laubach, J. Rufus Mosely, E. Stanley Jones, Glenn Clark, et al. *Together*. New York: Abingdon-Cokesbury, 1946.
Jones, Thomas E. *Creative Pioneering*. Philadelphia: American Friends Service Committee, 1941?.
Kagawa, Toyohiko. *Brotherhood Economics*. New York: Harper, 1936.
———. *Meditations on the Cross*. Translated by Helen F. Topping and Marion R. Draper. Chicago: Clark, 1935.
———. *Songs from the Slums*. Interpreted by Lois J. Erickson, introduction by Sherwood Eddy. Nashville: Cokesbury, 1935.
Kelly, Thomas R. *A Testament of Devotion*. Edited with a biographical memoir by Douglas Steere. New York: Harper, 1941.
Kennedy, Charles Rann. *The Terrible Meek*. New York: Harper, 1912.
Kepler, Thomas S. *The Fellowship of the Saints: An Anthology of Christian Devotional Literature*. New York: Abingdon-Cokesbury, 1948.
Kite, Florence L. *When Friends Sing: Notes on "A Hymnal for Friends."* Philadelphia: Friends General Conference, 1942.
Knox, John. "Re-examining Pacifism." In *Religion and the Present Crisis*, edited by John Knox, 30–47. Chicago: University of Chicago Press, 1942.
Kohl, Herbert, and Judith Kohl. "How This Book Came About." In *The Long Haul: An Autobiography*, by Miles Horton, xi–xvii. New York: Doubleday, 1990.
Laffin, Arthur J., and Anne Montgomery, eds. *Swords into Plowshares: Nonviolent Direct Action for Disarmament, Peace, Social Justice*, rev. ed. Marion, S.D.: Fortkamp, 1996.

Lansbury, George. *My Pilgrimage for Peace*. New York: Henry Holt, 1938. Reprint, Garland Library of War and Peace. New York: Garland, 1972.

Laubach, Frank C. *Channels of Spiritual Power*. Westwood, N.J.: Fleming Revell, 1954.

———. *The Game with Minutes*. N.p: privately printed, 1956.

———. *The Game with Minutes: Practicing the Presence of God*. N.p.: Lutterworth, 1959.

———. *Letters by a Modern Mystic: Excerpts from Letters Written at Dansalan, Lake Lanao, Philippine Islands to His Father*. New York: Student Volunteer Movement, 1937.

———. *Prayer: The Mightiest Force in the World*. New York: Fleming Revell, 1946.

———. *Wake Up or Blow Up! America: Lift the World or Lose It!* New York: Fleming Revell, 1951.

Lawrence, Brother (Nicholas Herman). *The Practice of the Presence of God: The Best Rule of a Holy Life*. Introduction by Hannah Whitall Smith. New York: Fleming Revell, 1895 [i.e., 1897].

———. *The Practice of the Presence of God*. Translated by Donald Attwater, with an introduction by Dorothy Day. Springfield, Ill.: Templegate Publishers, 1974.

Lester, Muriel. *Dare You Face Facts?* New York: Harper, 1940.

———. *It Occurred to Me*. New York: Harper, 1937.

———. *It So Happened*. New York: Harper, 1947.

———. *Kill or Cure?* Nashville: Cokesbury, 1937.

———. *Training*. New York: Abingdon-Cokesbury, 1940.

———. *Ways of Praying*. New York: Abingdon-Cokesbury, 1931.

Lieberman, Joshua. *Creative Camping*. New York: Association Press, 1931.

Limbert, Paul. "What Children Think About War." Offprint from *Progressive Education*, Feb. 1933.

Littlefield, Milton S., ed. *Hymns of the Christian Life*. New York: A. S. Barnes, 1931.

The Little Flowers of St. Francis. Translated by Raphael Brown. Garden City, N.Y.: Doubleday, 1958.

Lobingier, Elizabeth Miller. *Ship East—Ship West*. New York: Friendship Press, 1937.

Lobingier, Elizabeth Miller, and John Leslie Lobingier. *Educating for Peace*. Boston: Pilgrim, 1930.

Lobingier, John Leslie. *How Big Is Your World?* Boston: Pilgrim, 1931.

———. *Is War the Way?* Boston: Pilgrim, 1935.

Losey, Jessie L. *And the World Forgot: A Pageant for Peace*. Chicago: Dramatic Publishing, 1940.

Lotz, Philip Henry, ed. *Women Leaders*. Creative Personalities, vol. 2. New York: Association Press, 1940.

Luccock, Halford E., and Frances Brentano, eds. *The Questing Spirit: Religion in the Literature of Our Time*. New York: Coward-McCann, 1947.

Macgregor, G. H. C. *The New Testament Basis of Pacifism*. London: J. Clarke, 1936. Reprint, New York: Fellowship of Reconciliation, 1941.

———. *The New Testament Basis of Pacifism*. New and rev. ed. New York: Fellowship of Reconciliation, 1954.

———. *The Relevance of the Impossible*. London: Fellowship of Reconciliation, 1941.

Macintosh, Douglas Clyde. *Social Religion*. New York: Charles Scribner's Sons, 1939.

MacKaye, Hazel. *Good Will, the Magician*. New York: National Child Welfare Association Press, [1923?].

Manshardt, Clifford. *The Terrible Meek: An Appreciation of Mohandas K. Gandhi*. Hinsdale, Ill.: H. Regnery, 1948.

Marsh, J. B. T. *The Story of the Jubilee Singers; With Their Songs*. Rev. ed. Boston: Houghton, Osgood and Co., 1880.

Marshall, Hallie, et al. *The Ruby Bridges Story*. Wonderful World of Disney. New York: Disney, 1998.

Mathews, Shailer. *The Faith of Modernism*. New York: Macmillan, 1925.

Mattoon, Laura I., and Helen D. Bragdon. *Services for the Open*. New York: Century, 1923.

McCutchan, Robert Guy. *Our Hymnody: A Manual of the Methodist Hymnal*. New York: Methodist Book Concern, 1937.

McCutcheon, John. "Christmas in the Trenches." *Live at Wolf Trap*. Rounder CD 0283. Cambridge, Mass: Rounder, 1991.

McPherson, Imogene M. *Educating Children for Peace*. New York: Abingdon, 1936.

———. *Learning About War and Peace: A Textbook for Juniors in Vacation Church Schools*. St. Louis: Bethany Press for the Interdenominational Committee on Co-operative Publication of Vacation Church School Curriculum, 1937.

Methodist Episcopal Church. World Peace Commission. [Report.] In *Journal of the 31st Delegated Conference of the Methodist Episcopal Church*, 1932, 1637–42.

The Methodist Hymnal: Official Hymnal of the Methodist Church. New York: Methodist Publishing House, 1939.

The Methodist Hymnal: Official Hymnal of the Methodist Episcopal Church, the Methodist Episcopal Church, South, and the Methodist Protestant Church. New York: Methodist Book Concern, 1935.

Meyer, Ernest Louis. *Hey! Yellowbacks!: The War Diary of a Conscientious Objector*. New York: John Day, 1930.

Miller, Elizabeth Erwin. *Dramatization of Bible Stories*. Chicago: University of Chicago Press, 1918.

Miller, Francis P., ed. *Religion on the Campus: The Report of the National Student*

Conference, Milwaukee, Dec. 28, 1926–Jan. 1, 1927. New York: Association Press, 1927.

Moore, Howard W. *Plowing My Own Furrow*. New York: Norton, 1985.

Morgan, Arthur E. *Small Community Economics*. Yellow Springs, Ohio: Community Service, [1943].

Morrison, Charles Clayton. *The Outlawry of War: A Constructive Policy for World Peace*. Foreword by John Dewey. Chicago: Willett, Clark & Colby, 1927.

Murphy, Carol R. *The Roots of Pendle Hill*. Pendle Hill Pamphlet 223. Wallingford, Pa.: Pendle Hill, 1979.

Mussey, Mabel Hay Barrows. *Social Hymns of Brotherhood and Aspiration*. New York: A. S. Barnes, 1914.

Muste, A. J. *The Essays of A. J. Muste*. Edited by Nat Hentoff. Indianapolis: Bobbs-Merrill, 1967.

———. *Non-Violence in an Aggressive World*. New York: Harper, 1940.

———. *Not By Might: Christianity, The Way to Human Decency*. New York: Harper, 1947.

Muste, Constance. "Pacifists on Soap-Boxes." *Fellowship*, Sept. 1950, 9–15, 32.

Mygatt, Tracy. *Good Friday*. New York: 1919.

———. *The New Star*. N.p.: privately printed, n.d.

National Jubilee Melodies. 16th ed. Nashville: National Baptist Publishing Board, [1925?].

Nearing, Scott, and Helen Nearing. *Living the Good Life*. Harborside, Me.: Social Science Institute, 1954.

The New Century Hymnal. Cleveland: Pilgrim, 1995.

New Worship and Song, with Worship Services and Source Materials. Boston: Pilgrim, 1942.

Niebuhr, Hulda. *Greatness Passing By: Stories to Tell to Boys and Girls*. New York: Charles Scribner's Sons, 1931.

Niebuhr, Reinhold. Circular letter May 27, 1932, reproduced in Myles Horton, *The Long Haul*, 61–62.

———. *Moral Man and Immoral Society: A Study in Ethics and Politics*. New York: Scribner, 1932.

Northern Baptist Convention. Women's American Baptist Home Mission Society. [Report.] In *Annual of the Northern Baptist Convention*, 1928, 408.

Oberholzer, Ellis Paxson. *The Book of the Pageant*. Philadelphia: George W. Jacobs & Co., 1908.

Pacifist Handbook. Philadelphia: Peace Section, American Friends Service Committee; Brethren Board of Christian Education; Fellowship of Reconciliation, General Commission on World Peace of the Methodist Church, Women's International League for Peace and Freedom et al., 1939.

Pacifist Living—Today and Tomorrow. Philadelphia: Peace Section, American Friends Service Committee, 1941.

Pacifist Study Exchange, March 1942.

Page, Kirby. *Jesus or Christianity: A Study in Contrasts*. Garden City, N.Y.: Doubleday, Doran, 1929.

———. *Kirby Page, Social Evangelist*. Edited by Harold E. Fey. Nyack, N.Y.: Fellowship Press, 1975.

———. *The Light Is Still Shining in the Darkness*. La Habra, Calif.: privately printed, 1946.

———. *Living Abundantly: A Study of Creative Pioneer Groups through Twenty-seven Centuries of Exploration of Pathways to Joyous and Abundant Life*. New York: Farrar and Rinehart, 1944.

———. *Living Courageously*. New York: Farrar and Rinehart, 1936.

———. *Living Creatively*. New York: Farrar and Rinehart, 1932.

———. *Living Prayerfully*. New York: Farrar and Rinehart, 1941.

———. *Living Triumphantly*. New York: Farrar and Rinehart, 1934.

———. *A New Economic Order*. New York: Harcourt, Brace, 1930.

———. *Now Is the Time to Prevent a Third World War*. La Habra, Calif.: privately printed, 1946.

———. *The Personality of Jesus: Pathways by Which He Climbed the Heights of Life*. New York: Association Press, 1932.

———. *Recent Gains in American Civilization*. New York: Harcourt, Brace, 1928.

———. *Religious Resources for Personal Living and Social Action*. New York: Farrar and Rinehart, 1939.

———. *The Sword or the Cross, Which Should Be the Weapon for the Christian Militant?* Chicago: Christian Century Press, 1921.

———. *War: Its Causes, Consequences and Cure*. New York: George H. Doran, 1923.

Paths of Peace. Books I–IV. Oxford: Oxford University Press, 1924–30.

Peace Pilgrim. *Peace Pilgrim: Her Life and Work in Her Own Words*. Santa Fe: Ocean Tree Books, 1991.

Peace Study Outline: Problems of Applied Pacifism. Philadelphia: Prepared by the Peace Commission of the Friends World Committee for Consultation (American Section), [1941].

[Phillimore, Cecily Spencer-Smith]. *By an Unknown Disciple*. New York: George H. Doran, 1919.

Peterson, Frederick. *Creative Re-education*. New York: G. P. Putnam's Sons, 1936.

Phillips, Grace Darling. *Far Peoples*. Chicago: University of Chicago Press, 1929.

Phillips, Mary. *How to Grow a Peace Garden*. Lemont, Ill.: Peace Garden Nursery, 1954.

Pierce, Edith Lovejoy. Foreword to Philippe Vernier, *Not as the World Giveth*. New York: Fellowship Publications, 1947.
The Pilgrim Hymnal. Rev. ed. Boston: Pilgrim, 1935.
———. Boston: Pilgrim, 1958.
Pohl, Frederick G. *Gas*. New York: privately printed, 1921.
Ponsonby, Arthur. *Falsehood in War Time*. New York: E. P. Dutton, 1928.
Porter, David R. *Worship Resources for Youth*. New York: Association Press, 1948.
Prayers for the Church Service League. 5th ed. [Boston]: Episcopal Diocese of Massachusetts, 1937.
Program Suggestions for World Peace. New York: Dept. of International Justice and Good Will, Federal Council of the Churches of Christ in America, 1934.
Rauschenbusch, Walter. *Christianity and the Social Crisis*. New York: Macmillan, 1907.
———. *Christianizing the Social Order*. New York: Macmillan, 1912.
———. *Prayers of the Social Awakening*. Boston: Pilgrim, 1910.
Raven, Charles E. *The Theological Basis of Christian Pacifism*. New York: Fellowship Publications, 1951.
Read, Herbert. *Education for Peace*. New York: Scribner, 1949.
"Reconstructing Our World." *First-day School Lessons*. Philadelphia: Friends General Conference, First Month 1941, 1–68.
Redefer, Frederick L. *Child Education: A Corrective of the Adult's War Spirit*. New York: World Peaceways, [1934].
Regen, Rosalie. "Bad Mother." In *Peaceful Heroes*, edited by Rosalie Regen, 169–89. Philadelphia: Religious Education Committee, Friends General Conference, 1962.
Rex, Ruth Irwin. *We Worship*. New York: Century, 1930.
Richards, Edward. "The Test of Faith: A Chapter in Non-Resistance." *Atlantic Monthly*, May 1923, 617–27.
A Righteous Faith for a Just and Durable Peace. New York: Federal Council of the Churches of Christ in the U.S.A., Commission to Study the Basis of a Just and Durable Peace, 1942.
Ritter, Scott. *Waging Peace: The Art of War for the Antiwar Movement*. New York: Nation Books, 2007.
Rockwell, Ethel Genner. *All We Like Sheep: A Peace Play in One Act*. Boston: Baker's Plays, 1936.
Rodeheaver, Homer A. *Golden Bells*. Chicago: The Rodeheaver Co., 1923.
Rogers, Ingrid, ed. *Swords Into Plowshares: A Collection of Plays about Peace and Social Justice*. Elgin, Ill.: Brethren Press, 1983.
Rosenhaupt, Hans Wilhelm. *How to Wage Peace: A Handbook for Action*. New York: John Day, 1949.
Roth, Philip. *The Plot Against America*. Boston: Houghton Mifflin, 2004.

Sabatier, Paul. *Life of St. Francis of Assisi*. Translated by Louise Seymour Houghton. New York: Charles Scribner's Sons, 1894.

———. *Vie de Saint François d'Assise*. Paris: Fischbacher, 1893.

Sandburg, Carl. *The American Songbag*. New York: Harcourt, Brace, 1927.

Sanford, A. P., ed. *Peace Plays*. New York: Dodd, Mead, 1932.

Schweitzer, Albert. *Out of My Life and Thought: An Autobiography*. Translated by C. Campion. New York: Henry Holt, 1933.

Sheldon, Charles. *In His Steps*. New York: Burt and Co., 1896.

Shridharani, Krishnalal. *My India, My America*. New York: Duell, Sloan, and Pierce, 1941.

———. *War without Violence: A Study of Gandhi's Method and Its Accomplishments*. New York: Harcourt, Brace, 1939.

Simmons, Thomas. *The Unseen Shore: Memories of a Christian Science Childhood*. Boston: Beacon, 1991.

Sinclair, Upton. *Co-op: A Novel of Living Together*. New York: Farrar and Rinehart, 1936.

Small, Fred. "Scrambled Eggs and Prayers." On *No Limit*. Rounder Records 4018, ©1985, Pine Barrens Music (BMI).

Smith, H. Augustine, ed. *The American Student Hymnal*. New York: Century, 1928.

———. *Hymnal for American Youth*. New York: Century, 1919.

———. *New Church Hymnal*. New York: Century, 1937.

———. *The New Hymnal for American Youth*. New York: Century, 1930.

Smith, H. Augustine, and Grace Widney Mabee. *Hymns of Service*. New York: Century, 1924.

Speak Truth to Power: A Quaker Search for an Alternative to Violence: A Study of International Conflict. [Philadelphia]: American Friends Service Committee, [1955].

Sperry, Willard L. *Strangers and Pilgrims: Studies in Classics of Christian Devotion*. Boston: Little, Brown, 1939.

Stassen, Glen. *Just Peacemaking: Ten Practices for Abolishing War*. 2nd ed. Cleveland: Pilgrim, 2004.

———. *Living the Sermon on the Mount*. San Francisco: Jossey-Bass, 2006.

Steere, Douglas. *Cells for Peace*. New York: Fellowship of Reconciliation, 1947.

———. *Mutual Irradiation*. Wallingford, Pa.: Pendle Hill, 1971.

———. *The Peace Team*. New York: Fellowship of Reconciliation, ca. 1938.

Stories of Creative Living. Philadelphia: Judson, 1938.

Suttner, Bertha von. "Spiritual Testament." In *Selected Articles on War—Cause and Cure*, edited by Julia E. Johnsen, 7–9. New York: H. W. Wilson, 1926.

Swayne, Amelia W. *The Observance of Easter*. Philadelphia: Committee on Religious Education, Friends General Conference, 1939.

———. *The Sermon on the Mount*. Philadelphia: Committee on Religious Education, Friends General Conference, 1950.

Sweeney, Jon M. *Born Again and Again: Surprising Gifts of a Fundamentalist Childhood*. Orleans, Mass.: Paraclete, 2005.

Syracuse Peace Council. *Peace Education in Public Schools*. Syracuse, N.Y.: The Council, 1938.

Thomas, Norman. *The Challenge of War: An Economic Interpretation*. New York: League of Industrial Democracy, 1924.

———. *The Conscientious Objector in America*. New York: B. W. Huebsch, 1923.

Thomas, Wendell. *There Is But One Individual: A Religion for Today's World*. Burnsville, N.C.: Celo Press, 1961.

Trueblood, D. Elton. "The Quaker Way." *Atlantic Monthly*, Dec. 1940, 740–46.

Ulstein, Stefan. *Growing Up Fundamentalist: Journeys in Legalism and Grace*. Downers Grove, Ill.: Intervarsity, 1995.

Underhill, Evelyn. *Mysticism*. 1st ed. London: Methuen & Co., 1911.

———. *Mysticism*. 12th ed. London: Methuen & Co., 1930.

———. *Practical Mysticism: A Little Book for Normal People*. New York: E. P. Dutton, 1915.

Van Dyck, Harry R. *Exercise of Conscience: A World War II Objector Remembers*. Buffalo: Prometheus Books, 1990.

Van Kirk, Walter W. *Highways to International Good Will*. New York: Abingdon, 1930.

———. *Religion Renounces War*. Chicago: Willett, Clark, 1934.

Vernier, Philippe. *Not As the World Giveth*. Translated by Edith Lovejoy Pierce. New York: Fellowship Publications, 1947.

———. *With the Master: A Book of Meditations*. Translated by Edith Lovejoy Pierce. New York: Fellowship Publications, 1943.

Wallace, Archer. *Blazing New Trails*. New York: Doubleday, 1928.

———. *Heroes of Peace*. Garden City: Doubleday, 1929.

Webb, Kenneth B., and Susan H. Webb. *Summer Magic: What Children Gain from Camp*. New York: Association Press, 1953.

Willimon, William H. "Bless You, Mrs. Degrafinried." *Christian Century*, Mar. 14, 1984, 269–70.

Wilson, Dorothy Clarke. *The Friendly Kingdom: A Play in One Act*. Boston: Baker's Plays, 1940.

Wilson, E. Raymond. *Thus Far on My Journey*. Richmond, Ind.: Friends United Press, 1976.

———. *Uphill for Peace*. Richmond, Ind.: Friends United Press, 1975.

Wilson, Louis. *The Testing Hour*. Chicago: Dramatic Publishing Co., 1936.

Wink, Walter. *Jesus and Nonviolence: A Third Way*. Minneapolis: Fortress, 2003.

———. *The Powers*. 3 vols. Philadelphia: Fortress, 1984–92.

Winkler, Agnes K. *The Unknown Soldier Speaks*. New York: Community Church of New York, n.d.

Wiser, Art. "Morning at Macedonia." *Fellowship*, Nov. 1952, 13–17, 32.

With Children Leading. Philadelphia: Friends' Peace Committee of Philadelphia Yearly Meeting and Religious Education Committee of Arch Street Yearly Meeting, 1941.

Woolman, John. *A Plea for the Poor; or, A Word of Remembrance and Caution to the Rich*, 1793. In Phillips P. Moulton, ed. *The Journal and Major Essays of John Woolman*. Library of Protestant Thought. New York: Oxford University Press, 1971.

The Words of Christ Commonly Quoted For or Against War: A Compendium Prepared for Study Groups. Federal Council of Churches, 1929. Reprint, Chicago: Commission on World Peace, Methodist Church, [1941].

World Citizenship and the Religious Program. Philadelphia: Women's International League for Peace and Freedom, 1935.

Worship in Song: A Friends Hymnal. Philadelphia: Friends General Conference, 1996.

Wren, Brian. *What Language Shall I Borrow? God-Talk in Worship: A Male Response to Feminist Theology*. New York: Crossroad, 1989.

Yarnall, Elizabeth Biddle. "People Who Went to Prison Because They Were Good." *Changing Swords into Plowshares*. Modern Church School Series no. 9, 5–11. Boston: Pilgrim, 1937.

Young People and a New World. [pamphlet]. New York: FOR, [1929].

SECONDARY SOURCES

Aarne, Antti. *Verzeichnis der Märchentypen*. Folklore Fellows Communications no. 3. Helsingfors [now Helsinki]: Academia Scientiarum Fennica, 1910.

Abrams, Ray H. *Preachers Present Arms*. New York: Round Table Press, 1933.

Ahlstrom, Sydney E. *A Religious History of the American People*. New Haven: Yale University Press, 1972.

Albanese, Catherine. *America, Religions and Religion*. Belmont, Calif.: Wadsworth, 1981.

———. *Nature Religion in America: From the Algonkian Indians to the New Age*. Chicago: University of Chicago Press, 1990.

Alonso, Harriet Hyman. *Peace as a Women's Issue: A History of the U.S. Movement for World Peace and Women's Rights*. Syracuse Studies on Peace and Conflict Resolution. Syracuse, N.Y.: Syracuse University Press, 1993.

Anderson, Clifford V. "Camping History." In *Introduction to Christian Camping*, edited by Werner C. Graendorf and Lloyd D. Matson, 33–47. Duluth, Minn.: Camping Guideposts, 1984.

Anderson, Jervis. *Bayard Rustin: Troubles I've Seen: A Biography*. New York: HarperCollins, 1997.

Anderson, Richard C. *Peace Was in Their Hearts: Conscientious Objectors in World War II*. Watsonville, Calif.: Correlan Publications, 1994.

Appelbaum, Patricia. "Protestant Mysticism: Pacifists and the 'Practice of the Presence.'" *Quaker History* 94:2 (Fall 2005): 1–24.

Appleby, R. Scott. "The Fundamentalism of the Enclave: Catholic and Protestant Oppositional Movements in the United States." In *New Dimensions in American Religious History*, edited by Jay P. Nolan and James M. Wind, 231–60. Grand Rapids: Eerdmans, 1993.

"Arthur Holt Memorial Issue." *CTS Register*, March 1942.

Atkins, Gaius Glenn, and Frederick L. Fagley. *History of American Congregationalism*. Boston: Pilgrim, 1942.

Bacon, Margaret Hope. *One Woman's Passion for Peace and Justice: The Life of Mildred Scott Olmsted*. Syracuse Studies on Peace and Conflict Resolution. Syracuse, N.Y.: Syracuse University Press, 1993.

———. *The Quiet Rebels: The Story of Quakers in America*. Philadelphia: New Society, 1985.

Barbour, Hugh, and J. William Frost. *The Quakers*. Denominations in America, 3. New York: Greenwood Press, 1988.

Barbour, Hugh, et al. "Liberal Pastors and New Intellectual Meetings 1900–1945." In *Quaker Crosscurrents: Three Hundred Years of Friends in the New York Yearly Meetings*, edited by Hugh Barbour et al., 222–38. Syracuse, N.Y.: Syracuse University Press, 1995.

Bassett, Thomas. "Migration of Friends to the Upper Hudson and Champlain Valley." In *Quaker Crosscurrents: Three Hundred Years of Friends in the New York Yearly Meetings*, edited by Hugh Barbour et al., 30–36. Syracuse, N.Y.: Syracuse University Press, 1995.

Bednarowski, Mary Farrell. *New Religions and the Theological Imagination in America*. Bloomington: Indiana University Press, 1989.

Bell, Catherine. *Ritual Theory, Ritual Practice*. New York: Oxford University Press, 1992.

Bell, John. *Landscape and Desire: Bread and Puppet Pageants in the 1990s*. Glover, Vt.: Bread and Puppet Press, 1997.

Bendroth, Margaret Lamberts. *A School of the Church*. Grand Rapids: Eerdmans, forthcoming in 2008.

Benefiel, Margaret, and Rebecca Darden Phipps. "Practical Mysticism: Quakers and Social Transformation." In *Mysticism and Social Transformation*, edited by Janet K. Ruffing, RSM, 129–42. Syracuse, N.Y.: Syracuse University Press, 2001.

Benson, Louis F. *The English Hymn: Its Development and Use*. New York: George H. Doran, 1915. Reprint, Richmond, Va.: John Knox Press, 1962.

Berry, Brian Joe Lobley. *America's Utopian Experiments: Communal Havens from Long-Wave Crises*. Hanover, N.H.: University Press of New England, 1992.

Berry, Paul, and Mark Rostridge. *Vera Brittain: A Life*. London: Chatto & Windus, 1995.

Betz, Hans Dieter. *The Sermon on the Mount: A Commentary on the Sermon on the Mount, Including the Sermon on the Plain*. Hermeneia Series. Minneapolis: Fortress, 1995.

Blumhofer, Edith, and Mark A. Noll, eds. *Singing the Lord's Song in a Strange Land: Hymnody in the History of North American Protestantism*. Religion and American Culture. Tuscaloosa: University of Alabama, 2004.

Boyer, Paul. *By the Bomb's Early Light: American Thought and Culture at the Dawn of the Atomic Age*. New York: Pantheon, 1985.

Brasher, Brenda. *Godly Women: Fundamentalism and Female Power*. New Brunswick, N.J.: Rutgers University Press, 1998.

Braude, Ann. "Women's History *Is* American Religious History." In *Retelling U.S. Religious History*, edited by Thomas A. Tweed, 87–107. Berkeley: University of California Press, 1997.

Brecht, Stefan. *Peter Schumann's Bread and Puppet Theatre*. New York: Routledge, Chapman and Hall, 1988.

Brereton, Virginia Lieson. *From Sin to Salvation: Stories of Women's Conversions, 1800 to the Present*. Bloomington: Indiana University Press, 1991.

Brock, Peter. *Pacifism in the United States: From the Colonial Era to the First World War*. Princeton, N.J.: Princeton University Press, 1968.

———. *Pioneers of the Peaceable Kingdom*. Princeton, N.J.: Princeton University Press, 1968.

———. *Twentieth-Century Pacifism*. New Perspectives in Political Science. New York: Van Nostrand Reinhold, 1970.

Brock, Peter, and Nigel Young. *Pacifism in the 20th Century*. Syracuse, N.Y.: Syracuse University Press, 1999.

Brown, Elisabeth Potts, and Susan Mosher Stuard. *Witnesses for Change: Quaker Women Over Three Centuries*. New Brunswick, N.J.: Rutgers University Press, 1989.

Bunting, James F., et al. "The YMCA from 1939 to 1979." *Journal of Ecumenical Studies* 16 (Winter 1979): 87–93.

Burgeson, Dorothy. "Ahimsa." *Mather Record*, Jan. 17, 1941.

Burkhardt, Jean. "Drawing Strength from the Past: The Student Movement of the YMCA's of the U.S.A., 1970–1995." *Journal of Ecumenical Studies* 32:4 (1995): 505–7.

Bush, Perry. *Two Kingdoms, Two Loyalties: Mennonite Pacifism in Modern America*. Baltimore: Johns Hopkins University Press, 1998.

Bussey, Gertrude, and Margaret Tims. *Pioneers for Peace: The Women's International League for Peace and Freedom, 1915–1965*. Oxford, England: Alden, 1980.

Byrne, Donald E., Jr. "Folklore and the Study of American Religion." In *Encyclopedia of the American Religious Experience*, edited by Charles Lippy and Peter Williams. New York: Scribner, 1986.

Cadoux, C. J. *The Early Christian Attitude to War: A Contribution to the History of Christian Ethics*. With a foreword by the Rev. W. E. Orchard. London: Headley Bros., 1919. Reprint, New York: Seabury Press, 1982.

Caldwell, Patricia. *The Puritan Conversion Narrative: The Beginnings of American Expression*. Cambridge: Cambridge University Press, 1983.

Cantwell, Robert. *When We Were Good: The Folk Revival*. Cambridge, Mass.: Harvard University Press, 1996.

Carpenter, Joel A. *Revive Us Again: The Reawakening of American Fundamentalism*. New York: Oxford University Press, 1997.

Carter, Paul A. *The Decline and Revival of the Social Gospel: Social and Political Liberalism in American Protestant Churches, 1920–1940*. Ithaca, N.Y.: Cornell University Press, 1954.

Cazden, Elizabeth. "The Modernist Reinvention of Quakerism, 1920–1950." M.A. thesis, Andover Newton Theological School, 1997.

Chang, Patricia Mei Yin. "Sect." In *Contemporary American Religion*. Vol. 2, edited by Wade Clark Roof, 655–56. New York: Macmillan, 2000.

Chatfield, Charles. *The American Peace Movement: Ideals and Activism*. New York: Twayne, 1992.

———. *For Peace and Justice: Pacifism in America, 1914–1941*. Knoxville: University of Tennessee Press, 1971.

———. Introduction to Harold Studley Gray, *Character "Bad": The Story of a Conscientious Objector, as Told in the Letters of Harold Studley Gray*. [New York: Harper, 1934.] Reprint, New York: Garland, 1971.

Cheney, Liana de Girolami. "Peace." In *Encyclopedia of Comparative Iconography: Themes Depicted in Works of Art*. Vol. 2, edited by Helene E. Roberts, 701–6. Chicago: Fitzroy Dearborn, 1998.

Chew, Samuel Claggett. *The Virtues Reconciled: An Iconographic Study*. Toronto: University of Toronto Press, 1947.

Childs, Brevard. *The Book of Exodus: A Critical Theological Commentary*. Old Testament Library. Philadelphia: Westminster, 1974.

Clark, Christopher. *The Communitarian Moment: The Radical Challenge of the Northampton Association*. Ithaca, N.Y.: Cornell University Press, 1995.

Clark, Miles. *Glenn Clark: His Life and Writings*. Nashville: Abingdon, 1975.

Clements, Ronald E. *Isaiah 1–39*. New Century Bible Commentary. London: Marshall, Morgan & Scott; Grand Rapids: Eerdmans, 1980.

Cleveland Public Library. *Index to Negro Spirituals*. Chicago: Center for Black Music Research, Columbia College, 1991.

Conway, Jill Ker. "Convention versus Self-Revelation: Five Types of Autobiography by Women of the Progressive Era." Project on Women and Social Change, Smith College, June 13, 1983. Cited in Carolyn G. Heilbrun, *Writing a Woman's Life*, New York: Norton, 1988.

Curti, Merle. *Peace or War: The American Struggle, 1636–1936*. New York: Norton, 1936.

Dahlberg, Keith. *Edwin T. Dahlberg: Pastor, Peacemaker, Prophet*. Valley Forge, Pa.: Judson Press, 1998.

Dan, Joseph. "Exemplum." *Encyclopedia Judaica*. Vol. 6, 1020–21. New York: Macmillan, 1972.

Davis, Allen F. *American Heroine: The Life and Legend of Jane Addams*. New York: Oxford University Press, 1973.

Davis, Natalie Zemon. "From 'Popular Religion' to Religious Cultures." In *Reformation Europe: A Guide to Research*, edited by Steven Ozment, 321–41. St. Louis: Center for Reformation Research, 1982.

DeBenedetti, Charles. *The Peace Reform in American History*. Bloomington: Indiana University Press, 1980.

Dekar, Paul. *For the Healing of the Nations: Baptist Peacemakers*. Macon, Ga.: Smith & Helwys, 1993.

D'Emilio, John. *Lost Prophet: The Life and Times of Bayard Rustin*. New York: Free Press, 2003.

Dorrien, Gary. *The Making of American Liberal Theology*. 3 vols. Grand Rapids: Eerdmans, 2001–6.

Driedger, Leo, and Donald B. Kraybill. *Mennonite Peacemaking: From Quietism to Activism*. Scottdale, Pa.: Herald Press, 1994.

Driver, Tom F. *The Magic of Ritual: Our Need for Liberating Rites that Transform Our Lives and Our Communities*. San Francisco: Harper, 1991.

Dupré, Louis. "Mysticism" [first edition]. In Lindsay Jones, ed., *Encyclopedia of Religion*, 2nd ed. Vol. 9, 6341–55. Detroit: Thomson Gale, 2005.

Dyck, Willibrord-Christiaan van, O.F.M.Cap. "A Prayer in Search of an Author." Translated by Edward Hagman, O.F.M.Cap. *Greyfriars Review* 10:3 (Nov. 1996): 257–64.

Eagen, Eileen. *Class, Culture, and the Classroom: The Student Peace Movement of the 1930s*. Philadelphia: Temple University Press, 1981.

Early, Frances. *A World Without War: How U.S. Feminists and Pacifists Resisted World War I*. Syracuse, N.Y.: Syracuse University Press, 1997.

Eells, Eleanor. *History of Organized Camping: The First 100 Years.* Martinsville, Ind.: American Camping Association, 1986.

Eichenberg, Fritz. *The Wood and the Graver: The Work of Fritz Eichenberg.* New York: Clarkson N. Potter, 1977.

———. *Works of Mercy.* Edited by Robert Ellsberg. Maryknoll, N.Y.: Orbis, 1992.

Eller, Cynthia. *Conscientious Objectors and the Second World War.* New York: Praeger, 1991.

Epstein, Barbara. *The Politics of Domesticity: Women, Evangelism, and Temperance in Nineteenth-Century America.* Middletown, Conn.: Wesleyan University Press, 1981.

Evans, Christopher. *Social Gospel Liberalism and the Ministry of Ernest Fremont Tittle.* Lewiston, N.Y.: Edwin Mellen, 1996.

Fager, Chuck. "Liberal Friends (Re) Discover Fox." *Quaker History* 93:1 (Spring 2004): 40–52.

Ferm, Vergilius, ed. *Contemporary American Theology: Theological Autobiographies.* Vol. 1. New York: Round Table Press, 1932.

Findlay, James F. *Church People in the Struggle: The National Council of Churches and the Black Freedom Movement, 1950–1970.* New York: Oxford University Press, 1993.

Finke, Roger. "The Illusion of Shifting Demand: Supply-Side Interpretations of American Religious History." In *Retelling U.S. Religious History*, edited by Thomas A. Tweed, 108–24. Berkeley: University of California Press, 1997.

Finke, Roger, and Rodney Stark. *The Churching of America, 1776–1990: Winners and Losers in Our Religious Economy.* New Brunswick, N.J.: Rutgers University Press, 1992.

Fitzgerald, Maureen. "Losing Their Religion: Women, the State, and the Ascension of Secular Discourse, 1890–1930." In *Women and Twentieth-Century Protestantism*, edited by Margaret Lamberts Bendroth and Virginia Lieson Brereton, 280–303. Urbana: University of Illinois Press, 2002.

Fogarty, Robert S. *Dictionary of American Communal and Utopian History.* Westport, Conn.: Greenwood, 1980.

Forest, Jim. "Fritz Eichenberg: Artist of the Peaceable Kingdom." In Fritz Eichenberg, *Works of Mercy*, edited by Robert Ellsberg, 13–25. Maryknoll, N.Y.: Orbis, 1992.

Foster, Carrie A. *The Women and the Warriors: The U.S. Section of the Women's International League for Peace and Freedom, 1915–1946.* Athens, Ga.: University of Georgia Press, 1995.

Fox, Richard Wightman. *Jesus in America: Personal Savior, Cultural Hero, National Obsession.* New York: Harper, 2004.

———. *Reinhold Niebuhr: A Biography.* New York: Pantheon, 1985.

Frazer, Heather T., and John O'Sullivan. *"We Have Just Begun to Not Fight": An Oral History of Conscientious Objectors in Civilian Public Service during World War II*. Twayne's Oral History Series, 18. New York: Twayne, 1996.

Freemantle, Anne. *The Protestant Mystics*. Boston: Little, Brown, 1964.

Friends in Civilian Public Service: Quaker Conscientious Objectors in World War II Look Back and Look Ahead: A Conference, Nov. 4–7, 1996. Wallingford, Pa.: Pendle Hill, 1998.

Frost, Jennifer. "Conscientious Objection and Popular Culture: The Case of Lew Ayres." In *Challenge to Mars: Essays on Pacifism from 1918 to 1945*, edited by Peter Brock and Thomas P. Socknat, 360–69. Toronto: University of Toronto Press, 1999.

Fuller, Faith. *Briars in the Cotton Patch: The Story of Koinonia Farm*. Americus, Ga.: Cotton Patch Productions, 2004, film.

Gara, Larry, and Lenna Mae Gara. *A Few Small Candles: War Resisters of World War II Tell Their Stories*. Kent, Ohio: Kent State University Press, 1999.

Glassberg, David. *American Historical Pageantry: The Uses of Tradition in the Early Twentieth Century*. Chapel Hill: University of North Carolina Press, 1990.

Goossen, Rachel Waltner. "Pacifist Professional Women on the Job in the United States." In *Challenge to Mars: Essays on Pacifism from 1918 to 1945*, edited by Peter Brock and Thomas P. Socknat, 331–45. Toronto: University of Toronto Press, 1999.

———. *Women Against the Good War: Conscientious Objection and Gender on the American Home Front*. Chapel Hill: University of North Carolina Press, 1997.

Gottwald, Norman K. *The Hebrew Bible: A Socio-Literary Introduction*. Philadelphia: Fortress, 1985.

Gould, Rebecca Kneale. *At Home in Nature: Modern Homesteading and Spiritual Practice in America*. Berkeley: University of California Press, 2005.

———. "Getting (Not Too) Close to Nature: Modern Homesteading as Lived Religion in America." In *Lived Religion in America: Toward a History of Practice*, edited by David D. Hall, 217–42. Princeton, N.J.: Princeton University Press, 1997.

Gray, Elizabeth Janet. *Penn*. New York: Viking, 1938, repr. 1944, 1947, 1986.

Griffith, R. Marie. *God's Daughters: Evangelical Women and the Power of Submission*. Berkeley: University of California Press, 1997.

Grimes, Ronald L. *Beginnings in Ritual Studies*. Rev. ed. Studies in Comparative Religion, ed. Frederick M. Denny. Columbia: University of South Carolina Press, 1995.

———. "Forum: American Spirituality." *Religion and American Culture* 9:2 (1999): 131–57.

Haines, Deborah L. "Friends General Conference: A Brief Historical Overview." *Quaker History* 89:2 (Fall 2000): 1–16.

Hall, David D. *Lived Religion in America: Toward a History of Practice*. Princeton, N.J.: Princeton University Press, 1997.

Hallie, Philip. *Lest Innocent Blood Be Shed: The Story of the Village of Le Chambon and How Goodness Happened There*. New York: Harper & Row, 1979.

Hamm, Thomas D. *The Transformation of American Quakerism: Orthodox Friends, 1800–1907*. Bloomington: Indiana University Press, 1988.

Heilbrun, Carolyn. *Writing a Woman's Life*. New York: Norton, 1988.

Heineman, John L., ed. *Readings in European History, 1789 to the Present*. Dubuque, Iowa: Kendall/Hunt, 1994.

Henriksen, Margot A. *Dr. Strangelove's America*. Berkeley: University of California Press, 1997.

Hirst, Margaret E. *The Quakers in Peace and War: An Account of their Peace Principles and Practice*. London: Swarthmore, 1972.

Hobbs, June Hadden. *I Sing for I Cannot Be Silent: The Feminization of American Hymnody*. Pittsburgh: University of Pittsburgh Press, 1997.

Hopkins, C. Howard. *History of the Y.M.C.A. in North America*. New York: Association Press, 1951.

———. *John R. Mott, 1865–1955: A Biography*. Grand Rapids: Eerdmans, 1979.

Horsley, Richard A. *Jesus and the Spiral of Violence: Popular Jewish Resistance in Roman Palestine*. San Francisco: Harper & Row, 1987.

Horton, Aimee Isgrig. *The Highlander Folk School: A History of its Major Programs, 1932–1961*. Brooklyn, N.Y.: Carlson, 1989.

Hull, William I., ed. *William Penn's Plan for a League of Nations*. Philadelphia: American Friends Service Committee, 1919.

Hutchison, William R., ed. *Between the Times: The Travail of the Protestant Establishment in America, 1900–1960*. Cambridge Studies in Religion and American Public Life. New York: Cambridge University Press, 1989.

———. *Errand to the World: American Protestant Thought and Foreign Missions*. Chicago: University of Chicago Press, 1987.

———. *The Modernist Impulse in American Protestantism*. Durham, N.C.: Duke University Press, 1992.

———. "Protestantism as Establishment." In *Between the Times: The Travail of the Protestant Establishment in America, 1900–1960*, edited by William R. Hutchison, 3–18. Cambridge: Cambridge University Press, 1989.

Jeffreys-Jones, Rhodri. *Changing Differences: Women and the Shaping of American Foreign Policy, 1917–1994*. New Brunswick, N.J.: Rutgers University Press, 1995.

Johnson, James Weldon. *The Books of American Negro Spirituals*. New York: Da Capo, 1977. Reprint, *The Book of American Negro Spirituals* (1925) and *The Second Book of American Negro Spirituals* (1926).

Jonas, Gerald. *On Doing Good: The Quaker Experiment*. New York: Scribner, 1971.

Josephson, Harold, ed. *Biographical Dictionary of Modern Peace Leaders*. Westport, Conn.: Greenwood, 1985.
Jülicher, Adolf. *Die Gleichnisreden Jesu*. Leipzig: Mohr, 1899.
Kanter, Rosabeth Moss. *Commitment and Community: Communes and Utopias in Sociological Perspective*. Cambridge, Mass.: Harvard University Press, 1972.
―――, ed. *Communes: Creating and Managing the Collective Life*. New York: Harper, 1973.
Kaplan, Judy, and Linn Shapiro. "Growing Up Red: Children of the Left Meet and Remember." *Radical History Review* 31 (1984): 72–83.
―――. *Red Diapers: Growing Up on the Communist Left*. Urbana: University of Illinois Press, 1998.
Kapur, Sudarshan. *Raising Up a Prophet: The African-American Encounter with Gandhi*. Boston: Beacon, 1992.
Katz, Neil H. "Radical Pacifism and the Contemporary American Peace Movement: The Committee for Nonviolent Action, 1957–1967." Ph.D. diss., University of Maryland, 1974.
Keim, Albert N. *The CPS Story: An Illustrated History of Civilian Public Service*. Intercourse, Pa.: Good Books, 1990.
Keller, Phyllis. *States of Belonging*. Cambridge, Mass.: Harvard University Press, 1979.
King, William McGuire. "The Reform Establishment and the Ambiguities of Influence." In *Between the Times: The Travail of the Protestant Establishment in America, 1900–1960*, edited by William R. Hutchison, 122–40. Cambridge: Cambridge University Press, 1989.
K'Meyer, Tracy Elaine. *Interracialism and Christian Community in the Postwar South: The Story of Koinonia Farm*. Charlottesville: University Press of Virginia, 1997.
Kniss, Fred. *Disquiet in the Land: Cultural Conflict in American Mennonite Communities*. New Brunswick, N.J.: Rutgers University Press, 1997.
Kuhn, Thomas. *The Structure of Scientific Revolutions*. Chicago: University of Chicago Press, 1962.
Ladd-Taylor, Molly, and Lauri Umansky, eds. *"Bad" Mothers: The Politics of Blame in Twentieth-Century America*. New York: New York University Press, 1998.
Lambert, Frank. *Inventing the "Great Awakening"*. Princeton, N.J.: Princeton University Press, 1999.
Lampe, Peter. *From Paul to Valentinus: Christians at Rome in the First Two Centuries*. Translated by Michael Steinhouser. Minneapolis: Fortress, 2003.
Lears, T. J. Jackson. *No Place of Grace: Antimodernism and the Transformation of American Culture, 1880–1920*. New York: Pantheon, 1981.
Lee, Dallas. *The Cotton Patch Evidence*. New York: Harper & Row, 1971.

Lester, Muriel. *Ambassador of Reconciliation: A Muriel Lester Reader*. Edited by Richard Deats. Philadelphia: New Society Publishers, 1991.

Levine, Daniel. *Bayard Rustin and the Civil Rights Movement*. New Brunswick, N.J.: Rutgers, 2000.

Levine, David O. *The American College and the Culture of Aspiration, 1915–1940*. Ithaca, N.Y.: Cornell University Press, 1986.

Lightfoot, Sara Lawrence. *Balm in Gilead: Journey of a Healer*. Radcliffe Biography Series. Reading, Mass.: Addison-Wesley, 1998.

Lippy, Charles H. "Communitarianism." In *Encyclopedia of the American Religious Experience*, edited by Charles H. Lippy and Peter Williams, 859–73. New York: Scribner, 1988.

Lotz, David W., with Donald W. Shriver Jr. and John F. Wilson, eds. *Altered Landscapes: Christianity in America, 1935–1985*. Grand Rapids: Eerdmans, 1989.

Lynd, Staughton, and Alice Lynd. *Nonviolence in America: A Documentary History*. Rev. ed. Maryknoll, N.Y.: Orbis, 1995.

Lynn, Susan. *Progressive Women in Conservative Times: Racial Justice, Peace, and Feminism, 1945 to the 1960s*. New Brunswick, N.J.: Rutgers University Press, 1992.

Lyons, John D. *Exemplum: The Rhetoric of Example in Early Modern France and Italy*. Princeton, N.J.: Princeton University Press, 1989.

Maffly-Kipp, Laurie F. "Communitarianism." In *The Encyclopedia of American Religious History*, edited by Edward L. Queen II, Stephen R. Prothero, and Gardiner H. Shattuck Jr., vol. 1, 153–55. New York: Facts on File, 1996.

Marini, Stephen. *Sacred Song in America: Religion, Music, and Public Culture*. Urbana: University of Illinois Press, 2003.

Marsden, George M. *Fundamentalism and American Culture: The Shaping of Twentieth-Century Evangelicalism, 1870–1925*. New York: Oxford University Press, 1980.

Mather, Eleanore Price. *Pendle Hill: A Quaker Experiment in Education and Community*. Wallingford, Pa.: Pendle Hill, 1980.

McDannell, Colleen. *Material Christianity: Religion and Popular Culture in America*. New Haven: Yale University Press, 1995.

McLoughlin, William G. *The Meaning of Henry Ward Beecher: An Essay on the Shifting Culture of Mid-Victorian America, 1840–1870*. New York: Knopf, 1970.

McNeal, Patricia. *Harder Than War: Catholic Peacemaking in Twentieth-Century America*. New Brunswick, N.J.: Rutgers University Press, 1992.

Meier, August, and Elliott Rudwick. *CORE: A Study in the Civil Rights Movement*. New York: Oxford University Press, 1973.

Melton, J. Gordon. *Religious Leaders of America*. 2nd ed. Detroit: Gale Group, 1999.

Meyer, Donald B. *The Protestant Search for Political Realism, 1919–1941*. Westport, Conn.: Greenwood, 1973.

Miller, Lawrence McK. *Witness for Humanity: A Biography of Clarence E. Pickett*. Wallingford, Pa.: Pendle Hill, 1999.

Miller, Robert Moats. *American Protestantism and Social Issues, 1919-1939*. Chapel Hill: University of North Carolina Press, 1958.

———. *The History of American Methodism*. Vol. 3 of *Methodism and American Society*. Nashville: Abingdon, 1964.

———. *How Shall They Hear Without a Preacher?: The Life of Ernest Fremont Tittle*. Chapel Hill: University of North Carolina Press, 1971.

Miller, Timothy. *The Quest for Utopia in Twentieth-Century America*. Vol. 1: 1900-1960. Syracuse, N.Y.: Syracuse University Press, 1998.

Miller, William D. *A Harsh and Dreadful Love: Dorothy Day and the Catholic Worker Movement*. New York: Liveright, 1973.

Mittelman, Karen Sue. "'A Spirit that Touches the Problems of Today': Women and Social Reform in the Philadelphia Young Women's Christian Association, 1920-1945." Ph.D. diss., University of Pennsylvania, 1987.

Morgan, David. Introduction to David Morgan, ed., *Icons of American Protestantism: The Art of Warner Sallman*. New Haven: Yale University Press, 1996.

———. *Protestants and Pictures: Religion, Visual Culture, and the Age of American Mass Production*. New York: Oxford University Press, 1999.

———. *Visual Piety: A History and Theory of Popular Religious Images*. Berkeley: University of California Press, 1998.

Mosher, John Albert. *The Exemplum in the Early Religious and Didactic Literature of England*. New York: Columbia University Press, 1911.

Muelder, Walter G. *Methodism and Society in the Twentieth Century*. Vol. 2 of *Methodism and Society*. Nashville: Abingdon, 1961.

Mullin, Robert Bruce. *The Puritan as Yankee: A Life of Horace Bushnell*. Grand Rapids: Eerdmans, 2002.

Murray, Peter, and Linda Murray. *Oxford Companion to Christian Art and Architecture*. Oxford: Oxford University Press, 1996.

Nelson, John K., *The Peace Prophets: American Pacifist Thought, 1919-1941*. James Sprunt Studies in History and Political Science, vol. 49. Chapel Hill: University of North Carolina Press, 1967.

Nutt, Rick L. *Toward Peacemaking: Presbyterians in the South and National Security, 1945-1983*. Tuscaloosa: University of Alabama Press, 1994.

Orser, W. Edward. "The Macedonia Cooperative Community (1937-1958) and the Quest for a Communal Center." *Prospects* 4 (1978): 369-87.

———. *Searching for a Viable Alternative: The Macedonia Cooperative Community, 1937-1958*. American Cultural Heritage Series, 6. New York: Burt Franklin, 1981.

Orsi, Robert. "Everyday Miracles: The Study of Lived Religion." In *Lived Religion* in America: Toward a History of Practice, edited by David D. Hall, 3–21. Princeton, N.J.: Princeton University Press, 1997.

Pelikan, Jaroslav. *Jesus Through the Centuries: His Place in the History of Culture*. New Haven: Yale University Press, 1985.

Pencak, William A., and Daniel K. Richter. *Friends and Enemies in Penn's Woods: Indians, Colonists, and the Racial Construction of Pennsylvania*. University Park: Pennsylvania State University Press, 2004.

Pierce, Nathaniel W., and Paul L. Ward. *The Voice of Conscience: A Loud and Unusual Noise?: The Episcopal Peace Fellowship, 1939–1989*. Washington, D.C.: Episcopal Peace Fellowship, 1989.

Pinker, Steven. *How the Mind Works*. New York: Norton, 1997.

Pitzer, Donald E., ed. *America's Communal Utopias*. Chapel Hill: University of North Carolina Press, 1997.

———. "Appendix: America's Communal Utopias Founded by 1965." In *America's Communal Utopias*, edited by Donald E. Pitzer, 449–94. Chapel Hill: University of North Carolina Press, 1997.

Poloma, Margaret. *Main Street Mystics: The Toronto Blessing and Reviving Pentecostalism*. Lanham, Md.: AltaMira, 2003.

Poulenc, Jérôme, O.F.M., "The Modern Inspiration for the Prayer." Translated by Edward Hagman, O.F.M.Cap. *Greyfriars Review* 10:3 (Nov. 1996): 265–68.

Powell, Richard J. "Biblical and Spiritual Motifs." In *I Tell My Heart: The Art of Horace Pippin*, edited by Judith E. Stein, 124–35. Philadelphia: Pennsylvania Academy of the Fine Arts, 1993.

Prothero, Stephen. *American Jesus: How the Son of God Became a National Icon*. New York: Farrar Straus Giroux, 2003.

Randall, Mercedes, *Improper Bostonian: Emily Greene Balch*. New York: Twayne, 1964.

Robert, Dana L. *American Women in Mission: A Social History of Their Thought and Practice*. The Modern Mission Era, 1792–1992: An Appraisal. Edited by Wilbert F. Shenk. Macon, Ga.: Mercer University Press, 1996.

Roberts, Nancy L. *American Peace Writers, Editors, and Periodicals: A Dictionary*. New York: Greenwood, 1991.

———. *Dorothy Day and the Catholic Worker*. Albany: State University of New York, 1984.

Robinson, David, ed. *William Ellery Channing: Selected Writings*. Sources of American Spirituality. New York: Paulist, 1985.

Robinson, Jo Ann Ooiman. *Abraham Went Out: A Biography of A. J. Muste*. Philadelphia: Temple University Press, 1981.

Rodriguez, O. "Lawrence of the Resurrection." *New Catholic Encyclopedia*. 2nd ed. Detroit: Thomson-Gale, 2003, vol. 8, 569.

Rosen, Susan Grant. "'Minds for Christ': The Christian Association at Smith

College, 1910-1955." Paper presented at the Women and Twentieth-Century Protestantism Conference, Chicago, April 25, 1998.

Ruddick, Sara. *Maternal Thinking: Toward a Politics of Peace*. Boston: Beacon, 1989.

Rufus M. Jones, January 25, 1863-June 16, 1948: In Memoriam. Haverford, Pa.: Haverford College, 1950.

Rupp, Leila J., and Verta Taylor. *Survival in the Doldrums: The American Women's Rights Movements, 1945 to the 1960s*. New York: Oxford University Press, 1987.

Schlissel, Lillian D., ed. *Conscience in America: A Documentary History of Conscientious Objection in America, 1757-1967*. New York: E. P. Dutton, 1968.

Schmaltz, Alfred. "The Council for Social Action." In *The Congregational Churches*, edited by Frederick L. Fagley, 116-18. New York: Commission on Evangelism and Devotional Life, 1938.

Schmidt, Leigh Eric. "The Making of Modern 'Mysticism.'" *Journal of the American Academy of Religion* 71:2 (June 2003): 273-302.

———. *Restless Souls: The Making of American Spirituality from Emerson to Oprah*. San Francisco: Harper, 2005.

Schulz, Frieder. "The So-Called Prayer of St. Francis." Translated by Peter J. Colosi. *Greyfriars Review* 10:3 (Nov. 1996): 237-55.

Scott, Joan Firor. "Gender: A Useful Category of Historical Analysis." *American Historical Review* 91 (Dec. 1986): 1053-75.

Segal, Howard P. "Morgan, Arthur Ernest." In *American National Biography*, edited by John A. Garraty and Mark C. Carnes, 15:820-22. New York: Oxford University Press, 1999.

Shattuck, Gardiner H., Jr. "Christian Church (Disciples of Christ)." In *The Encyclopedia of American Religious History*, edited by Edward L. Queen II, Stephen R. Prothero, and Gardiner H. Shattuck Jr., 114-15. New York: Facts on File, 1996.

Silk, Mark. *Unsecular Media: Making News of Religion in America*. Urbana: University of Illinois Press, 1995.

Simon, Ronald T., and Marc Estrin. *Rehearsing with Gods: Photographs and Essays on the Bread & Puppet Theatre*. White River Junction, Vt.: Chelsea Green, 2004.

Simpson, Anne Key, *Hard Trials: The Life and Music of Harry T. Burleigh*. Metuchen, N.J.: Scarecrow, 1990.

Sivan, Emmanuel. "The Enclave Culture." In *Fundamentalisms Comprehended*, edited by Martin E. Marty and R. Scott Appleby, 5:11-68. Chicago: University of Chicago Press, 1995.

Smith, Allen. "The Peace Movement at the Local Level: The Syracuse Peace Council, 1936-1973." *Peace and Change* 23:1 (1998): 1-26.

———. "The Renewal Movement: The Peace Testimony and Modern Quakerism." *Quaker History* 85:2 (Fall 1996): 1-23.

Soderlund, Jean R., ed. *William Penn and the Founding of Pennsylvania, 1680–1684: A Documentary History*. Philadelphia: University of Pennsylvania Press, 1983.

Solomon, Barbara Miller. "Dilemmas of Pacifist Women, Quakers and Others, in World Wars I and II." In *Witnesses for Change: Quaker Women over Three Centuries*, edited by Elisabeth Potts Brown and Susan Mosher Stuard, 123–56. New Brunswick, N.J.: Rutgers University Press, 1989.

Spady, James O'Neal. "Colonialism and the Discursive Antecedents of 'Penn's Treaty with the Indians.'" In *Friends and Enemies in Penn's Woods: Indians, Colonists, and the Racial Construction of Pennsylvania*, edited by William A. Pencak and Daniel K. Richter, 18–40. University Park: Pennsylvania State University Press, 2004.

Steere, Douglas. "A Biographical Memoir." In *A Testament of Devotion*, edited by Thomas R. Kelly, 1–28. New York: Harper, 1941.

Stephen, Caroline. *Quaker Strongholds*. London: K. Paul, Trench, Trubner, 1890.

Stewart-Winter, Timothy. "Not a Soldier, Not a Slacker: Conscientious Objectors and Male Citizenship in the United States during the Second World War." *Gender and History* 19:3 (Nov. 2007): 519–42.

Stowe, David W. *How Sweet the Sound: Music in the Spiritual Lives of Americans*. Cambridge, Mass.: Harvard University Press, 2004.

Sweet, William Warren. *Methodism in American History*. Nashville: Abingdon, 1954.

Swerdlow, Amy. *Women Strike for Peace: Traditional Motherhood and Radical Politics in the 1960s*. Women in Culture and Society, ed. Catharine R. Stimpson. Chicago: University of Chicago Press, 1993.

Taylor, Verta. "Social Movement Continuity: The Women's Movement in Abeyance." *American Sociological Review* 54 (Oct. 1989): 761–75.

Tebbel, John. *The Golden Age Between Two Wars, 1920–1940*. Vol. 3 of *A History of Book Publishing in the United States*. New York: R. R. Bowker, 1978.

Thompson, Stith. *The Folktale*. New York: Holt, Rinehart and Winston, 1946.

———. *Motif-Index of Folk-Literature*. Bloomington: Indiana University Press, 1961.

Thurer, Shari. *The Myths of Motherhood: How Culture Reinvents the Good Mother*. Boston: Houghton Mifflin, 1994.

Toelken, Barre, *The Dynamics of Folklore*. Rev. and expanded ed. Logan, Utah: Utah State University Press, 1996.

Tweed, Thomas A., and Stephen Prothero, eds. *Asian Religions in America: A Documentary History*. New York: Oxford University Press, 1999.

Van Slyck, Abigail A. *A Manufactured Wilderness: Summer Camps and the Shaping of American Youth, 1890–1960*. Architecture, Landscape, and American Culture Series. Minneapolis: University of Minnesota Press, 2006.

Von Rohr, John. *The Shaping of American Congregationalism 1620–1957*. Boston: Pilgrim, 1992.

Wallis, Jill. *Mother of World Peace: The Life of Muriel Lester*. Enfield Locks: Hisarlik Press, 1993.

———. *Valiant for Peace: A History of the Fellowship of Reconciliation, 1914–1989*. London: Fellowship of Reconciliation, 1991.

Ward, Patricia A. "Madame Guyon and Experiential Theology in America." *Church History* 67:3 (1998): 484–98.

Weekley, Carolyn J. *The Kingdoms of Edward Hicks*. Williamsburg, Va.: Colonial Williamsburg Foundation, 1999.

White, James F. *Christian Worship in North America: A Retrospective, 1955–1995*. Collegeville, Minn.: Liturgical Press, 1997.

———. "The Missing Jewel of the Evangelical Church." *Christian Worship in North America: A Retrospective, 1955–1995*. Collegeville, Minn: Liturgical Press, 1997.

Wildberger, Hans. *Isaiah 1–12: A Commentary*. Translated by Thomas H. Trapp, Continental Commentaries. Minneapolis: Fortress, 1991.

Will, Herman. *A Will for Peace: Peace Action in the United Methodist Church: A History*. Washington, D.C.: General Board of Church and Society of the United Methodist Church, 1984.

Wilson, Bryan R. *The Social Dimensions of Sectarianism: Sects and New Religious Movements in Contemporary Society*. Oxford: Clarendon Press, 1990.

Wink, Walter, ed. *Peace Is the Way: Writings on Nonviolence from the Fellowship of Reconciliation*. Maryknoll, N.Y.: Orbis, 2000.

Wittner, Lawrence S. *Rebels Against War: The American Peace Movement, 1933–1983*. Rev. ed. Philadelphia: Temple University Press, 1984.

Worrall, Arthur J. "New York Quaker Settlements and Immigrants." In *Quaker Crosscurrents: Three Hundred Years of Friends in the New York Yearly Meetings*, edited by Hugh Barbour, Christopher Densmore, Elizabeth H. Moger, Nancy C. Sorel, Alson D. Van Wagner, and Arthur J. Worrall, 25–47. Syracuse, N.Y.: Syracuse University Press, 1995.

Wuthnow, Robert. *The Restructuring of American Religion: Society and Faith Since World War II*. Princeton, N.J.: Princeton University Press, 1988.

Yearbook of American Churches, 1949–60. New York: Round Table Press, 1949–60.

Yoder, John Howard. *Nevertheless: The Varieties and Shortcomings of Religious Pacifism*. Rev. and expanded ed. Scottdale, Pa.: Herald Press, 1992.

Youngs, J. William T. *The Congregationalists*. Denominations in America, no. 4. Westport, Conn.: Greenwood, 1992.

Zeiger, Susan. "Teaching Peace: Lessons from a Peace Studies Curriculum of the Progressive Era." *Peace and Change* 25:1 (2000): 52–69.

Ziegler, Valarie H. *The Advocates of Peace in Antebellum America*. Religion in North America. Bloomington: Indiana University Press, 1992.

Index

Abeyance structures, 34, 42, 144, 154, 203
Abingdon Press, 30, 122. *See also* Methodists
Addams, Jane, 134, 156, 167, 178, 248 (n. 34), 260 (n. 14), 267 (n. 14), 270 (n. 37). *See also* Heroes
African Methodist Episcopal Church, 188
Ahimsa Farm, 131, 140, 149–50, 151, 156–57, 159, 160, 263 (n. 34)
"Ain't Gonna Study War No More." *See* "I Ain't Gonna Study War No More"
Alcoholics Anonymous, 71
Allen, Devere, 27, 273 (n. 63)
Allen, Ernest Bourner, 59
"America the Beautiful," 85, 236 (n. 55)
American Baptist Historical Society, 245 (n. 2)
American Baptist Publication Society, 122
American Civil Liberties Union, 241 (n. 20)
American Friends Service Committee (AFSC), 40, 70, 131, 254 (n. 52); projects, 32, 130, 147, 148, 231 (n. 74), 264 (n. 52); persons associated with, 35, 39, 41, 188
American Legion, 185, 186
American Peace Society, 170
Amish. *See* Anabaptists
Anabaptists, 144, 154; Mennonites, 27, 37, 39, 46, 150, 207; Brethren, Church of the, 27, 37, 39, 46, 207; Amish, 44; Hutterites, 153; Bruderhof, 153, 161, 162, 208, 263 (n. 36)
Anglicans. *See* Episcopalians
Another Mother for Peace, 185
Antiheroes, 167–68, 198, 199
Antimodernism: pacifist culture and, 3, 42, 49–50, 108–9, 111, 127, 142, 155–56, 206; in U.S. culture, 49, 73, 127, 145–46, 206; examples, 103, 117, 121, 123, 187, 264 (n. 55)
Antioch College, 149, 259 (n. 6), 264 (n. 34), 264 (n. 46)
Army Corps of Engineers, 9
Arnold, Eberhard, 153
Art for World Friendship, 246 (n. 18)
Asilomar, Calif., 32, 34
Association of Catholic Conscientious Objectors, 37

Association Press, 29, 30, 166, 247 (n. 27). *See also* Young Men's Christian Association
Authority, struggles over, 159–60, 190
Axling, William, 266 (n. 7)

Baber, Zonia, 96, 101, 171, 246 (n. 18), 268 (nn. 25, 26)
Bailey, Alice, 135
Baker, Henry, 57
Baker, Walter H. (publishers), 80
Balch, Emily Greene, 35, 223 (n. 3)
Baptists, 26, 48, 101, 115, 229 (n. 54), 260 (n. 6). *See also* Northern Baptist Convention
Barton, Bruce, 82, 91
Bednarowski, Mary Farrell, 233 (n. 26)
Beecher, Henry Ward, 47
Beethoven, Ludwig van, 86, 247 (nn. 26, 28)
Bell, Catherine, 87
Benavente, Marcolino, 169
Benedict, Saint, 104
Benedictines, 162
Benson, Louis F., 56
Berrigan, Daniel and Philip, 214
Beyond War, 214
Bible references: Luke, 52, 59, 63, 70, 82, 240 (n. 9), 241 (n. 18); Mark, 52, 63, 64, 83, 241 (n. 8); Matthew, 52, 63, 64, 92, 240 (n. 9); Revelation, 62; John, 63, 86, 239 (n. 33), 241 (n. 18); Romans, 64, 65, 237 (n. 7); Micah, 66, 75, 93–97; Leviticus, 83; Isaiah, 94, 98, 240 (n. 9); I Corinthians, 239 (n. 33). *See also* Gardens; Good will; Lord's Prayer; Noah's Ark; Peaceable Kingdom; Sermon on the Mount; Sixth Commandment; Swords and plowshares

Biblical literalism. *See* Fundamentalism
Black Mountain College, 261 (n. 15)
Black Power, 214
Blanshard, Brand, 255 (n. 77)
Blue Ridge Assembly, North Carolina, 32
Body, 24, 76, 156; in conscientious objection, 20, 23, 36; in drama, 73, 86–89; in mysticism, 116, 117, 118, 119; for Richard Gregg, 134, 135–36; in nonviolent direct action, 190, 191
Boeckel, Florence Brewer, 8, 27, 57, 81, 83, 93, 173, 210, 271 (n. 50)
Book of Common Prayer, 77, 78
Borsodi, Ralph, 148, 153, 159, 160, 260 (n. 15)
Bowne, Borden Parker, 47
Bread and Puppet Theater, 214, 243 (n. 37)
Brethren, Church of the, 27, 37, 39, 46, 207
Bridges, Ruby, 213
Brinton, Howard, 122, 125, 251 (nn. 9, 10, 15), 265 (n. 66)
Brittain, Vera, 10, 272 (n. 53)
Bro, Margueritte Harmon, 41, 278 (n. 35)
Broadway Tabernacle, New York, 150
Brooks, Phillips, 16
Brookwood Labor College, 148
Broomell, Anna Pettit, 176, 267 (n. 37), 271 (n. 50)
Brown, Kenneth Irving, 11, 20, 223 (n. 4)
Bruderhof. *See* Anabaptists
Bryn Gweled, 149, 151, 261 (n. 18), 227 (n. 19). *See also* Cooperative housing
Buddhism, 127, 135, 207

Burcham, George, 35, 153
Burleigh, Harry T., 9
Burleigh, William H., 57
Burrows, Edward, 33

Cadoux, C. J., 134, 209
Calbeck, Margaret, 33
Camps and camping, 29–30, 32–33, 80, 112–13, 118, 187; history, 228 (n. 40); rituals in, 228 (n. 40)
Camps Farthest Out. *See* Clark, Glenn
Carlen, Robert, 107
Carpenter, Joel, 127
Carson, Rachel, 187
Cary, Stephen, 131
Catholics. *See* Catholic Worker movement; Roman Catholics
Catholic Worker, The, 104
Catholic Worker movement, 66, 103, 151, 162, 204, 208, 209, 261 (n. 17). *See also* Day, Dorothy
Cell groups, 38–39, 42, 133, 230 (n. 63), 231 (nn. 66, 67, 69), 261 (n. 17)
Celo Community, 147, 187
Cérésole, Pierre, 167, 210
Chalmers, Allan Knight, 41, 150
Chautauqua, 228 (n. 31)
Chatfield, Charles, 228 (n. 39), 256–57 (n. 6)
Chatterjee, Manmatha, 149, 265 (n. 58)
Children, 77, 139; drama for, 81, 83, 84, 85, 196; as symbols, 83, 89, 94, 102, 107, 179, 180–81; literature for, 98, 173–74, 176; parents' activism and, 151, 160, 197–98, 202, 213, 277 (n. 35); Swann family, 184, 187, 191, 195, 198; maternalist pacifism and, 200–201. *See also* Education; International friendship; Mothers and motherhood
Christ. *See* Jesus
"Christian ashrams." *See* Jones, E. Stanley
Christian Century, The, 30, 41, 194
Christian Church (Disciples of Christ), 5, 25; pacifists in, 11, 29, 41, 228 (n. 29); history, 12; worship, 57, 75, 240 (n. 10); Disciples Peace Fellowship, 69
Christian Endeavor, 29, 57
Christian Peacemakers, 214
"Christian realism." *See* Neo-orthodoxy
Christian Science, 229 (n. 54)
"Christ of the Andes," 82, 169–70, 176, 270 (n. 37)
Church of the Messiah. *See* Community Church of New York
Civilian Public Service (CPS), 51, 91, 199, 259 (n. 6); described, 8, 36–38; and pacifist vernacular, 67–68, 230 (nn. 57, 61); practices in, 110, 139; and cooperative living, 122, 150, 152–53, 262 (n. 31)
Clark, Christopher, 154
Clark, Glenn, 112, 113, 118–19, 122, 123, 251 (n. 7), 253 (n. 45), 254 (n. 65)
Cleghorn, Sarah, 27, 122, 123, 148, 210, 255 (nn. 67, 78)
Cloud of Unknowing, The, 122
Coffin, William Sloane, 203
Committee for Non-Violent Action (CNVA), 87, 190, 203, 264 (n. 54)
Commonwealth College, 261 (n. 15)
Communitarianism: U.S. history of, 144–45. *See also* Cooperative farming; Cooperative living
Community Church of New York, 94, 244 (n. 2)

Concord Park, Trevose, Pa., 187
Conference of Pacifist Farming Communities, 151, 162
Conferences, 31–33, 41–42, 42, 80, 96
Congregational Christian Churches of the United States. *See* Congregationalists
Congregationalists, 5, 25, 31, 34, 37, 118, 261 (n. 22); pacifists, 27, 28, 116, 234 (n. 29), 251 (n. 15); Council for Social Action, 32, 33, 37, 147, 228 (n. 39); theology and worship, 48, 63, 234 (n. 36)
Congress of Racial Equality (CORE), 87, 150, 187
Conscientious objection, 28, 35, 123, 161, 223 (n. 6); Civilian Public Service, 8, 36–38, 41, 152–53; Harold Gray and, 10, 11, 20–24; in World War II, 33, 36, 131, 186; articulation of beliefs, 41, 66, 67–68, 69, 230 (n. 61); in worship and drama, 78, 82, 86; in stories, 177–78; and women, 199–200; and gender, 278 (n. 44). *See also* Civilian Public Service; National Committee for Conscientious Objectors
Consistent living, 37–38, 98, 130, 164, 165, 166, 203. *See also* Way of life
Continuing revelation. *See* Progressive revelation
Conversion: to pacifism, 13–15, 29–34, 52, 186, 275 (n. 9); Protestant meanings of, 16–17, 47, 60, 65, 135, 227 (n. 17). *See also* Evangelicalism
Cooperation. *See* Cooperative economics; Cooperative living; Social Gospel
Cooperative economics, 49, 50, 67, 100, 147, 261 (n. 17). *See also* Economics
Cooperative farming: Harold Gray and, 12, 223 (n. 8); and iconography, 91, 102; pacifist movement, 143–44, 149–62; religious aspects of, 144, 145–46, 158–59, 161–62. *See also* Farms and farming; *names of individual farms*
Cooperative housing, 149, 151, 153, 187. *See also* Bryn Gweled; Skyview Acres
Cooperative League of the United States, 147
Cooperative living, 50, 166, 260 (n. 4), 261 (n. 17); and paradigm shift, 38, 42, 67, 143–44; mainline Protestant advocacy of, 49, 50, 146–49; and heroism, 98, 100, 111; pacifist movement and, 149–62; Swann family and, 187–88
Cooperatives, urban, 115, 150–51
Cortright, David, 214
Craft, 84, 86, 97, 104, 109
Craig, Mildred, 157
Crane, Henry Hitt, 41
Creativity: pacifist watchword, 52, 54, 61, 69, 118, 138, 152, 156, 166, 234 (n. 26); pacifist value, 68, 86, 122, 167, 178
Crucifixion, 14, 82, 120, 182, 208. *See also* Suffering

Damien, Father (Joseph de Veuster), 167, 247 (n. 26), 267 (n. 9)
Davis, Jerome, 147, 260 (n. 7)
Davis-DuBois, Rachel, 243 (n. 43)
Day, Albert Edward, 27, 241 (n. 20)
Day, Dorothy, 103, 167, 200, 208,

209. See also *Catholic Worker, The*; Catholic Worker movement
Decision-making. *See* Scrupulosity
Dellinger, David, 63, 151, 204
Delta Cooperative Farm, 147
Detrick, Fort. *See* Vigil at Fort Detrick
Disciples of Christ. *See* Christian Church (Disciples of Christ)
Disciples Peace Fellowship. *See* Christian Church (Disciples of Christ)
Discussion, 13, 29, 80, 81; as practice, 128, 129, 130–32, 134, 140–41; in cooperatives, 149, 154, 157, 158, 159, 160
Dix, Beulah Marie, 81
Dolls, 72, 245 (n. 2), 248 (n. 34)
Dorrien, Gary, 7, 45, 222 (n. 13)
Douglas, Mary, 265 (n. 64)
Dove, 84, 89, 92, 104
Drama, 69, 73–74, 83, 184–85, 241 (n. 21); church, 74, 80, 242 (n. 24); as cultural transmission, 86–87; iconography and, 91, 96; stories and, 170, 172, 173. *See also* Pageantry; Plays; Ritual
Driver, Tom R., 244 (nn. 54, 59)
Drummond, Henry, 16
Dunkers. *See* Brethren, Church of the
Duveneck, Josephine Whitney, 123–24, 125

Easton, N.Y., 179
Economics: nonviolence and, 4, 211–12; religious aspects of, 8, 15, 48–49, 53, 65; alternative, 12, 98, 133, 139, 155; war and, 52, 92–93. *See also* Cooperative economics
Eddy, Sherwood, 16, 29; and Harold Gray, 13, 14; activities, 27, 31, 147, 148, 266 (n. 7); and Kirby Page, 51, 52
Eden, Garden of, 107, 108
Education: peace, 27, 30, 132, 170, 176, 190, 196, 210; Sunday school, 27, 84, 170, 189; progressive, 73, 136, 148, 155, 226 (n. 9), 245 (n. 4); drama as, 80, 86, 87, 197
Educational communities, 148
Edwin, John F., Jr., 272 (n. 2)
Eichel, Seymour, 161
Eichenberg, Fritz, 102–6
Ellsberg, Robert, 249 (n. 42)
Emergency Peace Campaign, 26, 61, 257 (n. 6)
Emerson, Ralph Waldo, 16, 111
Emmanuel movement, 255 (n. 67)
Enclave culture, 265 (n. 64)
English, Martin, 151
Enzer, Erica, 200
Episcopalians, 25; pacifists, 26, 27, 33, 77, 123, 241 (n. 20); theology and worship, 58, 232 (n. 77), 240 (n. 6)
Episcopal Pacifist Fellowship, 36, 110, 259 (n. 50)
Episcopal Peace Fellowship. *See* Episcopal Pacifist Fellowship
Epworth League, 41, 228 (n. 39), 242 (n. 33)
Evangelicalism, 56, 120; relation to liberalism, 5, 7, 48, 75, 79, 206–7; and mysticism, 112, 113, 115. *See also* Conversion
Evolution, 46, 47–48, 60, 63, 75
Exempla, 163–83, 196, 197

Fager, Chuck, 255 (n. 77)
Farmer, James, 150
Farms and farming, 35, 104, 140, 203;

in iconography, 94, 104, 109, 161. *See also* Cooperative farming
Fast for Peace, 131
Fasting, 11, 23, 150, 188, 191
Federal Council of Churches, 25, 69, 80
Fell, Leonard, 270 (n. 46)
Fellowship, 27, 30, 38, 41, 52, 68, 70, 131, 194, 214. *See also* Fellowship of Reconciliation
Fellowship Farms, 151
Fellowship House (Philadelphia), 101, 140
Fellowship Houses, 151
Fellowship of Intentional Communities, 159
Fellowship of Reconciliation (FOR), 161, 209; description, 4, 27–28, 232 (n. 79); members, 12, 117, 241 (n. 20), 243 (n. 43), 258 (n. 47); leadership, 27, 31, 41, 114, 148; and paradigm shift, 36, 38, 229 (n. 54); and pacifist expression, 41, 68, 69, 80, 110, 130, 150, 176; Niebuhr and, 50; Rural Life Committee, 143. *See also* Fellowship
Fénelon, François de Salignac de la Mothe-, 122, 255 (n. 78)
Fey, Harold, 11, 41, 111, 227 (n. 29)
Fichter, Richard, 161
I Corinthians. *See* Bible references
Fisk Jubilee Singers, 222 (n. 16)
Fleming Revell (publishers), 30, 113, 251 (n. 9)
Folk arts, 32, 57, 73, 81, 102, 187, 203; and paradigm shift, 133, 137–38, 140–41; in cooperatives, 150, 155, 158
Folk dancing, 137, 139
Folk group, 6, 140, 142, 204, 206

Folk process, 16, 73, 139–40, 163–64, 173, 174–76
Folk schools, 137, 148, 151, 258 (n. 36). *See also* Highlander Folk School
Folk singing, 57, 102, 135, 137, 141
Fosdick, Harry Emerson, 26, 52, 58, 70, 81, 93, 271 (n. 50); and liberal theology, 16, 47, 48, 58, 63; "Unknown Soldier" sermon, 82, 134
Fox, George, 125
Franciscans, 154, 162
Francis of Assisi, Saint: "Prayer of St. Francis," 1–2, 8, 79, 124; meaning in pacifist culture, 8; as model, 30, 68, 104, 113, 155, 162; imagery, 91, 96, 104, 107, 247 (n. 23); as peace hero, 98, 101, 134, 165, 247 (n. 26), 277 (n. 34); persons compared to, 118, 167, 252 (n. 29); in exemplum, 180
Freedom, 14, 19, 22, 23, 60, 70, 103, 191
French, Samuel (publishers), 80
French and Indian War, 172
Friends, Society of (Quakers), 27, 30, 31, 98, 101, 162, 203, 208; and mainline Protestantism, 5, 112, 176, 204; members, 26, 27, 35, 38, 66, 69, 103, 106, 120, 123, 124, 178, 188, 227 (n. 19), 260 (n. 6), 277 (n. 34); and conscientious objection, 28, 35, 37, 131; and paradigm shift, 35, 36, 39–41, 103, 124–26, 206, 207, 265 (n. 65); and theology, 39, 40, 46, 48, 69, 188; hymnody, 56, 57, 58; and art, 103, 249 (n. 41); and mysticism, 112, 124–26, 255 (n. 77); and antimodernism, 127; and exempla, 172, 176, 179–80, 196. *See also* American Friends Service Committee; Friends General Conference; Friends Ser-

vice Committee (British); Pendle Hill; Wider Quaker Fellowship
Friends Committee on National Legislation, 32
Friends General Conference, 5, 39, 40, 125
Friends Service Committee (British), 40
Fry, Elizabeth, 178, 247 (n. 26)
Fry, Ruth, 181, 272 (n. 53)
Fundamentalism, 7, 43–44, 62, 63, 206; biblical literalism, 18, 62, 64

Gandhi, Mohandas, 41, 146, 155, 203, 241 (n. 20); as hero, 96, 98, 104, 114, 134, 165, 166, 208; iconography, 100–101; influence, 139, 149–50, 259 (n. 51). *See also* Nonviolent direct action
Gardens, 101–2, 107, 108, 171, 187
Garrison, William Lloyd, 46
Gender, 76, 137, 139, 236 (n. 50); in plays and exempla, 98, 167, 177, 178, 183, 198–99; in peace movement, 209, 210, 275 (n. 16), 278 (nn. 44, 45)
Glassberg, David, 73, 87
Glen Gardner homesteads, 153
Goddard, Alvin, 31
Good will, 18, 81, 85, 97–98, 134, 186; in hymnody, 58, 59, 60; in pacifist vernacular, 61, 67, 69–70; in exempla, 165, 166, 171. *See also* Bible references
Goodwill Day, 240 (n. 41)
Gould, Rebecca Kneale, 145, 146, 260 (n. 15), 265 (n. 66)
Gower, Jean Milne, 82
Grace Cathedral, San Francisco, 244 (n. 2)

Gray, Harold Studley, 10–24, 60, 72, 111, 134, 147, 148, 277 (n. 34); compared to Marjorie Swann, 184, 186, 191–92, 201
Gregg, Richard, 27, 128–42, 148, 210, 213; writings, 10, 115, 122, 146, 149, 158, 176; practices, 38, 152, 155, 158
Griscom, Anna, 69, 176, 271 (n. 50), 272 (n. 54)
Groton, Conn., 188, 242 (n. 27)
Guyon, Mme Jeanne-Marie de la Motte, 122, 251 (n. 9), 252 (n. 16)

Hagedorn, Hermann, 165, 266 (n. 5)
Hagiography. *See* Sainthood
Haines, Vesta, 271 (n. 50)
Ham, Marion Franklin, 236–37 (n. 56)
Harkness, Georgia, 27, 112, 183, 224 (n. 24), 251 (n. 15), 254 (n. 64)
Harlem Ashram, 41, 110, 149, 150, 160, 234 (n. 26), 261 (n. 23), 265 (n. 61)
Hartman, Doris and Justin, 247 (n. 28)
Harvey, Arthur, 190
Haslam, Herbert, 101
Hassler, Alfred, 41, 153
Hauerwas, Stanley, 214
Havens, Joseph, 131
Haverford College, 39, 120
Heard, Gerald, 110, 115, 122, 149, 152, 212, 271 (n. 50); and Allan Hunter, 166; as mystic, 234 (n. 29), 251 (n. 15)
Hennacy, Ammon, 66
Heroes: modern, 53, 58, 85, 97–98, 247 (nn. 26, 27); women, 98, 167, 196, 247 (n. 27); paradigm shift and, 98–101, 134, 165–68, 247 (nn. 28, 30), 277 (n. 34). *See also* Sainthood; *names of individual heroes*
Hicks, Edward, 106, 107

Highlander Folk School, 141, 148, 203, 260 (n. 14)
Hilltop Farm, 151
Hinduism, 124, 127, 207, 251 (n. 15)
Hiroshima Day, 102
Hodgkin, Henry, 14, 27, 148, 224 (n. 20)
Holmes, John Haynes, 26, 27, 30, 58, 64, 94; and drama, 80, 81, 82, 83, 86
Holt, Arthur, 267 (n. 10)
Holy Family, 104
Holy Mountain. *See* Peaceable Kingdom
Holy Spirit, 92, 125, 189
Homesteading. *See* Communitarianism; Cooperative farming
Horton, Myles, 148, 260 (n. 14)
Housman, Laurence, 176
Hunter, Allan, 27, 111, 122, 178, 250 (n. 1), 254 (n. 64); and paradigm shift, 100–101, 166–67; peace team, 166, 231 (n. 69)
Hutchison, William R., 7
Hutterites. *See* Anabaptists
Huxley, Aldous, 251 (n. 15)
Hymns: general use, 16, 27, 75–76, 135, 149, 234 (n. 36), 235 (n. 40); and pacifist theology, 55–60, 236 (n. 55); in Quakerism, 56, 57, 234 (n. 35), 235 (nn. 39, 45), 249 (n. 41); individual hymns, 57–60, 79, 85, 244 (n. 50), 255 (n. 38)

"I Ain't Gonna Study War No More," 1, 66, 79, 196, 270 (n. 37). *See also* Spirituals
Imitatio Christi, 8, 17, 61, 64, 146, 208. *See also* Jesus: emphasis on life and teaching of; Way of life
Industrial Workers of the World, 59

"In Flanders Fields," 236 (n. 55)
Intentional communities. *See* Communitarianism; Cooperative farming; Cooperative living; Cooperatives, urban
Intercollegian, 31
Intercontinental ballistic missiles (ICBMs), 190
International friendship, 56, 77, 81, 86, 160, 165, 173, 186, 248 (n. 34). *See also* Missions
Inter-Seminary League, 28
Iraq, 214, 271 (n. 52)
Isaiah. *See* Bible references
Islam, 116, 117

Jail. *See* Prison
James, William, 124
Jehovah's Witnesses, 37
Jesus: in liberal theology, 7, 14–15, 17, 18, 20, 40, 47, 52–53, 71, 189, 207; emphasis on life and teaching of, 25, 30, 62–64, 65–69, 131, 153, 237 (nn. 1, 2, 12); in pacifist expression, 77, 79, 82, 101, 134, 169, 172, 179; and alternative lifeways, 103, 147, 154, 155, 158, 162, 212. *See also* Imitatio Christi; Sermon on the Mount
Jews, 186, 253 (n. 37); in CPS camps, 37
John, Gospel of. *See* Bible references
John the Evangelist, Saint, 247 (n. 24). *See also* Bible references
Johnson, James Weldon, 9
Johnston, Georgina, 72
Jones, E. Stanley, 132, 148–49, 150, 231 (n. 66), 251 (n. 15), 254 (n. 65), 260 (n. 7), 261 (n. 17)
Jones, Edgar L., 209, 230 (n. 56)
Jones, Rufus M., 167, 176, 251 (n. 7),

271 (n. 50); and Society of Friends, 39–40, 125, 148, 231 (n. 71); and mysticism, 112, 118, 120, 125
Jones, Thomas E., 152
Jordan, Clarence, 151, 159
Justice, 35, 50, 85, 212

Kagawa, Toyohiko, 50, 81, 118, 134, 155, 260 (n. 7); as hero, 98, 100–101, 114, 166–67; and cooperatives, 147; life, 166, 210
Kaplan, Judy, 198
Katz, Neil H., 275 (n. 13)
Kellogg-Briand Peace Pact, 77, 98, 241 (n. 14)
Kelly, Thomas, 111, 112–13, 119–21, 122, 124, 212
Kennedy, Charles Rann, 80, 82, 241 (n. 20)
Kepler, Thomas, 122
King, Coretta Scott, 187
King, Martin Luther, Jr., 208
Kingdom of God: in Protestant use, 18, 47, 53, 56, 59, 61, 89, 148, 166; religiously open use, 121, 135, 158, 159, 182
Kingsley Hall, 115
Kingwood cooperative, 153, 259 (n. 50)
Kipling, Rudyard, 57, 58
Kiwanis Clubs, 171, 268 (n. 26), 275 (n. 6)
Koinonia Farm, 149, 151, 153, 154, 158, 159–60, 187, 265 (n. 61)
Kramer, Wendell, 153
Kropotkin, Petr, 146–47
Kuenzli, Alfred E., 230 (n. 56)

Labor Temple, 151, 259 (n. 26)
Landes, Carl J., 143, 150, 151, 261 (nn. 19, 22), 265 (n. 58)

Lane's End Homestead, 260 (n. 15)
Lansbury, George, 61, 267 (n. 11)
Laubach, Frank, 30; as hero, 98, 100–101; and mysticism, 113, 116–17, 118, 119, 122, 251 (n. 13); and speech, 117, 121, 252 (n. 33)
Lawrence, Brother (Nicholas Herman), 30, 113–14, 115, 116, 117, 118, 122, 203
Lawrence, Charles and Margaret, 153
Lawrence, Reginald, 80, 81
League of Free Nations Association, 94
League of Nations, 172
Lecturing, 12, 29, 31, 41, 51, 52, 53, 139, 166, 228 (n. 31)
Lester, Muriel, 27, 111, 152, 208, 238 (n. 21), 250 (n. 7), 252 (nn. 15, 21), 271 (n. 50); and peace teams, 38, 231 (n. 69); and cooperatives, 50, 115, 150, 151; as hero, 98, 100–101, 167, 209, 247 (n. 27); and mysticism, 112–13, 114–16, 119, 124
Leviticus. *See* Bible references
Liberalism. *See* Protestant liberalism
Liberation, 190
Light, 19–20, 22, 123, 125
Limbert, Paul, 170
Lindbergh, Charles, 49, 85, 97–98, 108, 171, 247 (nn. 24, 25, 26)
Lisle Fellowship, 41
Little, Henry, 161
Lobingier, Elizabeth Miller, 80, 101, 176, 210, 272 (nn. 50, 54)
Lobingier, John Leslie, 170, 210, 234 (n. 29), 272 (nn. 50, 54)
Loomis, Mildred, 260 (n. 15)
Lord's Prayer, 149
Love, 85, 156, 203, 239 (n. 33); in liberal theology, 17, 47, 59, 60, 186,

189; power of, 19, 53, 79; critiques of, 50, 51, 135; in pacifist vernacular, 67, 68–69; in stories, 69, 167, 178, 179; in mysticism, 114, 120, 121, 123; as force, 118–19, 165, 174, 181, 182; in Quakerism, 125, 131; in umbrella theology, 158–59
Loyola, Ignatius, 79
Luitweiler, Bob, 151
Luke, Gospel of. *See* Bible references
Lunde, Erling H., 23, 238 (n. 16)
Lutherans, 5, 229 (n. 54), 266 (n. 5), 267 (n. 37)
Lynch, Frederick, 26, 170
Lynd, Staughton and Alice, 2, 211, 221 (n. 4)
Lynn, Susan, 278 (n. 45)

Macedonia Cooperative Farm, 147, 152, 154, 157, 158, 160, 265 (n. 61); religious life, 153, 159
Macgregor, G. H. C., 64, 132, 209
Macintosh, D. C., 47
MacKaye, Hazel, 81
Manual work, 138–39. *See also* Gandhi, Mohandas
Mark, Gospel of. *See* Bible references
Markham, Edwin, 76
Marlatt, Earl, 79, 236 (n. 55)
Martyrdom, 19, 181, 198
Mary, Virgin, 104, 267 (n. 14)
Maternalist pacifism, 86, 185, 193, 194, 200–201
Mathews, Shailer, 45, 47
Matthew, Gospel of. *See* Bible references
May Valley cooperative, 154, 263 (n. 36)
McPherson, Imogene M., 176, 210, 269 (n. 37), 271 (n. 50)

Meadville Fellowship of Peace, 81, 242 (n. 27)
Means and ends, 13, 14, 17, 134
Meditation, 41, 110, 124, 192, 203; in worship, 53, 78–79, 126; in mysticism, 122, 127; Richard Gregg and, 133, 135, 137–38, 140–41; in cooperative living, 149, 150, 157, 159. *See also* Friends, Society of; Mysticism
Mendenhall, O. W., 34–35
Mendicancy. *See* Franciscans
Mennonites. *See* Anabaptists
Merom Institute, 261 (n. 22)
Methodist Episcopal Church. *See* Methodists
Methodist Episcopal Church, First, of Meadville, Pa., 246 (n. 15)
Methodists, 5, 66, 67, 110, 122, 176, 241 (n. 20), 271 (n. 50); and pacifism, 25, 31, 35, 37, 48; pacifists, 27, 28, 33, 35, 148, 150, 153, 156, 160, 251 (n. 15); hymnody and worship, 58, 75, 240 (nn. 5, 6); Marjorie Swann and, 186, 188. *See also* African Methodist Episcopal Church; Trinity Methodist Church, Springfield, Mass.
Metropolitan Federation of Daily Vacation Bible Schools, 85
Meyer, Karl, 277 (n. 30)
Micah. *See* Bible references
Miller, Elizabeth. *See* Lobingier, Elizabeth Miller
Miller, Timothy, 145, 146, 259 (n. 4), 261 (n. 8)
Ministers' No War Committee, 26
Missionaries, 98, 100, 102, 116–17, 148–49, 150, 151, 162
Missions: term, 70; in mainline practices, 75, 84, 90, 96, 245 (n. 2); and

pacifism, 111, 170, 210, 268 (n. 30). *See also* Missionaries; International friendship

Missions, 30

Mitchell, Morris, 38, 147, 148, 152, 160, 210, 265 (n. 58)

Modernism: defined, 7; in pacifist theology, 18, 49, 60, 71; in Quakerism, 39, 40, 207; in mainline theology, 49, 50, 205; in pacifist expression, 55, 121, 135, 165, 208. *See also* Protestant liberalism; Social Gospel

Modernity, 46, 47, 49, 85, 94, 112, 208

Molinos, Miguel de, 122

Monasticism, 161–62

Moore, Howard, 22, 23, 225 (n. 52)

Moore, Thomas, 34–35, 36, 40, 263 (n. 34)

Morgan, Arthur E., 38, 66, 146, 147, 148, 149, 151, 152, 187; life, 210, 259 (n. 6)

Morgan, David, 3, 90, 91

Morrison, Charles Clayton, 11, 19, 227 (n. 29)

Mothers and motherhood, 76; as peace symbol, 86, 89, 104, 107; "bad," 184, 274 (n. 1), 279 (n. 53); and activism, 185, 192–94, 202. *See also* Children; Maternalist pacifism

Motifs (folklore), 175–81

Motive, 31

Muelder, Walter, 33

Mullin, James, 29

Muslims. *See* Islam

Mussey, Mabel, 57, 235 (n. 40)

Muste, A. J., 27, 31, 37, 69, 111, 132, 196, 209; and School of Nonviolence, 38, 262 (n. 31); and paradigm shift, 39, 150, 151, 152, 162; and mysticism, 110, 255 (n. 78); Brookwood Labor College led by, 148; and Labor Temple, 262 (n. 26)

Mygatt, Tracy, 26, 77, 80, 82, 123, 241 (n. 20)

Mysticism: and mainline Protestantism, 7, 47, 56, 111, 112, 127, 148, 166; Kirby Page and, 7, 53, 55, 78–79; and Quakerism, 39, 40, 112, 120, 124–26, 148, 255 (nn. 77, 78); in pacifist expression, 69, 92, 101, 139, 152, 157, 187; texts, 110–22 passim; and antimodernism, 111, 112, 121, 127; practices, 111–26 passim, 139, 152; and social action, 112, 120–21, 123, 125, 152; prominent mystics, 112–21, 148, 166, 210, 251 (n. 15); and umbrella theology, 116, 146, 167, 187; orthodox theology in, 120–21; lay mystics, 122–24. *See also* Meditation

Nation, The, 31

National Association of Evangelicals, 206

National Cathedral, Washington, D.C., 244 (n. 2)

National Committee for a Sane Nuclear Policy (SANE), 275 (n. 12)

National Committee for Conscientious Objectors, 186

National Council for Prevention of War (NCPW), 26, 31, 80, 92, 130, 161

National Council of Methodist Youth, 28

National Study Conference on the Churches and World Peace, 64

Nature, 96, 98, 189, 206; liberal Protestantism and, 47, 76, 212; Kirby Page and, 55, 78; gardens, 101–2; farms, 145–46, 155, 156, 212

Nearing, Helen and Scott, 146, 159, 265 (n. 67)
Nelson, Juanita, 194
Neo-orthodoxy, 35, 45, 50–51, 54–55, 70, 121, 205. *See also* Niebuhr, Reinhold; Sin
Newark Ashram, 151
New England Committee for Nonviolent Action (NECNVA), 187, 188
New School for Social Research, 103
New Thought, 118, 253 (n. 45)
New York Times, 194
New York Tribune, 94
Niebuhr, Reinhold, 27, 29, 68, 147, 148, 240 (n. 43); *Moral Man and Immoral Society*, 50–51. *See also* Neo-orthodoxy
Noah's Ark, 107
Nobel Peace Prize, 40
Nonresistance, 45, 46, 62, 18
Nonviolent direct action, 67, 150, 154, 213, 214; body and ritual in, 72–73, 87–88, 136, 192; Marjorie Swann and, 187, 189–92. *See also* Gandhi, Mohandas
Northern Baptist Convention, 5, 25, 30, 37, 57, 75. *See also* Baptists
Nye Commission, 246 (n. 21)

Oak Ridge, Tenn., 187
Omaha Action, 184, 189–95
Omaha World-Herald, 194
Orchard, W. E., 14, 15, 16, 67, 224 (n. 20)
Oxenham, John, 58, 79
Oxford Group (Moral Rearmament), 266 (n. 5)

Pacifist Handbook, 26
Page, Kirby, 11, 26, 37, 60, 91, 134, 148, 212; worship service, 1–2, 7, 78–79; associates, 13, 14, 50, 61; theology, 16, 52–53, 55, 147; influence, 29, 32, 62, 176, 260 (n. 7), 271 (n. 50); life and work, 51–55, 209; practice, 53–54, 130; mysticism, 54–55, 250 (n. 7)
Pageantry, 73, 77–78, 84–86, 214, 243 (n. 37). *See also* Drama; Plays; Ritual
Palmer, Albert W., 26
Pax Christi, 257 (n. 24)
Peaceable Kingdom, 75, 92, 102, 104–8, 109, 214, 246 (n. 15), 249 (n. 47), 250 (n. 53)
Peace caravans, 130, 256–57 (n. 6)
Peace gardens, 101, 246 (n. 18), 248 (n. 34); Peace Garden (Lemont, Illinois), 102
Peace House, 93
Peacemaker, 190, 194
Peacemakers movement, 38, 39, 42, 153, 194
Peace monuments, 171, 268 (n. 26)
Peace Pilgrim, 123, 248 (n. 31)
Peale, Norman Vincent, 253 (n. 45)
Pendle Hill, 103, 112, 125, 148, 151, 251 (n. 15), 260 (n. 6), 265 (n. 66)
Penn, William, 82, 101, 106, 171–72, 179
Penney, Marjorie, 101
Pentecostalism, 117, 123, 126, 127, 251 (n. 9)
Perfectionism, 22, 67, 69, 165, 208
Personalist theology, 47, 48
Personality, 18, 48, 63, 103, 134
Phillips, Mary, 102, 108
Pickett, Clarence, 147, 273–74 (n. 66)
Pilgrim Fellowship, 41
Pinker, Steven, 202, 279 (n. 53)
Pippin, Horace, 107

Pitzer, Donald E., 261 (n. 18)
Plays, 79–83, 176, 196–99, 241 (n. 22), 242 (n. 24). *See also* Drama; Pageantry; Ritual
Pledging, 28, 77, 170
Plowshares movement, 214, 246 (n. 20)
Pohl, Frederick G., 81
Poteat, Edwin McNeill, 26
Presbyterian Church in the U.S.A. *See* Presbyterians
Presbyterians, 5, 25, 118, 262 (n. 26); pacifists, 26, 28, 33, 34, 37; hymnals, 56, 234 (n. 26); peace education, 127, 271 (n. 50)
Priesthood, 162
Print and publishing, 30–31, 41, 42, 122, 132, 134, 209, 227 (n. 26). *See also* Reading; *names of publishers*
Prison: cultural meaning of, 10, 156, 161, 197, 200, 211, 277 (n. 34); Harold Gray and, 11, 21, 23, 225 (n. 57); pacifists in, 69, 82, 110, 116, 161, 166, 167, 255 (n. 69); nonpacifists in, 158, 163; Marjorie Swann and, 184, 191, 193, 196, 276 (n. 19)
Progressive revelation, 39, 48, 64
Protestant Episcopal Church. *See* Episcopalians
Protestant liberalism, 12, 173–74, 203, 209; and Quakerism, 5, 36, 39–40, 69, 112, 207; described, 6–7, 45, 60; hymnody and worship, 7, 57, 58, 75, 79, 244 (n. 54); in pacifist religious thought, 15–20, 52–53, 67–71, 103, 135, 155–59, 189; and social networks, 30, 35, 41; theology, 46–48, 51; critiques, 49–50, 182, 208; Bible interpretation, 62–63; and iconography, 92, 94, 98, 102; and mysticism, 111, 112, 114, 117, 118, 120, 123; and persuasion, 128, 130; and Richard Gregg, 134–35, 137; and cooperative living, 144, 146, 158–59; and Marjorie Swann, 184, 186, 187, 188, 189. *See also* Evangelicalism; Modernism; Nature; Social Gospel; "Umbrella theology"
Providence Farm, 147

Quakers. *See* Friends, Society of

Race, 172, 187, 189, 211, 225 (n. 49); interracial cooperatives, 149, 151, 154; in art, 249 (nn. 46, 49), 250 (n. 54)
Raitt, Mary Page, 130
Rauschenbusch, Walter, 16, 49, 260 (n. 7), 271 (n. 50)
Rawson, Edward B., 255 (n. 77)
Read, Herbert, 132
Reading, 60, 134, 149, 157, 158. *See also* Print and publishing
Redbook, 195, 196
Regen, Rosalie, 184, 211, 274 (n. 1)
Religious openness, 108, 115, 117, 121, 148, 188. *See also* "Umbrella theology"
Revelation, Book of. *See* Bible references
Richards, Edward, 270 (n. 45), 272 (n. 59)
Ritter, Scott, 214
Ritual, 87–88, 119, 175, 197, 210–11; Protestants and, 74, 76–79, 86–87; post paradigm shift, 102, 139–41, 192, 206. *See also* Drama; Pageantry; Plays
Riverside Church, New York, 244 (n. 2)

Robbins, Jhan and June, 195, 274 (n. 1)
Rochdale cooperatives, 146, 152
Rockefeller, Abby Aldrich, 249 (n. 48)
Rodeheaver, Homer, 8
Rolland, Romain, 16, 30
Roman Catholics, 63, 88, 94, 113, 186, 209, 253 (n. 37), 261 (n. 17); in CPS camps, 37. *See also* Catholic Worker movement
Romans, Letter to the. *See* Bible references
Rotary Clubs, 171, 275 (n. 6)
Royden, Maude, 14, 224 (n. 20)
Rural Cooperative Community Conference, 151
Rural ideal, 8, 32, 97, 104, 155, 161, 206
Rush-Bagot Agreement, 101, 171, 248 (n. 32)
Ruskin, John, 103, 146, 246 (n. 20)
Ruskin College, 261 (n. 15)
Rustin, Bayard, 38, 150, 212, 262 (n. 31)

Sabatier, Paul, 222 (n. 15)
Saint Francis Acres, 153, 159
Sainthood, 97, 98, 100, 108, 114, 164. *See also* Heroes
Saline Valley Farms, 12, 147, 223 (n. 8)
Sandburg, Carl, 8, 9
SANE. *See* National Committee for a Sane Nuclear Policy
Sayre, John Nevin, 26, 27, 51, 148, 229 (n. 54)
Schmidt, Leigh Eric, 3, 111, 113
School of Living, 41, 148, 151, 156, 260 (n. 15). *See also* Schools of Community Living; Schools of Pacifist Living
Schools of Community Living, 37–38, 260 (n. 13)

Schools of Pacifist Living, 122, 152, 262 (n. 31)
Schweitzer, Albert, 100, 101, 166, 270 (n. 43)
Scott, Coretta. *See* King, Coretta Scott
Scrupulosity, 13, 20–22, 23–24, 54, 131, 160, 190, 208, 275 (n. 16)
Sectarianism, 3, 42–43, 205–6
Seeger, Dan, 41
Seminaries, 26, 34, 80, 225–26 (n. 3)
Sermon on the Mount, 65–66, 75, 86, 92–93, 97, 154–55, 238 (nn. 17, 21); cited, 46, 86, 149, 241 (n. 18); visual imagery, 246 (n. 22). *See also* Jesus: emphasis on life and teaching of
Service, 55, 59, 147, 165; as mainline Protestant term, 12, 19, 56, 57; in pacifist vernacular, 61, 67, 69, 70, 240 (n. 44)
Shakespeare, William, 91, 247 (n. 23)
Shapiro, Linn, 198
Sheehan, Cindy, 214
Sheldon, Charles, 17
Shridharani, Krishnalal, 149, 261 (n. 20)
Siegmund-Schultze, Friedrich, 267 (n. 11)
Silk, Mark, 168, 175
Silver Bay, New York, 32
Sin: sense of, 16–17, 19, 54, 58, 60, 114, 252 (n. 21); resistance to idea of, 57, 58, 69, 114. *See also* Neo-orthodoxy
Sinclair, Upton, 147
Singsen, Mary Ellen, 29, 32
Sixth Commandment, 64, 65, 238 (n. 14)
Skyview Acres, 149, 153. *See also* Cooperative housing
Small, Fred, 163–64
Smith College Peace Fellowship, 30

Smith, H. Augustine, 80
Smith, Jay Holmes, 67, 110, 149, 150, 151, 160, 261–62 (n. 23)
Smucker, Donovan, 150
Social Action, 31
Social Gospel, 12–13, 16, 48–50, 51–52, 59, 70, 144, 147, 188. *See also* Modernism; Protestant liberalism
Socialism, 27, 28, 30, 49–50, 51, 133
Sojourners, 214
Somalia, 213, 257 (n. 24)
Spinning jenny, 266 (n. 4)
Spirituals, 8–9, 57, 102, 137
Stassen, Glen, 214
Steere, Douglas, 27, 122, 152, 235 (n. 44), 255 (n. 78); teaches mysticism, 38, 110, 125, 148, 251 (n. 15); and peace teams, 38–39
Stewart-Winter, Timothy, 278 (n. 44)
Student Christian Associations, 11, 28–30, 31, 35, 41, 151, 204, 206
Student Christian Movement (SCM). *See* Student Christian Associations
Student Volunteer Movement (SVM), 28–29, 32
"Study War No More." *See* "I Ain't Gonna Study War No More"
Suffering, 13, 17, 19, 53, 103, 120, 166; ambivalence about, 182, 208, 253 (n. 44). *See also* Crucifixion
Survey, The, 57
Swann, Barbara and Judy, 195
Swann, Carol, 195, 198
Swann, Marjorie, 184–202, 203, 208, 210
Swann, Robert, 186–88, 191, 193, 195
Swayne, Amelia, 66
Swerdlow, Amy, 200, 274 (n. 3), 278 (n. 49)
Swomley, John, 27, 67, 131, 150, 151

Swords and plowshares: in performance, 1, 75, 77, 82–83, 84, 86; in hymn texts, 58, 59; in pacifist vernacular, 66; in iconography, 89, 93–97, 109; in manual work, 138

Tagore, Rabindranath, 76, 135
Templin, Ralph and Lila, 149, 151, 156, 260 (n. 15)
Tennyson, Alfred, 76, 243 (n. 47)
Theater. *See* Drama; Plays
Theosophy, 123, 135
Thomas, Evan, 20, 22, 225 (n. 52)
Thomas, John, 230 (n. 60)
Thoreau, Henry David, 41, 46, 145, 209
Thurman, Howard, 9, 27, 29, 254 (n. 65)
Tittle, Ernest Fremont, 83, 186
Tolstoy, Leo, 16, 30, 41, 46, 132, 134, 144, 209, 267 (n. 8)
Topoi. *See* Topos
Topos, 163, 168, 169–83; as folklore, 175
Trabuco College, 148
Trinity Methodist Church, Springfield, Mass., 94, 97, 247 (n. 23)
Trocmé, André, 210, 267 (n. 12)
Tuolumne Co-op Farm (TCF), 35, 153, 154, 157, 159, 262 (n. 34), 265 (n. 59)

"Umbrella theology," 3, 70–71, 111, 135, 158–59, 162, 188, 207; implicit, 39, 40–41, 67–69, 101, 103, 108, 116, 126, 144, 161. *See also* Religious openness
Underhill, Evelyn, 118, 122, 124, 254 (n. 64), 256 (n. 78)
Unitarians, 5, 30, 58, 94, 188, 229 (n. 54), 241 (n. 20)
"Unknown Soldier" theme, 82, 134

Vale, The, cooperative, 159
Van Dusen, Henry Pitney, 27, 112
Van Dyke, Henry, 76
Van Kirk, Walter, 230 (n. 57), 241 (n. 14)
Vedanta. *See* Hinduism
Vernier, Philippe, 167, 210
Veterans and pacifism, 36, 40, 230 (n. 56)
Vigil at Fort Detrick, 188
Villard, Oswald Garrison, 31
Vocation, 209
Voluntary poverty, 103–4, 166
Voluntown, Conn. *See* New England Community for Nonviolent Action

Wald, Lillian, 101
Wallace, Archer, 165
Walton, George A., 255 (n. 78)
War Resisters League (WRL), 26, 77, 229 (n. 53), 241 (n. 20)
Way of life, 71, 108, 114, 122, 152, 164; in liberal Protestantism, 15, 16, 17, 47, 52, 55, 56, 76; post-paradigm shift, 39, 41, 132–34, 143, 154–55, 156, 158–59; in pacifist vernacular, 67–68; in Quakerism, 125, 207. *See also* Consistent living
White, Anna, 273 (n. 61)
Whitman, Walt, 76
Whittier College, 35
Wider Quaker Fellowship, 40, 125, 207, 231 (n. 75)
Will, Herman and Margarita, 30
Willett, Clark (publishers), 166
Wilson, Dorothy Clarke, 83
Wilson, E. Raymond, 32, 227 (n. 19), 272 (n. 53)
Wilson, Louis, 83

Wink, Walter, 214
Winter, Miriam Therese, 236 (n. 55)
Wiser, Art, 158
Witherspoon, Frances, 26, 77
Witness for Peace, 214
Women Strike for Peace (WSP), 185, 200, 201, 279 (n. 49)
Women's International League for Peace and Freedom (WILPF), 35, 161, 229 (n. 53), 248 (n. 34); projects, 27, 102, 246 (n. 18), 257 (n. 6), 277 (n. 35); and religion, 57, 210
Woods, Charles Coke, 59
Woolman, John, 134, 263 (n. 44), 270 (n. 43)
World Peace Posters, 129
World Peaceways, 27, 80, 91
World-Telegram, 93
World Tomorrow, The, 27, 30, 50, 52, 91, 130
Worship: peace services, 1–2, 7–8, 74–79; drama and, 80, 86–87; definitions of, 103, 126, 225 (n. 58)

Yarnall, Elizabeth Biddle, 277 (n. 34)
Yellow Springs, Ohio, 187, 259 (n. 6), 260 (n. 15)
Young, Wilmer and Mildred, 264 (n. 54)
Young Men's Christian Association (YMCA), 3, 15, 57, 113, 130, 252 (n. 15); participants, 11, 13, 34, 35, 51, 120, 166, 225 (n. 52), 227 (n. 19); description, 12–13; student branch, 28–30
Young Women's Christian Association (YWCA), 28–30, 34, 35, 80, 227 (n. 20)

www.ingramcontent.com/pod-product-compliance
Lightning Source LLC
Chambersburg PA
CBHW030106010526
44116CB00005B/113